Education Facility Security Handbook

DON PHILPOTT AND MICHAEL W. KUENSTLE

GOVERNMENT INSTITUTES
An imprint of
The Scarecrow Press, Inc.
Lanham • Maryland • Toronto • Plymouth, UK
2007

 GOVERNMENT
INSTITUTES

Published in the United States of America
by Government Institutes, an imprint of The Scarecrow Press, Inc.
A wholly owned subsidiary of
The Rowman & Littlefield Publishing Group, Inc.
4501 Forbes Boulevard, Suite 200
Lanham, Maryland 20706
http://www.govinstpress.com/

Estover Road
Plymouth PL6 7PY
United Kingdom

British Library Cataloguing in Publication Information Available

Library of Congress Cataloging-in-Publication Data

Philpott, Don.
    Education facility security handbook / Don Philpott and Michael W. Kuenstle.
      p. cm.
    Includes bibliographical references.
    ISBN-13: 978-0-86587-167-0 (cloth : alk. paper)
    ISBN-10: 0-86587-167-1 (cloth : alk. paper)
    1. Schools—Security measures—United States.   2. Schools—United States—Safety measures.
I. Kuenstle, Michael W.   II. Title.
    LB2866.P55   2007
    371.7'82—dc22   2007022477

∞™ The paper used in this publication meets the minimum requirements of
American National Standard for Information Sciences—Permanence of
Paper for Printed Library Materials, ANSI/NISO Z39.48-1992.
Manufactured in the United States of America.

Contents

Acknowledgments

This handbook has drawn heavily on the authoritative materials published by the Centers for Disease Control, Department of Defense, Department of Education, Department of Health and Human Services, Department of Homeland Security, Federal Emergency Management Agency, Florida Department of Education, the Government Accountability Office, and the General Services Administrations. These materials are in the public domain, but accreditation has been given both in the text and in the bibliography if you need additional information.

The author also wishes to acknowledge the assistance of various members of staff of the Division of Facilities Management, The School District of Palm Beach County, Florida, one of the largest and most progressive school districts in the country. In particular the author would also like to acknowledge the considerable contribution of Joseph M. Sanches, chief of facilities management, and Don Thrasher, school board police and technical inspector.

Don Philpott

* * *

The 2003 Florida Safe School Design Guidelines presented here were originally developed as part of a sponsored research project accomplished at the University of Florida School of Architecture in collaboration with the Florida Department of Education, Office of Educational Facilities. The purpose of these Guidelines was to serve as an update and eventual replacement of the existing 1993 Florida Safe School Design Guidelines written by The Florida Center for Community Design and Research, University of South Florida. Portions of the 1993 document were incorporated into these new Guidelines.

We owe special thanks to many dedicated individuals for their contributions and support in preparing the Guidelines. Professor Nancy M. Clark from the School of Architecture served as Co-PI for research on the project and provided an astute knowledge of relevant building codes, design, planning, and construction issues. Her technical writing skills were an enormous contribution to the project. If she had not taken on this task, the documents would probably not exist.

Professor Richard Schneider, PhD, AICP, from the Department of Urban and Regional Planning served as senior researcher for the project and was instrumental in providing a clear and critical research approach and methodology. His years of planning experience combined with his depth of knowledge on the subject of crime prevention through environmental design proved to be invaluable.

We acknowledge the following school facilities design professionals for their review and advice during the development of the new Guidelines. Thomas W. Reynolds, AIA, served as a professional consultant to the project and William "Billy" Brame, AIA, and Phillip Rickman, AIA, represented end-users of the document.

Thanks are due to Jon Hamrick and the members of the Department of Education Steering Committee, Julie Collins, John Davis, Wayne Elmore, Chief Tom Gavin, Hank Henry, McGlade Holloway, Dave Lesansky, and Bill Reese, for their critical review, input, and perseverance.

Graduate research assistants Everett Henderson and Phyllis Henderson assisted with the production of the drawings and Larry Squires assisted in the initial literature review. The Florida Department of Education provided funding to support their work on the project.

Finally, I am grateful to co-author Don Philpott for the opportunity and encouragement to work with him on this important and timely Handbook.

Michael W. Kuenstle

Introduction

Each weekday, about a quarter of the population of the United States attends a place of education, either as students, teachers, or support staff. There are more than 60 million students and teachers involved in the nation's schools, and almost 20 million more attend public and private universities and colleges of higher education.

Our schools and colleges are the nation's most valuable asset—and one of the most vulnerable. Almost every week brings new horror stories of campus shootings or other violence.

During the past decade, more than three hundred violent deaths have occurred in or near school campuses. The incidents don't fit any neat patterns; they have occurred at one-classroom rural schools, inner-city high schools, and suburban elementary schools. Some of the more high-profile incidents in recent years include:

- An attack at a one-classroom Amish school in Pennsylvania by a thirty-two-year-old male who shot ten girls ages six to thirteen, killing five of them, before committing suicide.
- The Columbine High School massacre in Colorado when two male students went on a shooting rampage, killing twelve other students and a teacher and wounding twenty-four others, before killing themselves.
- The Red Lake High School shootings in northern Minnesota when a male student killed his grandfather and grandfather's parents before driving to his high school,

Our Schools and Colleges

- Approximately 55 million kindergarten to grade 12 students
- 6 million adults working as teachers or staff
- 117,000 public and private schools
- 16 million students in higher education
- 327,000 education buildings and offices in the fifty states and Washington, D.C.

where he shot more than fifteen people, including a teacher, a security officer, and five students who all died.

While these incidents attracted enormous publicity, violence or the threat of violence, especially gang-related, is a regular occurrence in and around many inner-city schools, while bullying, drugs, and vandalism continue to be major concerns almost everywhere.

Now there is the additional threat of terrorism. While no U.S. school has, to date, suffered a terrorist attack, schools must be considered viable targets for several reasons. Schools are a "soft and highly visible" target—accessible and easy to attack with little protection. Imagine the fear and panic that an attack would cause, not just locally but nationwide. An attack would certainly attract national and international media coverage, as did the deadly attack by Chechen terrorists at a school in Beslan in southern Russia in 2004. An attack would also almost certainly mean more police and other security personnel being diverted to protect schools, leaving other targets vulnerable.

Even if schools are not the target of terrorism, they could be affected by an attack. On September 11, 2001, four elementary schools and three high schools located within six blocks of the World Trade Center were just beginning classes when the first plane hit the north tower. Thousands of children were exposed to the dust clouds from the collapsing buildings. Even those children not in the immediate vicinity experienced a great deal of anxiety. Children in at least three states (New York, New Jersey, and Connecticut) had parents working in or around the World Trade Center that day. In the Washington, D.C., area, schools faced similar situations after the Pentagon was attacked.

Schools are an integral part of our community, and many are used for meetings and events, as polling stations in elections, and as health care centers. In many parts of the country that are prone to bad weather—floods, tornadoes, hurricanes, and the like—schools are often used as emergency evacuation shelters or command centers, and in the event of a major pandemic, such as avian flu, many would also be used as vaccination and treatment centers.

This book is concerned with protecting our students, teachers, administrators and other staff, and helping to keep them safe, whether it is from natural or man-made disaster.

The handbook is divided into three parts. The first provides a basic security overview and discusses how to identify critical assets and then conduct risk-threat assessments. You cannot incorporate safety and secure elements into your design until you know what you are protecting and the threats faced.

The second part looks at planning and design considerations and best practices that have been incorporated into new school designs. These include elements specifically designed to protect schools and education facilities against various natural hazards—such as earthquake, flooding, tornadoes, and hurricanes—as well as design principles used to make schools safer and more secure.

These guidelines cover external and internal design considerations, from site selection and parking to room layouts, protecting systems and equipment, and installing surveillance and other controls and alarm systems. Obviously many areas are covered by local and national building codes and these have to be complied with, but when considering design elements to improve safety and security, layout is probably the most critical element.

The first two parts of the book are concerned with planning, designing, and building a safe and secure education facility. The third part is about implementing "people" policies and practices to make our schools and colleges safer. These various practices can help reduce drug and alcohol abuse, bullying and vandalism, as well as other violence and crime.

This book does not claim to be an original work. Almost all the materials have been drawn from other sources, most of them in the public domain. What this handbook does set out to do, however, is to incorporate the best elements of design and "people" policies from these various sources into a single publication.

In the process, we hope that we can make a modest contribution to building and maintaining a safer and more secure environment for our nation's students and those who work with them.

About the Authors

Don Philpott is editor of *Homeland Defense Journal* and has been writing, reporting, and broadcasting on international events, trouble spots, and major news stories for almost forty years. For twenty years he was a senior correspondent with Press Association—Reuters, the wire service, and traveled the world on assignments including Northern Ireland, Lebanon, Israel, South Africa, and Asia.

He writes for magazines and newspapers in the United States and Europe and is a regular contributor to radio and television programs on security and other issues. He is the author of more than sixty books on a wide range of subjects and has had more than five thousand articles printed in publications around the world. His most recent books are *Terror—Is America Safe?* and *The Integrated Physical Security Handbook,* both published in June 2006. He has written special reports on "Protecting the Athens Olympics," "The Threat from Dirty Bombs," "Anti-Terrorism Measures in the UK," "Nanotechnology and the U.S. Military," and "The Global Impact of the London Bombings."

Born in the UK, he is now an American citizen working out of Orlando, Florida.

Michael W. Kuenstle, AIA, is an architect and professor at the University of Florida. He received his graduate architecture degree from Columbia University in 1991 and his bachelor of architecture degree from the University of Houston in 1989. He served as Adjunct Associate Professor at the New York Institute of Technology from 1990 to 1993 and has served as assistant and associate professor in the School of Architecture at the University of Florida since 1993. He is co-founder and principal partner in the architecture firm of Clark + Kuenstle Associates, Inc. and has received numerous design awards from the American Institute of Architects for his building projects throughout the United States and Canada. He received his early technical training in the Chicago office of Skidmore, Owings and Merrill and has continued to work on building design projects in New York, Los Angeles, Atlanta, and Toronto and most recently in Florida, where he now practices and teaches architecture full-time.

His current work and research focus on issues related to school facilities design, coastal construction, and building simulation modeling. While at the University of Florida he has successfully completed two significant research projects for the Florida

Department of Education; the first resulted in a complete update and rewrite of the *Florida Safe School Design Guidelines* and the second resulted in the publication of *The Florida Building Code Handbook for New Educational Facilities Construction*. Additionally, he has published numerous papers and given speeches on his research. Kuenstle is a member of the American Institute of Architects and currently serves as a state director to the Florida Association of the American Institute of Architects.

Security Basics

First Steps

In an ideal world, there would be no school crime, and the safety of each staff member and student would be ensured. However, the reality is that so many things are outside the control of the school administrator that such a task is virtually impossible. To attempt to predict the disruptive behavior of a student, a staff member, an intruder, or a terrorist is unrealistic, said Ronald D. Stephens, executive director of the National School Safety Center, which was established by the Departments of Education and Justice to address the growing problem of violence in U.S. schools.

"There are two types of school administrators: those who have faced a crisis and those who are about to," he added. "This nation's educational system has its foundation at the local level. Education is a federal concern, a state function, and a local responsibility. Assigning such responsibility to parents, students, educators, and other citizens closest to the need for schooling is both appropriate and demanding.

"No greater challenge exists today than creating safe schools or restoring schools to tranquil and safe places of learning. The challenge requires a major strategic commitment and involves placing school safety at the top of the educational agenda. Without safe schools, teachers cannot teach and students cannot learn. A safe school is foundational to the success of the academic mission. A safe school is also one that is prepared to respond to the unthinkable crisis," Stephens said.

School or Fortress?

School safety is a major issue in communities across the country, particularly in those areas that are near strategically rich terrorist targets. The question facing schools and communities alike is: How far must schools go to create a safe and welcoming environment without turning our nation's schools into armed camps?

For the most part, schools were not designed to be defended. They were designed as open places of learning and respect where teachers could teach and students could learn. Today, security is an integral part of new school building plans, but contingency planning and preparedness are still the keys to secure and safe school environments.

Developing a school safety plan and implementing safety and security policies and procedures are discussed in Section 3. There are, however, a number of initial decisions that have to be made.

Regardless of the size of a school construction program, certain steps are necessary and certain procedures must be followed. These will vary greatly in scope between the design of a small elementary school and the development of a multi-school program of new and remedial construction. Review and regulation procedures by outside agencies will also vary. Internal district decisions as to the design and construction process (e.g., conventional architect design and competitive construction bid, design/build or construction manager) will affect the scope and timing of some of the activities.

However, regardless of the size and scope of the project, the following steps should be taken; for a small project, they may entail relatively informal meetings among a few district staff, the school board, and others; for a large program, formal procedures must be established.

- Conduct an in-house assessment of the educational needs, with the assistance of a public education committee and consultants. Public committees continue throughout the programming and design process, acquiring specialist members as necessary at different stages for a large program.
- Determine the size and scope of the proposed program. (In a small district, an architect, who may later become the design architect, may be employed to assist the school district with this task.)
- Conduct an assessment of the site needs to determine the size and availability of sites (and lease/purchase as necessary).
- Develop educational specifications, both in-house and/or consultants.
- Conduct an assessment of financial needs.
- Identify financial resources, including alternative sources of funding (e.g., state and federal programs, local taxes, bond issues).
- Ensure funding (e.g., pass bond issue).
- Appoint a district building program management staff (appointed officials or a committee).
- Determine the design and construction process (i.e., conventional design and bid, design/build or construction management).
- Select and hire architects and other special design consultants or design/build team members; the timing of hiring will vary, depending on the number of projects, whether programming is involved, and other variables.
- Develop building programs, including building size, room size, equipment, and environmental requirements; this may be done in-house, and/or architects or independent program consultants may assist.
- Appoint the district staff and public stakeholders committee for the design phase.
- Develop designs (architects), together with cost estimates. Hold public meetings with architects and encourage public input into the design, together with district progress reviews.

- Design completion, district review of contract documents.
- Submit construction documents to the district and any permitting agencies for review and approval.
- Submit documents to building department and other required agencies.
- Select the contractor (bidding) or finalize design/build or construction management contracts.
- School construction.
- School district administration of construction contract.
- Observation by architect and inspection as required.
- School completed by contractor.
- School inspected and accepted by architect.
- School inspected and accepted by school district.
- School commissioned and occupied.

The sequence of the above steps may vary, depending on the complexity of the program; some steps may be implemented simultaneously.

Asset Protection and Risk-Threat Assessment

CRITICAL ASSETS

An essential element of the planning and design process is to identify your critical assets.

An asset is a resource of value requiring protection. An asset can be tangible (e.g., students, faculty, staff, school buildings, facilities, equipment, activities, operations, or information) or intangible (e.g., processes or a school's reputation). In order to achieve the greatest risk reduction at the least cost, identifying and prioritizing a school's critical assets is a vital first step in the process to identify the best mitigation measures to improve its level of protection, whether from a natural disaster or terrorist attack.

For instance, a school's main function is to teach, and its critical assets are the teachers and students. Also important are the computers and other teaching aids that are used, as well as the ancillary staff—but these are not as important as the teachers themselves. So you have to not only identify your critical assets, you have to prioritize them as well.

Recognizing that people are a school's most critical asset, the process described below will help identify and prioritize school infrastructure where people are most at risk and require protection. In order to conduct productive interviews, a list of areas to be covered should be generated and prioritized prior to the actual interviews.

Thorough planning and research to generate relevant questions will aid the process and yield better results. Identifying a school's critical assets is accomplished in a two-step process:

Step 1: Define and understand the school's core functions and processes

Basic questions

1. What is your current security situation?
   You must find out about the crime rate in your area and any current terrorist threats or alerts. You must know if your facility has been burgled or if current or former employees have made threats.
2. Site—Neighbors
   You must review all the facilities in your neighborhood to see which, if any, pose a threat to you. Are there high-risk targets that might be attacked and, if so, what would the impact be on your facility and your ability to continue operating?
3. Site—Location
   Walk around your perimeter and determine if your immediate surrounds are secure.
4. Site—Perimeter
   Focus on your perimeter—does it offer adequate protection, what are the vulnerabilities?
5. Perimeter Security
   Check out your perimeter physical security systems—are they adequate?
6. Building Usage
   It is essential to know everything about your building—who uses it, the main access points, traffic flow, different security levels, portals, and so on.
7. Building Structure
   Consult with your experts to determine if the building structure is safe or if physical hardening is needed.
8. Utility Systems
   Utility systems are critical but often overlooked. You must know what utilities are used, how they enter the building, where they are vulnerable, if there is on-site storage, backup systems, and so on.
9. People
   In almost all cases, people are your most critical asset, whether they are employees, students, or visitors. You must know who uses the building and when, how they access and exit it, where they go when they are inside, and whether their movement is controlled. You must also know what procedures are in place to screen staff and to train them in the event of an emergency.
10. Communications and Information Technology (IT)
    A key element of your integrated physical security plan is the protection of your IT, communications, and information systems. Even though communications is a critical part of integrated physical security (IPS), it is often covered in a separate plan. That is why IPS is so important because it must incorporate all these separate threads into one cohesive and all-encompassing plan.

11. Equipment Operations and Maintenance
   You must know all about the equipment used in the building, how it operates, and what the maintenance schedules are. If you do not know this information, make sure that the people who do have it are on your planning team.

12. External Security Systems
   You must examine all your external security systems—are they adequate, are they integrated? Do they support your deter, detect, and delay objectives?

13. Internal Security Systems
   As with external security systems, you have to do a comprehensive evaluation of all internal security systems. Are they adequate for the job at hand, are there newer systems that could be implemented, are there areas that should be protected that are not currently covered?

14. Security System Documents
   An essential part of your IPS is to ensure that all security system documents are kept up to date, and that they are in a secure environment yet are available to the proper authorities in the event of an emergency.

15. Security Master Plan
   As with your security system documents, you have to ensure that your security master plan is regularly reviewed and revised to accommodate changing circumstances and new threats. It should be a constantly evolving and improving document.

16. Compliance
   You must ensure that all modifications comply with all relevant codes.

Step 2: Identify school infrastructure
       —Critical components/assets
       —Critical information systems and data
       —Life safety systems and safe haven areas
       —Security systems

IDENTIFYING SCHOOL CORE FUNCTIONS

The initial step of an asset value assessment is the determination of core functions and processes necessary for the school to continue to operate or provide services after an incident. The reason for identifying core functions/processes is to focus the design team and school administrators on what a school does, how it does it, and how various threats can affect the school. This provides more discussion and results in a better understanding of asset value. Factors that should be considered include:

• What are the school's primary services or outputs?
• What critical activities take place at the school?

- Who are the school's occupants or visitors?
- What inputs from external organizations are required for a school's success?

IDENTIFYING SCHOOL INFRASTRUCTURE

After the core functions and processes are identified, an evaluation of school infrastructure is the next step. To help identify and value-rank infrastructure, the following should be considered, keeping in mind that the most vital asset for every school is its people:

- Identify how many people may be injured or killed during an incident—earthquake, terrorist attack, and so on—that directly affects the infrastructure.
- Identify what happens to school functions, services, or student satisfaction if a specific asset is lost or degraded. (Can primary services continue?)
- Determine the impact on other organizational assets if the component is lost or cannot function.
- Determine if critical or sensitive information is stored or handled at the school.
- Determine if backups exist for the school's assets.
- Determine the availability of replacements.
- Determine the potential for injuries or deaths from any catastrophic event at the school's assets.
- Identify any critical faculty, staff, or administration system whose loss would degrade or seriously complicate the safety of students, faculty, and staff during an emergency. (Consider first responders or the personnel responsible for shelter operations at a school that is a designated shelter for natural hazards.)
- Determine if the school's assets can be replaced, and identify replacement costs if the school building is lost.
- Identify the locations of key equipment.
- Determine the locations of personnel work areas and systems within a school.
- Identify the locations of any personnel operating "outside" a school's controlled areas.
- Determine the location, availability, and readiness condition of emergency response assets, and the state of training of school staff in their use.
- Determine, in detail, the physical locations of critical support architectures:
  —Communications and IT (the flow of critical information)
  —Utilities (e.g., facility power, water, air conditioning, etc.)
  —Lines of communication that provide access to external resources and provide movement of students and faculty (e.g., road, rail, air transportation)

QUANTIFYING ASSET VALUE

After identifying the school's assets or resources of value requiring protection, they should be assigned a value. Asset value is the degree of debilitating impact that would be caused by the incapacity or destruction of the school's assets.

ASSET VALUE SCALE

Asset Value	
Very High	10
High	8–9
Medium High	7
Medium	5–6
Medium Low	4
Low	2–3
Very Low	1

Source: FEMA

Very High—Loss or damage of the school's assets would have exceptionally grave consequences, such as extensive loss of life, widespread severe injuries, or total loss of primary services and core functions and processes.

High—Loss or damage of the school's assets would have grave consequences, such as loss of life, severe injuries, loss of primary services, or major loss of core functions and processes for an extended period of time.

Medium High—Loss or damage of the school's assets would have serious consequences, such as serious injuries or impairment of core functions and processes for an extended period of time.

Medium—Loss or damage of the school's assets would have moderate to serious consequences, such as injuries or impairment of core functions and processes.

Medium Low—Loss or damage of the school's assets would have moderate consequences, such as minor injuries or minor impairment of core functions and processes.

Low—Loss or damage of the school's assets would have minor consequences or impact, such as a slight impact on core functions and processes for a short period of time.

Very Low—Loss or damage of the school's assets would have negligible consequences or impact.

RISK ASSESSMENT

The risk assessment uses the threat, asset value, and vulnerability assessments to determine the level of risk for each critical asset against each applicable threat. This takes into account the likelihood of the threat occurring (probability) and the effects (consequences) of the occurrence if the critical asset is damaged or destroyed.

The risk assessment provides security consultants, engineers, designers, and architects with a relative risk profile that defines which assets are at the greatest risk against specific threats.

Any threat subjects an organization to risk. Therefore, when a threat is exhibited a risk rating needs to be applied in order to understand how to manage the risk. A threat management team should have processes and procedures in place for measuring the probability of loss and the severity of loss, in light of a threat.

The following primary risk types should be considered in determining risk exposure:

- Mission or function risks
- Asset risks
- Security risks

Remember that the aim in developing your secure facility design is to identify all critical assets—tangible and intangible—and reduce the risks to them to an acceptable level. You must take into account the following crucial elements: deterrence, detection, delay, and response and then recovery and reassessment. All are mitigation measures. These are the foundations on which any physical security plan must be built.

- **Deterrence**—provides countermeasures, such as policies, procedures, and technical devices and controls to defend against attacks on the assets being protected.
- **Detection**—monitors for potential breakdowns in protective mechanisms that could result in security breaches.
- **Delay**—provides measures that in the event of a breach delay intruders long enough to allow them to be apprehended before they achieve their objective.
- **Response**—procedures and actions for responding to a breach. Note: Because total protection is almost impossible to achieve, a security program that does not also incorporate detection and delay is incomplete. To be effective, all three concepts must be elements of a cycle that work together continuously.
- **Recovery**—your plan to continue operations as normally as possible following an incident. Mitigation planning is part of your response and recovery with the aim of minimizing the effects of any incident.
- **Reassessment**—crucial and an ongoing process. Before implementing any changes, you need to revisit your strategic plan to ensure that goals and objectives will be met. Whenever there are changed circumstances or when new threats are identified, revisit your strategic plan and conduct a reassessment to see what additional measures, if any, are needed.

After identifying asset value, the next step in the assessment process is to conduct a threat/hazard assessment wherein the threats or hazards are identified, defined, and quantified. A threat assessment is a continual process of compiling and examining all available information concerning potential threats and man-made hazards. It can be broken down into two processes: (1) defining threats, and (2) identifying threat event profiles and tactics.

THREAT IDENTIFICATION

Now that you know what you are protecting, you must identify what threats you face and from where these threats might come. This means identifying all internal and external threats and hazards and understanding why they might affect you. These threats include everything from internal pilfering and violence from a disgruntled student to external threats, such as theft, trespassing, natural disasters, and terrorism. When you have identified your various adversaries, you can determine the probability of attack and the degree of threat that each one poses.

Schools are particularly vulnerable to attack because they are site constrained, perimeters can be easily penetrated, there are clearly defined heavy-traffic patterns when students and staff arrive and leave school, and often there is very little security during the hours of darkness.

INFORMATION YOU NEED TO DEFINE THREAT

- Type of adversary and tactics
- Potential actions of adversary
- Motivations of adversary
- Capabilities of adversary

THREAT DEFINITION

A threat (hazard) is any indication, circumstance, or event with the potential to cause loss of or damage to an asset. It is important to understand who are the people who want to cause harm, or who, by process, materials, or proximity, can cause indirect harm to a school building. With the goal of reducing the potential risk of a school building, the design team and school administration should seek threat assessment information from local law enforcement, the local office of the Federal Bureau of Investigation (FBI), State Health Departments, the Department of Homeland Security (DHS), and the Homeland Security Offices (HSOs) at the state level.

In many areas of the country, there are coordinating committees that facilitate the sharing of information on threats. Local fire departments and hazardous materials (HazMat) units will frequently understand the threat of technological hazards due to hazardous materials on school grounds, as well as those in surrounding industries that could cause a collateral threat to schools. In many jurisdictions, the HazMat unit is part of the fire department.

Design Basis Threat

Design basis threat (DBT) was originally developed to protect the nation's nuclear industry, but the principles can be applied to any facility that needs to implement a physical security plan. Whether you are building a new school or retrofitting an existing one, DBT helps you identify all your likely threats and adversaries, their strengths and capabilities, what their targets might be, the likelihood of them attacking you, and if so, how. When you have answered these questions and identified all threats, you are better able to design and incorporate safeguards to protect your facility and its critical assets.

Defining a School's Threats

Any security strategy must incorporate the constraints of the facility so that all strengths, weaknesses, and idiosyncrasies are realized and provided for. How risks are approached will largely be driven by facility constraints. If theft and vandalism are primary risks for your school, answers to questions regarding the physical plant will determine the optimal security measures. Is the school new or old? Are the windows particularly vulnerable? Does everyone who ever worked at the school still have keys? What is the nighttime lighting like? Does the interior intrusion sensor system work well, or do the local police ignore the alarms due to a high false-alarm rate? Are visitors forced or merely requested to go through the front office before accessing the rest of the school?

If outsiders on campus are a primary concern, it will be necessary to recognize the facility's ability to control unauthorized access. How many entry points are there into the buildings? Are gangs present in the area? Are the school grounds open and accessible to anyone, or do fences or buildings restrict access? Is there easy access to the school roof? Where are hiding places within the building or on the premises? Is the student population small enough so that most of the staff would recognize most of the students and parents?

If issues of violence are a major concern, a thorough understanding of employees, student profiles, and neighborhood characteristics will be necessary. What is the crime rate in the neighborhood? Is the school administration well liked by the students? Are teachers allowed access to the school at night? Are students allowed off campus at lunchtime? How much spending money do students generally have? Are popular hangouts for young people close by and does management of business establishments collaborate with the school? Are expelled or suspended students sent home or to an alternative school? How many incidents of violence have occurred at the school over the past four years? What is the general reputation of the school, and how does it appear to an outsider? Are your most vocal parents pro-security or pro-privacy? Do your students like and respect your security personnel well enough to pass them pieces of information regarding security concerns? Once the school's threats, assets, and environmental constraints are identified, the security needs can be prioritized, so the school's security goals are understood by all those involved.

Identifying security needs and then securing the funding to pay for them are usually unrelated at most schools. Schools have to have a "Plan B," for program design, which may be the perfect "Plan A"—but spread out over several years of implementation. If the desirable strategies (e.g., fencing, sensors, locker searches, speed bumps) are too costly or unpalatable to the community, a school may then need to modify the facility constraints (e.g., back entrances locked from the outside, no open campus for students, no teacher access after 10:00 p.m., all computer equipment bolted down, no lockers for students, and so forth).

Most school districts or school boards will be more supportive of security measures and the requested funding if they are well educated about the most likely risks faced each year and the options available. A security staff should not have the wide-open charter to "keep everything and everybody safe." A school board should be briefed as often as once a month as to what the current security goals are and what strategies are recommended, realizing that these will and must continue to evolve. If a school board member is clearly aware of a school's most important concerns and what is required to achieve them, then he or she is less likely to be swayed by an irate parent into making a decision that will handicap reasonable security efforts.

Source: National Institute of Justice

Consult local law enforcement, the FBI, the DHS, and other government agencies to help develop your DBT.

As an example, the nuclear industry is charged with doing DBT assessments to mitigate threats equivalent to:

- The events of September 11, 2001
- A physical, cyber, biochemical, or other terrorist threat
- An attack on a facility by multiple coordinated teams of a large number of individuals
- An attack assisted by several persons employed at the facility
- A suicide attack
- A water-based or air-based threat
- The use of explosive devices of considerable size and other modern weaponry
- An attack by persons with a sophisticated knowledge of sensitive nuclear facility operations
- Fire, especially a fire of long duration
- Any other threat that the Nuclear Regulatory Commission determines should be included as an element of the DBT

Your school may not be as high risk as a nuclear power plant, but the methodology used to identify adversaries, their motivations, their strengths, their capabilities, and how they might attack you are just as applicable to your facility.

The three basic elements of crime prevention through environmental design (CPTED) are natural access controls, natural surveillance, and territorial reinforcement. Natural access controls include landscaping and fencing to control entry to an area. In design terms, natural surveillance means giving people maximum visibility in order to see and be seen in the spaces around them. Territorial reinforcement uses buildings and other structures to establish "ownership," that is, it enables people to determine who belongs there and who doesn't. There are great lessons to be learned from CPTED, and applying its elements and techniques is a good way of reducing potential security threats.

Threats and Possible Solutions

OUTSIDERS ON CAMPUS

- Posted signs regarding penalties for trespassing
- Enclosed campus (fencing)
- Guard at main entry gate to campus
- Greeters in strategic locations
- Student IDs or badges
- Vehicle parking stickers
- Uniforms or dress codes
- Exterior doors locked from the outside
- A challenge procedure for anyone out of class
- Cameras in remote locations
- School laid out so all visitors must pass through front office
- Temporary "fading" badges issued to all visitors

FIGHTS ON CAMPUS

- Cameras
- Duress alarms
- Whistles

VANDALISM

- Graffiti-resistant sealers
- Glass-break sensors
- Aesthetically pleasing wall murals (these usually are not hit by graffiti)
- Law enforcement officers living on campus
- Eight-foot fencing
- Well-lit campus at night

THEFT

- Interior intrusion detection sensors
- Property marking (including microdots) to deter theft
- Bars on windows
- Reinforced doors
- Elimination of access points up to rooftops
- Cameras

- Doors with hinge-pins on secure side
- Bolting down computers and TVs
- Locating high-value assets in interior rooms
- Key control
- Biometric entry into rooms with high-value assets
- Law enforcement officer living on campus

DRUGS

- Drug detection swipes
- Hair analysis kits for drug use detection (intended for parental application)
- Drug dogs
- Removal of lockers
- Random searches
- Vapor detection of drugs

ALCOHOL

- No open campus at lunch
- Breathalyzer® test equipment
- No access to vehicles
- No lockers
- Clear or open mesh backpacks
- Saliva test kits

WEAPONS

- Walk-through metal detectors
- Hand-held metal detectors
- Vapor detection of gunpowder
- Crimestopper hotline with rewards for information
- Gunpowder detection swipes
- Random locker, backpack, and vehicle searches
- X-ray inspection of bookbags and purses

MALICIOUS ACTS

- Setback of all school buildings from vehicle areas
- Inaccessibility of air intake and water source

continued

continued
- All adults on campus required to have a badge
- Vehicle barriers near main entries and student gathering areas

PARKING LOT PROBLEMS

- Cameras
- Parking decals
- Fencing
- Card ID systems for parking-lot entry
- Parking lots sectioned off for different student schedules
- Sensors in parking areas that should have no access during the school day
- Roving guards
- Bike patrol

FALSE FIRE ALARMS

- Sophisticated alarm systems that allow assessment of alarms (and cancellation if false) before they become audible
- Boxes installed over alarm pulls that alarm locally (screamer boxes)

BOMB THREATS

- Caller ID on phone system
- Crimestopper program with big rewards for information
- Recording all phone calls, with a message regarding this at the beginning of each incoming call
- All incoming calls routed through a district office
- Phone company support
- No pay phones on campus
- Policy to extend the school year when plagued with bomb threats and subsequent evacuations

BUS PROBLEMS

- Video cameras and recorders within enclosures on buses
- IDs required to get on school buses
- Security aides on buses
- Smaller buses
- Duress alarm system or radios for bus drivers

> **TEACHER SAFETY**
>
> - Duress alarms
> - Roving patrols
> - Classroom doors left open during class
> - Cameras in black boxes in classrooms
> - Controlled access to classroom areas

Design Basis Threat Worksheet

Objective: Identify & document who you are protecting your facility against

Purpose: This chart will capture who your potential adversaries are and what are their potential capabilities

Action 1:   Data Gathering
In order to narrow your threats to the most realistic ones your first step would be a Data collection activity. There are several sources you will need to draw upon: your local law enforcement (FBI, Sheriff etc), other similar facility type facilities, neighboring facilities, and the like.

Question   *Is there historical data that would identify potential threats to your facility*

Question   *Do the law enforcement authorities have specific intelligence that could narrow the list of potential threats*

Question   *Talk to similar facilities—are they aware of specific risks to your facility type*

Question   *Talk to your local community, neighbors—have there been any recent events that could profile potential adversarial profiles*

Action 2:   Develop your adversary list based on the above data gathering
A—List your potential adversaries
B—What is there motive to execute their attack
C—What the adversaries profile—how many, armed, on foot, equipped with hand tools
D—Identify what is the realistic probability of an attack
Vulnerability   Low—very slim chances
                    Medium—could happen
                    High—highly probable

Note: *Action 2D is critical because the core team will need to establish what adversaries to protect the facility against; a scenario based analysis will be done for each realistic adversary type and actions will be taken to protect the facility against these specific threats.*
*As a core team you will need to define the threshold for your DBT (for example **Medium** probability and above).*

Example	A Adversary List/type	B Motive	C Profile/ Characteristics	Probability of Attack		
				Low	Medium	High
1	Insider	Disgruntled Employee	Alone, has access to critical assets			H
2	Vandal	Just for Kicks	Adolescent group of 3 to 5		M	
3	Terrorist	Media, Sent on a Mission	Alone, suicide bomber	L		

Source: *The Integrated Physical Security Handbook,* by Don Philpott & Shuki Einstein, published by *Homeland Defense Journal,* 2006

Vulnerability Assessment

Having identified your critical assets and who might attack them, you now have to determine how vulnerable those assets are to attack. How effective is your existing security? Do you have any physical security in place? Conduct a security inventory based on the master assessment checklist.

- What is your current security situation?
- Are you at risk from your neighbors?
- How secure is your location?
- What is your current perimeter security?
- How structurally safe is your facility?
- Are your utilities secure and, if so, how?
- What communications/IT protection do you have?
- Is your equipment protected?
- What external security protection do you have?
- What internal security protection do you have?

Note: There are many methodologies for conducting risk assessment and they may use different criteria. Seek advice to decide which methodology is best for you. For instance, some funding sources may require that a particular methodology is used or some methodologies may be more appropriate for your type of enterprise and so on.

Major Steps in Conducting a Vulnerability Assessment

- Characterize facility
- Identify assets or "targets"
- Identify credible threats against assets
- Analyze undesired events

- Analyze likelihood of occurrence
- Identify consequence of loss
- Evaluate ranked list of vulnerabilities
- Identify impact on facility mission—low, medium, high

Determining the Vulnerability Rating

This task involves determining a vulnerability rating that reflects the weakness of functions, systems, and sites in regard to a particular threat. Weakness includes the lack of redundancies that will make the building system operational after an attack.

Redundancy Factor

A terrorist selects the weapon and tactic that will cause harm to people, destroy the infrastructure, or functionally defeat the target. The function and infrastructure vulnerability analysis will identify the geographic distribution within the building and interdependencies between critical assets. Ideally, the functions should have geographic dispersion, as well as a recovery site or alternate work location. However, some critical functions and infrastructure do not have a backup, or will be determined to be collocated and create what are called single-point vulnerabilities. Identification and protection of these single-point vulnerabilities are key aspects of the assessment process. Concerns related to common system vulnerabilities are:

- No redundancy
- Redundant systems feed into single critical node
- Critical components of redundant systems collocated
- Inadequate capacity or endurance in post-attack environment

Identification and protection of these single-point vulnerabilities will help you to determine a more accurate vulnerability rating for your assessment.

Once vulnerabilities have been identified, they also need to be rated so that you can prioritize them, as the examples below illustrate.

Very High—One or more major weaknesses have been identified that make the school's assets extremely susceptible to an aggressor or hazard.

High—One or more significant weaknesses have been identified that make the school's assets highly susceptible to an aggressor or hazard.

Medium High—An important weakness has been identified that makes the school's assets very susceptible to an aggressor or hazard.

Medium—A weakness has been identified that makes the school's assets fairly susceptible to an aggressor or hazard.

Medium Low—A weakness has been identified that makes the school's assets somewhat susceptible to an aggressor or hazard.

Figure 1–1.   Common Systems Vulnerabilities

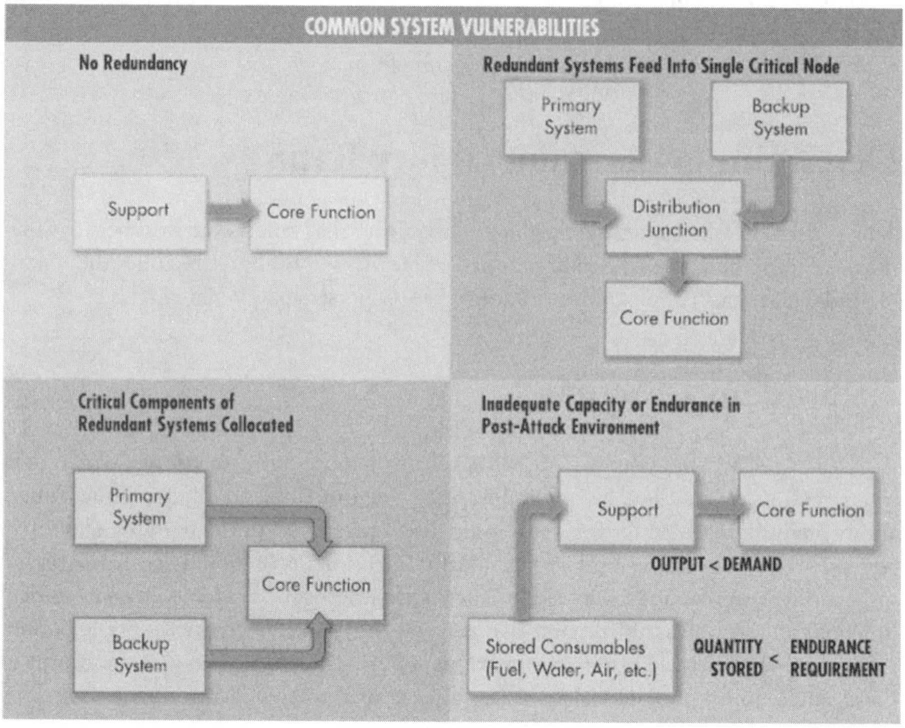

Source: FEMA 452 Risk Assessment Series: A How-To Guide to Mitigate Potential Terrorist Attacks against Buildings, January 2005

Low—A minor weakness has been identified that slightly increases the susceptibility of the school's assets to an aggressor or hazard.

Very Low—No weaknesses exist.

There are numerous methodologies and techniques for conducting a risk assessment. One approach is to assemble the results of the asset value assessment, threat assessment, and vulnerability assessment, and determine a numeric value of risk for each asset and threat/hazard pair in accordance with the following formula:

$$\text{Risk} = \text{Asset Value} \times \text{Threat Rating} \times \text{Vulnerability Rating}$$

Very High—The potential for loss or damage of the school's assets is so great as to expect exceptionally grave consequences, such as extensive loss of life, widespread severe injuries, or total loss of primary services and core functions and processes.

High—The potential for loss or damage of the school's assets is so great as to expect grave consequences, such as loss of life, severe injuries, loss of primary services, or major loss of core functions and processes for an extended period of time.

Table 1-1: Asset Threat/Hazard

ASSET	THREAT/HAZARD									
	Terrorist Act		Armed Attack		Unauthorized Entry		Low Level CBR Attack		Cyber-terrorism	
	Stationary Vehicle Bomb		Attack by Small Arms		Forced Entry at Night to Damage School Property		Hydrogen Sulfide "Stink Bomb"		Electronic Attack to Destroy or Alter School Academic Records	
	Vulnerability Rating		Vulnerability Rating		Vulnerability Rating		Vulnerability Rating		Vulnerability Rating	
Students	VH	10	H	9	VL	1	MH	7	VL	1
Faculty	VH	10	H	9	VL	1	MH	7	ML	4
Staff	VH	10	H	9	ML	4	MH	7	ML	4
Designated Shelter (safe haven)	H	9	L	3	ML	4	L	3	VL	1
Main School Building	VH	10	ML	4	M	5	L	3	VL	1
Teaching Functions	VH	10	VH	10	ML	4	H	9	L	3
IT/Communications Systems	VH	10	M	5	MH	7	L	2	MH	7
Utilities Associated with Shelter	H	8	ML	4	L	2	VL	1	VL	1
Utility Systems (gas, electrical, sewer/water)	MH	7	ML	4	M	5	L	2	VL	1
Nurses Station	H	9	H	8	M	6	L	3	VL	1
School/Student Records	H	9	L	3	M	6	L	2	MH	7
Transportation (buses and parking)	VH	10	H	9	M	6	L	3	VL	1
Security Equipment (metal detectors, badge equipment)	H	9	MH	7	M	6	L	2	VL	1
Administrative Functions	VH	10	H	8	M	6	MH	7	M	5
Temporary Classrooms (trailers)	VH	10	VH	10	MH	7	ML	4	VL	1
Food Service (cafeteria/kitchen)	VH	10	H	8	M	5	MH	7	VL	1
Library	VH	10	VH	10	MH	7	MH	7	ML	4
Custodial Functions	VH	10	ML	4	M	6	ML	4	VL	1
Science Laboratories	VH	10	M	5	H	8	L	3	VL	1
Vocational Equipment (shops)	VH	10	ML	4	H	8	L	3	VL	1
Indoor Sports Facilities	VH	10	ML	4	H	8	M	6	VL	1
Outdoor Sports Facilities	M	5	L	2	MH	7	L	2	VL	1

VH = Very High; H = High; MH = Medium High; M = Medium; ML = Medium Low; L = Low; VL = Very Low

Source: FEMA 428. Risk Management Series: Primer to Design Safe School Projects in case of Terrorist Attack, December 2003

Table 1–2:   Risk Rating

Risk	Risk Rating
≥ 261	Very High
201 - 260	High
141 - 200	Medium High
101 - 140	Medium
61 - 100	Medium Low
31 - 60	Low
1 - 30	Very Low

Source: FEMA 428. Risk Management Series: Primer to Design Safe
School Projects in case of Terrorist Attack, December 2003

Medium High—The potential for loss or damage of the school's assets is such as to expect serious consequences (e.g., serious injuries or impairment of core functions and processes for an extended period of time).

Medium—The potential for loss or damage of the school's assets is such as to expect serious consequences (e.g., injuries or impairment of core functions and processes).

Medium Low—The potential for loss or damage of the school's assets is such as to expect only moderate consequences (e.g., minor injuries or minor impairment of core functions and processes).

Low—The potential for loss or damage of the school's assets is such as to expect only minor consequences or impact (e.g., a slight impact on core functions and processes for a short period of time).

Very Low—The potential for loss or damage of the school's assets is so low that there would only be negligible consequences or impact.

Because of the large amount of information in a risk assessment matrix, it is useful to assign a color code (red, yellow, or green) based on the total numeric value of risk determined. As a minimum, mitigation measures to reduce risk and create an acceptable level of protection should be considered for those critical assets determined to be at highest risk.

Risk management is the process of selecting and implementing mitigation measures to achieve an acceptable level of risk at an acceptable cost. Because it is cost-prohibitive to protect against the entire range of possible threats, it is important to develop a realistic prioritization of mitigation measures. When considering mitigation measures, the following factors should be considered:

• Results of the risk assessment, including asset value and asset vulnerabilities
• Costs of the mitigation measures
• The value of risk reduction to the school
• Frequency with which the benefits of the mitigation measures will be realized
• The deterrence or preventive value of the mitigation measures
• The expected lifespan of the mitigation measures and the time value of money

Table 1–3:   Threat Hazard Assessment

	Threat/Hazard				
	Terrorist Act	Armed Attack	Unauthorized Entry	Low Level CBR Attack	Cyber-terrorism
	Stationary Vehicle Bomb	Attack by Small Arms	Forced Entry at Night to Damage School Property	Hydrogen Sulfide "Stink Bomb"	Electronic Attack to Destroy or Alter School Academic Records
Students/Faculty/Staff	200	360	50	490	140
Asset Value Rating	10	10	10	10	10
Threat Rating	2	4	5	7	7
Vulnerability Rating	10	9	1	7	2
Designated Shelter (safe haven)	180	120	200	210	70
Asset Value Rating	10	10	10	10	10
Threat Rating	2	4	5	7	7
Vulnerability Rating	9	3	4	3	1
Main School Building	180	144	225	189	63
Asset Value Rating	9	9	9	9	9
Threat Rating	2	4	5	7	7
Vulnerability Rating	10	4	5	3	1
Teaching Functions	60	120	60	189	63
Asset Value Rating	3	3	3	3	3
Threat Rating	2	4	5	7	7
Vulnerability Rating	10	10	4	9	3
IT/Communications Systems	160	160	280	112	392
Asset Value Rating	8	8	8	8	8
Threat Rating	2	4	5	7	7
Vulnerability Rating	10	5	7	2	7
Utilities Associated with Shelter	112	112	70	49	49
Asset Value Rating	7	7	7	7	7
Threat Rating	2	4	5	7	7
Vulnerability Rating	8	4	2	1	1
Utility Systems (gas, electrical, sewer/water)	98	112	175	98	49
Asset Value Rating	7	7	7	7	7
Threat Rating	2	4	5	7	7
Vulnerability Rating	7	4	5	2	1
Nurses Station	126	224	210	147	49
Asset Value Rating	7	7	7	7	7
Threat Rating	2	4	5	7	7
Vulnerability Rating	9	8	6	3	1

Source: FEMA 428. Risk Management Series: Primer to Design Safe School Projects in Case of Terrorist Attack, December 2003

Table 1–3:   Continued

	Threat/Hazard				
	Terrorist Act	Armed Attack	Unauthorized Entry	Low Level CBR Attack	Cyber-terrorism
	Stationary Vehicle Bomb	Attack by Small Arms	Forced Entry at Night to Damage School Property	Hydrogen Sulfide "Stink Bomb"	Electronic Attack to Destroy or Alter School Academic Records
School/Student Records	126	84	210	98	343
Asset Value Rating	7	7	7	7	7
Threat Rating	2	4	5	7	7
Vulnerability Rating	9	3	6	2	7
Transportation (buses and parking)	140	252	210	147	49
Asset Value Rating	7	7	7	7	7
Threat Rating	2	4	5	7	7
Vulnerability Rating	10	9	6	3	1
Security Equipment (metal detectors, badge equipment)	126	196	210	98	49
Asset Value Rating	7	7	7	7	7
Threat Rating	2	4	5	7	7
Vulnerability Rating	9	7	6	2	1
Administrative Functions	100	160	150	245	175
Asset Value Rating	5	5	5	5	5
Threat Rating	2	4	5	7	7
Vulnerability Rating	10	8	6	7	5
Temporary Classrooms (trailers)	80	160	140	112	28
Asset Value Rating	4	4	4	4	4
Threat Rating	2	4	5	7	7
Vulnerability Rating	10	10	7	4	1
Food Service (cafeteria/kitchen)	80	128	100	196	28
Asset Value Rating	4	4	4	4	4
Threat Rating	2	4	5	7	7
Vulnerability Rating	10	8	5	7	1
Library	60	120	105	147	84
Asset Value Rating	3	3	3	3	3
Threat Rating	2	4	5	7	7
Vulnerability Rating	10	10	7	7	4
Custodial Functions	60	48	90	84	21
Asset Value Rating	3	3	3	3	3
Threat Rating	2	4	5	7	7
Vulnerability Rating	10	4	6	4	1

Table 1–3:   Continued

	Threat/Hazard				
	Terrorist Act	Armed Attack	Unauthorized Entry	Low Level CBR Attack	Cyber-terrorism
	Stationary Vehicle Bomb	Attack by Small Arms	Forced Entry at Night to Damage School Property	Hydrogen Sulfide "Stink Bomb"	Electronic Attack to Destroy or Alter School Academic Records
Science Laboratories	60	60	120	63	21
Asset Value Rating	3	3	3	3	3
Threat Rating	2	4	5	7	7
Vulnerability Rating	10	5	8	3	1
Vocational Equipment (shops)	60	48	120	63	21
Asset Value Rating	3	3	3	3	3
Threat Rating	2	4	5	7	7
Vulnerability Rating	10	4	8	3	1
Indoor Sports Facilities	40	32	80	84	14
Asset Value Rating	2	2	2	2	2
Threat Rating	2	4	5	7	7
Vulnerability Rating	10	4	8	6	1
Outdoor Sports Facilities	10	8	35	14	7
Asset Value Rating	1	1	1	1	1
Threat Rating	2	4	5	7	7
Vulnerability Rating	5	2	7	2	1

To evaluate prospective mitigation measures, the design team should first calculate new values of risk based on how the installation or use of mitigation measures would change vulnerability and/or asset values. Some mitigation measures will affect multiple asset/threat risk values. After the amount of risk reduction each mitigation measure will produce has been calculated, the cost of each mitigation measure should be estimated. The final step is to perform a benefit/cost analysis to determine which mitigation measures will produce the greatest reduction of risk at an acceptable cost.

Facility Design

Facility Design Principles—In the Past

Schools are typically in use for long periods of time; as a result, teaching continues to be conducted in facilities that were designed and constructed at the beginning of the twentieth century. Early twentieth-century school design was based on late nineteenth-century models and was relatively static until after World War II. Schools ranged from one-room rural schoolhouses to major symbolic civic structures in large cities. Other inner-city schools were more modest, inserted into small sites on busy streets and constrained by budget limits.

The typical city school was one to three stories in height and consisted of rows of classrooms on either side of a wide, noisy corridor lined with metal lockers; there were asphalt play courts, and, sometimes, rooftop recreational areas. The larger schools sometimes had a library, special rooms for art and science, a shop, and an auditorium.

The surge to meet the school construction demands of the postwar baby boom was primarily a suburban development. Much larger sites were available, schools were one or two stories in height, auditoriums became multiuse buildings, and large parking lots appeared. However, many rural schools were located far away from towns and their resources, such as fire departments and other services.

But the fundamental school program of classrooms along double-loaded corridors did not change very much. However, in warm climates, the one-story finger plan school, constructed of wood and a small quantity of steel, was both economical and more human, and the noisy tiled double-loaded corridor became a covered walk, open to the air, with the classrooms on one side and a grassed court on the other. Compact versions of these plans appeared as schools became larger and sites smaller.

Inner-city high schools were usually large facilities, housing two thousand to three thousand students (basically small towns with complex social, economic, and class systems. In the 1960s and 1970s, some design experiments were tried, such as team teaching, which spawned large open classrooms with poor acoustics.

Some of the new, large high schools were built as air-conditioned enclosures, with many windowless classrooms, in buildings similar to the shopping malls that replaced the main street retail centers. At the same time, by adding prefabricated classrooms to accommodate a surge in enrollment, many schools were expanded. Although the pre-fabricated classrooms were originally intended as temporary space, many are now used as permanent classrooms. Schools built in the 1980s and 1990s assumed a wide variety of forms, often combining classrooms into clusters and focusing on providing an attractive learning environment. However, demographic needs, shortage of afford-able land, and limited funding has also resulted in the adaptation of existing non-educational buildings into schools.

Present School Design

New statements of design principles are beginning to emerge, although some of the fol-lowing represent perennial concerns:

- The building should provide for health, safety, and security.
- The learning environment should enhance teaching and learning and accommodate the needs of all learners.
- The learning environment should serve as the center of the community.
- The learning environment should result from a planning/design process that involves all stakeholders.
- The learning environment should allow for flexibility and adaptability to changing needs.
- The learning environment should make effective use of all available resources.

These principles lead, in turn, to a number of current design principles, including:

- Design for protection against natural hazards
- Increased design attention to occupant security
- Careful lighting design and increased use of day lighting and comfort control
- Design for durability
- Long-life/loose-fit approach: design for internal change and flexibility
- Design for sustainability, including energy efficiency and the use of "green" materials

Some new schools already respond to these needs, and, indeed, their originators, school districts, communities, and designers are among those defining the schools of the next decade. Some of the changes are the result of ideology and analysis; others are enforced by the effort to provide an improved learning environment and enhanced learning resources in an increasingly financially limited school construction economy. Some school districts will be hard pressed to provide a minimal learning environment with buildings of the utmost simplicity, while meeting the requirements for health, safety, and security.

Future School Design

Schools will continue to vary widely in size; however, even in the suburbs, land has become scarce and expensive. New schools will be more compact and the sprawling one-story campus will become less common. The desire for more supportive environments and the rejection of traditional school plans will result in more imaginative and often more complex layouts. Moreover, the move to repopulate the inner cities will result in the construction of even more dense and compact schools.

However, many educational researchers believe that students improve their learning skills in smaller schools. Although small schools may be economically unrealistic, methods of organization are being explored that provide some of the benefits of small size within a large physical complex. Some schools are organized into "learning academies" for each grade, with classrooms that can expand and contract and other activity rooms of various sizes.

Other researchers believe that the conventional library will disappear. The trend in many new schools is for the library to take the form of a multimedia center and material collections, including laptop computers that are distributed from mobile units to "classroom clusters."

Schools are increasingly seen as community resources that go beyond the educational functions. Adult education and community events now take place on evenings, on weekends, and throughout the traditional vacation periods; therefore, the school day and week have been expanded. These uses are seen as ways of finding affordable methods of enhancing community-service resources by ensuring that a facility's utilization is maximized.

Indications are that the school building will probably increase in importance to the community, as its roles expand beyond that of merely providing a K–12 education for students during a school year. At the same time, modern technology means that today's schools, already far more complex than the relatively simple buildings of a few decades ago, will tend to be more fragile and consequently more vulnerable to nature's and society's threats unless special attention is paid to their design and construction.

The natural hazards will remain: earthquakes and tornadoes will continue to be, for some locations, a source of worry and fear. Besides protecting their occupants, schools in earthquake-prone regions are often used as post-earthquake shelters. In California, this is particularly appropriate because the State's Field Act, enacted in 1933, following the Long Beach earthquake, requires that public schools be designed by a licensed architect or engineer, their plans checked, and the construction on site inspected by staff of the Department of State of Architecture. Elsewhere, floods and high winds are a familiar threat that also must be addressed by knowledgeable design and good construction practice. Schools, or designated areas within them, located in hurricane- and tornado-prone areas are increasingly being constructed to provide shelter for the occupants.

Multi-hazard and Performance-based Design

The concept of multi-hazard design is that designers need to understand the fundamental characteristics of hazards and how they interact, so that design for protection becomes integrated with all the other design demands.

Performance-based design suggests that, rather than relying on the building code for protection against hazards, a more systematic investigation is conducted to ensure that the specific concerns of building owners and occupants are addressed.

Building codes focus on providing life safety, and property protection is secondary: performance-based design provides additional levels of protection that cover property damage and functional interruption within a financially feasible context.

However, it is important to identify all hazards and their frequency, and careful consideration of design against hazards must be integrated with all other design issues and be present from the inception of the site selection and building design process.

Although the basic issues to be considered in planning a school construction program are, more or less, common to all school districts, the processes used differ greatly, because each school district has its own approach. Districts vary in size, from a rural district responsible for only a few elementary schools, to a city district or statewide system overseeing a complex program of all school types and sizes, including new design and construction, renovations, and additions. A district may have had a long-term program of school construction and be familiar with programming, financing, hiring designers, bidding procedures, contract administration, and commissioning a new building, but another district may not have constructed a new school for decades and have no staff members familiar with the process.

Layout and Design

The single most important goal in planning a site to resist terrorism and security threats is the protection of life, property, and operations. Decision making in support of this purpose should be based, first and foremost, on a comprehensive assessment of the man-made threats and hazards so that planning and design countermeasures are appropriate and effective in the reduction of vulnerability and risk.

Because the economics of development dictate the construction of schools, security concerns should be evaluated carefully. Conflicts sometimes arise between security site design and conventional site design. For example, open circulation and common spaces, which are desirable for conventional school design, are often undesirable for security design. To maximize safety, security, and sustainability, designers should implement a holistic approach to site design that integrates form and function to achieve a balance among the various design elements and objectives. Even if resources are limited, significant value can be added to a project by integrating security considerations into the more traditional design tasks in such a way that they complement, rather than compete with, the other elements.

In most cases, sound site planning will increase the land area needed for individual school buildings and maximize the protection measures to be adopted. While your school may not be a target, are you close to a high-risk target that, if attacked, would impact you? When designing a school, the designer should consider external and internal land-use design concerns, including the characteristics of the surrounding area (e.g., construction type, occupancies, and the nature and intensity of adjacent activities), as well as the implications of these characteristics for the protection of the students, faculty, and staff on the school site under consideration.

When designing new school buildings or evaluating existing schools, the designer should evaluate key protection measures to ensure they are appropriate, desirable, and cost-effective in terms of mitigating the risk of potential terrorist attacks. Security measures must be evaluated carefully to understand which measures are truly beneficial and which are not practical.

When making decisions about site antiterrorism and security, designers should consider the following:

- Adjacent land use and zoning plans for potential development that would impact security within the school (assess by using land-use maps and Geographic Information Systems [GISs])
- Building footprint(s) relative to total land available
- Building location(s) or, if undeveloped, suitable building location(s) relative to the site perimeter and adjacent land uses; distance between the perimeter fence and improved areas off site
- Access via foot, road, rail, water, and air; suitability to support a secure perimeter
- Current and planned infrastructure and its vulnerabilities, including easements, tunnels, pipes, and rights-of-way
- Infrastructure nodes that constitute single-point vulnerabilities
- Adjacent land uses and occupancies that could enable or facilitate attacks or that are potential targets themselves and, thus, present collateral damage or cascading failure hazards
- Proximity to fire and police stations, hospitals, shelters, and other critical facilities that could be of use in an attack
- Presence of natural physical barriers, such as water features, dense vegetation, and terrain that could provide access control and/or shielding, or suitability of the site for the incorporation of such features
- Topographic and climatic characteristics that could affect the performance of chemical agents and other weapons
- Observability from outside site boundaries; ability of vegetation in proximity to building or site to screen covert activity

Layout

The overall layout of a school site (e.g., the placement and form of its buildings, infra-structures, and amenities) is the starting point for development. Choices made during this stage of the design process will steer decision making for the other elements of the site. A number of aspects of site layout and building type present security considerations and are discussed below.

CLUSTERED VERSUS DISPERSED FUNCTIONS

There is a strong correlation between building functions and building layout and forms. Typically, the former dictates the other two. Depending on the site characteristics, the occupancy requirements, and other factors, school buildings may cluster key functions in one particular area or have these functions designed in a more dispersed manner. Both patterns have compelling strengths and weaknesses in terms of security.

Concentrating key functions in one place may create a target-rich environment and increase the risk of collateral impacts. Additionally, it increases the potential for the establishment of more single-point vulnerabilities. If several key functions are grouped in a particular area of the building (i.e., the mechanical rooms, stairs, telephone switch room, and loading docks) and this area is attacked, the school may be closed for a substantial period of time, even if the attack is not severe and the rest of the school remains unharmed. However, grouping high-risk activities, concentrations of personnel, and critical functions into a cluster can help maximize standoff from the perimeter and create a "defensible space." This also helps to reduce the number of access and surveillance points and minimize the size of the perimeter needed to protect the school areas.

In contrast, the dispersal of key functions reduces the risk that an attack on any one part of the site will impact the other parts. However, this could also have an isolating effect and reduce the effectiveness of on-site surveillance, increase the complexity of security systems and emergency response, and create a less defensible space.

To the extent that site, economic, and other factors allow, the designer should consolidate school designs that are functionally compatible and have similar threat levels. For example, visitor areas and receiving/loading areas constitute a school's innermost line of defense, because they are the first places where people and materials enter the school building. Logically, they should be physically separated from other key functions, such as the main operational areas or where people concentrate.

SCHOOL BUILDING ORIENTATION

The orientation of a school building can have significant impact on its performance, not only in terms of energy efficiency, but also the ability to protect occupants. A school building's orientation relative to its surroundings defines its relationship to that area. In aesthetic terms, a school building can open up to the area or turn its back; it can be inviting to those outside or "hunker down" defensively. The physical positioning of a building relative to its surroundings may seem subtle, but can be a greater determinant of this intangible quality than exterior aesthetics. Nevertheless, the proximity of a vulnerable facade to a parking area, street, adjacent site, or other area that is accessible to vehicles and/or difficult to observe can greatly contribute to its vulnerability. This illustrates one way in which protective requirements can be at odds with otherwise good design. A strong, blank wall with no glazing will protect students, faculty staff, property, and operations within from a blast, but the lack of windows removes virtually all opportunity for the faculty and staff to monitor activities outside and take appropriate actions in a timely manner. Designers should consider such trade-offs early in the design process, in an effort to determine the acceptable level of risk.

OPEN SPACE

The incorporation of open space into school site design presents a number of benefits. First and foremost is the ability to easily monitor an area and detect intruders, vehicles, and weapons. Closely related to this benefit is the standoff value of open space, so every additional increment of distance provides increasingly more protection. In addition, pervious open space allows storm-water to percolate back into the ground, reducing the need for culverts, drainage pipes, manholes, and other covert site access and weapon concealment opportunities. Also, if the open space is impassible for vehicles (as in the case of a wetland or densely vegetated area), it can provide not only environmental and aesthetic amenities, but prevent vehicle intrusion as well.

INFRASTRUCTURE AND LIFELINES

Providing power, gas, water, wastewater, and communications services is one of the most basic requirements of any school development. At the site scale, all critical lifelines should have at least one layer of redundancy, or backup. By eliminating single-point vulnerabilities, designers will reduce the chance that service will be interrupted if an attack damages or destroys a lifeline either outside the school perimeter or on site. It is important to note that co-locating a backup lifeline with its primary lifeline does not eliminate single-point vulnerability; only physical separation can substantially increase the likelihood of continuity of service.

Additionally, all controls, interconnections, exposed lines, and other vulnerable elements of school infrastructure systems should be protected from access and exploitation by surveillance and/or physical countermeasures. Service entrances and other secondary access points should be monitored and access-controlled; special attention should also be paid to any locations where multiple systems or primary and backup systems come together, such as control rooms and mechanical spaces. Again, these facilities should be designed for maximum observability, including the use of opportunity reduction and target hardening strategies, where appropriate, and should be equipped with adequate lighting and emergency communications capabilities wherever possible.

Structure

The structure provides support for all the elements of a building and ensures that the building can sustain all the loads and forces that it will encounter during its life. Often concealed behind ceilings, exterior cladding, and decorative facing materials, the structure plays a critical role in providing a safe and secure school building.

Because of the relatively small size of most school buildings and the simplicity of design of the traditional school, with numerous internal walls, structural design is relatively simple. A well-designed and constructed school should not collapse unless struck by a severe tornado or terrorist attack.

Most suburban schools built in the last few decades are typically one or two stories in height, with light steel frames or mixed structures of steel and wood frames and also with some concrete or concrete masonry walls. Except in the western states and the Atlantic and Gulf coasts, concrete masonry walls may have nominal or no steel reinforcing. Reinforced masonry perimeter and/or interior classroom separation walls sometimes are used as shear walls to provide lateral support. First floors are generally concrete slab-on-grade.

Many schools may have long-span gymnasiums or assembly spaces, using glued-laminated wood beams, steel trusses, or pre-cast reinforced concrete tees or double tees. In these long-span structures, large diaphragm and wind uplift forces must be transmitted to the perimeter walls or frames, and the design and construction of wall/roof connections are critical.

Typical prefabricated teaching spaces are usually classroom-sized wood frame boxes; they are air-conditioned where necessary, and generally have minimally adequate lighting and electrical services. They provide an economical way of solving a problem, but rows of prefabricated classroom boxes do not provide an appropriate long-term learning and social environment. Also, they are typically less resistant to natural hazards.

Inner-city schools may be three or four stories in height and are often built on congested sites. Structurally, they are usually constructed of reinforced masonry, reinforced concrete, and/or steel frames, and sometimes are a mix of these types of systems.

Older structures (i.e., pre–World War II) often had unreinforced masonry walls with wood floors and roof structures. Another common type was a lightly reinforced concrete frame infilled with hollow tile or masonry for walls, together with a wood floor and roof structure. Small schools were often of wood frame construction throughout, and basements and crawl spaces were common in these structures. Older structures are particularly vulnerable to natural hazards. Unreinforced masonry structures have performed very poorly in earthquakes and high winds, as have older reinforced concrete frames with infill. Older wood frame structures are often deficient in their design and construction detailing and are frequently weakened by insect attack or dry rot.

Nonstructural Systems and Components

Nonstructural systems and components are architectural elements, such as ceilings and partitions; mechanical, plumbing, and electrical items that provide utilities and services to the building; and cladding and roofing that provide weather protection and insulation.

A wide variety of exterior cladding materials are used for schools. The most common include brick or concrete masonry, stucco on metal or wood stud frame walls, exterior insulation finish systems (EIFS), and various natural and synthetic sidings on wood frame structures. Metal or stucco-faced insulated panels are also used. Metal and glass curtain walls are used infrequently, generally in an urban setting.

Newer schools usually have suspended grid ceilings that support light acoustic panels and inset lighting fixtures. Pendant fixtures are also used, in the form of rows of linear fluorescent fixtures or single high-intensity (HID) fixtures. The latter are often large in size when used in assembly spaces or gymnasiums. Incandescent fixtures may still be found in older school buildings, but are a source of high-energy use and should be replaced.

Non-load-bearing partitions are often of hollow tile or concrete masonry: however, especially in the western states, partitions are of gypsum board over wood or metal framing, although concrete masonry or tile may be used in restrooms or other service areas.

School mechanical systems are relatively simple. Older schools and some new ones employ perimeter hot water heating together with natural ventilation or forced air.

Very old schools may still employ steam heating, but most of these systems should have been replaced by hydronic systems. Newer schools, particularly when large, often employ forced air heating, ventilating, and cooling systems. Concern for energy conservation has resulted in the use of innovative systems, including a return to the use of natural ventilation and day lighting.

Plumbing tends to be concentrated in restroom areas, although science, art spaces, and school kitchens require more complex plumbing services. Specialized plumbing will also be found in mechanical/boiler rooms, the water service and fire protection service entrances, and domestic water heaters.

Electrical services have become increasingly complex with the need for ready access to power and communications services. The trend in communications devices to become wireless may serve to slightly reduce the extent of hard-wired communications. Fire alarm and security services, however, require increasingly extensive electrical and electronic services.

Fixed classroom desks and teacher units have been replaced by lighter mobile furniture. Libraries still require extensive shelving, although ready access to the Internet may tend to reduce the use of hard-copy materials.

Some special spaces, such as science labs, shop, and art rooms, need storage for hazardous chemicals and utilize heavy equipment; they are vulnerable to earthquake damage. Music spaces and gymnasiums all have special equipment and storage needs, some of which would be costly to replace in the event of damage.

Prescriptive Approach to Codes

The traditional approach used in building codes in the United States has been that of prescriptive-based codes. Prescriptive-based codes are quantitative and rely on fixed

Definitions of Performance-Based Design

Performance-based design is an evolving concept. The term as currently used has multiple definitions. Three common ones are:

- A design approach that meets the life safety and building performance intents of the traditional code, while providing designers and building officials with a more systematic way to evaluate alternative design options currently available in codes. In this regard, performance-based design facilitates innovation and makes it easier for designers to propose new building systems not covered by existing code provisions.
- A design approach that identifies and selects a performance level from several performance level options. Some provisions in the current version of the International Building Code (IBC) are sometimes called performance-based because they incorporate distinctions between performance goals for different building uses. These performance options are conceived to achieve higher-than-code-minimum design requirements.
- A design approach that provides designers with tools to achieve specific performance objectives such that the performance of a structure can be reliably predicted. In the hazards area, this approach has been highly developed for seismic design although considerable research is still necessary to ensure the requisite reliability and predictability that would allow a performance-based code to be possible.

values that are prescribed by the codes and intended to achieve a reasonable level of fire and life safety, as well as reasonable levels of safety from other hazards, such as earthquakes, floods, and high winds. Prescriptive requirements are based on broad classifications of buildings and occupancies, and are typically stated in terms of fixed values, such as travel distance, fire resistance ratings, allowable area and height, and structural design (e.g., dead loads, live loads, snow loads, rain loads, earthquake loads, wind loads, etc.).

Prescriptive codes provide limited rules for addressing various design and construction issues (e.g., establishing limits on the allowable area and height of a building based upon construction type and occupancy classification). One of the current prescriptive building codes limits the basic area of a noncombustible, unprotected school building to 14,500 square feet. Why are this building and its occupants considered reasonably safe or acceptable at 14,500 square feet and unsafe or unacceptable at 15,000 square feet? This traditional approach is assumed to provide an "acceptable level of risk."

This is not to say that buildings designed and built under the prescriptive-based codes are unsafe, but it is important to understand that the requirements in the prescriptive-based codes are judged to be only the minimum necessary to safeguard the public health, safety, and general welfare. In some instances, it may be desirable, appropriate, and even necessary to raise the level of safety above the prescribed minimums.

Under the prescriptive approach, all schools are essentially treated alike. Thus, the requirements for an elementary school with five hundred students are the same as those for a high school with five hundred students, although clearly there are differences in these buildings due to the age of the occupants and their ability to take proper and appropriate action under various emergency conditions.

Another issue involving school buildings is the use of the facility for purposes other than education. In many communities, school buildings are designated as emergency shelters to be used in the event of a natural or man-made disaster event. The "normal" prescriptive code approach does not address the building features and systems necessary for the continuity of service required for an emergency shelter (for security, flooding, high wind, or hazardous material release issues).

How can the issues, such as these and others, be addressed? An innovative procedure that is becoming increasingly adopted is the use of a performance-based approach to improve or supplement the prescriptive requirements.

Performance-Based Approach

Although having detailed requirements for "performance" is relatively new to the building and fire codes used in the United States, the concept is not. The various "prescriptive" building, fire, and life safety codes have all contained provisions for what was known as "alternative methods and materials" or "equivalencies." These code provisions allow for the use of methods, equipment, or materials not specified or prescribed in the code, provided the code official approves the alternative. It is under these provisions of the traditional codes that the performance-based design approach can be undertaken.

Under the concept of an alternative method and material, or equivalency, the code official must approve the alternative or equivalency if it can be shown to be equivalent in quality, strength, effectiveness, fire resistance, durability, and safety. The proponent of the alternative method, or equivalence, is responsible for providing all necessary documentation to the code official. Based on the ability of the code official to permit alternate methods and materials in the existing prescriptive codes, performance-based codes simply offer the code official a system with which to accept alternative designs based on performance. In other words, this is nothing new to the code official; it is just a more formal way to review designs.

As mentioned previously, taking a "performance" approach is not new to building design because decisions based upon performance occur in almost every project. As an example, constructing corridor walls out of either gypsum board and steel studs or concrete masonry units (CMUs) will meet the prescriptive code requirements for a rated corridor in an educational occupancy. However, from a "performance" standpoint, the concrete masonry assembly is more desirable due to its ability to withstand the normal wear and tear of such occupancy. Another example would be the selection of the heating, ventilating, and air conditioning (HVAC) system.

Although either rooftop units or central boilers/chillers might provide the requisite thermal performance, lifecycle cost analysis might support the choice of the central boiler/chiller.

Performance-based design provides a structured way of making decisions that is particularly applicable to the issue of life safety and damage reduction from natural and man-made hazards. From a designer's standpoint, the performance-based codes provide a more formalized system to develop, document, and submit alternative materials and methods, or equivalencies.

Unlike relying solely on a prescriptive code, performance-based design addresses an individual building's unique aspects or uses, and specific and stakeholder needs.

Stakeholders include everyone who has an interest in the successful completion of a school project (i.e., the school board members, responsible officials, members of the design team, the builders, the community at large, parents, and the code enforcement officials). The design team is a subgroup of the stakeholders, which includes individuals such as representatives of the architect, officials from the school district, and other pertinent consultants.

It is critical to the proper development, approval, and implementation of any performance-based design for all of the stakeholders to be actively involved in the process. Because the stakeholders establish the acceptable level of risk, it is crucial that all of them be involved in the project from the earliest stages. It is also important that the stakeholders realize that an incident in a school facility can be measured in more ways than just monetary. The loss of a school facility for any reason can have organizational, legal, political, social, and psychological impacts.

The performance-based procedure provides the basis for the development and selection of design options, based upon the needs of the specific project, to augment the broad occupancy classification requirements. The approach structures a comparison of safety levels provided by various alternative designs, and also provides a mechanism for determining what level of safety, at what cost, is acceptable to the stakeholders. Performance-based design aims at property protection and life safety strategies in which the systems are integrated, rather than designed in isolation.

Acceptable Risk and Performance Levels

The performance-based design process begins with establishing the acceptable risk and appropriate performance levels for the building and its systems. The basic concept of acceptable risk is the maximum level of damage to the building that can be tolerated, related to a realistic risk event scenario or probability. For each hazard, there are methods of measuring the magnitude of events and their probability, as well as terminology to describe levels of damage or performance levels. There are four performance levels, each of which addresses structural damage, nonstructural systems, occupant hazards, overall extent of damage, and hazardous materials. The types of damage that are defined will vary according to the type of hazard that is being addressed. The ICC Performance Code for Buildings and Facilities formalized four design performance levels in terms of tolerable limits to the building, its contents, and its occupants that apply to all types of hazards. These levels are as follows:

Mild Impact. At the mild impact level, there is no structural damage and the building is safe to occupy; injuries are minimal in number and minor in nature; damage to the building and contents is minimal in extent and minor in cost; and minimal hazardous materials are released into the environment.

Moderate Impact. At the moderate level, there is moderate, repairable structural damage, and some delay in re-occupancy can be expected; injuries may be locally significant, but generally moderate in numbers and in nature; there is a low likelihood of a single life loss and very low likelihood of multiple life loss; and some hazardous materials are released into the environment, but the risk to the community is minimal.

High Impact. At the high impact level, it is expected that there will be significant damage to structural elements, but with no falling debris. Significant delays in re-occupancy can be expected. Nonstructural systems needed for normal building use are also significantly damaged and inoperable. Emergency systems may be damaged, but remain operational. Injuries to occupants may be locally significant with a high risk to life, but are generally moderate in numbers and nature. There is a moderate likelihood of a single life loss, with a low probability of multiple life loss. Hazardous materials are released into the environment with localized relocation required.

Severe Impact. With severe impact, there will be substantial structural damage, and repair may not be technically possible. The building is not safe for re-occupancy, because re-occupancy could cause collapse. Nonstructural systems for normal use may be completely nonfunctional, and emergency systems may be substantially damaged and nonfunctional. Injuries to occupants may be high in number and significant in nature. Significant hazards to life may exist. There is a high likelihood of single life loss and a moderate likelihood of multiple life loss. Significant hazardous materials may be released into the environment, with relocation needed beyond the immediate vicinity.

Correlation between Performance Groups and Tolerated Levels of Damage

The provisions of the ICC Performance Code for Building and Facilities correlate the performance groups and the tolerated levels of damage. Events are classified as small, medium, large, or very large. Each hazard will have its own definitions that modify these generic magnitudes. Building groups in the ICC Performance Code include:

- Group I—Buildings that represent a low hazard to human life in the event of failure
- Group II—All buildings except Groups I, III, and IV
- Group III—Buildings with a substantial hazard to human life, including schools or day-care centers with a capacity greater than 250
- Group IV—Buildings designed as essential facilities, including designated earthquake, hurricane, or other emergency shelters

Using an elementary school with an occupant load of less than 250 as an example (Group II), it can be seen that there is a significant difference in the level of performance required when the building is to be used as a designated emergency shelter

(Group IV). These performance levels clearly are not addressed by the prescriptive code requirements.

For hazards, such as earthquakes and winds, it may be desirable to set different performance objectives for nonstructural versus structural design. Although the prescriptive code may provide acceptable structural safety, it may be cost-effective to spend a small additional amount of resources to enhance the attachment and bracing of key nonstructural components and provide for independent inspection of their installation. Local information on the characteristics of flood may suggest that it is prudent to allow an increased factor of safety above the expected flood elevation at the property. Similarly, local experience may suggest that projects should be designed for higher wind speeds than the code values.

Design Guidelines

FUNDAMENTAL IDEAS AND ORIENTATION

The guidelines presented here were developed by the Florida Department of Education. They are based on the fundamental idea that the proper design and management of the physical environment can help prevent and deter criminal behavior in Florida's schools and community colleges. The growing body of scientific evidence to support this suggestion comes from the field of place-based crime prevention, which early on produced theories of Defensible Space (Newman 1973), Crime Prevention through Environmental Design (CPTED) (Jeffrey 1971, 1977; Crowe 2000), Environmental Criminology (Brantingham 1981), and Situational Crime Prevention (Clarke 1997). These initial, interconnected approaches to crime prevention have produced a modern stream of research and applications that explore crime prevention strategies relative to educational institutions and their unique place in society (see, for example, Schneider et al., 2000; American Institute of Architects 2001; Duke 2001; National Crime Prevention Council 2002). This work is applicable to Florida schools and community colleges and these guidelines illustrate—through text and drawings—how school architects, facility managers, risk managers, planners, and others can translate these crime prevention ideas into action. This guide also is intended to serve school resource officers, school administrators, and the general public, as well.

RESEARCH APPROACH

The guidelines are based on research and studies of schools and crime prevention from across the United States and the world, on on-site visits to schools and community colleges throughout Florida conducted by the research team, and on survey responses gathered between May 15 and August 14, 2002, from a wide variety of individuals who have day-to-day responsibilities dealing with school and community college design, safety, and administrative issues (see Appendix 2 at the end of this section).

ORGANIZATION OF THE GUIDELINES

The organizing scheme of the guidelines is to move from the largest level or scale of concern—the school or community college "Site Design"—progressively down to the smallest and most specific scale of concern—"Systems and Equipment." In so doing, the guidelines present the design principles identified in Section 423, 7 (h) of the 2001 Florida Building Code—"*Natural Access Control, Natural Surveillance and Territorial Integrity*" and, where applicable, related "*Management*" concerns that are either identified in the code principles or are suggested by them.

To facilitate ease of use and cross referencing to the Florida Building Code's principles, the guidelines provide *bullet points* that summarize the most significant elements within each scale of interest and that are keyed, in order of their presentation, to each design principle in the Florida Building Code. For example, at the first and largest scale of concern, "Site Design," the guidelines focus on "Natural Access Control," which is the first design principle identified by the Florida Building Code. Each subsequent element, such as "Site Perimeter," is numbered for reference purposes. Following the bullet points, the Guidelines present a more detailed discussion of the points in relation to the major heading. So, for example, under "Site Design" Section 1.7 "Landscaping," the text discusses factors that "must be considered when planning landscape arrangements on school campuses."

Drawings and graphics are provided adjacent to the text that illustrate the most salient design (and, in some cases, management) aspects pertaining to each principle identified. It is important to note that the drawings are for illustrative purposes only and are not meant to provide prescriptive design solutions.

THE LINKAGE BETWEEN DESIGN AND MANAGEMENT

The scientific literature dealing with place-based crime prevention demonstrates that the design and management of places go hand in hand. It is easy to think of these as separate concerns, but they are intimately connected in "real world" application. This is especially germane to schools and community colleges, where day-to-day uses of places can easily affect their original design intent. One simple example to illustrate this is the design of windows facing building entryways to facilitate surveillance, a fundamental crime prevention principle. If administrators allow staff or students to obstruct the windows (by closing blinds or covering them with posters), their effectiveness is severely compromised. Management policies and practices must, therefore, be linked to design so as to complement crime prevention and deterrence on a continuing basis. That being said, we emphasize that these guidelines are not intended to dictate management practices or policy, which must remain the province of individual school districts, community colleges, and their respective administrators. Rather, our concern is to highlight the importance of thinking through the connections between design and management so that local administrators can better appreciate the implications that their decisions may have on facility design and use, and ultimately on crime prevention.

SCOPE OF THE GUIDELINES: CONFLICTS AND CONTRADICTIONS

While the guidelines seek to be as specific as possible, because of the great variety of conditions found in Florida schools and community colleges, they are necessarily presented to address issues in a general manner. In that sense, the guidelines do not differentiate between new construction and old construction, or between elementary schools, middle schools, high schools, and community colleges. The research team recognizes, however, that there are indeed differences among regions of Florida, urban and rural areas, and among design, construction, management, budget, and crime issues that affect each of these levels and types of institutions. Administrators are advised to make specific adjustments based upon the unique need of their school or community college. Where possible, the guidelines suggest approaches or strategies that may be useful to them in that process.

References

American Institute of Architects. *Building Security by Design: A Primer for Architects, Design Professionals, and Their Clients.* Washington, D.C., November 2001.

Brantingham, P. J., & P. L. Brantingham. *Environmental Criminology.* Beverly Hills, Calif.: Sage, 1981.

Clarke, R. V. *Situational Crime Prevention: Successful Case Studies.* 2nd ed. Albany, N.Y.: Harrow and Heston, 1997.

Crowe, T. *Crime Prevention Through Environmental Design.* 2nd ed. Beverly Hills, Calif.: Sage, 2000.

Duke, D. L.. *Creating Safe Schools for All Children.* Boston: Allyn and Bacon, 2001.

Jeffrey, C. R. *Defensible Space: Crime Prevention Through Urban Design.* New York: Macmillan, 1977.

National Crime Prevention Council. "Safer Schools and Communities by Design: The CPTED Approach." Atlanta, Ga., April 2002.

Newman, O. *Defensible Space: Crime Prevention Through Urban Design.* New York: Macmillan, 1973.

Schneider, T., H. Walker, & J. Sprague. *Safe School Design: A Handbook for Educational Leaders.* Eugene, Ore.: ERIC Clearinghouse on Educational Management, 2000.

Crime Prevention Through Environmental Design

CPTED is a crime reduction technique that has several key elements applicable to the analysis of building function and site design against physical attack. Architects, city planners, landscape and interior designers, and law enforcement use it with the objective of creating a climate of safety in a community by designing a physical environment that positively influences human behavior. Although CPTED principles are not incorporated into the assessment process presented in this primer, it is useful to briefly discuss CPTED because it is often entwined with terrorism protection measures.

Definition of Terms

ACCESS CONTROL:

The general design/management strategy is intended to decrease opportunity for crime by denying or increasing the effort required to approach a target or gain entry to a target area. This may also create or increase the perception of risk to the offender. Access control is generally categorized into three types—natural, mechanical, and organized:

> **Natural:** the use of design, including spatial definition and designation strategies, to deny or increase the effort and risk of entry and detection to offenders. Natural access-control strategies tend to be more cost-effective when they are "designed into" the structure beginning with the initial, schematic planning phases than added by retrofit.

> **Mechanical:** the use of locks, hardened or reinforced doors, gates, fences, bollards, or other similar "target hardening" devices or structures to deny or increase the effort and risk of entry and detection to offenders. Electronic devices associated with surveillance strategies below may also complement these.

> **Organized:** the use of human guardianship (whether formal, as in the employment of police or private security personnel, or informal, as when regular employees or residents control a target's site entry) to protect a target or target area by denying entry or increasing the real and perceived effort and risk of entry and detection to offenders.

MANAGEMENT:

Used here in terms of crime prevention theory and practice, management is the appropriate and effective use of resources, including personnel, equipment, and supplies, to preserve, sustain, or repair owned or controlled property so as to achieve crime prevention goals. Wilson and Kelling's "broken windows" theory (1982) suggested that small levels of environmental disorder (such as a broken window, graffiti, uncollected trash, etc.) provide "cues" that no one cares about places (and hence, they are attractive to offenders). There is a presumed developmental sequence to such disorder, such that small problems lead to larger ones, including the possibility of criminal behavior. The function of responsible management, in this context, is to maintain property under their control so as to not send out the "wrong" environmental cues.

continued

continued

SURVEILLANCE:

The general crime prevention strategy that seeks to decrease crime opportunity by keeping intruders under observation and/or by increasing their perception of the risk of being observed. Like "access control" above, surveillance is generally divided into three types—natural, mechanical, and organized:

> **Natural:** the use of design, including spatial definition and designation strategies, to increase the actual abilities of guardians to observe intruders, as well as to increase the *perception* of intruders that they may be observed by others. Examples here would include the placement of windows near building entryways and the design of entrance paths so that they put pedestrians in view of observers.

> **Mechanical:** the use of mechanical or electronic devices for observation purposes, such as mirrors, closed circuit television (CCTV), or sound recording devices. Visual observation is greatly facilitated by appropriate lighting, which can help reduce crime opportunity by increasing perceived risks relative to the chances of being observed and can also help reduce the fear of crime.

> **Organized:** the use of human guardianship (whether formal, as in the employment of police or private security personnel, or informal, as when regular employees or residents observe a target or target site) to increase the real and perceived effort and risk of entry and detection to offenders.

TERRITORIAL INTEGRITY:

A phrase derived from Oscar Newman's original notion of "**territoriality**" (1973), which focused on **the physical environment's capacity, through the design and marking of space, to create in users and residents the sense of *responsibility* for and *control* of that space, such that they will protect and defend it, if necessary.** Territorial integrity and territoriality are promoted by the clear definitions of boundaries, such that intruders (as well as "legitimate" users) can easily determine whether spaces are "public" or "private" in nature. In well-marked and bounded places, intruders can be easily observed and are likely to be challenged by legitimate users or by space guardians. Examples of markers are real space borders and barriers (such as fences and gates, which also serve as access-control devices), as well as symbolic markers of space, such as street pavers, ornamental gateposts, or entryways. Other space markers that augment territorial integrity include signs and posted maps, which also serve as way-finding devices and can be used for "rule setting" in places. Territorial integrity is further promoted by effective access-control and surveillance techniques, as defined above.

CPTED concepts have been successfully applied in a wide variety of applications, including streets, parks, museums, government buildings, houses, and commercial complexes. The approach is particularly applicable to schools, where outdated facilities are common. Most schools in the United States were built thirty to sixty or more years ago. Security issues were almost nonexistent at the time, and technology was dramatically different. As a result, building designs are not always compatible with today's more security-conscious environment.

According to CPTED principles, depending upon purely conventional physical security measures (e.g., security guards and metal detectors) to correct objectionable student behavior may have its limitations. Although employing physical security measures will no doubt increase the level of physical security, in some cases physical security measures employed as stand-alone measures may lead to a more negative environment, thereby enhancing violence. In short, employing stand-alone physical security measures may fail to address the underlying behavioral patterns that adversely affect the school environment. CPTED analysis focuses on creating changes to the physical and social environment that will reinforce positive behavior.

CPTED builds on three strategies:

- Territoriality (using buildings, fences, pavement, signs, and landscaping to express ownership)
- Natural surveillance (placing physical features, activities, and people to maximize visibility)
- Access control (the judicial placement of entrances, exits, fencing, landscaping, and lighting)

A CPTED analysis of a school evaluates crime rates, office-referral data, and school cohesiveness and stability, as well as core design shortcomings of the physical environment (e.g., blind hallways, uncontrolled entries, or abandoned areas that attract problem behavior). The application of CPTED principles starts with a threat and vulnerability analysis to determine the potential for attack and what needs to be protected. Protecting a school from physical attack by criminal behavior or terrorist activity, in many cases, only reflects a change in the level and types of threats. The CPTED process asks questions about territoriality, natural surveillance, and access control that can:

- Increase the effort to commit crime or terrorism
- Increase the risks associated with crime or terrorism
- Reduce the rewards associated with crime or terrorism
- Remove the excuses as to why people do not comply with the rules and behave inappropriately

The CPTED process provides direction to solve the challenges of crime and terrorism with organizational (people), mechanical (technology and hardware), and natural design (architecture and circulation flow) methods.

CPTED concepts can be integrated into expansion or reconstruction plans for existing buildings, as well as new buildings. Applying CPTED concepts from the beginning usually has minimal impact on costs, and the result is a safer school. Each school, district, and community should institute measures appropriate for their own circumstances because there is no single solution that will fit all schools.

Many CPTED crime prevention techniques for a school complement conventional terrorism and physical attack prevention measures. For example, as part of the CPTED strategy of improving territoriality, schools are encouraged to direct all visitors through one entrance that offers contact with a receptionist who can determine the purpose of the visit and the destination, and provide sign-in/sign-out and an ID tag prior to building access. These CPTED measures are similar to and complement physical security entry-control point stations.

However, in some cases, CPTED techniques can conflict with basic physical security principles. The CPTED strategy of natural surveillance calls for locating student parking in areas that allow ease of monitoring. A design that locates student parking close to the principal's office also reduces vehicle standoff and could create a vulnerability of the school structure to a vehicle bomb. In cases where CPTED techniques conflict with security principles, designers and school administrators should seek innovative solutions tailored to their unique situation.

1.1 SITE PERIMETER

Natural Access Control

- Clearly establish and define school property lines
- Secure the site perimeter, and limit access with selected entry points
- Create boundaries that delineate public, semipublic, semiprivate, and private spaces
- Establish clearly defined and secure boundaries between joint-use facilities and school
- Utilize fencing, where feasible, that does not permit footholds in order to deter unauthorized access

Natural Surveillance

- Avoid blocking lines of sight with fencing, signage, and landscaping
- Locate site entry points in areas of high visibility where they can be easily observed and monitored by staff and students in the course of their normal activities

Territorial Integrity

- Maintain school property to help establish pride of place and a sense of ownership
- Encourage activities on school grounds that promote community ownership and territorial integrity

Management

- Utilize fencing materials that resist graffiti

The location of a school and its relationship to its immediate surroundings is critical in evaluating safety and security concerns. While there is evidence showing that, by and large, schools and community college campuses tend to be safer places than the neighborhoods in which they are located, crime rates and types of crimes in schools, nevertheless, are affected by their surrounding environment. Despite this, each campus is unique and there are no formulas that can be applied to all. However, there are overarching design principles that are applicable to virtually all locations, whether rural, suburban, or inner-city urban. These principles apply not only to the relation of the school to its context, but also to its edges as well as to the connections or specific linkages, whether physical or perceptual, between the school and neighboring areas. These principles include: maximizing natural surveillance opportunities onto school grounds from surrounding areas; controlling access into and out of the campus; increasing, whenever possible, the sense of ownership that students, staff, and neighbors have in the school, clearly demarcating boundaries and spaces, minimizing undefined and "unowned" spaces, properly maintaining the property and grounds so that strong signals are sent that "someone cares about this place," and locating campus facilities and activities so that they are compatible with adjacent, off-site land uses and activities.

The site perimeter, which is the part of the school grounds that contacts the street and adjacent property, defines the initial impression of a school. How a school's site design responds to its immediate surroundings is evident in its treatment of its perimeter and edges. These edges communicate to the public messages of accessibility or inaccessibility. Therefore, a primary consideration in school site design is the clear definition of the school property lines. This definition can be achieved by utilizing lay-

Figure 2-1

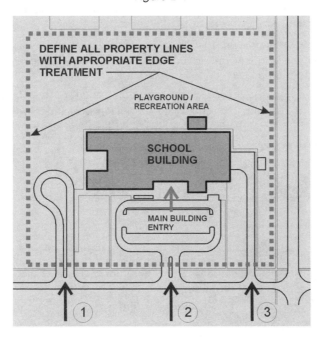

Figure 2–2

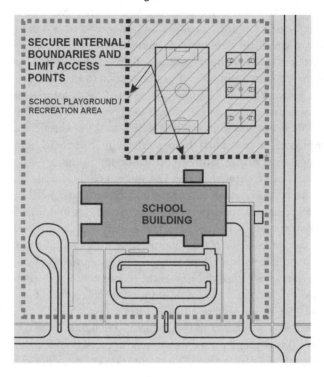

ered edge treatments, such as fencing, landscaping, and ground surface treatments. Symbolic markers, such as archways, entry posts, and student artworks, are also useful in creating psychological boundary delineations of the school's perimeter and edges.

Special consideration should be taken in the design of schools with joint-use or shared facilities, such as playgrounds and recreational areas, which are accessible to the community during and/or after school hours. In such circumstances, it is critical to delineate internal boundaries between the community and the school by establishing a distinct perimeter for both the school and the joint-use facilities with separate and secure access points. Properly designed joint-use facilities can reinforce neighborhood connections, ownership, and territorial integrity.

1.2 VEHICULAR ROUTES AND PARKING AREAS

Natural Access Control

- Restrict external access to parking areas to a limited number of controlled entrances
- Close unsupervised entrances during low-use times to reinforce the idea that access and parking are for school business only
- Provide clear signage and posted rules as to who is allowed to use parking facilities and when they are allowed to do so

Figure 2–3

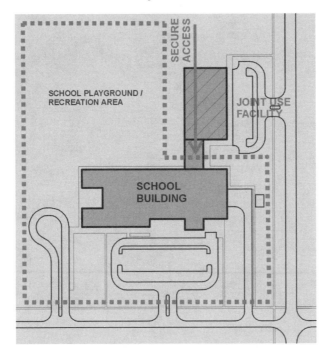

Standoff Distance

The most cost-effective solution for mitigating explosive effects on school buildings is to keep explosives as far away from them as possible. The distance between an asset and a threat is referred to as the standoff distance.

There is no ideal standoff distance; the type of threat, the type of construction, and desired level of protection determine it. The easiest and least costly opportunity for achieving appropriate levels of protection against terrorist threats is to incorporate sufficient standoff distance into school designs. Maximizing standoff distance also ensures that there is opportunity in the future to upgrade school buildings to meet increased threats or to accommodate higher levels of protection. Standoff distance must be coupled with appropriate building hardening as discussed in Section 3, to provide the necessary level of protection to the school.

For schools located in high-risk areas, additional considerations follow:

- The first mode of site protection is to create "keep out zones" that can ensure a minimum guaranteed distance between an explosion (i.e., from a vehicle) and the school structure.

continued

continued

Figure 2–4:   Explosives Environment

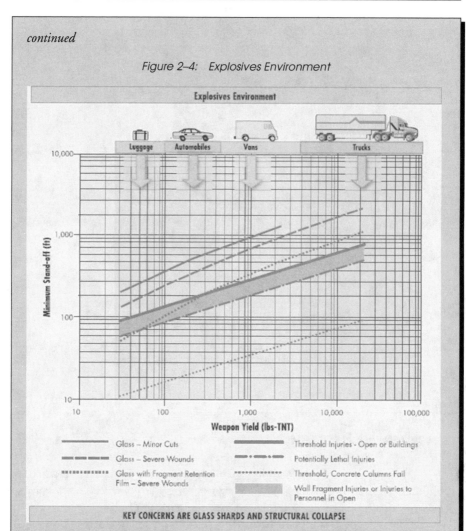

Source: FEMA 428. Risk Management Series: Primer to Design Safe School Projects in case of Terrorist Attack, December 2003

- The perimeter line is the outermost line that can be protected by the security measures incorporated during the school design process. It is recommended that the perimeter line be located as far as is practical from the building exterior. Many vulnerable school buildings are located in urban areas where only the exterior wall of the building stands between the outside world and the building occupants. In this case, the options are obviously limited. Often, the perimeter line can be pushed out to the edge of the sidewalk by means of bollards, planters, and other obstacles. To push this line even farther outward, restricting or eliminating parking along the curb often can be arranged with local authorities. In some extreme cases, elimination of loading zones and the closure of streets are options.

- "Keep out zones" can be achieved with perimeter barriers that cannot be compromised by vehicular ramming. A continuous line of security should be installed along the perimeter of the site to protect it from unscreened vehicles and to keep all vehicles as far away from the school as possible.
- The following critical building components should be located away from main entrances, vehicle circulation, and parking and maintenance areas. If this is not possible, harden as appropriate:
  - Emergency generator, including fuel systems, day tank, fire sprinkler, and water supply
  - Normal fuel storage
  - Telephone distribution and main switchgear
  - Fire pumps
  - Building control centers
  - Uninterrupted power supply (UPS) systems controlling critical functions
  - Main refrigeration systems if critical to building operation
  - Elevator machinery and controls
  - Shafts for stairs, elevators, and utilities
  - Critical distribution feeders for emergency power

Several architectural considerations can be implemented to mitigate the effects of a terrorist bombing on a school facility. These considerations often cost nothing or very little if implemented early in the design process.

The shape of the school building can contribute to the overall damage to the structure. For example, U- or L-shaped buildings tend to trap shock waves, which may exacerbate the effect of explosive blasts. For this reason, it is recommended that reentrant corners be avoided. In general, convex rather than concave shapes are preferred when designing the exterior of a school building. Other considerations follow:

- Orient school buildings horizontally rather than vertically to reduce their profile and exposure.
- Elevate the ground floors of school buildings above grade to prevent vehicles from being driven into the facility.
- Avoid eaves and overhangs, because they can be points of high local pressure and suction during blasts. When these elements are used, they should be designed to withstand blast effects.
- Locate utility systems away from likely areas of potential attack, such as loading docks, lobbies, and parking areas.
- Orient glazing perpendicular to the primary facade to reduce exposure to blast and projectiles.

continued

continued

- Avoid having exposed structural elements (e.g., columns) on the exterior of the school.
- Connect interior non-load-bearing walls to the structure with flexible connections.
- Place areas of high visitor activity away from key assets.
- Eliminate hiding places within the school building.
- Locate assets in areas where they are visible to more than one person.
- Use interior barriers to differentiate levels of security within a school building.
- Stagger doors located across from one another in interior hallways to limit the effects of a blast through the school structure.
- Provide foyers with reinforced concrete walls, and offset interior and exterior doors from each other in the foyer.
- Locate stairwells required for emergency as remotely as possible from areas where blast events might occur.
- Wherever possible, do not discharge stairs into lobbies, parking lots, or loading areas.
- Separate unsecured areas of the main school building as much as possible. For example, a separate lobby pavilion or loading dock area outside of the main footprint of the building provides enhanced protection against damages and potential building collapse in the event of an explosion.
- Place parking areas outside the main footprint of the school building to reduce the vulnerability to catastrophic collapse.

All new school buildings should be designed with the intent of reducing the potential for progressive collapse as a result of an abnormal loading event, regardless of the required level of protection. However, as with all mitigating efforts, there is no reason why your preferred solutions should not only be effective but aesthetically pleasing.

Entry control

In the case of a school, the objective of the design professional is to save lives by mitigating building damages and reducing the chances of a catastrophic collapse of the building at least until it is fully evacuated. Although there are many forms of attacks against a school, from the standpoint of school structural design, the vehicle bomb governs design because historically it has been used on multiple occasions by terrorists. Where a school perimeter barrier is required for security, it will be necessary to provide points of access through the perimeter for school users (i.e., students, faculty, staff, visitors, and service providers). An entry-control point or guard building serves as the designated point of entry for site access. It provides a point for implementation of desired/required levels of screening and access control. The objective of the entry-control point is to prevent unauthorized access to school grounds while maximizing the rate of authorized access by foot or vehicle. These measures will not be required for all schools; they may only be appropriate for schools considered at high risk. Designs should be flexible to allow implementation of increased security controls when schools are placed in high alert and easing of controls at lower threat levels. For a school considered to be at high risk, the following should be considered in the design of entry-control points:

- Design entry roads to schools so that they do not provide direct or straight-line vehicular access to the main building. Route major corridors away from key school areas and functions.
- Design access points at an angle to oncoming streets so that is difficult for a vehicle to gain enough speed to break through them.
- Minimize the number of access roads and entrances into a school.
- Provide a drop-off/pick-up lane for buses only.
- Minimize the number of driveways or parking lots that students will have to walk across to get to the school building.
- Designate an entry to the school for commercial, service, and delivery vehicles, preferably away from key school areas and functions, whenever possible.
- Design the entry-control point and guard building so that the authorization of approaching vehicles and occupants can be adequately assessed, and the safety of both gate guards and approaching vehicles can be maintained when a school is placed at high alert.
- Design (if they are required) traffic-calming strategies and barriers (road alignment, retractable bollards, swing gates, or speed bumps) to control vehicle speed and slow incoming vehicles before they reach the gate so that entry-control personnel have adequate time to respond to unauthorized activities.
- Provide inspection areas that are not visible to the public. Place appropriate landscape plantings to accomplish screening.
- Provide pullover lanes at site entry gates to check suspect vehicles. Also, provide a visitor/site-personnel inspection area to inspect vehicles prior to allowing access to the school site.
- Consider providing a walkway and turnstile for pedestrians and a dedicated bicycle lane.

- Locate visitor parking directly adjacent to main entry and administration
- Provide adequate space adjacent to the building for emergency vehicles
- Establish separate vehicular circulation routes to service and delivery areas, visitors' entry, bus drop-off, student parking, and staff parking
- Prohibit through-traffic on school campuses
- Provide a secure caged area for off-hour deliveries

Figure 2.5

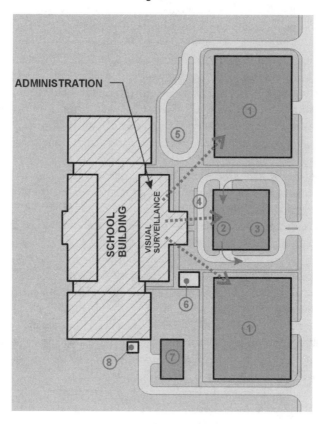

Figure 2.6

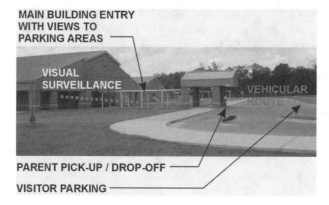

Figure 2.7

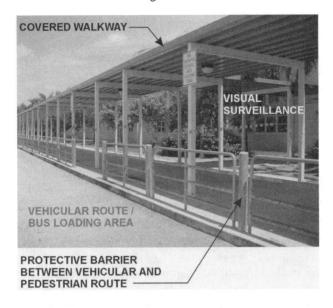

Figure 2.8

Natural Surveillance

- Locate parking areas in close proximity to school building or activity areas to facilitate natural surveillance
- Provide windows in classrooms and administration areas that overlook parking areas
- Provide adequate lighting in drop-off zones and parking areas
- Utilize zoned parking in limited controlled areas when appropriate
- Locate bus loading area so that it is visible to administration or adjacent to areas of surveillance
- Locate access to public transportation in areas that promote natural surveillance

Territorial Integrity

- Differentiate and identify parking spaces for students, faculty, staff, and visitors
- Provide designated primary routes and parking lots for after-hours use when applicable
- Clearly mark transition(s) from public streets onto school entry routes and into parking areas
- Provide clearly marked transitions from parking areas to pedestrian routes
- Minimize ambiguous and unassigned spaces at entry and parking areas
- Maintain a separation between pedestrian and vehicular traffic
- Provide blue-light emergency phones in parking lots on community college campuses

Management

- Supervise entrances and parking areas during peak-use times
- Utilize vandal-resistant lighting in parking areas and along vehicular routes
- Design parking lots that reduce opportunities for high-speed activity

Figure 2–9

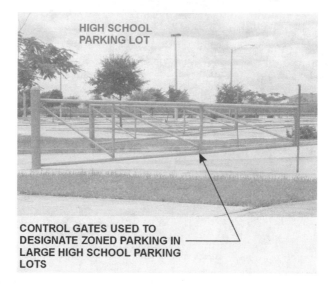

CONTROL GATES USED TO DESIGNATE ZONED PARKING IN LARGE HIGH SCHOOL PARKING LOTS

Figure 2–10

**PROVIDE ADEQUATE LIGHTING IN
PARKING LOTS USING VANDAL
RESISTANT TYPE FIXTURES**

Figure 2–11

**COMMUNITY COLLEGE CAMPUS
PARKING LOT**

Figure 2–12

COMMUNITY COLLEGE
CAMPUS

BLUE LIGHT EMERGENCY
PHONE

VEHICULAR AND PEDESTRIAN CIRCULATION

The movement of people and materials into, through, and out of a school facility is determined by the design of its access, circulation, and parking systems. Such systems should be designed to maximize efficiency while minimizing conflicts between vehicle and pedestrian modes. Designers should begin with an understanding of the school's transportation requirements based on an analysis of how the school will be used. This includes studying the number and types of access points that are required, bus requirements, the parking volume needed, where users need to go to and from, and the modes of transportation they will use. Several aspects of transportation planning can impact security and are discussed below.

ROADWAY NETWORK DESIGN

Streets are generally designed to minimize travel time and maximize safety, with the end result typically being a straight path between two or more endpoints. Although a straight line may be the most efficient course, designers should use caution when orienting streets relative to school buildings requiring high protection. Designers should design a roadway system to minimize vehicle velocity, thus using the roadway itself as a protective measure. This is accomplished through the use of several strategies. First, straight-line or perpendicular approaches to school buildings should not be used in a school at high risk, because these give vehicles the opportunity to gather the speed necessary to ram through protective barriers and crash into or penetrate buildings. Instead, approaches should be parallel to the facade, with berms, high curbs, appropriate trees, or other measures used to prevent vehicles from departing the roadway. A related technique for reducing vehicle speeds is the construction of serpentine (curving) roadways with tight radius corners. Existing streets can be retrofitted with barriers, bollards, swing gates, or other measures to force vehicles to travel in a serpentine path. Again, high curbs and other measures should be installed to keep vehicles from departing the roadway in an effort to avoid these countermeasures. Less radical than these techniques are traffic-calming strategies, which seek to use design measures to cue drivers as to the acceptable speed for an area. These include raised crosswalks, speed humps and speed tables, pavement treatments, bulbouts, and traffic circles. In addition to creating a more pedestrian-friendly environment, which increases "eyes on the street" surveillance, designing roadways to physically limit speed can have the added benefits of increasing safety and, subsequently, lowering liability. Designers should be aware, however, that many of these techniques can have detrimental effects for emergency response, including slowing response time, interfering with en route emergency medical treatment, and increasing the difficulty of maneuvering fire apparatus. They also may present problems for snow removal, and their outer ends should remain flat so that bicycles can proceed unimpeded.

Parking Issues

Vehicular routes and parking areas include the primary entry drive, parking lots, bus loading zones, parent drop-off/pickup areas, and service and delivery drives. Vehicular routes and parking lots must be designed to handle the rush of people and vehicles at the peak unloading and loading times at the beginning and end of each day. Other times, these areas may be completely empty and unsupervised, potentially providing opportunities for unwanted access.

In general, the safety and security of vehicular routes and parking areas benefit from the following design considerations. First, they should not be isolated from the school, but should be in close proximity to facilitate visual surveillance from classroom and administration areas. Second, these areas, especially classrooms, should be provided with windows that overlook vehicular routes and parking areas. Third, external access to parking areas should be restricted to a limited number of controlled entrances. Fourth, provisions must be made to ensure separation of vehicular and pedestrian circulation by creating barriers and well-defined routes. Fifth, unassigned and "unowned" spaces should be minimized as much as possible, especially in student parking zones. Sixth, entry areas and parking lots should have signs that spell out accepted usage and rules that describe what is and is not permitted. And finally, parking areas and vehicular routes should be adequately lit with vandal-resistant lighting.

The main entry drive area should be where visitors enter the school and parents pick up their children. This entry drive should be clearly visible from the administration office, where staff can keep an eye on who is coming and going during regular school hours. Also, it is important to provide a designated paved area adjacent to the building for emergency vehicles as per code requirements.

The bus loading area must be segregated from the main entry and other vehicular traffic according to code. However, when possible, the bus waiting area should still be visible from the administration area or some other point of natural surveillance, such as classrooms.

Parking lots are particularly susceptible to criminal activity. A primary factor is that these areas are typically the farthest from the central core of the campus. Because principals, school resource officers, and facility managers have consistently identified parking lots as venues for misbehavior, vandalism, and more serious crimes, adequate guardianship is essential. While this is particularly important at peak-use times, it should also be a priority, resources permitting, during off-peak periods, since parking lots contain an enormous trove of valuable targets for motivated offenders.

Locating parking lots near areas that promote natural surveillance, such as classrooms, can help mitigate criminal activity. It is important to provide a sufficient amount of windows in these areas to allow views of the lots. Special provision may have to be made for overflow lots for special and sporting events. When numerous lots exist, such as on large campuses, these lots should be clearly numbered or identified to avoid confusion. It is also recommended that designated parking lots be provided, especially for high schools, in order to monitor students who may leave campus during school hours. Such lots should be able to be secured and, if possible, supervised during peak-use times. In addition, design professionals should consider providing a designated "estranged spouses" parking lot for endangered or stalked adult students and school employees. This area should be centrally located and well protected at all times with constant monitoring.

When designing parking lots, particularly those that will be used by students, avoid long, straight layouts that allow cars to speed through the lot, endangering pedestrians. Traffic-calming devices can greatly reduce the potential for high-speed activity.

Community colleges have unique vehicular route and parking requirements for several reasons. The bulk of the student population is no longer delivered in groups to specific entry points. Instead, these students typically arrive individually, are usually required to park in areas located a substantial distance from the implied security zones of campus buildings, and often leave school after dark. It is, therefore, imperative that areas used in these circumstances have appropriate levels of lighting to help eliminate potential hiding places. In addition, in order to increase security on community college campuses, blue-light emergency phones should be located in all parking lots. It is important to place these phones in areas that are clearly visible and easily accessible.

For community colleges, public transportation also poses particular safety and security concerns. Public buses can provide a means to quickly enter and leave campus undetected and unmonitored. Therefore, access points to public transportation should be located near areas that promote natural surveillance whenever possible. Community colleges should also consider incorporating electronic surveillance, such as closed circuit television (CCTV), of these access points. Service and delivery drives should be separated from other vehicular routes. These areas should be able to be secured and should include a caged area for off-hour deliveries.

There are some key considerations regarding vehicular routes and parking areas when schools incorporate joint-use or shared facilities. Clearly marked designated parking lots should be provided for the public to avoid conflicts and confusion. In addition, routes and access points for the community should be well defined and separated from the school.

Finally, vehicular requirements for Enhanced Hurricane Protection Areas (EHPAs) or designated shelters must be taken into account in the design of school vehicular routes and parking areas. Since parking is not permitted within fifty feet of an EHPA during an emergency condition, provisions must be made to prevent confusion regarding where one can and cannot park during these times. In addition, clearly defined emergency vehicle access must be provided and located to avoid potential conflicts with other vehicular access routes and parking. Vehicular requirements for EHPA should not impede or obstruct designated areas for emergency equipment.

Surface lots can be designed and placed to keep vehicles away from school buildings, but they can consume large amounts of land and, if constructed of impervious materials, can contribute greatly to storm-water runoff. They can also be hazardous for pedestrians if dedicated pedestrian pathways are not provided.

PARKING RESTRICTIONS

Parking restrictions can help to keep potential threats away from a school building. In urban settings, however, curbside or underground parking is often necessary and sometimes difficult to control. Mitigating the risks associated with parking requires creative design measures, including parking restrictions, perimeter buffer zones, barriers, structural hardening, and other architectural and engineering solutions. The following considerations may help designers to implement parking measures for schools that may be at high risk:

- Locate vehicle parking areas away from school buildings to minimize blast effects from potential vehicle bombs.
- Provide separate parking areas for students, faculty, staff, and visitors who may be going in and out during the school day. (This allows the main student parking lot to be closed off during the school day.)
- If possible, locate visitor or general public parking near, but not on, the site itself.
- Locate general parking in areas that provide the fewest security risks to school personnel.
- Consider one-way circulation within a school parking lot to facilitate monitoring for potential aggressors.
- Locate parking within view of occupied school buildings while maintaining standoff.
- Prohibit parking within the standoff zone.
- Request appropriate permits to restrict parking in the curb lane for school vehicles or key employee parking only where distance from the building to the nearest curb provides insufficient setback and compensating design measures do not sufficiently protect the building from the assessed threat. If necessary, use structural features to prevent parking.
- Provide appropriate setback from parking on adjacent properties, if possible. Structural hardening may be required if the setback is insufficient. In new designs, it may be possible to adjust the location of the school building on the site to provide adequate setback from adjacent properties.
- When establishing parking areas, provide emergency communications systems (e.g., intercom, telephones, etc.) at readily identified, well-lit, CCTV-monitored locations to permit direct contact with security personnel.

- Provide parking lots with CCTV cameras connected to the security system and adequate lighting capable of displaying and videotaping lot activity.
- If possible, prohibit parking beneath or within a school building.
- If parking beneath a building is unavoidable, limit access to the parking areas and ensure they are secure, well lit, and free of places of concealment.
- Apply the following restrictions if parking within a school building is required:
  —Public parking with identification (ID) check
  —School vehicles and school employees and students only

LOADING DOCKS AND SERVICE ACCESS

Loading docks and service access areas are commonly required for a school building and are typically kept as invisible as possible. For this reason, special attention should be devoted to these service areas in order to avoid intruders. Design criteria for school loading docks and service access include the following:

- Separate by at least fifty feet loading docks and shipping and receiving areas in any direction from utility rooms, utility mains, and service entrances, including electrical, telephone/data, fire detection/alarm systems, fire suppression water mains, cooling and heating mains, and the like.
- Locate loading docks so that vehicles will not be allowed under the building. If this is not possible, the service area should be hardened for blast. Loading dock design should limit damage to adjacent areas and vent explosive forces to the exterior of the building.
- If loading zones or drive-through areas are necessary, monitor them and restrict height to keep out large vehicles.
- Avoid having driveways within or under school buildings.
- Provide adequate design to prevent extreme damage to loading docks. The floor of the loading dock does not need to be designed for blast resistance if the area below is not occupied and/or does not contain critical utilities. In certain cases, significant structural damage to the walls and ceiling of the loading dock may be acceptable; however, the areas adjacent to the loading dock should not experience severe structural damage or collapse.
- Provide signage to clearly mark separate entrances for deliveries.

CONTROLLED ACCESS ZONES

For a school at high risk, one method to attain the appropriate protection is with the creation of a controlled access zone. These zones define minimum distances between a school building and potential threats through the installation of barriers (such as bollards, planters, fountains, walls, and fences). The barriers are designed to withstand assaults by terrorist vehicles; however, their placement must be designed to allow for access by fire and rescue vehicles in the event of an emergency. Selection of barriers is based on operational considerations related to vehicle access and parking. Good design principles for high-risk schools endorse the complete surround of a school building with a standoff zone that has perimeters set at distances that consider threat levels, desired level of protection, building construction, and land availability. Entry into the controlled area should only be through an entry-control point.

When designing schools at high risk, controlled access zones may be exclusive or nonexclusive. An exclusive zone is the area surrounding a school building within the exclusive control of the building. Anyone entering an exclusive zone must have a purpose related to the building. A nonexclusive zone is either a public right-of-way or a particular area related to the main school building.

The following are some security considerations applicable to controlled access zones and enforcement:

- Design and select barriers based on threat capabilities.
- If the limited availability of land precludes the creation of an exclusive zone, the use of screening surrounding the school building is an alternative.
- Design and locate security devices to establish consistent rhythm patterns within the site. Incorporate subtle and aesthetically pleasing security measures to reach the desired level of protection.
- Locate security measures so that they do not impede the free access to school public entrances or internal pedestrian flow. Miscellaneous decorative elements (e.g., flag poles, fountains, pools, gardens, and similar features) may be located within access ways to slow movement or restrict access.
- Use a combination of barriers. Some barriers are fixed and obvious (fences and gates), while others are passive (sidewalks far away from buildings, curbs with grassy areas, etc.).
- Consider using landscape materials to create barriers that are soft and natural rather than man-made where physical barriers are required.
- Use vehicles as temporary physical barriers by placing them in front of buildings or across access roads.
- Maintain as much standoff distance as possible between potential vehicular bombs and the school building.
- Provide traffic obstacles near entry-control points to slow down traffic.
- Consider vehicle barriers at building entries and drives.
- Offset vehicle entrances from the direction of a vehicle's approach to force a reduction in speed.
- Position gates and perimeter boundary fences outside the blast vulnerability envelope, when possible.
- Provide a vehicle crash resistance system in the form of a low wall or earth berm, if the threat level warrants it.
- Design entry-control points (if provided) to screen the building from vehicles entering it.
- Provide passive vehicle barriers to keep stationary vehicle bombs at a distance from the school building.

- Use high curbs, low berms, shallow ditches, trees, shrubs, and other physical separations to keep stationary bombs at a distance.
- Do not allow vehicles to park next to perimeter walls of the secured area. Consider using bollards or other devices to keep vehicles away.
- Provide adequate lighting to aid in threat detection in controlled access zones.
- Use CCTV to control entry points, the site perimeter, and exclusive and nonexclusive zones.

1.3 EXTERIOR PEDESTRIAN ROUTES

Natural Access Control

- Design exterior sidewalks to clearly mark routes
- Direct all pedestrian circulation to a few selected entry points
- Provide designated routes and entry points for use after dark on community college campuses
- Provide clear signage for way-finding and access control

Figure 2–13

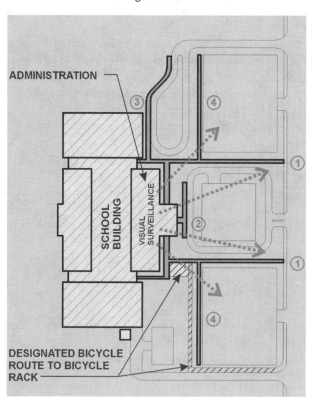

Figure 2–14

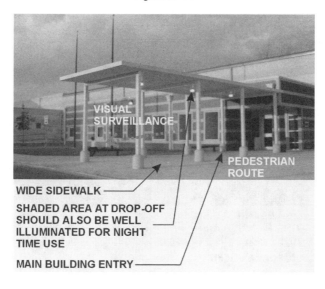

WIDE SIDEWALK

SHADED AREA AT DROP-OFF
SHOULD ALSO BE WELL
ILLUMINATED FOR NIGHT
TIME USE

MAIN BUILDING ENTRY

Figure 2–15

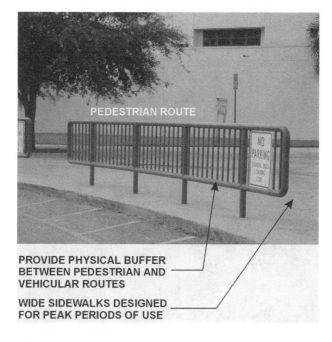

PROVIDE PHYSICAL BUFFER
BETWEEN PEDESTRIAN AND
VEHICULAR ROUTES

WIDE SIDEWALKS DESIGNED
FOR PEAK PERIODS OF USE

Figure 2–16

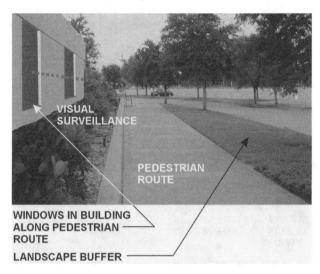

Figure 2–17

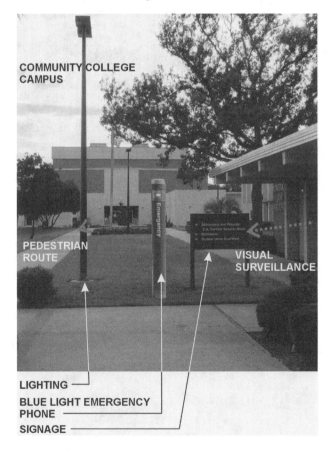

Natural Surveillance

- Minimize hiding places along pedestrian routes
- Avoid blocking lines of sight with fencing, signage, and landscaping
- Place exterior pedestrian routes so as to maximize surveillance from inside adjacent spaces
- Provide windows along exterior pedestrian routes
- Design lighting along exterior routes to reinforce natural surveillance, avoiding shadowed areas caused by uneven lighting and landscaping

Territorial Integrity

- Provide a physical buffer between sidewalks and vehicular routes with safety islands, landscape buffers, lights, or exterior furnishings
- Clearly demarcate pedestrian routes so that there are no ambiguous spaces along the way
- Utilize canopies to provide covered areas that are protected from the elements for students waiting to board buses or to be picked up by parents
- Provide paths from drop-off areas with sufficient width to accommodate peak periods of use
- Provide secure exterior assembly area(s) for gathering during an emergency
- Provide blue-light emergency phones along pedestrian routes on community college campuses

In survey research, adjacent sites off school grounds and parking lots were ranked the highest among all school locations as areas susceptible to security problems. Exterior walkways connect these areas to the core campus. The exterior walkway should be well defined with smooth walking surfaces and adequate lighting placed in locations that allow natural surveillance.

Public routes should be clearly marked and provided with signage and maps to reduce confusion and wandering visitors. Well-defined public pedestrian routes also make it easier to identify trespassing in unauthorized or restricted areas. Windows in school buildings should be located along exterior pedestrian routes, wherever possible, to encourage surveillance by teachers, administrators, staff, and students during their normal activities, thus reducing the potential for undetected trespassers, vandalism, and other such security concerns.

Paths from drop-off areas and routes to school entry points need to be wide enough to accommodate peak periods of use, thus preventing congestion, pushing, fighting, and accidents. Paving material should be nonskid, well marked, and non-glare. Canopies should be used to provide shaded and dry areas for students to wait to board buses or for those waiting to be picked up by parents. This can help reduce conflicts caused by the psychological irritation of standing in the hot sun or in the rain.

Planters along exterior routes should be designed to allow easy maintenance and prevent vandalism. Properly designed, these planters can integrate seating, lighting, and garbage containers, which will prevent damage to plants as well as eliminate stray refuse. Moreover, they can serve as surfaces for student art, thereby reinforcing territorial integrity.

Special consideration must be taken when designing exterior pedestrian routes for community colleges, which typically have large "campus plan" organizations with multiple access points surrounding their perimeter. In addition, because community colleges offer evening classes, provisions must be made to ensure campus security after dark. There are a few key design strategies to help enhance safety and security in these cases. First, community colleges should utilize blue-light emergency phones throughout the campus. These phones should be placed along pedestrian routes in visible locations with unobstructed access. Second, all access points should be well marked with adequate lighting. Finally, whenever feasible, limit such access points during evening hours by designating specific routes and entry points to be used after dark. It is important that these designated areas are clearly identified, well lit, and devoid of potential hiding places.

1.4 RECREATION AREAS

Natural Access Control

- Provide multiple enclosures around recreational areas to achieve greater access control
- Secure and limit access points between joint-use recreational facilities and the school
- Provide separate facilities related to recreational areas, such as restrooms, water fountains, and vending areas, when applicable

Natural Surveillance

- Locate recreational areas in a visible location, whenever possible
- Avoid blocking lines of sight into recreational areas with fencing, signage, and landscaping
- Utilize see-through fencing in recreational areas to enhance supervision
- Design lighting of recreational areas to reinforce natural surveillance

Territorial Integrity

- Clearly delineate boundaries between joint-use recreational facilities and the school

Management

- Locate hard-court play areas away from buildings
- Protect window openings located near hard-court play areas

Recreation areas and playgrounds have been cited in survey research as locations vulnerable to criminal activities, such as vandalism, trespassing, and assault and battery.

Physical Security Lighting

Security lighting can be provided for overall school ground/building illumination and the perimeter to allow security personnel to maintain visual assessment during darkness. It may provide both a real and psychological deterrent for continuous or periodic observation. Lighting is relatively inexpensive to maintain and may reduce the need for security personnel while enhancing personal protection by reducing opportunities for concealment and surprise by potential attackers.

Provide sufficient lighting at entry-control points to ensure adequate lighting for the area. Place lighting elements, where practical, as high as possible to give a broader, more natural light distribution. This requires fewer poles (less hazardous to drivers) and is more aesthetically pleasing than standard lighting.

The type of site lighting system used depends on the school's overall security requirements. Four types of lighting are used for security lighting systems:

- Continuous lighting is the most common security lighting system. It consists of a series of fixed lights arranged to flood a given area continuously during darkness with overlapping cones of light.
- Standby lighting has a layout similar to continuous lighting; however, the lights are not continuously lit, but are either automatically or manually turned on when suspicious activity is detected or suspected by the security personnel or alarm systems.
- Movable lighting consists of manually operated, movable searchlights that may be lit during hours of darkness or only as needed. The system normally is used to supplement continuous or standby lighting.
- Emergency lighting is a backup power system of lighting that may duplicate any or all of the above systems. Its use is limited to times of power failure or other emergencies that render the normal system inoperative. It depends on an alternative power source, such as installed or portable generators or batteries. Consider emergency/backup power for security lighting as determined to be appropriate.

Specific safety and security concerns in these areas include visibility and proximity to the school building, as well as securing and limiting access points. In addition, schools that include joint-use or shared recreational facilities for the community must make special provisions to ensure control of access to the school campus.

Strategic placement of recreational areas and playgrounds on school campuses can significantly enhance natural surveillance. These areas should always be placed in locations that permit unobstructed views from the school building. When possible, it is preferable to identify vantage points on school sites to locate buildings for unobstructed surveillance of recreational areas. Nighttime visual access to recreational areas

Figure 2–18

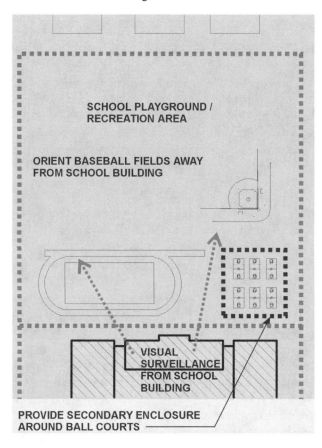

SCHOOL PLAYGROUND /
RECREATION AREA

ORIENT BASEBALL FIELDS AWAY
FROM SCHOOL BUILDING

VISUAL
SURVEILLANCE
FROM SCHOOL
BUILDING

PROVIDE SECONDARY ENCLOSURE
AROUND BALL COURTS

Figure 2–19

RECREATION
AREA

PROVIDE SECONDARY ENCLOSURE
WITH LIMITED ACCESS TO BALL
COURTS TO ENHANCE ACCESS
CONTROL

Figure 2–20

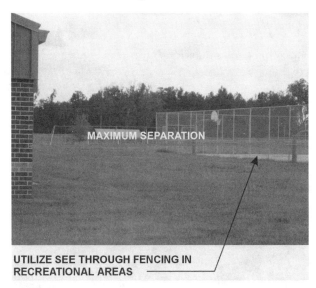

requires not only adequate illumination, but attention to the design of the edge conditions as well. Where play areas are adjacent to neighborhoods, fencing or street edge plants should have sufficient openings to allow visual sight lines to fields beyond. This allows the local community and passing patrol cars to monitor after-hour school recreational use.

As discussed in Section 1.1, joint-use facilities present special security concerns. Increasingly, Florida schools are sharing facilities with their surrounding community. In the case of joint-use recreational facilities, it is critical to eliminate ambiguity regarding the boundaries of the school campus and to differentiate the recreational facilities from the school by clearly marking and securing the edges of the campus. Access between the school and the shared recreational areas should be limited and located in a place that facilitates natural surveillance.

Many community colleges have a strong relationship with the surrounding community and often promote activity and use of their facilities. In these circumstances, recreational areas are open to the public and, therefore, some campuses may require internal separation of athletic and academic areas in order to control and limit unauthorized access.

Multiple enclosures around individual tennis courts, basketball courts, and other recreational areas can provide greater control. Additional layers of fencing make it more difficult to penetrate into these areas and remove or vandalize school property. Interior fences can be a strictly functional material, while the outer public fence can have a more aesthetically pleasing appearance when allowed by the budget. Fencing should permit maximum visibility into the play areas and, whenever possible, minimize climbing opportunities.

1.5 BIKE RACKS AND DUMPSTER ENCLOSURES

Natural Access Control

- Secure and enclose bike racks in lock-up areas
- Limit access to dumpsters

Figure 2–21

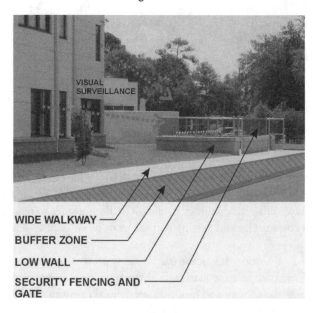

Figure 2–22

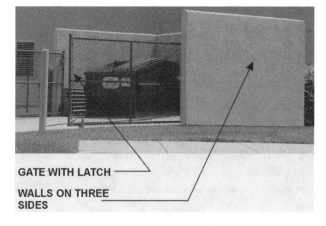

Natural Surveillance

- Minimize hiding places around bike racks and dumpster enclosures
- Locate bike racks near windows to enhance surveillance

Bike racks and lock-up areas should be located in a highly visible area near either the main entrance or where they can be easily observed by faculty, staff, and students during the course of normal activities. Enclose bike racks with see-through fencing and avoid blocking lines of sight to facilitate monitoring and surveillance.

Dumpsters should be secured and enclosed to prevent unauthorized access. If not enclosed in a designated service area, they should be surrounded on three sides by a high wall and provided with a gate that can be secured.

1.6 SIGNAGE

Natural Access Control

- Design signs with large, bold graphics and simple directions

Natural Surveillance

- Design signage to eliminate spaces that permit concealment
- Avoid blocking lines of sight with signage
- Design lighting to enhance natural surveillance near signage

Figure 2–23

Figure 2–24

DESIGN SIGNAGE TO
PREVENT CONCEALMENT

Territorial Integrity

- Include signage that directs visitors to the main entry and administrative office, as well as to an emergency contact point
- Clearly mark the entry with signs indicating to visitors what is expected of them

Signage is a critical element for controlling access and establishing territoriality on school campuses. Signs can be instrumental in minimizing lost and wandering visitors. Signs should have large lettering, bold graphics, and simple directions, and be well lit. It is also important to ensure that signs do not create hiding places.

Signage that includes maps and arrows in addition to text helps guide visitors along the appropriate route to the main entry. Signage should indicate to visitors what is expected of them, including rules governing access and impermissible behavior as well as applicable local and state regulations.

1.7 LANDSCAPING

Natural Access Control

- Utilize landscaping elements to control access and define public, semipublic, semi-private, and private areas
- Locate trees to avoid providing access to roofs

Natural Surveillance

- Design landscaping to minimize hiding places and shadowed areas
- Avoid blocking lines of sight with landscaping

Territorial Integrity

- Provide a safety barrier between sidewalks and vehicular routes with landscape buffers
- Utilize tree canopies to provide shaded areas

Signs are an important element of school security. They are meant to keep intruders out of restricted areas. Confusion over site circulation, parking, and entrance locations can contribute to a loss of site security. Signs should be provided off site and at school entrances; there should be on-site directional, parking, and cautionary signs for students, faculty, staff, visitors, service vehicles, and pedestrians. Unless required, signs should not identify sensitive areas. A comprehensive signage plan should include the following:

- Prepare entry-control procedures signs that explain current entry procedures for drivers and pedestrians.
- Prepare traffic regulatory and directional signs that control traffic flow and direct vehicles to specific appropriate points.
- Consider using street addresses or building numbers instead of detailed descriptive information inside the school grounds.
- Minimize the number of signs identifying high-risk areas; however, a significant number of warning signs should be erected to ensure that possible intruders are aware of entry into restricted areas.
- Minimize signs identifying critical utility complexes (e.g., power stations and significant gas, water, and sewer). Post easily understandable signs to minimize accidental entry by unauthorized visitors into critical areas.
- In areas where English is one of two or more languages commonly spoken, warning signs must contain the other language(s) in addition to English. The signs should be posted at intervals of no more than a hundred feet and should not be mounted on fences equipped with intrusion-detection equipment.
- Locate variable message signs, which give information to on-site/organization special events and visitors, far inside site perimeters.

- Incorporate the garden areas, landscaping, planting, and student artwork to enhance territorial integrity

Management

- Design low-maintenance landscaping
- Locate trees to prevent lay down or impact hazards

Several factors must be considered when planning landscape arrangements and plant selections on school campuses. In Florida's climate, landscaping can become an essential ingredient in the design of outdoor spaces. However, budget constraints may make it difficult to employ extensive landscaping strategies on school campuses. In addition, landscaping must be properly maintained. If it is not managed, landscaping can actually cause an unsafe school environment by creating places to hide, by blocking illumination and by interfering with lines of sight necessary for natural surveillance. Finally, misplaced landscape elements may also encourage vandalism. Therefore, care

Figure 2–25

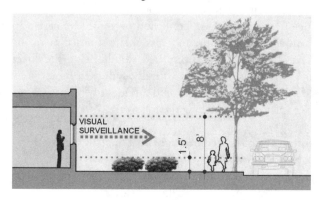

Figure 2–26

Figure 2–27

SPECIAL GARDEN AREAS CREATE A
SENSE OF PRIDE AND REINFORCE
TERRITORIALITY

must be taken when considering the use of landscaping on school campuses in safe school design.

Landscaping can be used as a method of access control. Like walls and fencing, a row of trees incorporated with low-level plants can define an edge that leads to an opening or entrance. When budget constraints are an issue, landscape materials that are less expensive, such as boulders, mulch, and timbers, can also effectively delineate spaces and control access. In order to ensure that landscaping does not obscure natural surveillance or create places to hide, tree canopies should be maintained above eight feet and shrubs should be trimmed to maintain a maximum height of eighteen inches.

Trees can also provide comfort and relief from the heat of Florida's subtropical sun, often far more economically than a built structure. However, it is important to position trees away from exits, access roads, and equipment areas to ensure that, if they should blow over or lose large branches, they will not block these areas. In addition, emergency drill areas should be free of trees to prevent danger to students in the event of a fire.

1.8 STORM-WATER

Natural Access Control

- Utilize retention ponds to limit access to school property
- Enclose retention areas with fencing that does not provide footholds for climbing, whenever possible

Other Landscaping Considerations

Designing to meet user needs while maintaining stewardship of the natural and built environments becomes increasingly more challenging when security requirements are factored in. Design principles at the school site should include an emphasis on selection of low-impact development techniques and environmental stewardship; compatibility of context and relationship with adjacent uses, forms, and styles; establishment of scale and identity through aesthetic design; connectivity among buildings, uses, activities, and transportation modes; resource conservation; cultural responsiveness; and the creation of appealing public spaces. These objectives are generally achieved through the work of two closely related disciplines, landscape design and urban design. For the purposes of this document, these two disciplines are virtually overlapping and will, therefore, be addressed together.

- Landscape design. Many landscape features can be used in school design to enhance security. Landscape design features should be used to create the level of protection without turning the school into a fortress. Elements, such as landforms, water features, and vegetation, are among the building blocks of attractive and welcoming spaces, and they can also be powerful tools for enhancing security. These features can be used not only to define or designate a space, but also to deter or prevent hostile surveillance or unauthorized access. Vegetative groupings and landforms can even provide some level of blast shielding. Stands of trees, earth berms, and similar countermeasures generally cannot replace setbacks, but they can offer supplementary protection. However, landscaping can also have detrimental impacts for safety and security, and designers should consider the unique requirements of the school project to ensure the landscape design elements that they choose will be appropriate and effective. With careful selection, placement, and maintenance, landscape elements can provide visual screening that protects school gathering areas and other activities from surveillance without creating concealment for covert activity. However, dense vegetation in close proximity to a school building can screen illicit activity and should be avoided. Additionally, thick ground cover, such as English ivy, or vegetation over four inches tall, such as monkey grass, can be used to conceal bombs and other weapons; in setback clear zones, vegetation should be selected and maintained with eliminating concealment opportunities in mind. Similarly, measures to screen visually detractive components such as transformers, trash compactors, and condensing units should be designed to minimize concealment opportunities for people and weapons.
- Urban design. Numerous urban design elements present opportunities to provide school security. The scale of the streetscape should be appropriate to its primary users, and it can be manipulated to increase the comfort level of

desired users while creating a less-inviting atmosphere for users with malicious intent. However, even at the pedestrian scale, certain operational requirements must be accommodated. For example, although efficient pedestrian and vehicle circulation systems are important for school functions and operations, they are also critical for emergency response, evacuation, and egress, and must be able to accommodate vehicles up to the largest fire apparatus in the community. Furthermore, despite an emphasis on downsizing the scale of the streetscape, it is critical to maintain the maximum standoff distance possible between vehicles and structures. At the school perimeter, walls and fences used for space definition may be hardened to resist the impact of a weapon-laden truck; however, planters, bollards, or decorative boulders could accomplish the same objective in a much more aesthetically pleasing manner. Such an approach also creates permeability, which would allow pedestrians and cyclists to more easily move through the space. Landscape and urban design inherently define the lines of sight in a space. These techniques seek to deny aggressors a line of sight to a potential target, either from on or off site. This increases the protection of sensitive information and operations by using standoff weapons. In addition to the use of various types of screening options, anti-surveillance measures (e.g., using building orientation, landscaping, screening, and landforms) to block sight lines can also be used.

Depending on the circumstances, landforms can be either beneficial or detrimental to anti-surveillance. Elevated sites may enhance surveillance of the surrounding area from inside the facility, but may also allow observation of on-site areas by adversaries. School buildings should not be sited immediately adjacent to higher surrounding terrain, unsecured buildings owned by unfamiliar parties, and vegetation, drainage channels, ditches, ridges, or culverts that can provide concealment. For high-risk school buildings, it may be necessary to provide additional protection by creating a clear zone immediately adjacent to the structure that is free of all visual obstructions or landscaping. The clear zone facilitates monitoring of the immediate vicinity and visual detection of attacks. Walkways and other circulation features within a clear zone should be located so that buildings do not block views of pedestrians and vehicles. If clear zones are implemented, it may be necessary to implement other anti-surveillance measures.

Natural Surveillance

• Avoid blocking lines of sight with fencing and landscaping around retention ponds

Territorial Integrity

• Utilize retention ponds to demarcate boundaries

Figure 2–28

ENCLOSE RETENTION POND
WITH FENCING AS
REQUIRED BY CODE

Figure 2–29

UTILIZE GRATING OR METAL
REBAR TO PREVENT ACCESS

Management

• Periodically inspect dry retention areas, which can provide places to hide

Storm-water retention areas, necessary in Florida to control flooding and to filter pollution from rainwater runoff, can be dry ponds or landscaped wet ponds. Both must be safely enclosed to prevent accidental drowning as per code requirements.

Wet retention ponds, while requiring more space, have many advantages. Designed to hold water even during the dry season, they can be used to form a physical barrier or moat to prevent trespassing to certain parts of the school. They can also help segregate play and pedestrian areas from areas of heavy vehicular traffic.

When dry ponds are not enclosed with fencing, protection of outflow structures should be addressed. Utilize grating or metal rebar to reduce the opening size and prevent access. Precautions should be taken to ensure that such protection does not impede the performance of the storm-water system.

1.9 SITE UTILITIES

Natural Access Control

• Secure site utilities and limit access

Natural Surveillance

• Locate site utilities to promote natural surveillance

Territorial Integrity

• Provide a designated area for equipment associated with the Enhanced Hurricane Protection Area (EHPA) requirements

Figure 2–30

Figure 2–31

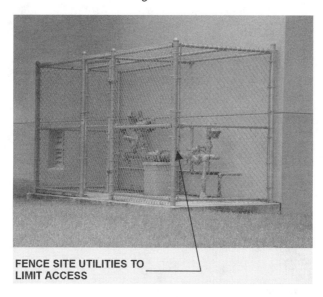

FENCE SITE UTILITIES TO
LIMIT ACCESS

Site utilities must be properly protected against criminal activities. It is important to ensure that these areas will not be damaged or interfered with in any way. Water and electrical supply, transformers, backflow preventers, and other site utilities should be secured to eliminate unauthorized access. Whenever possible, provide unobstructed views to these areas from the school building to enhance monitoring.

Enhanced Hurricane Protection Areas (EHPAs) or designated shelters present particular safety and security concerns, especially in terms of site design and emergency utilities. Designated shelters require special equipment, such as generators, water bladders, and sewer bladders. Designs should include adequate parking for required equipment in a designated area that can be secured to limit access. Care should be taken to locate these designated areas where they will not impede access into the shelter or obstruct emergency vehicle routes. In addition, designated equipment areas should be located to prevent lay down or impact damage from trees.

Building Design

2.1 BUILDING ORGANIZATION

Natural Access Control

- Tailor access-control solutions to fit the particular building organizational type utilized, such as a compact single/multistory plan, alphabet configurations, courtyard organization, or campus plan

More Site Utilities Considerations

Utility systems can suffer significant damage when subjected to the shock of an explosion. Some of these utilities may be critical for safely evacuating people from the school building. Their destruction could cause damage that is disproportionate to other building damage resulting from an explosion. To minimize the possibility of such hazards, apply the following measures:

- Where possible, provide underground, concealed, and protected utilities.
- Provide redundant utility systems (particularly electrical services) to support school security, life safety, and rescue functions.
- Consider quick connects for portable utility backup systems if redundant sources are not available.
- Prepare vulnerability assessments for all utility services to the school, including all utility lines, storm sewers, gas transmission lines, electricity transmission lines, and other utilities that may cross the site perimeter.
- Protect drinking water supplies from waterborne contaminants by securing access points, such as manholes. If warranted, maintain routine water testing to help detect waterborne contaminants.
- Minimize signs identifying critical utilities. Provide fencing to prevent unauthorized access and use landscape planting to conceal aboveground systems.
- Locate petroleum, oil, and lubricants storage tanks and operations buildings down-slope from all other occupied school buildings. Locate fuel storage tanks at least a hundred feet from buildings.
- Consider providing utility systems with redundant or loop service, particularly in the case of electrical systems. Where more than one source or service is not currently available, provisions should be made for future connections. In the interim, consider "quick connects" at the building for portable backup systems.
- Decentralize a school's communications resources, when possible; the use of multiple communication networks will strengthen the communications system's ability to withstand the effects of a terrorist attack.
- Place trash receptacles as far away from the building as possible; trash receptacles should not be placed within thirty feet of a building.
- Provide a school-wide public address system that extends from the interior to the exterior of buildings.
- Conceal and harden incoming utility systems within schools to provide blast protection, including burial or proper encasement wherever possible.
- Locate utility systems at least fifty feet from loading docks, front entrances, and parking areas.
- Route critical or fragile utilities, so that they are not on exterior walls or on walls shared with mailrooms.

continued

continued

- Ensure that the redundant utilities are not collocated or do not run in the same chases. This minimizes the possibility that both sets of utilities will be adversely affected by a single event.
- Ensure backup systems are located away from the systems components for which they provide backup.
- Mount all overhead utilities and other fixtures weighing thirty-one pounds (fourteen kilograms) or more to minimize the likelihood that they will fall and injure school occupants. Design all equipment mountings to resist forces of 0.5 times the equipment weight in any direction and 1.5 times the equipment weight in the downward direction. This standard does not preclude the need to design equipment mountings for forces required by other criteria, such as seismic standards.
- Ensure that access to crawl spaces, utility tunnels, and other means of under-school building access is controlled to limit opportunities for aggressors placing explosives underneath buildings.
- Screen, seal, or secure all utility penetrations of the site's perimeter to prevent their use as access points for unauthorized entry into the school site. If access is required for maintenance of utilities, secure all penetrations with screening, grating, latticework, or other similar devices.

Natural Surveillance

- Organize building components to promote natural surveillance of both the school campus and interior spaces within the building
- Organize building components to promote natural surveillance from adjacent neighborhoods

Territorial Integrity

- Locate the building(s) on the site to promote a connection to the neighborhood context, when possible

If properly designed, the overall organization of a school can enhance school and safety authorities' ability to maintain a secure environment and can also discourage vandalism, trespassing, and breaking and entering.

The contemporary "campus plan" evolved from the availability of inexpensive land and the lower cost of constructing single-story buildings. Maintaining security can be difficult in this type of building organization because the buildings are spread out, hindering surveillance and access control. One solution is to close gaps by linking all the buildings together with fencing and clearly marked routes. Limiting the points of access can also aid in securing the school campus plan by forcing visitors and late arrivers to enter through specific monitored places.

Figure 2–32

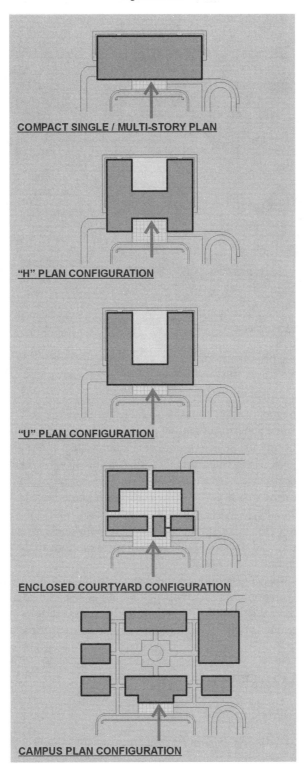

COMPACT SINGLE / MULTI-STORY PLAN

"H" PLAN CONFIGURATION

"U" PLAN CONFIGURATION

ENCLOSED COURTYARD CONFIGURATION

CAMPUS PLAN CONFIGURATION

Figure 2–33

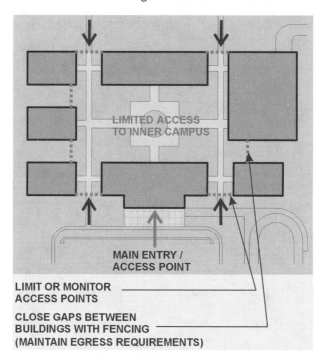

MAIN ENTRY /
ACCESS POINT

LIMIT OR MONITOR
ACCESS POINTS

CLOSE GAPS BETWEEN
BUILDINGS WITH FENCING
(MAINTAIN EGRESS REQUIREMENTS)

Traditional school plan organizations were relatively compact. This was a reaction to the environmental concerns of natural daylight and ventilation. The benefits of the compact plans include an efficient interior circulation system and a minimal amount of exterior surface area, which reduces maintenance requirements. When utilizing a compact building organization, precautions must be taken to ensure that the surrounding exterior environment is also secure. When schools become too introverted, students may be at risk once they leave the safety of the interior environment, since there is little to no surveillance of the school perimeter and recreational areas from inside the school building. Avoiding solid walls and providing extensive windows to the exterior will help make the surrounding exterior secure.

The narrow wings of traditional school organization lend themselves to common "alphabet" configurations. *U*- and *H*-shaped buildings result in courtyards protected on three sides. This makes monitoring activity in the courtyard easier and helps provide shade and shelter. These types of organization are also easy to lock and secure.

2.2 EXTERIOR COVERED WALKWAYS

Natural Access Control

- Design covered walkways to eliminate opportunities for gaining access to roofs, windows, or other upper-level areas

- Apply slippery finishes or coatings to columns
- Design landscaping and tree placement away from covered walkways to eliminate access to roofs, windows, or other upper-level areas

Figure 2–34

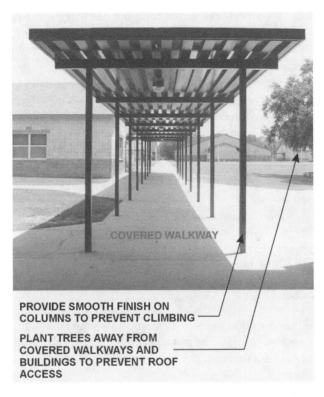

COVERED WALKWAY

PROVIDE SMOOTH FINISH ON
COLUMNS TO PREVENT CLIMBING

PLANT TREES AWAY FROM
COVERED WALKWAYS AND
BUILDINGS TO PREVENT ROOF
ACCESS

Figure 2–35

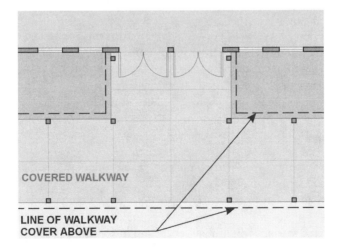

COVERED WALKWAY

LINE OF WALKWAY
COVER ABOVE

Natural Surveillance

- Avoid blocking lines of sight along exterior covered walkways
- Avoid using niches at entries
- Design lighting to reinforce natural surveillance along walkways

Covered walkways provide protection from the rain and sun for primary exterior circulation paths. However, if designed improperly, these structures can provide opportunities for criminal activity and unauthorized access. Columns and other supports should be designed to prevent climbing by using smooth building materials and finishes and by eliminating footholds. Low walls, trees, and planters should be located away from canopies to prevent access onto rooftops and into buildings through upper-level windows. Exterior covered walkways should also be designed to promote natural surveillance and should be provided with adequate illumination as a deterrent against criminal activity during normal use. Incorporate windows, whenever possible, that overlook covered walkways.

Exterior covered walkways should also be designed with "T" connections at entries to provide a continuously protected walkway without using niches, which can create hiding places. This will also ensure a clear path unobstructed by doors.

2.3 POINTS OF ENTRY

Natural Access Control

- Minimize the number of unmonitored entrances into the building
- Locate main point of entry at the front of the school near the administration area and visitor parking/drop-off area
- Avoid hidden entries
- Secure the secondary entries

Natural Surveillance

- Provide windows and glazed doors at main entry to enhance natural surveillance
- Utilize glazing extensively at administrative area to promote surveillance of main entry, as well as drop-off and visitor parking areas
- Eliminate places to hide at recessed secondary entries
- Design lighting at points of entry to reinforce natural surveillance

Territorial Integrity

- Design a well-defined main entry with signage and rules to direct all visitors to the administration area during school hours
- Design overhangs at the main entry to shelter a large number of people from sun and rain
- Provide covered seating areas at main entry and bus loading area

Figure 2–36

MAIN POINT OF ENTRY

**LOCATE ADMINISTRATION NEAR
MAIN POINT OF ENTRY AND
PROVIDE EXTENSIVE GLAZING TO
ENHANCE VISUAL SURVEILLANCE**

Figure 2–37

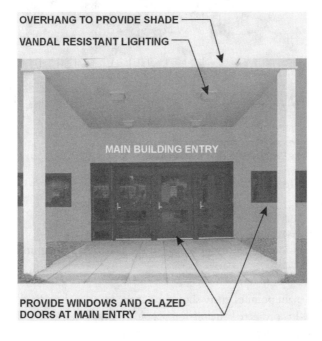

OVERHANG TO PROVIDE SHADE

VANDAL RESISTANT LIGHTING

MAIN BUILDING ENTRY

**PROVIDE WINDOWS AND GLAZED
DOORS AT MAIN ENTRY**

Figure 2–38

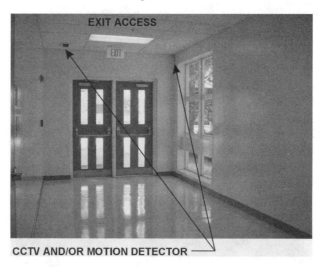

Figure 2–39

Management

- Provide vandal-resistant lighting
- Maintain operational integrity of sensor or timer lighting when utilized at points of entry

Ideally, the main point of entry should be at the front of the school and should provide a safe, well-lit, protected shelter for people entering the school. This area should also be easily visible from the administration area. Provide glazed doors and windows at this entry to enhance monitoring. The main entry should also be prominent and well marked to guide visitors to the administration office. In the case of community college campuses, where there are typically multiple buildings, each with its own entry, a well-defined primary entrance for each building can help direct visitors to this entry. Placing this primary entry in a location that promotes natural surveillance, such as a lobby, administration areas, or faculty offices whenever appropriate, can also help eliminate wandering visitors and trespassing, as well as provide general access control.

The entry overhang should be large enough to shelter a large number of people from the sun and rain. This can prevent heatstroke during the summer, as well as wet and slippery ground surfaces during storms. The overhang should drain to the sides away from where people might enter or where it meets the school building. Covered seating areas should be provided at the main entry and the bus-loading zone. Seating should be carefully located to eliminate opportunities for gaining access to the roof. The walkway must be wide enough to accommodate seating areas without obstructing normal pedestrian movement. Entries that pose safety concerns during peak hours include the primary points of entry and exit used by students at the start and end of the school day. Congestion at these entry points can cause pushing and fighting, especially in middle schools. Design wide sidewalks and entrances in these areas to reduce overcrowding.

According to survey data and site visits, secondary entries are a common problem area for school security. Even if properly designed as "exit only" access points, students frequently prop these doors open. Therefore, these access points should be placed in a visible location whenever possible and checked often. When feasible, secondary entries should be equipped with alarms to indicate when these doors are open. Secondary entries also require careful design to prevent them from becoming dark alcoves where someone can hide. While secondary exterior entries should remain recessed for weather protection, their alcoves can have improved visibility by the use of wide recesses or chamfered corners. These recesses should be limited by the same constraints applicable to interior room doors.

Points of entry should have adequate illumination with vandal-resistant fixtures. Consideration should be given to providing a sensor or timer light at delivery and service entries. When sensor or timer lighting is provided, care should be taken to ensure that they are operating properly by periodically checking these systems.

2.4 COURTYARDS

Natural Access Control

- Secure and limit entries to courtyards
- Place main entry to courtyards adjacent to administration or staff/faculty office spaces
- Design courtyards to eliminate unauthorized after-hours access

Natural Surveillance

- Provide windows with views into courtyards
- Maintain unobstructed lines of sight across courtyards

Territorial Integrity

- Minimize ambiguous or "unowned" spaces in courtyards
- Designate and clearly demarcate formal gathering areas for students
- Utilize student art, ground-surface treatments, and landscaped areas to reinforce territorial integrity

Figure 2–40

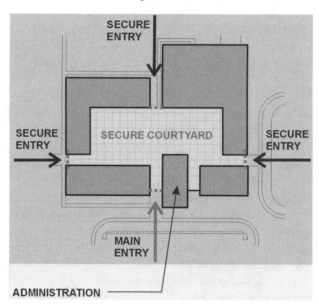

Figure 2–41

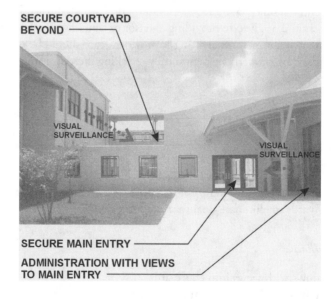

Figure 2–42

SECURE
COURTYARD
SIDE

"EXIT ONLY" TYPE DOORS
WITH PANIC HARDWARE
AND CLOSURE

ROLL-UP TYPE SECURITY
GRILLE

Figure 2–43

SHADED
COURTYARD
AREA

LANDSCAPING

SEATING

GROUND SURFACE
TREATMENT

The overall organization of the school can create a beneficial enclosure of exterior space. The traditional form of the courtyard school allows for uncomplicated supervision and control. An outdoor circulation arcade around the courtyard allows one person to oversee activities during class changes. The arcade also helps provide protection from the sun and rain.

Care must be taken to ensure access control in courtyards. Secure entries must be provided to limit access into and out of the courtyard area. The main entry should be located adjacent to the administration office. Since this area is always occupied during school hours, continuous observation of this entry can be maintained. Windows from administration office areas with views to the main entry should be provided. Increased surveillance of courtyards can also be achieved by providing windows in the building that look out into the courtyard.

Entries to courtyards used during peak hours of the day by students can present safety and security concerns. These courtyard entry areas should be wide to reduce congestion. Avoid using swinging doors that must be held open by students, a situation considered by principals and school resource officers to be a common cause of fighting, especially in middle schools. It is preferable to utilize roll-up security grilles with adjacent "exit only" doors. An alternative solution is to use wide gates that can be secured. In this case, it is important to design the gates to minimize climbing opportunities.

It is critical to design walls and fences surrounding courtyards high enough to prevent access after hours. They should be built with materials that do not provide footholds whenever possible and designed to resist climbing. Seating, planters, and landscaping should be located away from courtyard enclosures to eliminate opportunities for gaining unauthorized access into the courtyard.

2.5 RELOCATABLE/PORTABLE BUILDINGS

Natural Access Control

- Design exterior sidewalks that clearly mark routes to relocatable/portable buildings
- Screen spaces under relocatable/portable buildings to prevent access

Natural Surveillance

- Minimize hiding places around relocatable/portable buildings
- Design lighting to reinforce natural surveillance

Management

- Provide vandal-resistant lighting
- Provide appropriate emergency communications connections between the relocatable/portable buildings and school administration

Relocatable/portable buildings present similar safety and security concerns as the main school building. If not designed properly, these areas can actually promote a

Figure 2–44

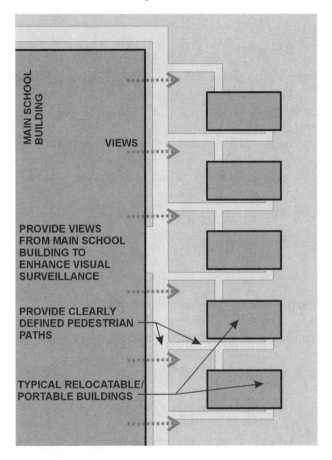

Figure 2–45

heightened sense of separation from the main building and, consequently, concerns about safety. It is important to eliminate hiding places, to enhance visual supervision of these buildings, and to be able to secure these buildings when necessary.

Relocatable/portable buildings should be well lit, with clearly defined and unambiguous routes to and from these areas. Whenever possible, provide windows from the main building overlooking these pedestrian paths to afford possibilities for surveillance. The buildings should be sufficiently separated for fire prevention and control, as well as to promote natural surveillance.

A common problem with relocatable/portable buildings is that they can provide places to hide underneath the structure. Therefore, whenever feasible, these areas should be screened with materials that will simultaneously prohibit access, maintain visibility, and allow for ventilation. This can be easily accomplished by utilizing see-through fencing.

2.6 DOORS

Natural Access Control

- Incorporate tamper-resistant doors and locks
- Utilize vestibules at entry doors, where possible, to increase security
- Design classroom doors with locksets that allow the door to be locked from either side and always opened from the inside

Natural Surveillance

- Design doors with view panels or sidelites to increase visibility of adjacent circulation spaces
- Avoid blind corners and dark niches, which can provide places to hide
- Design vestibule lighting for surveillance at night

Figure 2–46

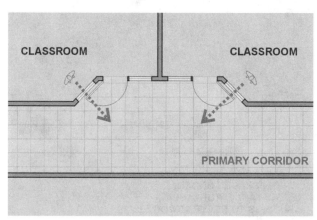

Figure 2–47

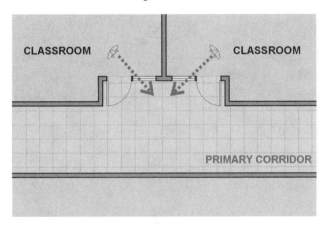

Figure 2–48

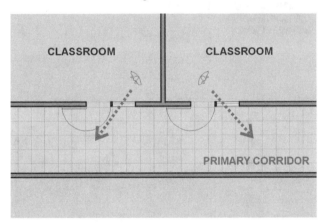

Management

• Provide kick plates at classroom, assembly, and circulation doors

Doors and hardware must conform to use and location requirements. In an emergency situation, classrooms should be able to be locked down quickly. Whenever feasible, classroom doors should be equipped with special classroom security locksets. This lockset function allows teachers to secure a door from inside the classroom without having to enter the corridor and also allows egress from the inside of the classroom at all times.

The use of hinges with non-removable pins and strike-plate covers reduces the potential for forced break-ins. Doors with view panels or sidelites increase safety by allowing a person to see what is on the other side of the door and also allow teachers to

Figure 2–49

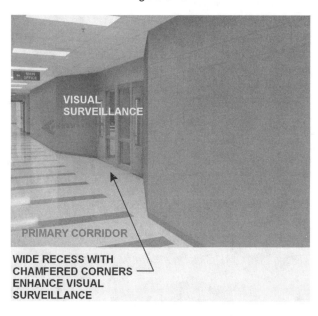

Figure 2–50

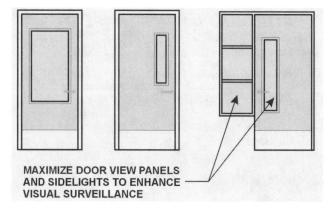

keep an eye on activity in adjacent circulation spaces. Kick plates should be provided for classroom, assembly, and circulation doors.

Doors along main corridors must either be located in a recess or must swing a full 180 degrees by code. These recesses can be dark and can provide opportunities for hiding. One solution is to chamfer the corners of the recess. However, due to budget constraints this may not be feasible. Another option is to create larger recessed areas in the corridor by coupling classrooms that share the same niche. This can greatly increase both surveillance and illumination. In all cases, provide adequate and well-designed lighting in these areas.

The use of multiple sets of doors to create vestibules can help reduce heated and air-conditioned air loss, as well as increase security. Lighting the vestibule at night illuminates activities and helps prevent entry through the second set of doors.

2.7 WINDOWS

Natural Access Control

• Design windows to deter after-hours access

Natural Surveillance

• Utilize extensive glazing, especially in classrooms and administration areas, to enhance natural surveillance

As mentioned in previous sections, strategic incorporation of windows and glazing in school buildings is an important aspect of safe school design and can be vital for enhancing access control and surveillance. However, care must also be taken to ensure that windows do not create security problems.

Windows not only let in light and air, but can also let in thieves if their design and placement is not carefully considered. Clerestory windows allow for ventilation, light, and privacy while minimizing wall penetrations. However, because they do not provide views to adjacent areas, clerestory windows should be utilized in conjunction with window designs that create opportunities for natural surveillance by staff and students

Figure 2–51

UTILIZE EXTENSIVE GLAZING AT MAIN ENTRY TO ENHANCE VISUAL SURVEILLANCE TO PARKING LOTS AND PEDESTRIAN ROUTES

Figure 2–52

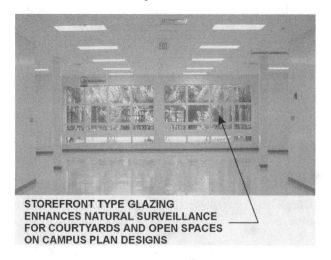

**STOREFRONT TYPE GLAZING
ENHANCES NATURAL SURVEILLANCE
FOR COURTYARDS AND OPEN SPACES
ON CAMPUS PLAN DESIGNS**

Figure 2–53

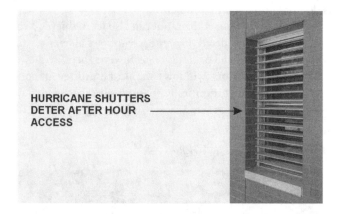

**HURRICANE SHUTTERS
DETER AFTER HOUR
ACCESS**

during the course of their normal activities. Window protection requirements for Enhanced Hurricane Protection Areas (EHPAs) or designated shelters, such as hurricane shutters and screens, can have an added benefit of deterring after-hours access.

Glazing in administration areas is especially critical to enable staff to monitor the main entrance, as well as other areas on the school campus. Another important location for windows is classrooms, where many eyes can have views of exterior areas, such as parking lots, exterior pedestrian routes, and recreational facilities. In addition, incorporating view panels and sidelites in classrooms and administration areas along corridors can also provide enhanced security. Whenever possible, extensive glazing should be utilized to permit views and surveillance of exterior areas, such as courtyards.

2.8 EXTERIOR WALLS

Natural Access Control

• Design screening walls and architectural features on exterior walls that do not allow footholds or handholds

Natural Surveillance

• Avoid blind corners and dark niches, which can provide places to hide

Management

• Design vandal-resistant walls
• Provide markings and game lines on walls near recreational and play areas to deter graffiti

Wall form, texture, and use influence safety concerns. Avoid utilizing walls that undulate or project into small wings, which can create niches and hiding places. When such niches occur, security can be enhanced by incorporating windows that have unobstructed lines of sight into these areas. In addition, these recesses or niches should also be well lit to enhance safety.

Screening walls of metal or decorative concrete block are often used to provide separation without compromising ventilation. However, they can become informal ladders that allow unauthorized access to the roof. This can be prevented by making sure that the screening wall provides no footholds and that the top section near the roof is smooth and cannot be climbed.

Figure 2.54

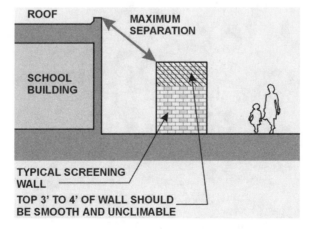

Walls in graffiti-prone areas should be made of a durable vandal-resistant material or be replaced with see-through fencing, when appropriate, to reduce maintenance and vandalism. Walls near recreation areas are often defaced by youths making markings for games, such as handball and street hockey. Provide markings and game lines beforehand, so that students will not be tempted to make their own.

2.9 ROOFS

Natural Access Control

- Avoid using building materials or designing architectural elements that provide access to roofs
- Apply slippery finishes or coatings to exterior pipes and columns
- Install locks on roof hatches
- Protect roof equipment from access and vandalism
- Minimize access through roof skylights

Natural Surveillance

- Design roof parapets to allow for surveillance from the ground, whenever possible

A key concept for safe school design is to minimize opportunities to gain access to school roofs and into the school from roofs through potential entry points. Avoid the use of permanent mounted roof access ladders, short walls adjacent to low canopy

Figure 2.55

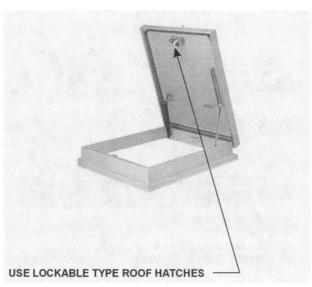

USE LOCKABLE TYPE ROOF HATCHES

Figure 2.56

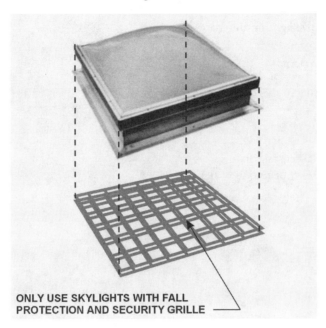

**ONLY USE SKYLIGHTS WITH FALL
PROTECTION AND SECURITY GRILLE**

roofs, screen walls and columns using decorative block, or other building materials that make climbing up to roofs easy.

Skylights can create opportunities to gain entry into the interior of school buildings. When utilized, they must be carefully designed to minimize access. Incorporating solid or fixed diffusers within the light well, or adding cages over skylights, can prevent entry at these points, as well as eliminate the possibility of someone accidentally falling through the glass.

Roof equipment, such as heating, ventilation, and air conditioning (HVAC) cooling towers, should be protected with enclosures to prevent vandalism. Whenever possible, provide roof access from a secure room within the building and utilize lockable-type roof hatches to eliminate unauthorized access onto the roof or into the building.

2.10 LIGHTING

Natural Access Control

- Design lighting that does not provide footholds or handholds for climbing
- Secure and protect fixtures to reduce vandalism

Natural Surveillance

- Design uniform and consistent levels of lighting

- Avoid pockets of shadow and uneven lighting created by niches, landscaped areas, and fencing
- Avoid excessive lighting and glare

Territorial Integrity

- Utilize lighting to maximize use of public facilities

Management

- Utilize vandal-resistant fixtures
- Maintain proper operation of lighting

Figure 2.57

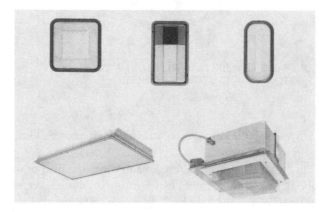

Figure 2.58

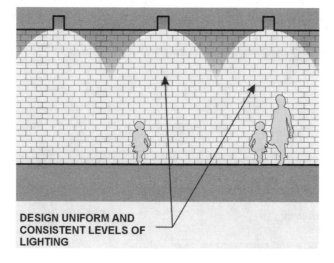

DESIGN UNIFORM AND CONSISTENT LEVELS OF LIGHTING

Figure 2.59

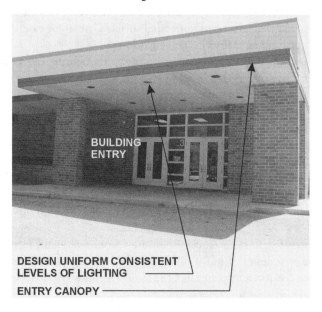

BUILDING ENTRY

DESIGN UNIFORM CONSISTENT LEVELS OF LIGHTING

ENTRY CANOPY

Figure 2.60

COVERED WALKWAY

UTILIZE VANDAL RESISTANT TYPE LIGHT FIXTURES

The use of artificial illumination can help deter criminal activity and reduce accidents. Key issues are the accessibility of the fixtures, the level of illumination, the reduction of shadows, and the lighting of horizontal surfaces. Areas for careful consideration of lighting include lobbies, stairwells, and corridors.

There are currently two approaches to after-hours lighting on school campuses. The first approach promotes full lighting and the second encourages darkened campuses. The advantages to a lighted campus include enhanced surveillance of the school by the community and law enforcement and protection of staff after hours. In addition, a lighted campus can also encourage use of facilities by the public after hours. On the other hand, there is evidence to suggest that a darkened campus may also have security benefits, especially with regards to vandalism and theft. On a dark campus, light sources from intruders will be apparent to external surveillance. A compromise to complete blackout is the utilization of motion-response and timer lighting. The choice of one approach over another requires a thorough assessment of the unique and specific needs of the school.

Maintenance of lighting is crucial to ensure school safety and security. A school's lighting may be well designed but, if inadequately maintained, will fail to perform as intended. Check for proper operation of motion-response systems, burned-out light bulbs, and correct settings for timer lighting.

Light fixtures are frequent targets of vandalism. The damage or theft of a fixture can leave an area vulnerable to safety and security problems. Therefore, the proper selection and installation of fixtures is critical. Fixtures should not provide footholds or handholds for scaling a wall. They should be flush-mounted or recessed whenever possible and covered with an impact-resistant material.

Light fixtures should be located so that they do not block lines of sight or create hiding places. In addition, it is important to consider lighting design relative to elements, such as low walls or landscaping, so that shadows and dark areas will not inadvertently be created. Campus lighting should also be carefully designed to avoid excess illumination of adjacent neighborhoods.

Interior Spaces

3.1 LOBBIES AND RECEPTION AREAS

Natural Access Control

- Position a primary control point in the lobby between the main entry and all other areas of the school
- Direct all visitors through this single control point at the main entry
- Locate a staffed administration area or desk adjacent to the main entry and connected to the lobby
- Design lobby areas that can be easily secured

Natural Surveillance

• Utilize extensive interior glazing and windows in the lobby area to encourage natural surveillance

Territorial Integrity

• Provide an escape route from staffed administration reception area for emergency egress out of the lobby area

To control access and limit intrusion, visitors should be guided to a single control point and required to pass directly through to administration reception areas when entering or leaving the building. Lobbies should also be designed for ease of security after hours and during emergencies.

The combination of a main entry with a carefully located and constantly staffed administration area can enhance supervision of school entries, stairs, and hallways without the need for an additional assigned monitor.

This area should be positioned to allow for unobstructed surveillance of lobby doors, stairwells, and perpendicular hallways. Placing the administrative area on an exterior wall allows additional surveillance and a distant view of outside areas, especially visitor parking, drop-off areas, and exterior routes leading up to the main entrance. When feasible and appropriate, consider providing security camera(s) in the lobby area for electronic surveillance to enhance access control.

Figure 2.61

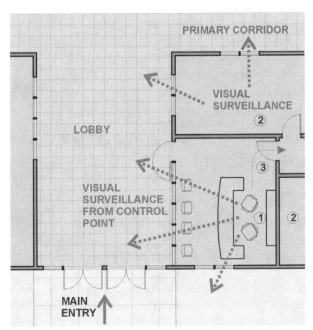

Figure 2.62

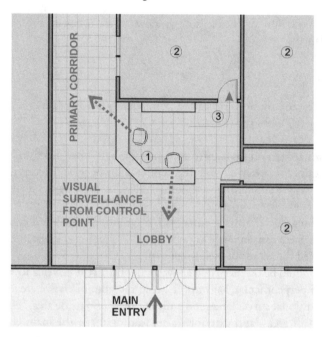

3.2 ADMINISTRATION AREAS

Natural Access Control

- Locate administration areas adjacent to the main entry and lobby
- Provide the reception/visitor information area with adequate protection by utilizing a counter and, when necessary, a protective shield
- Secure the faculty offices, student records, and clinic supplies

Natural Surveillance

- Incorporate extensive interior glazing in administration areas to provide unobstructed views and natural surveillance

Territorial Integrity

- Design and locate the administration area to reinforce its role as the guardian of the school facility
- Provide seating at reception/visitor information areas

The visitors' information counter, faculty offices, student records, and clinics need to have a high degree of security while maintaining a "sense of accessibility" to students,

Figure 2.63

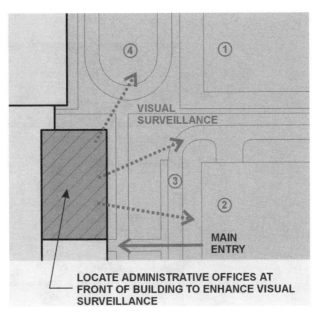

LOCATE ADMINISTRATIVE OFFICES AT
FRONT OF BUILDING TO ENHANCE VISUAL
SURVEILLANCE

parents, and visitors. Administration areas should be adjacent to main entry areas and designed to allow a visual connection through windows between administrators and students or visitors.

The reception/visitor information area should be provided with the minimum protection of a counter. In certain circumstances, a protective shield of Plexiglass may be required, especially in areas where funds are collected. This area should include interior glazing to provide surveillance of main access corridors and main entry.

When appropriate, consider providing a safe room in the administration area. This room should consist of a lockable door and a working telephone. In addition, two remote exits should be provided from the principal's office, one of which could be a window to the exterior. Faculty offices and student records should be separated from the reception area and accessible through lockable corridor doors. Student records should be stored in a fire-resistant vault within a locked room.

Schools might also consider providing an emergency kit, which should be located within the administration area in a locked cabinet. This kit would include items that administrators use during emergency situations, such as keys, facility information including site plans, floor plans, evacuation maps, system control and shut-off information, radios and/or cell phones, medical supplies, attendance data, contact lists, and emergency numbers.

Clinic supplies and equipment should be locked in an observable storage closet located in the nurse's office.

Figure 2.64

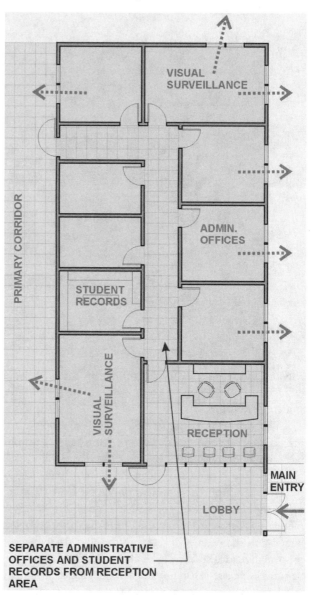

3.3 CORRIDORS

Natural Access Control

- Secure the exterior doors located along corridors to prevent unauthorized access into the building

Natural Surveillance

- Incorporate the interior glazing where possible to avoid long corridors with dead walls that block off natural surveillance
- Minimize hiding places and blind corners in corridors
- Avoid the use of segregated locker areas by locating lockers within main corridors or classrooms
- Recess lockers to eliminate hiding places

Territorial Integrity

- Increase corridor width beyond minimum requirements, when possible

According to survey research, principals, facility managers, and school resource officers cite corridors as the second-highest location within the school building for fighting. This is primarily due to overcrowding and congestion. It is, therefore, vital that corridors be carefully designed to accommodate large numbers of students during peak-use hours. Although a minimum corridor width is dictated by code, research has shown that this minimum width may not be sufficient. It is recommended that corridors be designed beyond the minimum width whenever feasible, especially where lockers are located. Corridors should also be well lighted and clearly defined without projections that might impede the flow of movement.

Designs that lead to sudden 90-degree turns should be avoided. These corners allow people to hide and, although costly, allow better visibility, as well as smoother pedestrian traffic flow. When budget constraints are an issue, strategically located convex mirrors can also help enhance surveillance and reduce conflicts.

Figure 2.65

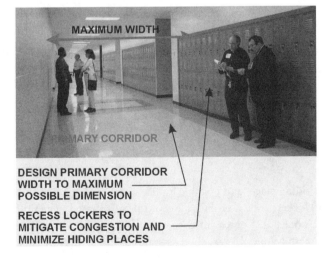

Figure 2.66

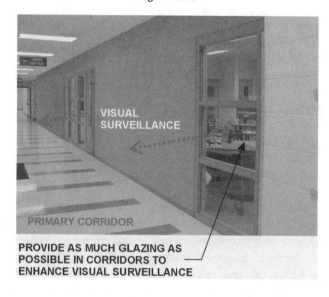

PROVIDE AS MUCH GLAZING AS
POSSIBLE IN CORRIDORS TO
ENHANCE VISUAL SURVEILLANCE

Figure 2.67

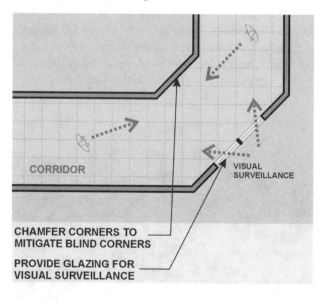

CHAMFER CORNERS TO
MITIGATE BLIND CORNERS

PROVIDE GLAZING FOR
VISUAL SURVEILLANCE

To reduce hiding places and possible injury, water coolers, vending machines, trash containers, and lockers should be either low profile or recessed to be flush with the wall. Avoid creating nooks and other small spaces along corridors that promote criminal activity. Any freestanding objects, such as stand-alone lockers or vending machines, should be mounted to the wall to avoid injury if they should fall over.

3.4 STAIRS AND STAIRWELLS

Natural Access Control

- Enclose entire area under all stairs
- Monitor doors leading to exterior from stairwells

Natural Surveillance

- Exterior stairs, balconies, ramps, and upper-level corridors should have open or see-through type handrails and guardrails to allow surveillance
- Avoid designing enclosed exterior stairwells, when possible
- Design lighting in stairs and stairwells to enhance surveillance

Territorial Integrity

- Increase stair width beyond minimum requirements, when possible

Stairs and stairwells pose similar safety and security issues as corridors. Because they are also susceptible to congestion during peak-use hours, consideration should be given to designing stairs and landings beyond the minimum code requirements.

Solid handrails create hiding places on stairs and landing areas. Open handrails allow visual access to areas on both sides of the stairwells. Handrails should be designed

Figure 2.68

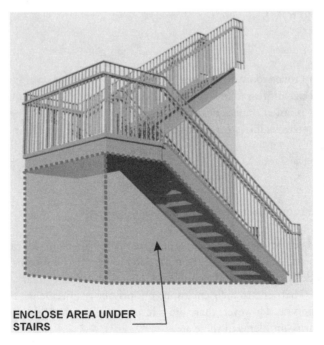

ENCLOSE AREA UNDER
STAIRS

Figure 2.69

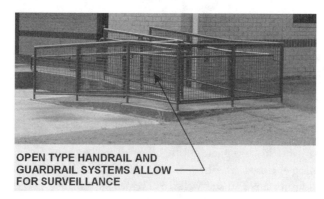

OPEN TYPE HANDRAIL AND
GUARDRAIL SYSTEMS ALLOW
FOR SURVEILLANCE

to discourage people from sliding on them, which can result in inadvertent damage or possible injury. The entire area under all stairs should be enclosed and made inaccessible for any use.

Attempts should be made to avoid enclosed exterior stairwells. If required, consideration should be given to providing these enclosed stairwells with electronic surveillance equipment whenever feasible. Doors leading to the exterior from stairwells are typically concealed and are, therefore, particularly vulnerable to unauthorized access. They should be monitored and checked by staff as much as possible. If the budget allows, equip these doors with alarms to indicate when a door has been opened.

3.5 TOILET ROOMS

Natural Surveillance

- Design group toilet rooms that open to the building interior with maze entries utilizing screen partitions rather than double-door entries
- Locate toilet room entrances near areas with natural surveillance
- Provide adequate facilities for after-school activities in locations adjacent to recreation areas

Management

- Utilize vandal-resistant materials, fixtures, and hardware

Research data indicates that toilet rooms are the fourth-highest locations for criminal activities on school campuses. The most common security concerns are vandalism, fighting, disorderly conduct, and alcohol and tobacco use. The primary factor for security problems is that, due to their enclosure and privacy requirements, toilet rooms are difficult to supervise. However, there are a few key design strategies to help mitigate safety and security problems in these areas.

Figure 2.70

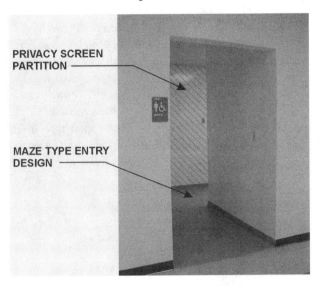

PRIVACY SCREEN
PARTITION

MAZE TYPE ENTRY
DESIGN

Figure 2.71

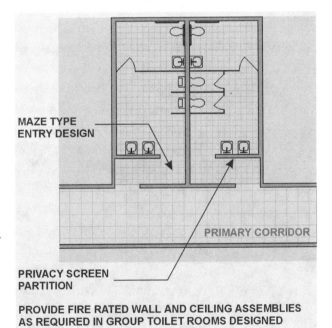

MAZE TYPE
ENTRY DESIGN

PRIMARY CORRIDOR

PRIVACY SCREEN
PARTITION

PROVIDE FIRE RATED WALL AND CEILING ASSEMBLIES
AS REQUIRED IN GROUP TOILET ROOMS DESIGNED
WITHOUT ENTRY DOORS

First, toilet room entrances should be located in places where natural surveillance can occur, such as primary corridors and administration areas. Facilities provided for after-school activities should also be designed to promote surveillance and should be able to be secured, when necessary. They should be highly visible from recreational areas. Second, utilizing privacy screen partitions with a maze-type entry design in interior group toilet rooms, when allowed by code, provides enhanced acoustical surveillance from adjoining corridors while preserving privacy. Third, the enclosed nature of the toilet room allows vandals the opportunity to damage fixtures. Therefore shelves, hand dryers, soap and paper towel dispensers, sanitary napkin dispensers, and trash containers should be heavy duty, recessed, and fire resistant, and have separate locks. Toilet room walls, floors, and ceilings should have a durable finish to withstand repeated cleaning of graffiti.

3.6 CLASSROOMS

Natural Access Control

- Design classrooms to be locked down quickly by faculty inside classrooms during an emergency situation

Natural Surveillance

- Provide extensive exterior windows from classrooms to enhance surveillance of school campus

Figure 2.72

PROVIDE WINDOWS BETWEEN TEACHER'S PLANNING ROOM AND CLASSROOM TO ENHANCE NATURAL SURVEILLANCE

Figure 2.73

PROVIDE EXTERIOR WINDOWS
IN CLASSROOMS TO ENHANCE
VISUAL SURVEILLANCE

- Provide interior windows and glazing between the classroom and the hallway to promote surveillance both into and out of the classroom
- Design retractable partitions to fully recess into walls to eliminate hiding places

Classrooms are a common location on school campuses for fighting, theft, and disorderly conduct. Therefore, it is important to design classrooms for easy monitoring and unobstructed visual supervision. Designs should include windows and glazing between hallways and classrooms to help increase surveillance. In classrooms that include retractable partitions, niches should be provided for housing partitions when they are in a retracted position. When applicable, lockers, built-in furniture, and storage units in classrooms should be designed so as not to obscure surveillance of the room or provide hiding places.

Incorporating windows along exterior walls of classrooms with views to the exterior enhances school security and promotes natural surveillance of the campus by staff and students during the course of their normal activities. This is particularly important for areas on campus that cannot be easily seen by the main administration office area.

In an emergency situation, classrooms should be able to be locked down quickly. Whenever possible, provide special classroom security locksets, which give teachers the ability to secure a door from inside the classroom without having to enter the corridor. This lockset function also allows egress from the room at all times.

3.7 LABS, SHOPS, AND COMPUTER ROOMS

Natural Access Control

- Locate labs, shops, and computer rooms with minimal direct access from the exterior whenever possible
- Provide a lockable room for storing equipment and supplies

Natural Surveillance

- Provide faculty and staff with direct visual access to workrooms and entry areas

Clear organization and unobstructed surveillance of workspaces is essential in the design of rooms where special equipment is being used. Since theft is a primary security issue associated with labs, shops, and computer rooms, faculty and staff should have direct visual access to workrooms and entries. Secondary access points, when they occur, should be well secured. In addition, valuable equipment and supplies should be protected in a lockable closet, visible to faculty and staff, to limit unauthorized access.

Figure 2.74

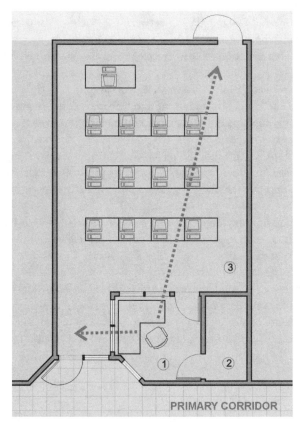

Figure 2.75

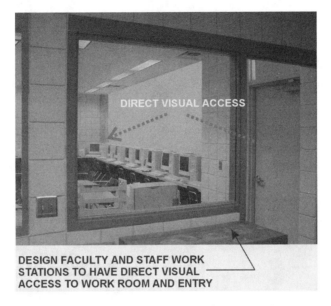

DIRECT VISUAL ACCESS

DESIGN FACULTY AND STAFF WORK
STATIONS TO HAVE DIRECT VISUAL
ACCESS TO WORK ROOM AND ENTRY

It is also important to limit access to chemicals, tools, and similar items that could be used for dangerous purposes.

Whenever feasible, entries to workspaces should be equipped with an alarm system to make breaking and entering difficult. To maximize security and minimize theft, rooms with computers and other costly equipment should have a limited number of windows. Direct access from the exterior should also be limited.

3.8 MUSIC ROOMS

Natural Access Control

- Provide unobstructed view of entrances to music room for access control
- Provide a lockable room for equipment and supplies

Natural Surveillance

- Locate lockable storage rooms to promote natural surveillance

As in the previous section, a principal security concern in the case of music rooms is theft. Music rooms or band practice areas also have similar programmatic considerations as auditoriums. It is important to facilitate visual supervision by one person over a large assembly of students and to properly secure equipment. Storage areas for equipment and supplies should be locked at all times and should be located in an area clearly visible to faculty and staff.

Figure 2.76

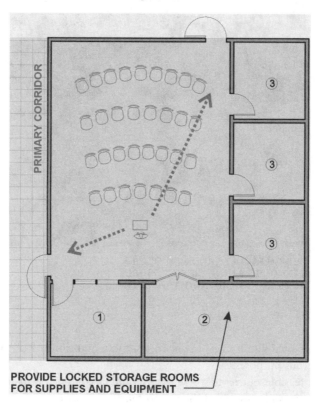

PROVIDE LOCKED STORAGE ROOMS
FOR SUPPLIES AND EQUIPMENT

Entrances to the music room should be able to be easily secured and located in a highly visible area. Special consideration should be given to providing access detection alarms to increase security. Storage units, built-in furniture, and similar accessories associated with music and band practice areas should not create places to hide or obstruct surveillance of any portion of the room.

3.9 CAFETERIAS

Natural Access Control

- Locate a well-defined control point near main entrance of cafeteria
- Design kitchen and serving areas, so that they can be secured both during and after-school hours

Natural Surveillance

- Control point at the main entrance should have unobstructed surveillance of entire cafeteria
- Design serving line and cashier area to be visible from dining area

Territorial Integrity

• Design cafeteria to eliminate traffic-flow conflicts and overcrowding

Educators and school resource officers cite cafeterias as the primary location on school campuses for fighting. Overly cramped and crowded designs can irritate and frustrate students. Because large groups of students move in and out of cafeterias at the

Figure 2.77

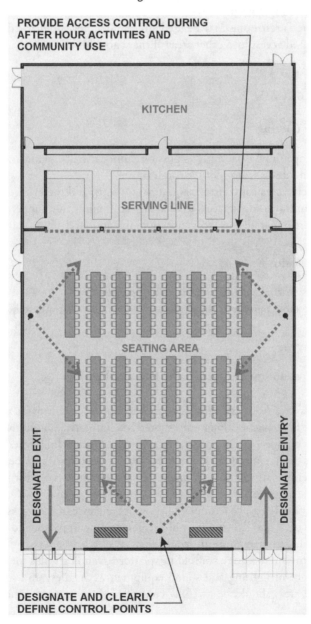

same time, it is critical to design circulation patterns that eliminate traffic-flow problems. Solutions include designing well-defined one-way entry and exit doors, as well as providing sufficient space between tables to allow ample circulation. It is also important to provide a designated control point near the main entrance and exit that has a clear line of sight of the whole cafeteria.

Due to the presence of cash, both at the cashier and with the students in line, the serving line should be visible from the dining area. The serving and kitchen areas of cafeterias should be able to be properly secured, since food may be a target of theft in schools. In addition, care must be taken to secure kitchen utensils, such as knives, which may be used for dangerous purposes.

Since cafeteria restrooms may be used after hours, they should be designed to prevent unauthorized access into other areas of the school building.

3.10 AUDITORIUMS

Natural Access Control

- Locate roof openings as far away as possible from catwalks, platforms, and scaffolding to prevent access from roof into auditorium
- Provide a secure area for controls, equipment, props, and tools
- Limit and control student access to catwalks, scaffolding, and upper-level platforms
- Provide secure, separate entrances for school use and after-hours activities

Natural Surveillance

- Avoid niches that provide hiding places along walls
- Design retractable partitions to fully recess into walls to eliminate hiding places

Territorial Integrity

- Design auditoriums to eliminate traffic-flow conflicts

Like any large school assembly area, auditoriums should provide clear sight lines and easy traffic flow. Niches along walls should be eliminated, and, if the auditorium is subdivided for dual use as classrooms, the partitions should fully recess into the wall. Partitions that do not recess can form a barrier for people to hide behind when the auditorium is empty, as well as providing cover to those intent on disrupting a general assembly.

The stage curtain can be left open to allow surveillance of the backstage area when not in use. Electrical and lighting controls, stage equipment, props, and tools should be placed in lockable storage rooms to reduce theft.

Auditoriums often require scaffolding, platforms, and catwalks for the installation and maintenance of lighting and sound equipment. For safety and security reasons, access to these areas should be carefully controlled. During times when students are

Figure 2.78

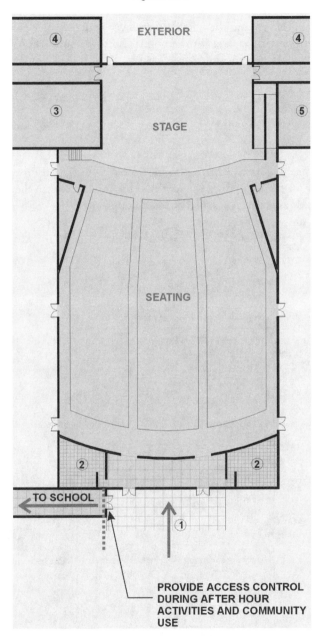

permitted in these areas, it is imperative that they are closely monitored and supervised. Care must also be taken not to locate roof openings close to these structures, as it is possible to gain entry into an auditorium by prying open a roof hatch or smoke vent and traveling via a scaffold down to floor level.

Auditoriums are often used for after-hours activities and are commonly used by the community as joint-use facilities. Therefore, dual main entrances should be provided. Design a direct entrance from the school for students and a separate entrance from the street or designated parking area for the public. Both entrances should be able to be properly secured for access control.

3.11 GYMNASIUMS

Natural Access Control

- Locate roof openings as far away as possible from architectural features that may provide a means for climbing from the roof into the interior within the gymnasium
- Utilize clerestories instead of skylights whenever possible
- Provide a secure area for equipment
- Provide secure separate entrances for school use and after-hours activities

Figure 2.79

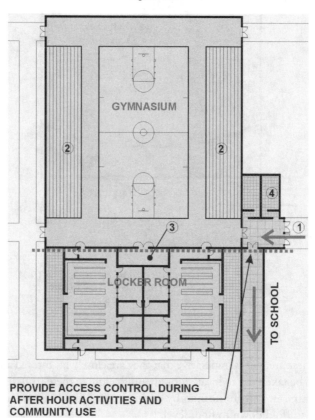

Figure 2.80

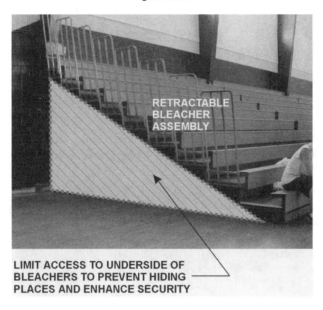

RETRACTABLE
BLEACHER
ASSEMBLY

LIMIT ACCESS TO UNDERSIDE OF
BLEACHERS TO PREVENT HIDING
PLACES AND ENHANCE SECURITY

Natural Surveillance

- Utilize retractable bleachers that can be secured when not in use
- Locate equipment storage rooms in an area that is visible to gym users and staff to promote surveillance

As in the case of auditoriums, gymnasiums require dual entrances to allow independent operation for school use and after-hours activities, as well as community use. This will restrict visitors from entering the school. Provide a direct entrance from the school for students and an entrance for the public from the street or designated parking lot. Both entrances should be able to be secured.

Like the auditorium, the gym is another large-span structure, and care must be taken to avoid opportunities for students to enter the school building through the roof and climbing down structural elements, such as trusses.

When skylights are used, they should be installed well clear of any means of climbing down to the gym floor. Clerestory windows can be used in place of skylights. However, they should be designed to prevent access from bleachers. In addition, structural members should not be accessible from either the floor or adjacent bleachers.

Retractable bleachers should be secured so as to prevent vandalism. Because these areas can also present opportunities for hiding, it is important to control and monitor access to the underside of bleachers.

Equipment rooms must be designed for access control. A secure and lockable area for storage of equipment should be provided. This area should be placed in a location where gym users, instructors, and coaches can see it during the course of their normal activities to enhance monitoring and surveillance.

3.12 LOCKER ROOMS

Natural Access Control

- Locate gym instructors' and coaches' offices near the main entrance to the locker room
- Utilize finishes that eliminate access to ceiling area

Natural Surveillance

- Provide windows in gym instructors' and coaches' offices with unobstructed views into locker areas
- Recess lockers to eliminate hiding places and limit access to ceiling areas
- Place lockers along the perimeter walls of locker room or limit locker height to enhance surveillance

Figure 2.81

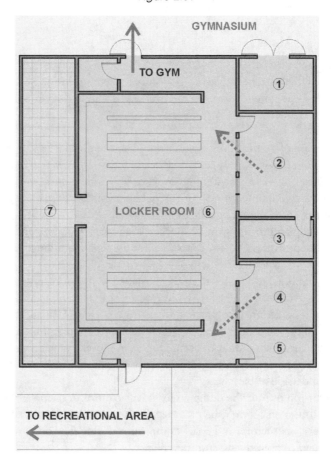

Figure 2.82

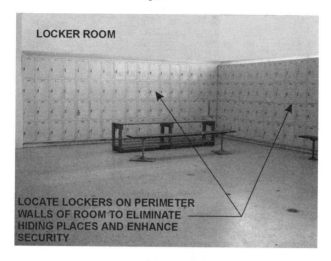

Figure 2.83

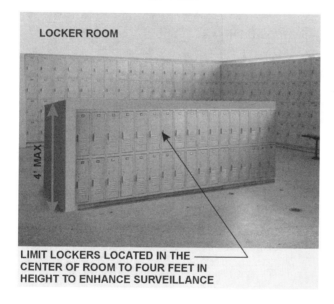

Management

• Utilize vandal-resistant materials, fixtures, and hardware

Educators and security officers have consistently cited locker rooms as school locations with a high level of security and safety problems. Theft, fighting, and vandalism are specific concerns. Due to the enclosure and privacy requirements of these areas, locker rooms can present opportunities for criminal activities. Therefore, these areas should be carefully organized and designed to promote as much access control and surveillance as is possible.

The gym instructors' and coaches' offices should be located adjacent to the main entry to the locker room and should have extensive glazing that overlooks the entire room. These offices should be able to be easily secured to control unauthorized access. It is preferable to place lockers along the perimeter walls of the locker room with a centralized and open changing space. However, this may not be feasible due to budget constraints and space limitations. When parallel rows of lockers are necessary, an alternative is to utilize lockers that do not exceed four feet in height, adequately spaced to avoid crowding, and to place the rows of lockers perpendicular to the office window wall and parallel to the faculty's line of sight to ensure an unobstructed view of this area. Lockers should be either recessed into the wall or sloped on top to minimize opportunities to gain access to ceiling areas. Recessed lockers can also eliminate places to hide.

Light fixture covers, windows, and mirrors should be impact resistant to prevent damage from vandalism. Acoustical ceiling tiles should not be used in any area of the locker room. Exposed concrete or plaster-finished ceilings eliminate the opportunity to use the space above as a hiding place for persons, stolen property, or controlled substances.

3.13 LIBRARIES AND MEDIA CENTERS

Natural Access Control

- Locate circulation desk and/or reception area near main entrance
- Design a separate lockable area for audiovisual and computer equipment to control access

Natural Surveillance

- A control point at the main entrance should have unobstructed surveillance of entire library/media center
- Maintain unobstructed lines of sight throughout library/media center and from the media specialist's office

Management

- Install detection devices and alarm systems, when possible

Library design should minimize opportunities for theft of materials and equipment, as well as minimize possible hiding places. Both goals can be met through the use of control points and the maintenance of clear sight lines.

The reception area or circulation librarian should be placed in a central location near the main entry to control student traffic. Low stacks that are well spaced and placed parallel to the circulation librarian's line of sight will aid in visual control, as well as reduce hiding places for storing stolen goods or controlled substances. Serious con-

Figure 2.84

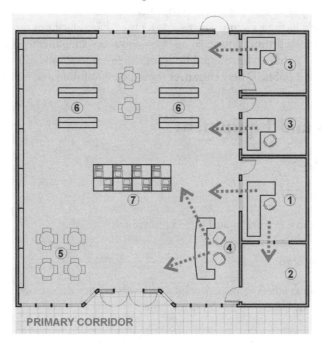

PRIMARY CORRIDOR

Figure 2.85

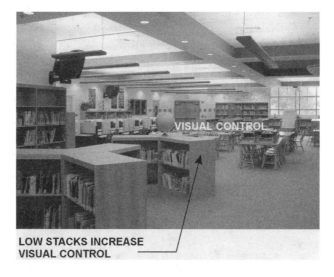

VISUAL CONTROL

LOW STACKS INCREASE
VISUAL CONTROL

sideration should be given to installing a book alarm system. When feasible and applicable, also consider providing alarms at secondary exits in libraries and media centers to enhance access control and to protect against theft.

Creating a lockable delivery/pickup area separate from general equipment storage can control access to audiovisual (AV) equipment.

School libraries and media centers may also be combined with public libraries or be used by the public in a joint-use arrangement. Special provisions for access control should be made in these circumstances. As in other shared facilities mentioned in previous sections, two distinct and separate main entrances, one direct entrance from the school and one entrance for the public from the exterior, should control access into the school by the public. These entrances should be monitored and easily secured.

Systems and Equipment

4.1 ELEVATORS

Natural Access Control

• Limit access to elevators to authorized individuals

Natural Surveillance

• Locate elevators adjacent to main circulation where they can be observed
• Provide adequate lighting in elevator lobbies

Figure 2.86

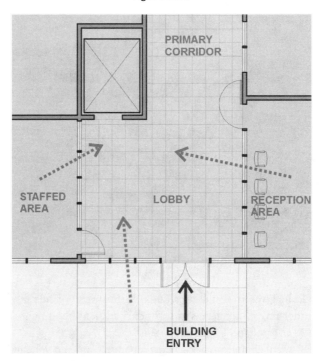

Territorial Integrity

• Provide electronic surveillance within elevator cabs when possible
• Provide vandal-resistant convex mirrors in elevator cabs

Elevators should be centrally located adjacent to main circulation spaces, that is, entry lobbies and primary corridors. A landing area that does not obstruct student traffic should be provided. Elevator lobbies should be well lit to enhance surveillance and security.

The use of elevators for criminal activities can be significantly deterred by faculty/staff surveillance of lobbies and corridors coupled with the use of electronic surveillance, such as closed circuit television (CCTV), within the elevator cabs. Convex mirrors placed in strategic locations within elevator cabs can eliminate hiding places and greatly increase security. These mirrors should be made of vandal-resistant materials.

4.2 HEATING, VENTILATION, AND AIR CONDITIONING/MECHANICAL EQUIPMENT

Natural Access Control

• Locate heating, ventilation, and air conditioning (HVAC)/mechanical equipment in a secured area accessible to authorized personnel only
• Provide a lockable enclosure for equipment, such as exterior condensing units
• Install flush-mounted vents in mechanical rooms
• Identify all critical electrical and communication distribution rooms as "Equipment Rooms"

Figure 2.87

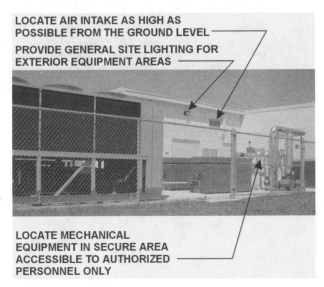

LOCATE AIR INTAKE AS HIGH AS POSSIBLE FROM THE GROUND LEVEL

PROVIDE GENERAL SITE LIGHTING FOR EXTERIOR EQUIPMENT AREAS

LOCATE MECHANICAL EQUIPMENT IN SECURE AREA ACCESSIBLE TO AUTHORIZED PERSONNEL ONLY

Figure 2.88

PROVIDE A SECURE
ENCLOSURE AROUND
CONDENSING UNITS

Figure 2.89

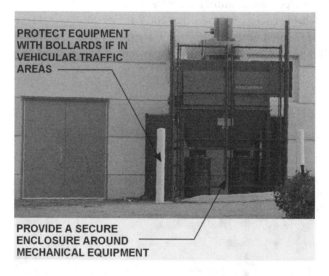

PROTECT EQUIPMENT
WITH BOLLARDS IF IN
VEHICULAR TRAFFIC
AREAS

PROVIDE A SECURE
ENCLOSURE AROUND
MECHANICAL EQUIPMENT

Natural Surveillance

• Locate lockable equipment enclosures in areas where general lighting occurs, when possible

The location for HVAC equipment should be accessible only to authorized personnel, but should also allow for proper ventilation. Mechanical equipment storage should have flush-mounted vents located out of reach. Spacing of vent slats should not allow persons to reach in or to pass objects through them, potentially causing damage to equipment or exhaust fans. Equipment should be protected with bollards when located adjacent to vehicular routes.

Secure exterior condensing units with enclosures designed using materials that provide protection from thrown projectiles. Fresh air intake, water and electrical supply, and backflow preventers should be secured to eliminate unauthorized access. Rooms containing electrical, telephone, computer distribution, security, fire, and other critical distribution equipment should be identified and labeled simply as "Equipment Rooms." This makes it difficult for an intruder to shut down the school and its communication network.

Locating these structures in areas where general site lighting is used will make nighttime surveillance easier without having to install direct lighting.

4.3 WATER FOUNTAINS

Natural Access Control

• Utilize wall-hung water fountains to prevent vandalism when possible

Natural Surveillance

• Locate water fountains near group toilet rooms in areas with natural surveillance

Figure 2.90

Figure 2.91

PROVIDE ROLL-UP TYPE SECURITY
GRILLE TO LIMIT ACCESS AFTER
SCHOOL HOURS

Water fountains need to be protected from vandalism. It is important to locate water fountains in areas where they can be monitored. Flush-mounted water fountains provide protection for the cooling system, but do not provide access for handicapped persons. Floor-mounted fountains are completely exposed, providing protection only to the side facing the wall. It is preferable to use wall-hung fountains that have in-wall cooling systems when possible. These fountains should have heavy-duty mounts to prevent damage due to vandalism.

Water fountains in exterior locations should be able to be easily secured to limit access after school hours when necessary. Place water fountains in a recessed area and provide a roll-up type security grille to control access and prevent vandalism.

4.4 VENDING MACHINES AND PUBLIC TELEPHONES

Natural Access Control

- Control student access to vending machines
- Design exterior vending machine areas that can be easily secured after school hours
- Locate public telephones in a centralized area

Natural Surveillance

- Locate vending machine areas in well-monitored areas with natural surveillance
- Recess vending machines into alcoves to prevent hiding places
- Locate public telephones in areas that facilitate supervision and surveillance

Figure 2.92

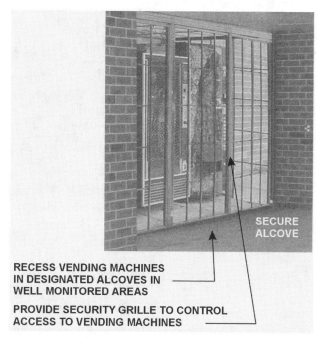

RECESS VENDING MACHINES
IN DESIGNATED ALCOVES IN
WELL MONITORED AREAS

PROVIDE SECURITY GRILLE TO CONTROL
ACCESS TO VENDING MACHINES

SECURE
ALCOVE

Figure 2.93

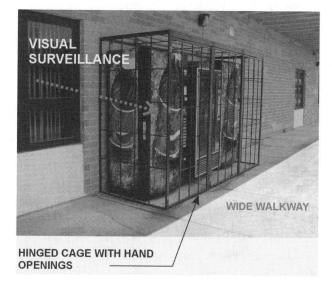

VISUAL
SURVEILLANCE

WIDE WALKWAY

HINGED CAGE WITH HAND
OPENINGS

Figure 2.94

VISUAL SURVEILLANCE

LOCATE PAY TELEPHONE IN
DIRECT LINE OF SIGHT OF
FULL-TIME STAFFED WORK
STATION

Vending machines are vulnerable to vandalism and theft, both during and after school hours. Provision should be made to protect vending machines located in schools and on school campuses. Public telephones can also provide opportunities for criminal activity. A common problem cited is the use of public telephones for bomb threats. Therefore, supervision of these areas is key to enhancing school security.

Controlling access to vending machines can be achieved in several ways. Providing a recess or alcove with a roll-up type security grille with hand openings can limit access to machines, as well as eliminate hiding places. These recesses can also be provided with doors to secure vending areas after school hours when necessary. A less-expensive alternative is to fit machines with hinged cages and hand openings that only allow students to reach in and make purchases. In either case, avoid placing vending areas in isolated areas. They should be located in well-lit areas where they can be monitored by faculty and staff in the course of their normal activities. Design wide corridors and walkways adjacent to vending machine areas to avoid conflicts and overcrowding.

Public telephones, especially on high school campuses, should be located in a centralized and highly visible location, such as adjacent to the administration areas. Providing a window with unobstructed lines of sight of the telephones in these locations can significantly reduce vandalism. Design wide corridors and walkways in these areas to prevent congestion.

4.5 FIRE CONTROL AND ALARMS

Natural Access Control

- Flush-mount sprinklers in ceilings
- Avoid blocking or obstructing paths of travel with fire control equipment

Natural Surveillance

- Locate fire extinguishers, fire alarms, and standpipe cabinets where they can be easily monitored

Figure 2.95

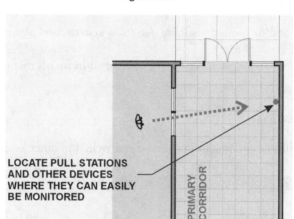

LOCATE PULL STATIONS AND OTHER DEVICES WHERE THEY CAN EASILY BE MONITORED

PRIMARY CORRIDOR

Figure 2.96

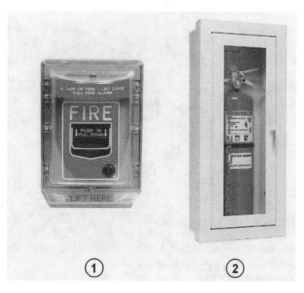

Fire control equipment includes such items as fire extinguishers, fire alarm pull stations, standpipe cabinets, and sprinklers.

Fire extinguisher and standpipe cabinets located in main circulation paths should be flush-mounted in walls adjacent to classrooms. Fire alarm pull stations should be located in areas that allow for unobstructed surveillance. Like vending machines and telephones, isolated equipment is more susceptible to vandalism and misuse. Providing tamper-proof covers for fire alarm pull stations can also deter misuse of the device. Fire sprinklers should also be flush-mounted in ceilings to avoid damage.

4.6 ALARM AND SURVEILLANCE SYSTEMS

Mechanical Access Control

- Utilize audio and/or motion sensitive detection systems and alarm systems, when possible
- Locate detection devices at critical entry points and in rooms that contain valuable equipment

Mechanical Surveillance

- Provide surveillance equipment in enclosed stairwells and other key locations, when possible

Management

- Maintained operational integrity of equipment

Figure 2.97

CCTV SHOULD BE INSTALLED IN
POTENTIAL PROBLEM AREAS IN
NEED OF INCREASED CONTROL

Figure 2.98

CCTV STRATEGICALLY POSITIONED
TO MONITOR VISITOR PARKING AND
BUILDING PERIMETER

Figure 2.99

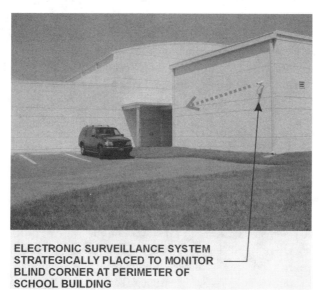

ELECTRONIC SURVEILLANCE SYSTEM
STRATEGICALLY PLACED TO MONITOR
BLIND CORNER AT PERIMETER OF
SCHOOL BUILDING

Both survey data and site visits confirm that increased surveillance and access control continues to be a significant issue for schools. Principals, facility managers, and school resource officers mention repeatedly that electronic surveillance systems, such as closed circuit television (CCTV), are a desirable addition to their campuses. Because the use of alarm and surveillance systems can greatly increase the safety and security of

"Security technologies are not the answer to all school security problems. However, many security products (e.g., cameras, sensors, and so forth) can be excellent tools if applied appropriately. They can provide school administrators or security officials with information that would not otherwise be available, free up manpower for more appropriate work, or be used to perform mundane tasks. Sometimes they can save money (compared to the long-term cost of personnel or the cost impact of not preventing a particular incident). Too often, though, these technologies are not applied appropriately in schools, are expected to do more than they are capable of, or are not well-maintained after initial installation. In these cases, technologies are certainly not cost-effective." National Institute of Justice, The Appropriate and Effective Use of Security Technologies in U.S. Schools.

schools, serious consideration should be given to incorporating mechanical as well as natural access control and surveillance.

Typical locations and conditions cited as potential problem areas in need of increased control include the lobby and main entrance, enclosed stairwells, courtyards, secondary access points, and blind corners and hidden areas along the building perimeter. Propped doors at secondary entrances are a particularly common occurrence and, since it is difficult for resource officers and staff to properly check these areas throughout the school day, providing alarms on these doors to alert staff should be a priority.

The use of sensors or alarmed security systems can reduce property loss and vandalism in schools after hours. Coordination with local police can help reduce response time, increasing the chances of apprehending persons while still on school grounds with property in hand. Expert contractors should handle the installation of electronic surveillance systems. They will strategically locate detection devices at key points throughout the school.

Closed Circuit Television

A properly integrated closed circuit television (CCTV) assessment system provides a rapid and cost-effective method for determining the cause of intrusion alarms. For surveillance, a properly designed CCTV system provides a cost-effective supplement to patrols. For large facilities, the cost of a CCTV system is more easily justified. It is important to recognize that CCTV alarm assessment systems and CCTV surveillance systems perform separate and distinct functions. The alarm assessment system is designed to respond rapidly, automatically, and predictably to the receipt of ESS alarms at the security center. The surveillance system is designed for use at the discretion of and under the control of the security center's console operator.

Installation of a closed circuit system has several additional benefits. The knowledge that a system is installed generally leads to behavioral improvements and greater peace of mind for students and faculty. It deters outsiders from coming on campus because they can be immediately recognized as such, and videotapes provide strong evidence that an incident took place, even if the student denies it.

Other systems that should be considered are metal detectors and hand-held scanners, identification cards and card readers, and duress alarms that not only alert security staff that an incident is taking place but pinpoint exactly where on campus.

Designing for Explosive and Chemical, Biological, and Radiological Attacks

PROTECTING AGAINST EXPLOSIVE, CHEMICAL, BIOLOGICAL, AND RADIOLOGICAL ATTACKS

Designing security into a building requires a complex series of trade-offs. Security concerns need to be balanced with many other design constraints, such as accessibility, initial and life-cycle costs, natural hazard mitigation, fire protection, energy efficiency, and aesthetics.

Because the probability of attack is very small, security measures should not interfere with daily operations of the building. On the other hand, because the effects of attack can be catastrophic, it is prudent to incorporate measures that may save lives and minimize business interruption in the unlikely event of an attack. The measures should be as unobtrusive as possible to provide an inviting, efficient environment that does not attract the undue attention of potential attackers. Security design needs to be part of an overall multi-hazard approach to ensure that it does not worsen the behavior of the building in the event of a fire, earthquake, or hurricane, which are far more prevalent hazards than are terrorist attacks.

Because of the severity of the types of hazards discussed, the goals of security-oriented design are by necessity modest. With regard to explosive attacks, the focus is on a damage-limiting or damage-mitigating approach rather than a blast-resistant approach. The goal is to incorporate some reasonable measures that will enhance the safety of the people within the building and facilitate rescue efforts in the unlikely event of attack.

Protection against terrorist attack is not an all-or-nothing proposition. Incremental measures taken early in design may be more fully developed at a later date. With a little forethought regarding, for instance, the space requirements needed to accommodate additional measures, the protection level can be enhanced as the need arises or the budget permits after construction is complete.

The Federal Emergency Management Agency (FEMA) advocates a holistic, multi-disciplinary approach to security design by considering the various building systems, including site, architecture, structure, and mechanical and electrical systems and providing general recommendations for the design professional with little or no background in this area.

If you are designing a new building you can strategically site it as far from the perimeter as you can and secure the perimeter against vehicular intrusion using landscaping or barrier methods. Incorporating these security elements into an existing facility requires a different design approach.

Best practices recommended by FEMA for new buildings are listed below. The security concepts involved, however, and the remedies are equally applicable to existing buildings and facilities.

- Place building as far from any secured perimeter as practical.
- Secure the perimeter against vehicular intrusion using landscaping or barrier methods.
- Use lightweight nonstructural elements on the building exterior and interior.
- Place unsecured areas exterior to the main structure or in the exterior bay.
- Incorporate measures to resist progressive collapse.
- Design exterior window systems and cladding so that the framing, connections, and supporting structure have a lateral-load-resistance that is equal to or higher than the transparency or panel.
- Place air intakes as far above the ground level as practical.
- Physically isolate vulnerable areas, such as the entries and delivery areas, from the rest of the structure by using floor-to-floor walls in these areas.
- Use redundant, separated mechanical/electrical control systems.

OVERVIEW OF POSSIBLE THREATS

Explosive Threats:

- Vehicle weapon
- Hand-delivered weapon

Airborne Chemical, Biological, and Radiological Threats:

- Large-scale, external, airborne release
- External release targeting building
- Internal release

Although it is possible that the dominant threat mode may change in the future, bombings have historically been a favorite tactic of terrorists. Ingredients for home-made bombs are easily obtained on the open market, as are the techniques for making bombs. Bombings are easy and quick to execute. Finally, the dramatic component of explosions in terms of the sheer destruction they cause creates a media sensation that is highly effective in transmitting the terrorists' message to the public.

EXPLOSIVE ATTACKS

From the standpoint of structural design, the vehicle bomb is the most important consideration. Vehicle bombs are able to deliver a sufficiently large quantity of explosives to cause potentially devastating structural damage. Security design intended to limit or mitigate damage from a vehicle bomb assumes that the bomb is detonated at a so-called critical location. For a vehicle bomb, the critical location is taken to be the closest point that a vehicle can approach, assuming all security measures are in place. This may be a parking area directly beneath the occupied building, the loading dock, the curb directly outside the facility, or a vehicle-access control gate where inspection takes place, depending on the level of protection incorporated into the design.

Another explosive attack threat is the small bomb that is hand delivered. Small weapons can cause the greatest damage when brought into vulnerable, unsecured areas of the building interior, such as the building lobby, mailroom, or retail spaces. Recent events around the world make it clear that there is an increased likelihood that bombs will be delivered by persons who are willing to sacrifice their own lives. Hand-carried explosives are typically on the order of five to ten pounds of TNT equivalent. However, larger charge weights, in the fifty to one hundred pounds TNT equivalent range, can be readily carried in rolling cases. Mail bombs are typically less than ten pounds of TNT equivalent.

In general, the largest credible explosive size is a function of the security measures in place. Each line of security may be thought of as a sieve, reducing the size of the weapon that may gain access. Therefore the largest weapons are considered in totally unsecured public space (such as in a vehicle on the nearest public street), and the smallest weapons are considered in the most secured areas of the building (such as in a briefcase smuggled past the screening station).

Two parameters define the design threat: the weapon size, measured in equivalent pounds of TNT, and the standoff. The standoff is the distance measured from the center of gravity of the charge to the component of interest.

The owner in collaboration with security and protective design consultants (engineers who specialize in the design of structures to mitigate the effects of explosions) usually select the design weapon size. Although there are few unclassified sources giving the sizes of weapons that have been used in previous attacks throughout the world, security consultants have valuable information that may be used to evaluate the range of charge weights that might be reasonably considered for the intended occupancy. Security consultants draw upon the experience of other countries, such as Great Britain and Israel, where terrorist attacks have been more prevalent, as well as data gathered by U.S. sources.

To put the weapon size into perspective, it should be noted that thousands of deliberate explosions occur every year within the United States, but the vast majority of them have weapon yields less than five pounds. The number of large-scale vehicle weapon attacks that have used hundreds of pounds of TNT during the past twenty years is very small by comparison.

The design vehicle weapon size will usually be much smaller than the largest credible threat. The design weapon size is typically measured in hundreds of pounds rather than thousands of pounds of TNT equivalent.

The decision is usually based on a trade-off between the largest credible attack directed against the building and the design constraints of the project. Further, it is common for the design pressures and impulses to be less than the actual peak pressures and impulses acting on the building. This is the approach that the federal government has taken in its design criteria for federally owned domestic office buildings.

There are several reasons for this choice:

1. The likely target is often not the building under design, but a high-risk building that is nearby. Historically, more building damage has been due to collateral effects than direct attack.
2. It is difficult to quantify the risk of man-made hazards. However, qualitatively it may be stated that the chance of a large-scale terrorist attack occurring is extremely low. A smaller explosive attack is far more likely.
3. Providing a level of protection that is consistent with standards adopted for federal office buildings enhances opportunities for leasing to government agencies in addition to providing a clear statement regarding the building's safety to other potential tenants.
4. The added robustness inherent in designing for a vehicle bomb of moderate size will improve the performance of the building under all explosion scenarios.

DESCRIPTION OF EXPLOSION FORCES

An explosion is an extremely rapid release of energy in the form of light, heat, sound, and a shockwave. The shockwave consists of highly compressed air that wave-reflects off the ground surface to produce a hemispherical propagation of the wave that travels outward from the source at supersonic velocities. As the shockwave expands, the incident or over-pressures decrease. When it encounters a surface that is in line of sight of the explosion, the wave is reflected, resulting in a tremendous amplification of pressure. Unlike acoustical waves, which reflect with an amplification factor of 2, shockwaves can reflect with an amplification factor of up to 13, due to the supersonic velocity of the shockwave at impact. The magnitude of the reflection factor is a function of the proximity of the explosion and the angle of incidence of the shockwave on the surface.

The pressures decay rapidly with time (exponentially), measured typically in thousandths of a second (milliseconds). Diffraction effects, caused by building features, such as reentrant corners and overhangs of the building, may act to confine the air blast, prolonging its duration.

Late in the explosive event, the shockwave becomes negative, followed by a partial vacuum, which creates suction behind the shockwave. Immediately following the vacuum, air rushes in, creating a powerful wind or drag pressure on all surfaces of the building. This wind picks up and carries flying debris in the vicinity of the detonation.

In an external explosion, a portion of the energy is also imparted to the ground, creating a crater and generating a ground shockwave analogous to a high-intensity, short-duration earthquake. The peak pressure is a function of the weapon size or yield and the cube of the distance.

The extent and severity of damage and injuries in an explosive event cannot be predicted with perfect certainty. For instance, two adjacent columns of a building may be roughly the same distance from the explosion, but only one fails because a fragment strikes it in a particular way that initiates collapse. The other, by chance, is not struck and remains in place. Similarly, glass failures may occur outside of the predicted areas due to air-blast diffraction effects caused by the arrangement of buildings and their heights in the vicinity of the explosion. The details of the physical setting surrounding a particular occupant may greatly influence the level of injury incurred. The position of the person, seated or standing, facing toward or away from the event as it happens, may result in injuries ranging from minor to severe. Despite these uncertainties, it is possible to calculate the expected extent of damage and injuries to be expected in an explosive event, based on the size of the explosion, distance from the event, and assumptions about the construction of the building. Additionally, there is strong evidence to support a relationship between injury patterns and structural damage patterns.

Damage due to the air-blast shockwave may be divided into direct air-blast effects and progressive collapse. Direct air-blast effects are damage caused by the high-intensity pressures of the air blast close to the explosion. These may induce localized failure of exterior walls, windows, roof systems, floor systems, and columns.

Progressive collapse refers to the spread of an initial local failure from element to element, eventually resulting in a disproportionate extent of collapse relative to the zone of initial damage. Localized damage due to direct air-blast effects may or may not progress, depending on the design and construction of the building. To produce a progressive collapse, the weapon must be in close proximity to a critical load-bearing element. Progressive collapse can propagate vertically upward or downward from the source of the explosion, and it can propagate laterally from bay to bay as well.

The pressures that an explosion exerts on building surfaces may be several orders of magnitude greater than the loads for which the building is designed. The shockwave also acts in directions that the building may not have been designed for, such as upward pressure on the floor system.

In terms of sequence of response, the air blast first impinges the exterior envelope of the building. The pressure wave pushes on the exterior walls and can cause wall failure and window breakage. As the shockwave continues to expand, it enters the structure, pushing both upward on the ceilings and downward on the floors.

Floor failure is common in large-scale, vehicle-delivered explosive attacks because floor slabs typically have a large surface area for the pressure to act on and a comparably small thickness. Floor failure is particularly common for close-in and internal explosions. The loss of a floor system increases the unbraced height of the supporting columns, which may lead to structural instability.

For hand-carried weapons that are brought into the building and placed on the floor away from a primary vertical load-bearing element, the response will be more localized, with damage and injuries extending a bay or two in each direction. Although the weapon is smaller, the air-blast effects are amplified due to multiple reflections from interior surfaces. Typical damage types that may be expected include:

- Localized failure of the floor system immediately below the weapon
- Damage and possible localized failure for the floor system above the weapon

- Damage and possible localized failure of nearby concrete and masonry walls
- Failure of nonstructural elements, such as partition walls, false ceilings, ductwork, and window treatments
- Flying debris generated by furniture, computer equipment, and other contents

More extensive damage, possibly leading to progressive collapse, may occur if the weapon is strategically placed directly against a primary load-bearing element, such as a column.

In comparison to other hazards, such as earthquake or wind, an explosive attack has several distinguishing features:

- The intensity of the localized pressures acting on building components can be several orders of magnitude greater than these other hazards. It is not uncommon for the peak pressure on the building from a vehicle weapon parked along the curb to be in excess of 100 psi. Major damage and failure of building components is expected, even for relatively small weapons, in close proximity to the building.
- Explosive pressures decay extremely rapidly with distance from the source. Pressures acting on the building, particularly on the side facing the explosion, may vary significantly, causing a wide range of damage types. As a result, air blast tends to cause more localized damage than other hazards that have a more global effect.
- The duration of the event is very short, measured in thousandths of a second (milliseconds). In terms of timing, the building is engulfed by the shockwave and direct air-blast damage occurs within tens to hundreds of milliseconds from the time of detonation due to the supersonic velocity of the shockwave and the nearly instantaneous response of the structural elements. By comparison, earthquake events last for seconds and wind loads may act on the building for minutes or longer.

CORRELATION BETWEEN DAMAGE AND INJURIES

Three types of building damage can lead to injuries and possible fatalities. The most severe building response is collapse. In past incidents, collapse has caused the most extensive fatalities. For the Oklahoma City bombing in 1995, nearly 90 percent of the building occupants who lost their lives were in the collapsed portion of the Alfred P. Murrah Federal Office Building. Many of the survivors in the collapsed region were on the lower floors and had been trapped in void spaces under concrete slabs.

Although the targeted building is at greatest risk of collapse, other nearby buildings may also collapse. For instance, in the Oklahoma City bombing, a total of nine buildings collapsed. Most of these were unreinforced masonry structures that fortunately were largely unoccupied at the time of the attack. In the bombing of the U.S. embassy in Nairobi, Kenya, in 1998, the collapse of the Uffundi building, a concrete building adjacent to the embassy, caused hundreds of fatalities.

For buildings that remain standing, the next most severe type of injury producing damage is flying debris generated by exterior cladding. Depending on the severity of the incident, fatalities may occur as a result of flying structural debris. Some examples of exterior wall failure causing injuries are listed below.

- In the Oklahoma City bombing, several persons lost their lives after being struck by structural debris generated by infill walls of a concrete-frame building in the Water Resources Building across the street from the Murrah Building.
- In the Khobar Towers bombing in 1996, high-velocity projectiles created by the failed exterior cladding on the wall that faced the weapon impacted most of the nineteen U.S. servicemen who lost their lives. The building was an all-pre-cast, reinforced concrete structure with robust connections between the slabs and walls. The numerous lines of vertical support, along with the ample lateral stability provided by the "egg crate" configuration of the structural system, prevented collapse.

Even if the building remains standing and no structural damage occurs, extensive injuries can occur due to nonstructural damage. Typically, for large-scale incidents, these types of injuries occur to persons who are in buildings that are within several blocks of the incident. Although these injuries are often not life threatening, many people can be affected, which impacts on the ability of local medical resources to adequately respond.

An example of nonstructural damage causing injuries is the extensive glass lacerations that occurred in the Oklahoma City bombing within the Regency Towers apartment building, which was approximately five hundred feet from the Murrah Building. In this incident, glass laceration injuries extended as far as ten blocks from the bombing. Another example is the bombing of the U.S. embassy in Nairobi, Kenya. The explosion occurred near one of the major intersections of the city, which was heavily populated at the time of the bombing, causing extensive glass lacerations to passersby. The ambassador, who was attending a meeting at an office building across from the embassy, sustained an eye injury as a result of extensive window failure in the building.

It is impractical to design a civilian structure to remain undamaged from a large explosion. The protective objectives are, therefore, related to the type of building and its function. For an office, retail, residential, or light industrial building, where the primary assets are the occupants, the objective is to minimize loss of life. Because of the severity of large-scale explosion incidents, the goals are, by necessity, modest. Moreover, it is recognized that the building will be unusable after the event. This approach is considered a damage-limiting or damage-mitigating approach to design.

To save lives, the primary goals of the design professional are to reduce building damage and to prevent progressive collapse of the building, at least until it can be fully evacuated. A secondary goal is to maintain emergency functions until evacuation is complete.

The design professional is able to reduce building damage by incorporating access controls that allow building security to keep large threats away from the building and to limit charge weights that can be brought into the building. Preventing the building from collapsing is the most important objective.

Historically, the majority of fatalities that occur in terrorist attacks directed against buildings are due to building collapse. Collapse prevention begins with awareness by architects and engineers that structural integrity against collapse is important enough to be routinely considered in design. Features to improve general structural resistance to collapse can be incorporated into common buildings at affordable cost. At a higher level, designing the building to prevent progressive collapse can be accomplished by the alternate-path method (i.e., design for the building to remain standing following the removal of specific elements) or by direct design of components for air-blast loading.

Furthermore, facilitating evacuation, rescue, and recovery efforts through effective placement, structural design, and redundancy of emergency exits and critical mechanical/electrical systems may optimize building design. Through effective structural design, the overall damage levels may be reduced to make it easier for occupants to get out and emergency responders to safely enter.

Beyond preventing collapse and facilitating evacuation/rescue, the objective is to reduce flying debris generated by failed exterior walls, windows, and other components to reduce the severity of injuries and the risk of fatalities. This may be accomplished through selection of appropriate materials and use of capacity-design methods to proportion elements and connections. A well-designed system will provide predictable damage modes, selected to minimize injuries.

Finally, good antiterrorist design is a multidisciplinary effort involving the architect, structural engineer, security professional, and the other design team members. It is also critical for security design to be incorporated as early as possible in the design process to ensure a cost-effective, attractive solution.

CHEMICAL, BIOLOGICAL, AND RADIOLOGICAL PROTECTION

This section discusses three types of airborne hazards.

1. A large exterior release originating some distance away from the building (includes delivery by aircraft).
2. A small localized exterior release at an air intake or other opening in the exterior envelope of the building.
3. A small interior release in a publicly accessible area, a major egress route, or other vulnerable area (such as the lobby, mailroom, or delivery receiving).

Like explosive threats, chemical, biological, and radiological (CBR) threats may be delivered externally or internally to the building. External ground-based threats may be released at a standoff distance from the building or may be delivered directly through an air intake or other opening. Interior threats may be delivered to accessible areas, such as the lobby, mailroom, or loading dock, or they may be released into a secured area, such as a primary egress route.

There may not be an official or obvious warning prior to a CBR event. While you should always follow any official warnings, the best defense is to be alert to signs of a release occurring near you. The air may be contaminated if you see a suspicious cloud or smoke near ground level, hear an air blast, smell strange odors, see birds or other small animals dying, or hear of more than one person complaining of eye, throat, or skin irritation or convulsing.

Chemicals will typically cause problems within seconds or minutes after exposure, but they can sometimes have delayed effects that will not appear for hours or days. Symptoms may include blurred or dimmed vision; eye, throat, or skin irritation; difficulty breathing; excess saliva or nausea.

Biological and some radioactive contaminants typically will take days to weeks before symptoms appear, so listen for official information regarding symptoms. With radioactive "dirty" bombs, the initial risk is from the explosion. Local responders may advise you to either shelter-in-place or evacuate. After the initial debris falls to the ground, leaving the area and washing will minimize your risk from the radiation.

Buildings provide a limited level of inherent protection against CBR threats. To some extent, the protection level is a function of how airtight the building is, but to a greater extent it is a function of the heating, ventilation, and air conditioning (HVAC) system's design and operating parameters.

The objectives of protective building design, as they relate to the CBR threat, are first to make it difficult for the terrorist to successfully execute a CBR attack and second, to minimize the impact of an attack (on life, health, property damage, loss of commerce) if it does occur.

In order to reduce the likelihood of an attack, use security and design features that limit the terrorist's ability to approach the building and successfully release the CBR contaminant. Some examples are listed below:

- Use security standoff, accessibility, and screening procedures similar to those identified in the explosive threat mitigation section.
- Recognize areas around HVAC equipment and other mechanical systems to be vulnerable areas requiring special security considerations.
- Locate outdoor air intakes high above ground level and at inaccessible locations.
- Prevent unauthorized access to all mechanical areas and equipment.
- Avoid the use of ground-level mechanical rooms accessible from outside the building. Where such room placement is unavoidable, doors and air vents leading to these rooms should be treated as vulnerable locations and appropriately secured.
- Treat operable ground-level windows as a vulnerability and either avoid their use or provide appropriate security precautions to minimize the vulnerability.
- Inside the building, minimize public access to HVAC return-air systems.

Air Intakes

Air intakes may be made less accessible by placing them as high as possible on the building exterior, with louvers flush with the exterior. All opportunities to reach air intakes through climbing should be eliminated. Ideally, there should be a smooth, vertical surface from the ground level to the intake louvers, without such features as high shrubbery, low roofs, canopies, or sunshades, as these features can enable climbing and concealment. To prevent opportunities for a weapon to be lobbed into the intake, the intake louver should be ideally flush with the wall. Otherwise, a surface sloped at least 45 degrees away from the building and further protected through the use of metal mesh (a.k.a. bird screen) should be used. Finally, closed circuit television (CCTV) surveillance and enhanced security is recommended at intakes.

In addition to providing protection against an airborne hazard delivered directly into the building, placing air intakes high above ground provides protection against ground-based standoff threats because the concentration of the airborne hazard diminishes somewhat with height. Because air-blast pressure decays with height, elevated air intakes also provide modest protection against explosion threats. Furthermore, many recognized sources of indoor-air contaminants (such as vehicle exhaust, standing water, lawn chemicals, trash, and rodents) tend to be located near ground level. Thus, elevated air intakes are a recommended practice in general for providing healthy indoor air quality.

In the event that a particular air intake does not service an occupied area, it may not be necessary to elevate it above ground level. However, if the unoccupied area is within an otherwise occupied building, the intake should either be elevated or significant precautions (tightly sealed construction between unoccupied/occupied areas, unoccupied area maintained at negative pressure relative to occupied area) should be put in place to ensure that contaminants are unable to penetrate into the occupied area of the building.

Mechanical Areas

Another simple measure is to tightly restrict access to building mechanical areas (such as mechanical rooms, roofs, and elevator equipment access). These areas provide access to equipment and systems (such as HVAC, elevator, building exhaust, and communication and control) that could be used or manipulated to assist in a CBR attack. Including these areas in those monitored by electronic security and by eliminating elevator stops at the levels that house this equipment may provide additional protection. For rooftop mechanical equipment, ways of restricting (or at least monitoring) access to the roof that do not violate fire codes should be pursued.

Return-Air Systems

Similar to the outdoor-air intake, HVAC return-air systems inside the building can be vulnerable to CBR attack. Buildings requiring public access have an increased vulnerability to such an attack. Design approaches that reduce this vulnerability include the use of ducted HVAC returns within public access areas and the careful placement of return-air louvers in secure locations not easily accessed by public occupants. The second objective is to have a design to minimize the impact of an attack.

For many buildings, especially those requiring public access, the ability to prevent a determined terrorist from initiating a CBR release will be a significant challenge. Compared to buildings in which campus security and internal access can be strictly controlled, public access buildings may require a greater emphasis on mitigation. However, even private access facilities can fall victim to an internal CBR release, whether through a security lapse or perhaps a delivered product (mail, package, equipment, or food). Examples of design methods to minimize the impact of a CBR attack are listed below:

- Public access routes to the building should be designed to channel pedestrians through points of noticeable security presence.

- The structural and HVAC design should isolate the most vulnerable public areas (entrance lobbies, mailrooms, load/delivery docks) both physically and in terms of potential contaminant migration.
- The HVAC and auxiliary air systems should carefully use positive and negative pressure relationships to influence contaminant migration routes.

Lobbies, Loading Docks, and Mail Sorting Areas

Vulnerable internal areas where airborne hazards may be brought into the building should be strategically located. These include lobbies, loading docks, and mail sorting areas. Where possible, place these functions outside of the footprint of the main building. When incorporated into the main building, these areas should be physically separated from other areas by floor-to-roof walls. Additionally, these areas should be maintained under negative pressure relative to the rest of the building, but at positive-to-neutral pressure relative to the outdoors. To assist in maintaining the desired pressure relationship, necessary openings (doors, windows, etc.) between secure and vulnerable areas should be equipped with sealing windows and doors, and wall openings due to ductwork, utilities, and other penetrations should be sealed. Where entries into vulnerable areas are frequent, the use of airlocks or vestibules may be necessary to maintain the desired pressure differentials.

Ductwork that travels through vulnerable areas should be sealed. Ideally, these areas should have separate air-handling units to isolate the hazard. Alternatively, the conditioned air supply to these areas may come from a central unit, as long as exhaust/return air from these areas is not allowed to mix into other portions of the building. In addition, emergency exhaust fans that can be activated upon internal CBR release within the vulnerable area will help to purge the hazard from the building and minimize its migration into other areas. Care must be taken that the discharge point for the exhaust system is not co-located with expected egress routes. Consideration should also be given to filtering this exhaust with High Efficiency Particulate Air (HEPA) filtration. For entrance lobbies that contain a security screening location, it is recommended that an airlock or vestibule be provided between the secured and unsecured areas.

Zoning of HVAC Systems

Large buildings usually have multiple HVAC zones, each zone with its own air-handling unit and duct system. In practice, these zones are not completely separated if they are on the same floor. Air circulates among zones through plenum returns, hallways, atria, and doorways that are normally left open. Depending upon the HVAC design and operation, airflow between zones on different floors can also occur through the intentional use of shared air-return/supply systems and through air migrations via stairs and elevator shafts.

Isolating the separate HVAC zones minimizes the potential spread of an airborne hazard within a building, reducing the number of people potentially exposed if there is an internal release. Zone separation also provides limited benefit against an external release, as it increases internal resistance to air movement produced by wind forces and chimney effect, thus reducing the rate of infiltration. In essence, isolating zones divides the building into separate environments, limiting the effects of a single release to an isolated portion of the building. Isolation of zones requires full-height walls between each zone and the adjacent zones and hallway doors.

Another recommendation is to isolate the return system (i.e., no shared returns). Strategically locate return air grilles in easily observable locations and preferably in areas with reduced public access. Both centralized and decentralized shutdown capabilities are advantageous.

To quickly shut down all HVAC systems at once in the event of an external threat, a single-switch control is recommended for all air exchange fans (including bathroom, kitchen, and other exhaust sources). In the event of a localized internal release, redundant decentralized shutdown capability is also recommended. Controls should be placed in a location easily accessed by the facility manager, security personnel, or emergency response personnel. Duplicative and separated control systems will add an increased degree of protection. Further protection may be achieved by placing low-leakage automatic dampers on air intakes and exhaust fans that do not already have back-draft dampers.

Positive Pressurization

Traditional good engineering practice for HVAC design strives to achieve a slight overpressure of 5–12 Pa (0.02inch–0.05-inch w.g.) within the building environment, relative to the outdoors. This design practice is intended to reduce uncontrolled infiltration into the building. When combined with effective filtration, this practice will also provide enhanced protection against external releases of CBR aerosols.

Using off-the-shelf technology (such as HEPA), manually triggered augmentation systems can be put into place to overpressure critical zones to intentionally impact routes of contaminant migration and/or to provide safe havens for sheltering-in-place. For egress routes, positive pressurization is also recommended, unless of course, the CBR source is placed within the egress route. Design parameters for such systems will depend upon many factors specific to the building and critical zone in question. Care must be taken that efforts to obtain a desired pressure relationship within one zone will not put occupants in another zone at increased risk. Lastly, the supply air used to pressurize the critical space must be appropriately filtered (see Filtration Systems on p. 151) or originate from a non-contaminated source in order to be beneficial.

Air Tightness

To limit the infiltration of contaminants from outside the building into the building envelope, building construction should be made as airtight as possible. Tight construction practices (weatherization techniques, tightly sealing windows, doors, wall construction, continuous vapor barriers, sealing interface between wall and window/door frames) will also help to maintain the desired pressure relationships between HVAC zones. To ensure that the construction of the building has been performed correctly, building commissioning is recommended throughout the construction process and prior to taking ownership to observe construction practices and to identify potential airflow trouble spots (cracks, seams, joints, and pores in the building envelope and along the lines separating unsecured from secured space) before they are covered with finish materials.

Filtration Systems

To offer effective protection, filtration systems should be specific to the particular contaminant's physical state and size. Chemical vapor/gas filtration (a.k.a. air cleaning) is currently a very expensive task (high initial and recurring costs) with a limited number of design professionals experienced in its implementation. Specific expertise should be sought if chemical filtration is desired. Possible application of the air cleaning approach to collective protection zones (with emergency activation) can assist in significantly reducing the cost, though the protection is limited to the reduced size of the zone.

Most traditional HVAC filtration systems focus on aerosol-type contaminants. The CBR threats in this category include radioactive "dirty" bombs, bio-aerosols, and some chemical threats. Riot-control agents and low-volatility nerve agents, for example, are generally distributed in aerosol form; however, a vapor component of these chemical agents could pass through a filtration system. HEPA filtration is currently considered adequate by most professionals to achieve sufficient protection from CBR particulates and aerosols. However, HEPA filtration systems generally have a higher acquisition cost than traditional HVAC filters, and they cause larger pressure drops within the HVAC system, resulting in increased energy requirements to maintain the same design airflow rate.

Due to recent improvements in filter media development, significant improvements in aerosol filtration can be achieved at relatively minimal increases in initial and operating costs. Also important is that incremental increases in filtration efficiency will generally provide incremental increases in protection from the aerosol contaminant. In 1999, the American Society of Heating, Refrigeration and Air Conditioning Engineers (ASHRAE) released Standard 52.2–1999. This standard provides a system for rating filters that quantifies filtration efficiency in different particle-size ranges to provide a composite efficiency value named the Minimum Efficiency Reporting Value (MERV).

MERV ratings range between 1 and 20, with a higher MERV indicating a more efficient filter. Using the MERV rating table, the desired filter efficiency may be selected according to the size of the contaminant under consideration. For example, a filter with a MERV of 13 or more will provide a 90 percent or greater reduction of most CBR aerosols (generally considered to be at least 1–3 μm in size or larger) within the filtered air stream with much lower acquisition and maintenance costs than HEPA filtration.

Efficiency of filtration systems is not the only concern. Air can become filtered only if it actually passes through the filter. Thus, filter-rack design, gasketing, and good-quality filter sources should all play a role in minimizing bypass around the filter. The use of return-air filtration systems and the strategic location of supply and return systems should also be carefully employed to maximize effective ventilation and filtration rates.

Detection Systems

Beyond the measures discussed above, there is the option of using detection systems as part of the protective design package. In general, affordable, timely, and practical detection systems specific to all CBR agents are not yet available. However, for aerosol contaminants, nonspecific detection equipment can be employed to activate response actions should a sudden spike in aerosol concentration of a specific size range be detected. If the spike were detected in an outdoor intake, for example, this could trigger possible response options, such as damper closure, system shutdown, bypass to alternate air intake, or rerouting the air through a special bank of filters. Such protective actions could occur until trained personnel could perform an investigation (check with adjacent alarms and review security tape covering outdoor air intake). Unless foul play was discovered, the entire process could be completed within ten minutes or less and without alarming occupants.

The initial cost of such a system is relatively modest (depending upon the number of detectors and response options incorporated into the design), but the maintenance requirements are relatively high. Similar monitoring systems could be employed to trigger appropriate responses in high-threat areas, such as mailrooms, shipping/receiving areas, or entrance lobbies. The approach could also be expanded to incorporate some of the newer chemical detection technologies, though the low-threshold requirements may generate a substantial number of false positives. As technology progresses, detector availability and specificity should continue to expand into the general marketplace.

Emergency Response Using Fire/HVAC Control Center

Certain operations that are managed at the Fire Control Center can play a protective role in the response to a CBR incident. Examples of such operations and how they could be used are given below.

Purge Fans. These can be used to purge an interior CBR release or to reduce indoor contaminant concentrations following building exposure to an external CBR source. (Note: In practice, some jurisdictions may recommend purging for chemical and radiological contaminants but not for biological contaminants, which may be communicable and/or medically treatable.)

Communication Systems. Building communication systems that allow specific instructions to be addressed to occupants in specific zones of the building can play a significant role in directing occupant response to either an internal or external release.

Pressurization Fans. These provide two functions. First, the ability to override and deactivate specific positive-pressure zones may be beneficial in the event that a known CBR source is placed into such an area. Second, areas designated for positive pressurization (generally for smoke protection) may also become beneficial havens for protection from internal and external CBR releases, if they are supplied by appropriately filtered air.

HVAC Controls. The ability to simultaneously and individually manipulate operation of all HVAC and exhaust equipment from a single location may be very useful during a CBR event. Individuals empowered to operate such controls must be trained in their use. The provision of simple floor-by-floor schematics showing equipment locations and the locations of supply and return louvers will aid the utility of this control option.

Elevator Controls. Depending upon their design and operation, the ability to recall elevators to the ground floor may assist in reducing contaminant migration during a CBR event.

EVOLVING TECHNOLOGIES

Many of the challenges relating to CBR terrorism prevention will be facilitated with the introduction of new technologies developed to address this emerging threat. As vendors and products come to market, it is important that the designer evaluate performance claims with a close level of scrutiny. Vendors should be willing to guarantee performance specs in writing and provide proof of testing (and show certified results) by an independent, reputable lab, and the testing conditions (such as flow rate, residence time, and incoming concentrations) should be consistent with what would be experienced within the owner's building. For CBR developments, proof of federal government testing and acceptance may be available.

CHEMICAL, BIOLOGICAL, AND
RADIOLOGICAL PROTECTIVE MEASURES

- Place air intakes servicing occupied areas as high as practically possible (minimum twelve feet above ground). General Services Administration (GSA) may require locating at fourth floor or above, when applicable.
- Restrict access to critical equipment.
- Isolate separate HVAC zones and return-air systems.
- Isolate HVAC supply and return-air systems in unsecured areas.
- Physically isolate unsecured areas from secured areas.
- Use positive pressurization of primary egress routes, safe havens, and/or other critical areas.
- Commission building throughout construction and prior to taking ownership.
- Provide redundant, easily accessible shutdown capabilities.
- For higher levels of protection, consider using contaminant-specific filtration and detection systems.
- Incorporate fast-acting, low-leaking dampers.
- Filter both return-air and outdoor-air for publicly accessible buildings.
- Select filter efficiencies based upon contaminant size. Use reputable filter media installed into tight-fitting, gasketed, and secure filter racks.
- For higher-threat areas (mailroom, receiving, reception/screening lobby):
  —Preferably locate these areas outside the main building footprint.
  —Provide separate HVAC, with isolated returns capable of 100 percent exhaust.

—Operate these areas at negative pressure relative to the secure portion of the building.

- Use airtight construction, vestibules, and air locks if there is a high traffic flow.
- Consider installation of an emergency exhaust fan to be activated upon suspected internal CBR release.
- Lock, secure, access-log, and control mechanical rooms.
- In public access areas, use air diffusers and return air grilles that are secure or under security observation.
- Zone the building communication system so that it is capable of delivering explicit instructions and has backup power.
- Create safe zones using enhanced filtration, tight construction, emergency power, dedicated communication systems, and appropriate supplies (food, water, first aid, and personal protective equipment).

Sample Specs

1. INTRUSION DETECTION AND SECURITY-ACCESS SYSTEM

MAIN CABINET

A. Steel construction #14 gauge, 36″ × 36″ × 6″ cabinet with hinged, lockable cover, ½″ thick plywood backboard, painted light gray.
1. Also allow a 4′ × 4′ empty space above or to either side of the main cabinet at a centerline of 7′ for additional security equipment.
B. Main cabinet shall be surface mounted.
C. The main security cabinet shall be located in the video control room; however, section 2.3 A. has priority.
D. The location of the main, head-end, security terminal cabinet shall not exceed 95′ from the antenna weather head.

BUILDING AND FLOOR DISTRIBUTION CABINETS

E. Steel construction #14 gauge, 12″ × 18″ × 6″ cabinet with hinged lockable cover, ½″ thick plywood backboard, painted light gray.
F. All distribution cabinets shall be surface mounted.

CONDUIT AND BOXES

G. Criteria for security antenna stub-out location:
1. This location will be based on the radio frequency assigned to the site and the direct line of sight from the antenna to the repeater location and will be selected at time of review.

2. The security system radio has a direct line of sight antenna to the repeater located at latitude (26, 35,20 N) and longitude (080, 12, 43 W) US 441 and Lantana Road.

H. Provide and install a 3″ raceway to outside of building at the antenna mounting structures designated location and terminated with a weather head.

1. The penetrating portion of conduit shall be a contiguous 10′ piece of rigid, with 6′ firmly supported at two joist points below the roof penetration and 4′ above the roof.

2. The raceway shall continue and terminate against the wall below the ceiling 90″ Above Finished Floor (AFF) over the main head-end terminal cabinet capped with an Electrical Metallic Tubing (EMT) set screw connector and fiber bushing.

I. Provide and install an antenna mounting structure located next to the antenna stub-out (refer to B on previous page).

1. Design the antenna mounting structure to support an antenna array consisting of six (6) 6—element Yagi 9dBd gain antennas model #460–6.

2. Structures shall meet ASCE-78 requirements.

3. Top of structures shall be no more than 49′ or 15 meters above grade.

J. Provide and install a building distribution cabinet for each building.

1. Provide and install a separate 2″ raceway from the main head-end cabinet for each building distribution cabinet.

2. For buildings with more than one level, provide a floor distribution cabinet for each additional floor level.

3. Feeding each of these cabinets with a separate 2″ conduit, from the building distribution cabinet.

4. If any floor level area is greater than 20,000 sq ft, additional floor distribution cabinets shall be provided; with no one cabinet feeding more than 20,000 sq ft.

5. Raceway shall not exceed 400′ without a pull box.

K. Provide and install ¾″ conduits from the distribution cabinets and distribute to feed all junction and mounting boxes in the distribution area.

1. Each ¾″ conduit shall feed no more than 16 wall sensor mounting box locations.

2. Each of these conduit runs shall leave and return to the cabinet (LOOPED).

L. Provide and install a separate ¾″ conduit from the main security terminal cabinet to the fire alarm main terminal cabinet.

M. Provide and install a separate ¾″ conduit from the nearest security distribution cabinet to all walk-in refrigeration units, and terminate this conduit to the unit's temperature sensor relay enclosure.

N. Provide and install a separate ¾″ conduit from the nearest security distribution cabinet to the emergency electric generator control panel.

O. Provide and install recessed mounted 4″ × 4″ × 2⅛″ boxes with flush single gang ring and single gang cover; mounted with the opening vertical, located 12″ to the side of the intercom speaker or clock; in rooms where clocks or speakers are designated.

1. If a projection screen will block the security device in this location, move the security junction box to clear the blockage to either side of the projection screen.

P. Provide and install recessed mounted $4'' \times 4'' \times 2\frac{1}{8}''$ sensor mounting boxes with single gang ring and single gang cover; mounted with the opening vertical, $90''$ above the floor and $25'$ from any exterior doors or exterior glass (susceptible to entry) at the following locations:

   1. All interior corridors
   2. Rooms that do not have a clock or speaker but have exterior doors or glass
   3. Electrical rooms, mechanical rooms, storage rooms, and the like, that may allow access through them to the interior of the building

Q. Provide and install recessed mounted $4'' \times 4'' \times 2\frac{1}{8}''$ sensor mounting boxes with single gang ring and single gang cover; mounted with the opening vertical, $90''$ above the floor and $15'$ from the entry/exit doors in the following areas:

   1. Cafeteria manager's office
   2. Media CCTV studio
   3. Media CCTV storage room
   4. PE storage room
   5. PE office
   6. Main telephone equipment room
   7. Clinic
   8. All corridors, approximately $65'$ apart
   9. All classrooms, workrooms, administrative areas, adjacent to all the video surveillance j-boxes, and other areas as defined in the SDPBC plan specific review process

R. Provide and install an additional $4\frac{11}{16}'' \times 4\frac{11}{16}'' \times 2\frac{1}{8}''$ box above suspended ceiling directly above each wall sensor-mounting box.

   1. Locate box no higher than $36''$ above the ceiling, in the same room as the wall-mounted boxes.

S. Provide and install two recessed mounted Knox-Boxes with UL listed tamper switches, $\frac{1}{4}''$ plate steel housing, $\frac{1}{8}''$ thick door with interior gasket seal. Both box and lock shall have $2''$ steel dust cover with tamper seal mounting capability. Finish color shall be aluminum for police and black for fire. The Knox-Box shall be mounted at $48''$ above the finished floor.

   1. The following Knox-Box is recommend: Manufactured by The Knox Company, Model 3221 for Fire Department and 3225 for Police Department with the recessed mounting kit (3240). All recessed mounting kit shell housings, including the cover plate and screw heads, are flush with the finish wall. The housing must be plumbed to ensure vertical alignment of the vault.
   2. Provide and install a $\frac{3}{4}''$ conduit from the back of the Knox Box to a $4\frac{11}{16}'' \times 4\frac{11}{16}'' \times 2\frac{1}{8}''$ box with cover, located above the nearest removable ceiling tile. Continue the conduit run to the nearest security distribution terminal cabinet.
   3. The school district's project manger shall coordinate with the Department of School Police and the contractor to transmit the Knox authorization forms, which will be provided by the Department of School Police to assure it is keyed to the PBCSD Master. The Knox authorization forms for the fire department Knox box must be obtained from the fire department having jurisdiction.

T. Provide and install a separate ¾" conduit from the main security cabinet to the main telephone room terminal board.

U. Provide and install a separate ¾" conduit from the back of the fire department's Knox Box to a $4^{11}\!/_{16}" \times 4^{11}\!/_{16}" \times 2\frac{1}{8}"$ box with cover, located above the nearest removable ceiling tile. Continue the conduit run to the nearest security distribution terminal cabinet.

V. Provide and install a ¾" conduit between all security distribution cabinets and all card access distribution cabinets at all terminal cabinet locations.

W. Provide and install six additional recessed mounted $4" \times 4" \times 2\frac{1}{8}"$ sensor mounting boxes with flush single gang ring and single gang cover; with the opening mounting vertical with ¾" conduit and run to nearest security junction box. (Estimate 100' of conduit for each run.) Wall-mount locations to be directed in field during construction prior to final above ceiling inspection.

POWER FEED

X. Provide and install a dedicated 120-volt normal power duplex outlet located adjacent to the upper portion of the main security system's cabinet.

Y. Provide and install a dedicated 120-volt duplex outlet fed from the optional branch of the generator power source, adjacent to the normal power receptacle.

EXECUTION

Installation

A. Install system in accordance with National Electrical Contractors Association (NECA) "Standard of Installation" and Section 16111.

B. Obtain a detail book from the SDPBC School Police Department Security Section for system specifics.

C. Permanently label all conduits as to plan room number destination, at all terminal cabinets.

D. Paint all security system junction box covers black.

E. Install ½" (black round indicators) of paper construction on ceiling tile grid work at all locations where security system boxes are located above the drop ceiling.

F. Permanently label all the security system terminal cabinets "security system."

G. Install 200-lb.-strength pull-string throughout the raceway system.

H. All junction boxes mounted above ceiling shall be mounted with the opening facing down, and shall have a reasonable immediate access pathway provided. Note: removal of a light fixture or other similar ceiling equipment is not considered as a reasonable access pathway.

I. The security system raceway shall be a separate raceway system and shall not interconnect with or be used by any other system without the authorization of The Department of School Police Security System Section or per DMS sections 16722, 16723, 16724 and 16725.

J. All conduit runs shall be as direct as possible in order to save on wiring cost and to reduce poor performance due to cable voltage loss.

2. Video Surveillance System

GENERAL

System Description

The video surveillance system shall include the furnishing and installation of main and distribution cabinets, conduit system, and power feeds.

Main Cabinet

A. Steel construction #14 gauge, 36″ × 36″ × 6″ cabinet with hinged, lockable cover, ½″ thick plywood backboard, painted light gray and shall be surface mounted.

Distribution Cabinets

B. Steel construction #14 gauge, 12″ × 18″ × 6″ cabinet with hinged lockable cover, ½″ thick plywood backboard, painted light gray and shall be surface mounted.

Conduit and Boxes

C. Provide and install a building distribution cabinet for each building.
   1. Provide and install a separate 2″ raceway from the main "head-end" cabinet for each building distribution cabinet.
      a. For buildings with more than one level, provide a floor distribution cabinet for each additional floor level.
      b. Feeding each of these cabinets with a separate 1½″ conduit from the building distribution cabinet.
      c. If any floor level area is greater than 20,000 sq ft, additional floor distribution cabinets shall be provided; with no one cabinet feeding more than 20,000 sq ft.
      d. Raceway shall not exceed 400′ without a pull box.
D. Provide and install feed conduits from each distribution cabinet to feed the mounting boxes designated for the area. Size each of the separate feeds as follows:
   1. ¾″ for a maximum of 2 mounting boxes.
   2. 1″ for a maximum of 4 mounting boxes.
   3. 1¼″ for a maximum of 6 mounting boxes.
   4. 1½″ for a maximum of 8 mounting boxes.
E. Provide and install 4¹¹⁄₁₆″ × 4¹¹⁄₁₆″ × 2⅛″ mounting boxes with covers at designated interior locations. If the area location has removable ceiling tile, the box shall be located above the tile.

1. If the location has a structure of fixed ceiling material, then flush-mount the box with a double gang mud ring and cover.

F. Provide and install $4^{11}/_{16}'' \times 4^{11}/_{16}'' \times 2^{1}/_{8}''$ flush-mounted mounting boxes with double gang mud ring and weatherproof covers; mounted with the opening vertical, at all designated exterior locations fed from additional $4^{11}/_{16}'' \times 4^{11}/_{16}'' \times 2^{1}/_{8}''$ boxes at the interior feed penetrations through the exterior walls.

G. Provide and install a 1″ conduit from the main VSS cabinet to the main "head-end" security cabinet.

H. Provide a ¾″ conduit from the main VSS cabinet to the main card access system cabinet.

I. Provide and install a 2″ conduit from the main video surveillance terminal cabinet to a brook's box located at designated entry gates.

1. All entry gates on school site will have a 2″ conduit run.
2. Exact location to be determined at the plan review.

J. Provide and install an additional $4^{11}/_{16}'' \times 4^{11}/_{16}'' \times 2^{1}/_{8}''$ box above suspended ceiling directly above each wall video-mounting box. Locate J-box no higher than 36″ above the ceiling grid and in the same room as the wall-mounted boxes.

Power Feed

K. Provide and install a dedicated 120-volt duplex outlet fed from the optional branch of the generator power source, adjacent to the normal power receptacle for the main cabinet.

L. Provide and install a dedicated 120-volt duplex outlet fed from the optional branch of the generator power source, adjacent to the lower portion of the entry terminal of each building.

EXECUTIONS

Installation

A. Install system in accordance with NECA "Standard of Installation" and Section 16111.

B. Obtain a detail book from the SDPBC School Police Department Security Section for system specifics.

C. Permanently label all conduits as to plan room number destination, at all terminal cabinets.

D. Paint all video surveillance system junction-box covers gold.

E. Install ½″ (gold round indicators) of paper construction on ceiling tile grid work at all locations where video surveillance system boxes are located above the drop ceiling.

F. Permanently label all the video surveillance system terminal cabinets "video-surveillance system."

G. Install 200-lb.-strength pull-string throughout the raceway system.

H. All junction boxes mounted above ceiling shall be mounted with the opening facing down, and shall have a reasonable immediate access pathway provided. Note: removal of a light fixture or other similar ceiling equipment is not considered as a reasonable access pathway.

I. The "Video-Surveillance System Raceway" shall not be used as part of any other raceway.

J. Provide and install six additional $4^{11}/_{16}'' \times 4^{11}/_{16}'' \times 2^{1}/_{8}''$ mounting boxes with flush single gang ring and single gang cover; with the opening mounting vertical with $^{3}/_{4}''$ conduit run to the nearest video terminal cabinet or junction box. (Estimate 100' of conduit for each run.) Mounting locations to be directed in field during construction prior to final above-ceiling inspection.

Location

K. Provide video junction boxes in the following locations.
   1. At all card reader locations
   2. Cafeteria main dining room
   3. Bus loop
   4. Main office reception area
   5. In all corridors
   6. Student pick-up/drop off
   7. Parking areas
   8. Gymnasium and gymnasium lobby
   9. Auditorium and auditorium lobby
   10. Other areas as defined in the project specific review process, by the SDPBC.

3. Emergency Radio Communications Systems

Conduit and boxes
Power wiring

System Description

Emergency radio communications systems shall include the furnishing and installation of raceway systems and power feeds for the emergency broadcast receiver, radio communications repeater station, hurricane shelter communications, and wireless propagation enhancement systems.

Conduit and Boxes

A. ALL SITES: If the Emergency Broadcast Receiver/Repeater is located at the main security terminal cabinet, then the following requirement (Item A only) is not required. If the Emergency Broadcast Receiver/Repeater is not located at the main security terminal cabinet, then: Provide and install a 1½" raceway to outside of building through the roof at the designated Emergency Broadcast Receiver/ Repeater antenna location and terminated with a weather head. The penetrating portion of conduit shall be a contiguous 10' piece of rigid, with 6' firmly supported at two joist points below the roof penetration and 4' above the roof. Continue this raceway and terminate into a 6" × 6" × 4" box located just above the ceiling at the designated Emergency Broadcast Receiver/Repeater "head-end" room location. Provide and install two ¾" conduits run from the 6" × 6" × 4" box and terminate into two flush-mounted 4¹¹⁄₁₆" × 4¹¹⁄₁₆" × 1½" boxes with single gang mud rings and single gang covers 48" AFF in their respective locations in the designated "head-end" room.

B. ALL BUILDINGS: Provide and install a 1½" raceway to outside of building through the roof at the buildings designated Wireless Propagation Enhancement location and terminate with a weather head. The penetrating portion of conduit shall be a contiguous 10' piece of rigid, with 6' firmly supported at two joist points below the roof penetration and 4' above the roof. Continue this raceway and terminate into a 6" × 6" × 4" box located just above the ceiling at the designated Wireless Propagation Enhancement "head-end" room location. For each floor of the respective building, provide and install one ¾" conduit run from the 6" × 6" × 4" box and terminate into one flush-mounted 4¹¹⁄₁₆" × 4¹¹⁄₁₆" × 1½" box with single gang mud rings and single gang covers 48" AFF in their respective locations in the designated "head-end" room.

C. HURRICANE SHELTERS:

1. Provide and install an antenna mounting structure located next to the Hurricane antenna stub-out location. Design the antenna mounting structure to support an antenna array of six 6-element Yagi 9dBd gain antennas model #460–6. Structure shall meet ASCE-78 requirements. Top of structure shall be at least 49' (15 meters) above grade.

2. Provide and install a 2" raceway to outside of building through the roof at the designated Hurricane Shelter antenna location and terminate with a weather head. Continue this raceway and terminate into a 6" × 6" × 4" box located just above the ceiling at the designated Hurricane Shelter "head-end" room location. Provide and install (2) ¾" conduits run from the 6" × 6" × 4" box and terminate into two flush-mounted 4¹¹⁄₁₆" × 4¹¹⁄₁₆" × 1½" boxes with single gang mud rings and single gang covers. Locate these boxes 80" AFF, parallel with 4" between each in the designated "head-end" room.

Power Feed

D. Provide and install a dedicated duplex 120-volt power receptacle fed from the life safety branch of emergency generator power source in each of the designated emergency broadcast receiver, radio communications repeater station, hurricane shelter communications, and wireless propagation enhancement systems "head-end" locations. Locate adjacent to the "head-end" single gang boxes.

EXECUTION

Installation

A. Install systems in accordance with NECA "Standard of Installation" and Section 16111.
B. Obtain a detail book from the SDPBC School Police Department Security Section for system specifics.
C. Install a 200-lb.-strength pull-string throughout the raceway systems.
D. All junction boxes mounted above ceiling shall be mounted with the opening facing down, and shall have a reasonable immediate access pathway provided. Note: removal of a light fixture or other similar ceiling equipment is not considered as a reasonable access pathway.
E. Antenna raceways shall not exceed 100′ from the weather head to the designated "head-end" locations.

Card Access System

A. Main cabinet
B. Terminal cabinet
C. Conduit and boxes
D. Power wiring

Main Cabinet

A. Steel construction #14 gauge, 36″ × 36″ × 6″ cabinet with hinged, lockable cover, ½″ thick plywood backboard, painted light gray and shall be surface mounted.

Distribution "Building and Floor" Cabinets

B. Steel construction #14 gauge, 24″ × 24″ × 6″ cabinet with hinged lockable cover, ½″ thick plywood backboard, painted light gray.

Conduit and Boxes

C. Provide and install the building and floor distribution cabinets for each building according to the following criteria:
    1. There must be one of these cabinets within 300′ of a controlled device.
    2. Each cabinet can feed no more than eight controlled devices and the cabinet must be located on the same floor as the controlled devices.
    3. The main cabinet can serve as the distribution cabinet for its area.
    4. Provide a 2″ raceway from the main cabinet to the next building and floor distribution cabinet.
    5. After all distribution cabinets are fed with this raceway, return the raceway to the main cabinet.

6. Raceway shall not exceed 400′ without a pull box.

7. For buildings with more than one floor provide a 2″ raceway from the first floor cabinet to feed each floor's cabinet.

8. If floors 2 or 3 have more than one cabinet, then feed cabinet (1) on that floor from the first floor cabinet with a 2″ then proceed to cabinet (2) on that floor with a 2″, and from there to the next floor cabinet.

D. Provide and install ¾″ conduits from the distribution cabinets and distribute to feed the junction and mounting boxes designated for the area. Each separate ¾″ feed will supply no more than two Controlled Device/Card Reader Feed locations.

E. Provide and install an elevator interface cabinet, 12″ × 12″ × 4″ with hinged lockable cover and a ½″ plywood backboard painted light gray with a 10-lug terminal strip mounted on the board at all designated elevator control panel locations. Feed this interface box from the ¾″ card access raceway. Provide and install a separate ¾″ raceway from the box into elevator control panel. Label this box "Card Access/Elevator Interface." The elevator contractor shall extend his control wiring from the elevator control panel to this interface box.

F. At all elevator stops provide 4¹¹⁄₁₆″ × 4¹¹⁄₁₆″ × 2⅛″ flush-mounted box with single gang mud ring with cover. Mount the box adjacent to the elevator call button box and use a ¾″ conduit to connect the two boxes together. Run a ¾″ conduit from the 4¹¹⁄₁₆″ × 4¹¹⁄₁₆″ × 2⅛″ box back to the nearest card access terminal cabinet and terminate.

G. At each controlled door, install the electric hardware's power supply above drop ceiling within 50′ of the hardware. In "separate" raceway, supply 120-volt feed to the power supply. Provide and install a ¾″ conduit from the supply box to a neutral 6″ × 6″ × 4″ distribution box located next to the supply. Feed this box from the ¾″ card access system raceway. Also from this neutral box, provide and install an additional ¾″ raceway along with (8) 18AWG and (2) 12AWG conductors run from the supply box to feed the electrical power transfer device. From the supply, using that wiring, connect the electric hardware through the electrical power transfer device.

H. Provide and extend raceway to feed 4¹¹⁄₁₆″ × 4¹¹⁄₁₆″ × 2⅛″ flush-mounted boxes with single gang mud ring and weatherproof covers; mounted with the opening vertical, at all designated card reader locations. Locate to the strike side of single doors and as designated for double doors, elevator control, and gates. Center 4′ above finished floor.

I. Provide and install a 2″ conduit from the main card access terminal cabinet to a brook's box located at designated entry gates. Exact location to be determined at the plan review.

J. Provide and install a 4¹¹⁄₁₆″ × 4¹¹⁄₁₆″ × 2⅛″ card access feed junction box with cover, at the interior side of all designated card access door locations. If the area location has removable ceiling tile, the box shall be located above the tile. If the location has a structure of fixed ceiling material, then flush-mount the box with a square to round mud ring and cover.

K. Provide and install a 4¹¹⁄₁₆″ × 4¹¹⁄₁₆″ × 2⅛″ flush-mounted box with single gang mud ring and weatherproof cover; mounted with the opening vertical at 60″ AFF as the designated "TeleEntry" mounting box.

L. Provide and install a $4^{11}/_{16}'' \times 4^{11}/_{16}'' \times 2^{1}/_{8}''$ flush-mounted box with single gang mud ring and weatherproof cover; mounted with the opening vertical at 60" AFF as the designated "Master Key Control Box" mounting box. This mounting box must have 24" × 24" free space for mounting the key box.

M. Provide and install a ¾" conduit from the main telephone room terminal board to the main card access cabinet.

N. Provide and install six additional recessed mounted $4^{11}/_{16}'' \times 4^{11}/_{16}'' \times 2^{1}/_{8}''$ mounting boxes with flush single gang ring and single gang cover; with the opening mounting vertical with ¾" conduit run to nearest card access junction box. (Estimate 100' of conduit for each run.) Wall-mount locations will be directed in field during construction, prior to final above-ceiling inspection.

Power Feeds

O. Provide a double duplex, dedicated 120-volt power receptacle fed from the optional branch of emergency generator power source, adjacent to the lower portion of the main terminal cabinet and each distribution cabinet.

P. Provide and install dedicated 120-volt power feeds from the optional branch of emergency generator source to all Electric Hardware Power supplies.

Installation

A. Install system in accordance with NECA "Standard of Installation" and Section 16111.

B. Obtain a detail book from the SDPBC School Police Department Security Section for system specifics.

C. Permanently label all conduits as to plan room number destination, at all terminal cabinets.

D. Paint all card access system junction box covers tan.

E. Install ½" (tan round indicators) of paper construction on ceiling tile grid work at all locations where card access system boxes are located above the drop ceiling.

F. Permanently label all the card access system terminal cabinets "card access system."

G. Install 200-lb.-strength pull-string throughout the raceway system.

H. The card access system raceway shall be a separate raceway and shall not interconnect with or be used by any other system without the authorization of the PBCSD School Police Department Security Section or per LCCCG sections 16722, 16723, 16724 and 16725.

I. All junction boxes mounted above ceiling shall be mounted with the opening facing down, and shall have a reasonable immediate access pathway provided. Note: removal of a light fixture or other similar ceiling equipment is not considered as a reasonable access pathway.

J. All conduit runs shall be as direct as possible in order to save on wiring costs and to reduce poor performance due to cable loss.

K. Refer to S.D.P.B.C. LCCCG Section 8700 for Card Access Door preparation.

Location

L. Provide a card reader/controlled device at each of the following locations. These are the minimum number of locations, and more locations could be added in the plans review process:

   1. Administrative main entry
   2. Main entry doors to facility, principal's office
   3. Bookkeeper's office
   4. Media center
   5. A/V storage room
   6. CCTV studio area
   7. Cafeteria main entries
   8. Cafeteria receiving area
   9. Cafeteria dry food storage area
   10. Cafeteria manager's office
   11. Elevator entry on all floors
   12. Gymnasium entries
   13. Auditorium entries
   14. Custodial receiving
   15. Video Surveillance Control Room Door
   16. School Police Office
   17. Other areas as defined in the SDPBC plan specific review process

Florida Department of Education Design and Construction Process

Executive Summary

INTRODUCTION

This is a summary of specific and general findings and recommendations based upon responses to survey instruments, field investigations at schools, and community colleges throughout Florida, and a review of the literature on safety and security in schools and community colleges. The "Methodology" and "Survey Results and Related Data Analysis" sections below provide a detailed description of the approaches used to gather the data and the results of that effort. Accompanying some of the findings here are general recommendations; others are spelled out in the *"Guidelines"* that precede this section and are highlighted in the bullet points associated with the graphics and the text.

SPECIFIC FINDINGS AND RECOMMENDATIONS

Findings:

KNOWLEDGE, USE, AND ASSESSMENT OF CPTED, SAFE SCHOOL DESIGN PRINCIPLES, AND THE EXISTING *GUIDELINES*

Survey respondents for this research were, by and large, much more aware of CPTED principles than were respondents to the survey conducted as part of the research preceding publication of the 1993 *Guidelines*. Awareness and use of the principles is credited to increased training through reference organizations and through articles in the trade and professional literature.

Despite higher knowledge and awareness levels of those principles generally, survey respondents and those interviewed in the field were considerably less aware of 1993 *Guidelines*. Design professional respondents were much more likely than other respondents to indicate that either Safe School Design principles or the *Guidelines* have been incorporated into the design and construction of public schools and community colleges.

MOST IMPORTANT FEATURES RELATIVE TO
SAFETY AND SECURITY ISSUES

When asked to identify the "most important" Safe School Design features relative to safety and security, the responses from the school district, community college, and design professional groups centered around *surveillance, access control,* and *territoriality* issues, in that order.

DOES SAFE SCHOOL DESIGN MAKE SCHOOLS SAFER?

Although some design professionals are critical of elements of the *Guidelines,* the great majority of all respondents believe that the use of Safe School Design principles and the *Guidelines* make schools and community colleges safer places. Some design professionals report difficulty fulfilling the design intent of "slippery finishes," "audio/motion detection systems," and providing for the "separation of after-school activities" from the core educational facility.

Recommendation:

Continue education programs focused on CPTED and Safe School Design principles as contained in the *Florida Safe School Design Guidelines* for school district risk/facility managers, community college risk/facility managers, and design professionals. Wherever possible, partner with organizations, such as the Florida Association of School Resources Officers (FASRO), to present educational programs about the *Guidelines* and their impacts on promoting school safety and security.

WHAT ARE SERIOUS CRIMES ON PUBLIC SCHOOL
AND COMMUNITY COLLEGE CAMPUSES?

Finding:

Principals report that *fighting, disorderly conduct,* and *vandalism* are the top three crimes on their campuses in terms of numbers of incidents while community college respondents say that *larceny/theft, vandalism,* and *breaking and entering* are the three crimes they perceive to be the most serious based on event frequency.

PREFERRED SCHOOL DESIGN TYPE

Finding:

A sizeable majority of respondents overall favor the one-story, centrally organized building group configuration over other plan types. However, only a plurality of principals and community college respondents favored this arrangement over others.

CRITICAL AREAS OF SCHOOL DESIGN

Finding:

Relative to critical areas of school design, *corridor surveillance* issues are the most important concerns among the respondent groups generally. These are followed by *perimeter enclosure* issues and by the perceived need to *minimize niches.* For public schools in particular, corridor surveillance is considered to be especially important. Community college risk/facility managers reported that their most critical areas of school design related to security are *exterior lighting, alarm systems,* and *interior lighting,* in that order.

WHAT SINGLE POLICY OR PROCEDURE CHANGE WOULD THEY RECOMMEND?

Finding:

All respondents were asked the open-ended question, "What single policy or procedural change would they recommend if funding were available?" Central themes that emerge from this very mixed collection of open-ended responses tend to center around the fundamental problems of *surveillance* and *access control,* which are interwoven issues.

PUBLIC ACCESS AFTER HOURS

Finding:

With the notable exception of community college respondents who were split almost evenly (50 percent "Yes," 45 percent "No," and 5 percent non-responsive), significant majorities within the other three respondent groups (ranging from 65 percent to 69 percent) believe that public access does make their institutions more prone to criminal activity.

POSTING SIGNS FOR ACCESS CONTROL

Finding:

Most respondents (64 percent) who answered this question report that their school, district, or community college had policies in place governing the posting of access-control signs during school hours; however, a significantly lower number (33 percent) report having policies for signage to deal with *after-hours* access.

CRIME BY LOCATION

Finding:

Several distinct peaks and valleys are evident. On the *high* side of the spectrum, respondents overall identify *parking lots, off-grounds/adjacent buildings, locker rooms,* and *restrooms* as the top four places for crimes and report *low* criminal activity on *rooftops of covered walkways,* on *building rooftops,* in *lobby/reception areas,* and at *main entrances.* The most crimes reported in parking lots are trespassing and vandalism. The most crimes reported in off-grounds/adjacent buildings are use of alcohol, tobacco, and drugs and fighting. For locker rooms, the most crimes reported are larceny/theft and fighting. The most crimes in restrooms are vandalism and the use of alcohol, tobacco, and drugs.

CRIME BY TIME

Finding:

All respondent groups for this question perceive that significantly more crimes occur *before school, after school, during the evening,* and *on weekends* than during *normal classroom hours* (including breaks between classes). This perception is consistent with earlier results showing that respondent groups (with the exception of community college risk/facility managers) overwhelmingly report the perception that after-hours access to public school campuses makes them more prone to crime.

OTHER SERIOUS CONCERNS ON PUBLIC SCHOOL AND COMMUNITY COLLEGE CAMPUSES

Finding:

Principals, school district risk/facility managers, community college risk/facility managers, and school resource officers were asked whether they had serious concerns relative to "*gang-related activities, hate crimes, bomb threats, terrorists, and violence in the workplace.*" Of the listed concerns, "bomb threats" registered the highest number of affirmative responses, with slightly over a fourth (26 percent, or forty individuals) of all those who answered this question saying that these were a serious concern at their schools. The second most serious concern was "violence in the workplace" which registered a positive response from 24.2 percent of the respondents (thirty-four individuals) who answered this question, and the third was *gang violence,* which was viewed by 19.3 percent of the respondents as a serious concern.

WHAT DESIGN CHANGES WOULD YOU IMPLEMENT IN YOUR SCHOOL/COMMUNITY COLLEGE TO MAKE IT SAFER?

Finding:

All of the respondent groups put *surveillance* issues clearly at the forefront, followed by *access control* (with the exception of school resource officers who combined *access control and territoriality* issues second), and *territoriality* third. Some respondents combined all of these, as well as *guardianship* and *management* issues, in their comments.

General Findings and Recommendations

SURVEILLANCE AND CCTV

Finding:

There is significant and growing interest in the use of closed circuit television (CCTV) to accomplish surveillance in both interior and exterior spaces at schools and community colleges.

Recommendation:

Continue emphasis on programs that focus on designs for natural surveillance, which should be the first strategy for surveillance. Nevertheless, a framework for the application and design integration of CCTV for security purposes should be developed for Florida public schools. A model could be the National Institute of Justice report, *The Appropriate and Effective Use of Security Technologies in U.S. Schools,* NCJ 178265, September 1999.

SMALL-SCALE DESIGN ELEMENTS

Finding:

Specific, small-scale elements may be important contributors to school and community college security. Examples include the design and placement of access-control signs and alarming secondary building entrances to warn administrators and school resource officers when doors are propped open.

Recommendation:

Support research into small-scale design changes in schools and community colleges.

COMMUNITY COLLEGES AND K–12

Finding:

Even though they are subject to the same Safe School Design Requirements found in Florida Building Code requirements, community colleges and public schools present very different security design profiles in that they have very different student populations and, for the most part, different campus plans and organization. As a consequence, they tend to have different crime and crime prevention issues.

Recommendation:

Future research should concentrate on community colleges and public school as separate entities insomuch as security design is concerned.

AFTER-HOURS ACCESS

Finding:

Respondents to our surveys, and especially those from public schools, report overwhelmingly that after-hours access to school campuses makes them more prone to crime, even though the co-location of public facilities is bound to increase in the future. School designers report that they have problems fulfilling the design intent of this aspect of Safe School Design. Moreover, most respondents believe that more crime takes place after normal daytime class hours than during that period.

Recommendation:

Increased research and continuing education should be devoted to the after-hours access issue.

SCHOOL CRIME AND LOCATION DATA

Finding:

There is a lack of Florida data that connects school design, location, and criminal acts.

Recommendation:

School Environment Safety Incident Reporting System (SESIR) data should include references to the specific locations where crimes are committed in schools.

STUDENT INTERVIEWS

Finding:

Field interviews and survey research about crime in Florida public schools and community colleges suggest that school children and community college students may be the best sources of information about crime on their campuses.

Recommendation:

Student interviews should be incorporated into research conducted for the updating and revision of future *Florida Safe School Design Guidelines.*

Building Vulnerability Assessment Checklist

Assessment Checklist

	Yes/No	Threat Assessment	Vulnerability Assessment	Risk Assessment	Mitigation Option
		High/ Medium/Low	GAP ANALYSIS High/ Medium/Low	High/ Medium/Low	GAP CLOSURE

1. Security Situation

Your current security situation

Are you in a high-crime area?

Are you a high-risk target for a terrorist attack?

Do you store goods, materials that would attract thieves, that is, jewelry store, drugs in a hospital?

Has your facility ever been broken into?

Has your facility ever been vandalized?

Have you suffered workplace violence?

Have you suffered computer/IT crime?

Do you have an integrated physical security plan?

Do you have an emergency management plan?

2. Site—Neighbors

Could your neighbors impact on your facility's security?

Are you at risk from facilities in the area, that is, power plants, government buildings, chemical plants, gas and oil facilities, high-risk targets?

Do nearby roads or railway lines pose a threat?

Do any immediate neighbors pose a threat, that is, could they be a target, do they handle toxic materials, is their security adequate?

Do neighborhood development plans impact you?

3. Site—Location
How secure is your location?

Is your facility in a favorable location, that is, good all-around views, not in a depression, not subject to frequent fogs?

Is your facility in a high-traffic urban area (vehicles and pedestrians)?

Can vehicles park close to your facility?

4. Site—Perimeter
Is your perimeter secure?

Is there an external perimeter, that is, fence or barriers?

Is there any standoff distance?

Are there too many access points to the facility?

Does vehicle traffic have access to the facility?

Is vehicle access controlled?

Is there pedestrian access to the facility?

Is pedestrian access controlled?

Is there potential access to the facility from utility paths, that is, manholes, tunnels?

Is there below-ground car parking?

Is below-ground car parking protected?

Is there good lighting around the facility, at doorways?

Is there adequate signage in the area?

Are fire hydrants accessible?

Do you have loading bays?

Are they controlled?

Are there nearby trashcans/mailboxes?

5. Perimeter Security
Do you have adequate perimeter security?

Is there perimeter security lighting?

Is there closed circuit TV surveillance?

Are access points monitored?

Assessment Checklist

	Yes/No	Threat Assessment	Vulnerability Assessment	Risk Assessment	Mitigation Option
			GAP ANALYSIS		GAP CLOSURE
		High/ Medium/Low	High/ Medium/Low	High/ Medium/Low	

6. Building Usage

Do you understand your building usage?

Is access to the building controlled?

Do staff/public use same access points?

Are all access points protected?

Does the building have multiple tenants?

Are public/private areas separated?

Does the public have access to restrooms/stairwells/elevators?

Are access points protected?

Are critical assets close to the main entrance?

Are critical building systems hardened?

Is internal traffic flow controlled?

Are critical assets under surveillance?

Are mailrooms located away from main entrance?

Is access to the mailroom controlled?

Can the mailroom be isolated?

Do you have safe rooms/areas?

Do you have different security levels?

Are there adequate portals between security levels?

7. Building Structure

How structurally safe is your facility?

Does the facility have any physical hardening, that is, reinforced walls, floors, doors?

Do the windows have strengthened glass?

Could the walls withstand an external or internal explosion?

Are non-weight-bearing walls reinforced?

Are critical elements subject to failure?

Is the structure vulnerable to collapse?

Are there adequate redundant load paths in the structure?

Is the loading dock able to withstand/contain an explosion?

Is the mailroom able to withstand/contain an explosion?

8. Utility Systems

Understanding your utilities

Do you know the source of domestic water, that is, utility, municipal, storage tank?

Is there a secure alternate drinking water supply?

Do you know how the water comes into the facility, that is, one point or multiple points?

Are the water entry points secure?

Do you know the source of water for the fire suppression system, that is, utility line, storage tanks, river?

Is the fire suppression system adequate?

Are sprinkler and standpipe connections adequate and redundant?

Are sewer systems accessible?

Are sewer systems protected?

Do you know what fuels the building relies on for critical operations?

Do you know how much fuel is stored on site?

Is storage secure and protected?

Do you know how fuel is delivered?

Are there alternate sources of fuel?

Do you know your normal source of electricity?

Is there a redundant electrical source?

Do you know how many electric service points there are?

Are these electric service points secure?

Are there provisions for emergency power?

Are there transformers or switchgear outside the building?

Assessment Checklist

	Yes/No	Threat Assessment	Vulnerability Assessment GAP ANALYSIS	Risk Assessment	Mitigation Option GAP CLOSURE
		High/Medium/Low	High/Medium/Low	High/Medium/Low	
Are they vulnerable to public access?					
Are they protected?					
Is the electrical room protected?					
Are critical electrical systems collocated with other building systems?					
Do you know how telephone and data communications come into the building?					
Are these access points secure?					
Are there redundancies in telephone and data communications?					
Is your fire alarm system reliant on external communications?					
Are fire alarm panels protected?					
Are fire alarm systems standalone or integrated with other systems?					
Are utility lines above ground/underground or buried?					
Are external air intakes accessible to the public?					
Are these air intakes protected?					
Can air intakes be closed/sealed?					
Do you have air monitors/sensors?					
Can sections of the AC be isolated?					
Is roof access limited?					
Are mechanical systems in secure areas?					
Are there smoke evacuation systems?					
Do you have fire barriers?					
Are there fire dampers at all fire barriers?					
Can elevators be shut down and isolated?					
Is access to building materials controlled?					

9. People

What do you know about your most critical asset?

Do you know who uses your facility, that is, staff, students, visitors, deliveries?

Do you know traffic flow patterns to and around the building?

Do you know traffic flows within the building?

Do employees carry ID cards?

Are there access controls for employees entering the building, that is, badges/cards?

Are there different security layers within the building?

Is access to these different layers controlled?

Are visitors screened and searched?

Do you have security staff?

Do you have front desk security?

Do you do background checks on all employees?

Do employees understand the need for security?

Do you practice security/fire/evacuation drills?

10. Communications and IT

How secure are your communications and IT?

Is the main telephone distribution room secure?

Does the room have an uninterruptible power supply?

Is communications wiring secure?

Are there redundant communication systems?

Is the IT main distribution location secure?

Do IT systems meet requirements for integrity, confidentiality, and availability?

Is there a disaster-recovery mirroring site?

Is backup for tapes/file storage safe?

Is there a mass-notification system to reach all building occupants, that is, public address, pagers?

Assessment Checklist	Yes/No	Threat Assessment	Vulnerability Assessment GAP ANALYSIS	Risk Assessment	Mitigation Option GAP CLOSURE
		High/ Medium/Low	High/ Medium/Low	High/ Medium/Low	

11. Equipment Operation and Maintenance

What do you need to know about your building systems?

Are there plans of all major systems?

Are these plans current?

Are there updated operations and maintenance manuals?

Have critical air systems been rebalanced?

Are mechanical/electrical/plumbing (MEP) systems tested and balanced on a regular basis?

Are there maintenance and service agreements for MEP?

Are backup power systems tested regularly?

Do all stairway and emergency exit lights work?

12. External Security Systems

Do you have the right external protection?

Are closed circuit TVs in use?

Are they monitored and recorded 24/7?

Do they have an uninterrupted power supply?

Do the cameras respond automatically to perimeter alarm events?

Do the cameras have built-in video motion capabilities?

Are panic/duress alarm buttons used?

Are there intercom call boxes in parking areas and along the building perimeter?

Is there adequate monitoring of the CCTV?

Are infrared camera illuminators used?

Are there exterior intrusion detection system sensors (IDS), that is, electromagnetic, fiber optic, active infrared, microwave?

Is GPS used to monitor vehicles?

13. Internal Security Systems
Do you have the right internal protection?

Are CCTVs used?

Are they monitored 24/7?

Do they monitor the whole building?

Are they programmed to respond automatically to interior building alarm events?

Is the transmission media, that is, fiber, telephone wire, wireless, secure?

Is there a security access-control system?

Are physical security systems integrated with IT networks?

What is the alternate backup power supply for the access-control systems?

Are panic/duress alarm buttons used?

Are there intercom call boxes in the building?

Are metal detectors/X-ray equipment used?

Are interior IDS sensors used?

Do you know what locks are used in the building, that is, manual, electromagnetic, keypad?

Are potentially hazardous materials kept on site?

Are there security procedures for handling mail?

Is there a designated security room?

Is there a backup security room?

Is there offsite 24/7 monitoring of IDSs?

Is the security room in a secure area?

Are there vaults or safes in the building?

Are they protected?

Assessment Checklist	Yes/No	Threat Assessment	Vulnerability Assessment GAP ANALYSIS	Risk Assessment	Mitigation Option GAP CLOSURE
		High/ Medium/Low	High/ Medium/Low	High/ Medium/Low	

14. Security System Documents

Are your critical documents current and available?

Are security system as-built drawings available?

Are security system manuals available?

Have security system design and drawing standards been developed?

Are security equipment selection criteria defined?

Have contingency plans been developed?

Has security system construction been prepared and standardized?

Have qualifications been determined for security consultants, system designers, engineers, installation vendors, and contractors?

15. Security Master Plan
Master plan critical issues

Is there a written system security plan for the building?

Has it been recently reviewed and revised?

Has the plan been communicated to key management?

Has the plan been benchmarked against related organizations and operational entities?

Has the security plan been tested and evaluated from cost-benefit and operational efficiency/effective perspectives?

Does the plan set out short-/medium-/long-term goals and objectives?

Have security operating and capital budgets been addressed?

Have all regulatory and industry guidelines been followed?

Does the security plan address the protection of people, property, critical assets, and information?

Does the plan address access control, response, surveillance, building hardening and protection against CBR and cyber-network attacks?

Do you know when the last security assessment was carried out?

Does the plan address all issues flagged by asset, threat, vulnerability, and risk assessments?

Crisis Management

School Safety Planning and Preparedness

> "Families trust schools to keep their children safe during the day. Thanks to the efforts of millions of teachers, principals and staff across America, the majority of schools remain a safe haven for our nation's youth. The unfortunate reality is, however, that school districts in this country may be touched either directly or indirectly by a crisis of some kind at any time."
>
> —The Office of Safe and Drug-Free Schools,
> U.S. Department of Education.

Natural disasters, such as floods, earthquakes, fires, and tornadoes, can strike a community with little or no warning. While still rare, school shootings, threatened or actual, are horrific and chilling when they occur. The harrowing events of September 11 and subsequent anthrax scares have ushered in a new age of terrorism. Communities across the country are struggling to understand and avert acts of terror.

Children and youth rely on and find great comfort in the adults who protect them. Teachers and staff must know how to help their students through a crisis and return them home safely. Knowing what to do when faced with a crisis can be the difference between calm and chaos, between courage and fear, between life and death. There are thousands of fires in schools every year, yet there is minimal damage to life and property because staff and students are prepared. This preparedness needs to be extended to all risks that schools face. Schools and districts need to be ready to handle crises, large and small, to keep our children and staff out of harm's way and ready to learn and teach.

The time to plan is now. If you do not have a crisis plan in place, develop one. If you have one, review, update, and practice it.

Crises range in scope and intensity from incidents that directly or indirectly affect a single student to ones that impact the entire community. Crises can happen before, during, or after school and on or off school campuses. The definition of a crisis varies with the unique needs, resources, and assets of a school and community. Staff and students may be severely affected by an incident in another city or state. The events of Columbine and September 11 left the entire nation feeling vulnerable.

The definition of a crisis is: "An unstable or crucial time or state of affairs in which a decisive change is impending, especially one with the distinct possibility of a highly undesirable outcome" (*Webster's Ninth Collegiate Dictionary*, 1987). Additionally, *Webster* notes that "crisis" comes from the Greek word meaning "decision." In essence, a crisis is a situation where schools could be faced with inadequate information, not enough time, and insufficient resources, but in which leaders must make one or many crucial decisions.

All districts and schools need a crisis team. One of the key functions of this team is to identify the types of crises that may occur in the district and schools and define what events would activate the plan. The team may consider many factors, such as the school's ability to handle a situation with internal resources and its experience in responding to past events. Plans need to address a range of events and hazards caused by nature and people.

PLANNING CONSIDERATIONS FOR SAFE SCHOOLS AND CRISIS RESPONSE

In the school's mission statement, identify the context for which the school wishes the academic learning to take place, using phrases like "to learn in a safe and secure environment free of violence, drugs, and fear." Such phrases enhance the school's legal position to create and enforce policies that promote a safe, caring, and disciplined school climate.

Identify a specific procedure for evaluating and responding to threats. Every campus should have a series of threat assessment protocols so that school officials can effectively work with mental health and law enforcement professionals in handling circumstances that could result in potential violence or harm. Also, make certain students are on your team. For the most part, students are the best information resources for inside threats. Recent studies by the Secret Service revealed that in the vast majority of student shootings, other students on the campus were aware of the event before it occurred. Having a tipline or safe reporting mechanism in place for students is critical.

Identify the potential disasters that could occur based on the school's setting and climate. Such disasters may include:

- Civil unrest/demonstrations/rioting
- Bomb threats/explosions
- Intruders/unauthorized visitors
- Hostage takings
- Sniper attacks
- Extortion
- Assault/battery/rape
- Weapons possessions

- Drug abuse/trafficking
- Gang-related violence/drive-by shootings
- Kidnappings/abductions
- Child abuse/neglect/molestation
- Medical emergencies
- Life-threatening illness
- Accidental injury or death
- Intentional injury or death
- Utility failures
- Chemical spills
- Fire
- Automobile accidents
- Severe weather
- Natural disasters: earthquake, flood, tornado, fire, hurricane, tsunami
- Mass-transit disasters: falling aircraft/train derailment/bus accidents

Control campus access. Minimize the number of campus entrance and exit points used daily. Access points to school grounds should be limited and supervised on a regular basis by individuals who are familiar with the student body. Campus traffic, both pedestrian and vehicular, should flow through areas that can be easily and naturally supervised. Delivery entrances used by vendors also should be checked regularly. Parking lots often have multiple entrances and exits, which contribute to the vandalism and defacement of vehicles and school property. Vehicular and pedestrian access should be carefully controlled. Perimeter fencing should be considered. Bus lots should be secured and monitored. Infrequently used rooms and closets should be locked. Access to utilities, roofs, and cleaning closets should be secured.

Identify specifically assigned roles and responsibilities. Specific policies and procedures that detail staff members' responsibilities for security should be developed. These responsibilities may include monitoring hallways and restrooms, patrolling parking lots, and providing supervision at before-school and after-school activities. Specific roles and responsibilities should also be assigned for times of crisis, including the appointment of a crisis team.

Identify whom to call in a crisis. Maintain an updated list of whom to call in case of various kinds of crises. Develop a close working partnership with these emergency responders. Know the extent of services offered by these agencies. Find out what to do when an emergency responder is not immediately available. Develop a close working partnership with law enforcement officials. Determine in advance who will lead, who will follow, and how searches, interrogations, and other issues will be handled. The counselor or psychologist can also be an important partner in the aftermath of a crisis.

Provide training for all members of the school community regarding cultural awareness and sensitivity. It is important to consider the impact of cultural influences on a school community's ability to create and maintain safe, secure, and peaceful schools. Cultural influences will directly affect the information, strategies, and resources that will be used in safe school planning. The sensitivity to cultural influences also applies to creating a plan to manage and respond to a crisis.

Establish an emergency operation communication system. In addition to campus intercoms and two-way radios, school officials must be able to communicate with law enforcement and outside telephone providers. This includes the use of cell phones.

Implement a uniform school crime reporting and record-keeping system. When school administrators know what crimes are being committed on their campus, when these are committed, and where and who is involved, they are better able to develop effective strategies and supervision procedures. In addition, it is important to conduct some level of crime analysis to determine what, if any, linkages exist among various aspects of criminal activity on the campus.

PREPARING FOR NATIONAL EMERGENCIES

Schools should stay informed about potential national security threats, be prepared for emergencies, and know how to react during an attack.

Identify potential and reliable sources of information to be accessed once a crisis situation develops. Prepare a plan that identifies the first and subsequent contacts you will make to access credible information and appropriate direction for action.

Perform an assessment of your school's risk during a national crisis. This includes:

- Evaluating health and medical on-site preparedness
- Checking the availability and accessibility of local emergency services, including HazMat (hazardous materials), fire, emergency medical, law enforcement, and local and federal emergency management agencies
- Identifying potential terrorist targets in your local community
- Identifying and taking inventory of potential informal contacts in the community who could provide food, water, shelter, medical aid, power sources, and other forms of emergency support
- Reviewing viable communications plans, such as phone chains and parent contact information

Be observant of the things transpiring on campus. During periods of high alert, an additional level of vigilance must be in place. Everyone who comes onto the campus must have a legitimate purpose. It is important to have a uniform screening policy for all visitors, including volunteer workers, vendors, and delivery/service personnel. All visitors should be required to sign in at the school office, state their specific business, and wear or visibly display a visitor's badge. Keep records. Watch for suspicious people, packages, and activities on or near your campus. Notify authorities of these observations. **In view of Homeland Security recommendations, it is especially important to pay added attention to the possibility of the following kinds of disasters. Review and revise your crisis plans accordingly.**

- Bomb threats/explosions
- Suicide bombings
- Intruders/unauthorized visitors

- Biological/radiological attacks
- Utility failures
- Mass-transit disasters: falling aircraft/train derailment/bus accidents

Assemble your crisis teams to reacquaint members with each other and with crisis plans and procedures. Enlist new team members as needed.

Provide training to all school staff members regarding crisis preparation. Detail each person's responsibilities during a crisis. Train them to be observant and watchful of suspicious or out-of-the-ordinary activity; how to identify and what to do with suspicious packages; how to turn off utilities and heating or air systems and who would be responsible for doing so; and basic first aid.

Conduct an inventory of campus provisions, including food, water, alternative power sources, materials for sealing doors and windows, and medical and first aid supplies that would need to be available during an emergency. Consider assembling emergency kits and food and water supplies for every classroom. Maintain an updated record of any hazardous chemicals and cleaning agents that may be stored on campus. Be sure that such materials are securely stored according to local and federal regulations.

Review and, if needed, revise existing plans for evacuation, alternative shelter, temporary lockdown, and shelter-in-place. Be prepared to put any combination of these into effect. It is possible that a situation would call for simultaneous lockdown of one section of the building while evacuating other parts of the school.

Keep parents informed of your crisis plans, procedures, and protective policies, particularly with regard to reuniting parents and children after a crisis event.

As appropriate to your community and degree of risk, conduct emergency drills for evacuation, lockdown, or shelter-in-place procedures so that staff and students are familiar with the appropriate response in an actual emergency.

> "Creating safe schools is a joint responsibility involving students, parents, teachers, school officials, local law enforcement, judges, emergency personnel, social service and a variety of other youth-serving professionals. The bottom line is if we are going to require young people to attend school, then it is our responsibility to provide them with a safe, secure and welcoming environment. In this time of heightened potential for terror, including the use of chemical, biological and radiological weapons in our community, it is more important than ever for our schools to be prepared to respond in appropriate ways."
>
> —Ronald Stephens, executive director of the
> National School Safety Center.

PLANNING FOR THE WORST

Every school should have a school safety emergency management plan developed in partnership with public safety agencies, including law enforcement, fire, public health, mental health, and local emergency preparedness agencies. The plan should address fire and natural and manmade disasters. A school's plan should be tailored to address the unique circumstances and needs of the individual school, and should be coordinated and integrated with community plans and the plans of local emergency preparedness agencies.

Because of the ever-present threat of terrorism, these plans should also consider chemical, biological, and radiation (CBR) attack scenarios and the associated procedures for communicating instructions to building occupants, identifying suitable shelter-in-place areas (if they exist), identifying appropriate use and selection of personal protective equipment (i.e., clothing, gloves, respirators), and directing emergency evacuations. This is dealt with in more detail later on.

The Sequence of Crisis Management

There are four phases of crisis management:

- Mitigation/prevention addresses what schools and districts can do to reduce or eliminate risk to life and property.
- Preparedness focuses on the process of planning for the worst-case scenario.
- Response is devoted to the steps to take during a crisis.
- Recovery deals with how to restore the learning and teaching environment after a crisis.

The U.S. Department of Education recommends that each school crisis plan should address these four major areas.

MITIGATION/PREVENTION:

- Conduct an assessment of each school building. Identify those factors that put the building, students, faculty, and staff at greater risk, such as proximity to rail tracks that regularly transport hazardous materials or facilities that produce highly toxic material or propane gas tanks, and develop a plan for reducing the risk. This can include plans to evacuate students away from these areas in times of crisis and to reposition propane tanks or other hazardous materials away from school buildings.
- Work with businesses and factories in close proximity to the school to ensure that the school's crisis plan is coordinated with their crisis plans.
- Ensure that a process is in place for controlling access and egress to the school. Require all persons who do not have authority to be in the school to sign in.
- Review traffic patterns, and where possible, keep cars, buses, and trucks away from school buildings.
- Review landscaping, and ensure that buildings are not obscured by overgrowth of bushes or shrubs where contraband can be placed or people can hide.

PREPAREDNESS:

- Have site plans for each school building readily available and ensure they are shared with first responders and agencies responsible for emergency preparedness.
- Ensure there are multiple evacuation routes and rallying points. First or second evacuation site options may be blocked or unavailable at the time of the crisis.
- Practice responding to crisis on a regular basis.
- Ensure a process is established for communicating during a crisis.
- Inspect equipment to ensure it operates during crisis situations.
- Have a plan for discharging students. Remember that, during a crisis, many parents and guardians may not be able to get to the school to pick up their children. Make sure every student has a secondary contact person and contact information readily available.
- Have a plan for communicating information to parents and for quelling rumors. Cultivate relationships with the media ahead of time, and identify a public information officer (PIO) to communicate with the media and the community during a crisis.
- Work with law enforcement officials and emergency preparedness agencies on a strategy for sharing key parts of the school crisis plans.

RESPONSE:

- Identify the type of crisis that is occurring, and determine the appropriate response.
- Develop a command structure for responding to a crisis. The roles and responsibilities for educators, law enforcement, fire officials, and other first responders in responding to different types of crisis need to be developed, coordinated, reviewed, and approved.
- Ensure all relevant staff maintains communications.

RECOVERY:

- Return to the business of teaching and learning as soon as possible.
- Identify and approve a team of credentialed mental health workers to provide mental health services to faculty and students after a crisis. Understand that recovery takes place over time and that the services of this team may be needed.

Crisis plans need to be customized to communities, districts, and schools to meet the unique needs of local residents and students. Crisis plans also need to address state and local school safety laws. Experts recommend against cutting and pasting plans from other schools and districts. Other plans can serve as useful models, but what is effective for a large inner-city school district, where the population is concentrated, may be ineffective for a rural community, where schools and first responders are far apart.

- Ensure that the team is adequately trained.
- The plan should include notification of parents about actions that the school intends to take to help students recover from the crisis.

CRISIS PLANNING ESSENTIALS

Crisis management is a continuous process in which all phases of the plan are being reviewed and revised. Good plans are never finished. They can always be updated based on experience, research, and changing vulnerabilities. Districts and schools may be in various stages of planning. These guidelines, developed by the U.S. Department of Education, provide the resources needed to start the planning process and can be used as a tool to review and improve existing plans.

Crisis planning may seem overwhelming. It takes time and effort, but it is manageable.

- Effective crisis planning begins with leadership at the top. Every governor, mayor, legislator, superintendent, and principal should work together to make school crisis planning a priority. Top leadership helps set the policy agenda, secures funds, and brings the necessary people together across agencies. Other leadership also needs to be identified—the teacher who is well loved in her school, the county's favorite school resource officer, or the caring school nurse. Leaders at the grassroots level will help your school community accept the planning process.
- Crisis plans should not be developed in a vacuum. They are a natural extension of ongoing school and community efforts to create safe learning environments. Good planning can enhance all school functions. Needs assessments and other data should feed into a crisis plan. Crisis plans should address incidents that could occur inside school buildings, on school grounds, and in the community. Coordination will avoid duplication and mixed messages, as well as reduce the burden on planners.
- School and districts should open the channels of communication well before a crisis. Relationships need to be built in advance so that emergency responders are familiar with your school. Cultivate a relationship with city emergency managers, public works officials, and health and mental health professionals now, and do not overlook local media. It is important that they understand how the district and schools will respond in a crisis.
- Crisis plans should be developed in partnership with other community groups, including law enforcement, fire safety officials, emergency medical services, as well as health and mental health professionals. Do not reinvent the wheel. These groups know what to do in an emergency and can be helpful in the development of your plan. Get their help to develop a coordinated plan of response.
- A common vocabulary is necessary. It is critical that school staff and emergency responders know each other's terminology. Work with emergency responders to develop a common vocabulary. The words used to give directions for evacuation, lockdown, and other actions should be clear and not hazard specific. The Federal Emergency Management Agency (FEMA) recommends using plain language to announce the need for action, for example, "evacuate" rather than "code blue." Many districts

note that with plain language everyone in the school building, including new staff, substitute teachers, and visitors, will know what type of response is called for. However, some districts have found it useful to use—but streamline—codes. Rather than do a code for each type of incident they use only one code for each type of response. With either approach, it is critical that terms and/or codes are used consistently across the district.

- Schools should tailor district crisis plans to meet individual school needs. In fact, a plan should not be one document. It should be a series of documents targeted to various audiences. For example, a school could use detailed response guides for planners, flipcharts for teachers, a crisis response toolbox for administrators, and wallet cards containing evacuation routes for bus drivers. Plans should be age appropriate. Elementary school children will behave very differently in a crisis from high school students.
- Plan for the diverse needs of children and staff. Our review of crisis plans found that few schools addressed children or staff with physical, sensory, motor, developmental, or mental challenges. Special attention is also needed for children with limited English proficiency. Outreach documents for families may be needed in several languages.
- Include all types of schools where appropriate. Be sure to include alternative, charter, and private schools in the planning process, as well as others who are involved with children before and after school.
- Provide teachers and staff with ready access to the plan so they can understand its components and act on them. People who have experienced a crisis often report that they go on "autopilot" during an incident. They need to know what to do in advance not only to get them through an incident but also to help alleviate panic and anxiety.
- Training and practice are essential for the successful implementation of crisis plans. Most students and staff know what to do in case of a fire because the law requires them to participate in routine fire drills, but would they know what to do in a different crisis? Many districts now require evacuation and lockdown drills in addition to state-mandated fire drills. Drills also allow your school to evaluate what works and what needs to be improved.

Crisis plans are living documents. They need to be reviewed and revised regularly. Analyzing how well a crisis plan worked in responding to an incident, whether a drill or a real event, is crucial. Documenting all actions taken while, during, and after an event helps in identifying the strengths and weaknesses of a plan. Use this information to strengthen the plan.

Crisis Planning Mitigation and Prevention

ACTION CHECKLIST

- Connect with community emergency responders to identify local hazards. Review the last safety audit to examine school buildings and grounds.

- Determine who is responsible for overseeing violence prevention strategies in your school.
- Encourage staff to provide input and feedback into the crisis planning process.
- Review incident data.
- Determine the major problems in your school with regard to student crime and violence.
- Assess how the school addresses these problems.
- Conduct an assessment to determine how these problems—as well as others—may impact your vulnerability to certain crises.

Although schools have no control over some of the hazards that may impact them, such as earthquakes or plane crashes, they can take actions to minimize or mitigate the impact of such incidents. Schools in earthquake-prone areas can mitigate the impact of a possible earthquake by securing bookcases and training students and staff what to do during tremors.

Schools cannot always control fights, bomb threats, and school shootings. However, they can take actions to reduce the likelihood of such events. Schools may institute policies, implement violence prevention programs, and take other steps to improve the culture and climate of their campuses.

School safety and emergency management experts often use the terms "prevention" and "mitigation" differently. Crises experts encourage schools to consider the full range of what they can do to avoid crises, when possible, or lessen their impact. Assessing and addressing the safety and integrity of facilities (window seals, heating, ventilation, and air conditioning [HVAC] systems, building structure), security (functioning locks, controlled access to the school), and the culture and climate of schools through policy and curricula are all important for preventing and mitigating possible future crises.

Mitigation and prevention require taking inventory of the dangers in a school and community and identifying what to do to prevent and reduce injury and property damage. For example:

- Establishing access-control procedures and providing IDs for students and staff might prevent a dangerous intruder from coming onto school grounds.
- Conducting hurricane drills can reduce injury to students and staff because they will know what to do to avoid harm. Also, schools in hurricane-prone areas can address structural weaknesses in their buildings.
- Planning responses to and training for incidents involving hazardous materials is important for schools near highways.

There are resources in every community that can help with this process. Firefighters, police, public works staff, facilities managers, and the district's insurance representative, for example, can help conduct a hazard assessment. That information will be very useful in identifying problems that need to be addressed in the preparedness process. Rely on emergency responders, public health agencies, and school nurses to develop plans for and provide training in medical triage and first aid.

FEMA has done considerable work to help states and communities in the area of mitigation planning. It notes that the goal of mitigation is to decrease the need for response, as opposed to simply increasing response capability.

"Mitigation is any sustained action taken to reduce or eliminate long-term risk to life and property from a hazard event. Mitigation . . . encourages long-term reduction of hazard vulnerability" (FEMA, 2002).

Mitigating emergencies is also important from a legal standpoint. If a school, district, or state does not take all necessary actions in good faith to create safe schools, it could be vulnerable to a lawsuit for negligence. It is important to make certain that the physical plant is up to local codes, as well as federal and state laws.

Mitigating or preventing a crisis involves both the district and the community. Contact the regional or state emergency management office to help get started and connect to efforts that are under way locally.

CREATING A SAFE AND ORDERLY LEARNING ENVIRONMENT

Creating a safe and orderly learning environment should not be new to any school and district. Identifying students (or in some cases staff) who may pose a danger to themselves or to others is sometimes called "threat assessment." The U.S. Department of Education and U.S. Secret Service have released a guide, *Threat Assessments in Schools: A Guide to Managing Threatening Situations and to Creating Safe School Climates,* that may be useful in working through the threat assessment process. The results of a threat assessment may guide prevention efforts, which may help avoid a crisis.

Many schools have curricula and programs aimed at preventing children and youth from initiating harmful behaviors. Social problem-solving or life skills programs, anti-bullying programs, and school-wide discipline efforts are common across the nation as a means of helping reduce violent behavior. The staff in charge of prevention in a school (counselors, teachers, health professionals, administrators) should be part of the crisis planning team. Information on effective and promising prevention programs is on the Office of Safe and Drug-Free Schools Web site (www.ed.gov/about/offices/list/osdfs/index.html).

Know the school building. Assess potential hazards on campus. Conduct regular safety audits of the physical plant. Be sure to include driveways, parking lots, playgrounds, outside structures, and fencing. A safety audit should be part of normal operations. This information should feed into mitigation planning.

Know the community. Mitigation requires assessment of local threats. Work with the local emergency management director to assess surrounding hazards. This includes the identification and assessment of the probability of natural disasters (tornadoes, hurricanes, earthquakes) and industrial and chemical accidents (water contamination or fuel spills). Locate major transportation routes and installations. For example, is the school on a flight path or near an airport? Is it near a railroad track that trains use to transport hazardous materials? Also address the potential hazards related to terrorism. Schools and districts should be active partners in community-wide risk assessment and mitigation planning. To help agencies work together, they may want to develop a memorandum of understanding (MOU) that outlines each agency's responsibility.

Bring together regional and local school leaders, among others. Given that mitigation/prevention are community activities, leadership and support of mitigation and prevention activities are necessary to ensure that the right people are at the planning table. Again, leadership begins at the top. Schools and districts will face an uphill battle if state and local governments are not supportive of their mitigation efforts.

Make regular school safety and security efforts part of mitigation/prevention practices. Consult the comprehensive school safety plan and its needs assessment activities to identify what types of incidents are common in the school.

Establish clear lines of communication. Because mitigation and prevention planning requires agencies and organizations to work together and share information, communication among stakeholders is critical. In addition to communications within the planning team, outside communications with families and the larger community are important to convey a visible message that schools and local governments are working together to ensure public safety. Press releases from the governor and chief state school officer that discuss the importance of crisis planning can help open the channels of communication with the public.

Preparedness

ACTION CHECKLIST

- Determine what crisis plans exist in the district, school, and community.
- Identify all stakeholders involved in crisis planning.
- Develop procedures for communicating with staff, students, families, and the media.
- Establish procedures to account for students during a crisis.
- Gather information that exists about the school facility, such as maps and the location of utility shutoffs.
- Identify the necessary equipment that needs to be assembled to assist staff in a crisis.

ACTION STEPS

Start by identifying who should be involved in developing the crisis plan. Include training and drills. Delegating responsibilities and breaking the process down into manageable steps will help planners develop the plan.

Identify and involve stakeholders. Identify the stakeholders to be involved in developing the crisis management plan (the people who are concerned about the safety of the school and the people who will assist when a crisis occurs). Ask stakeholders to provide feedback on sections of the plan that pertain to them. For instance, ask families to comment on procedures for communicating with them during a crisis.

During this process, create working relationships with emergency responders. It is important to learn how these organizations function and how you will work with each other during a crisis. Take time to learn the vocabulary, command structure, and culture of these groups. Some districts have found it useful to sign MOUs with these agencies that specify expectations, including roles and responsibilities.

It is essential to work with city and county emergency planners. You need to know the kinds of support municipalities can provide, as well as any plans the city has for schools during a crisis. For example, city and county planners may plan to use schools as emergency shelters, supply depots, or even morgues. Reviewing this information in advance will help you quickly integrate resources. Participating in local emergency planning gives school and district administrators insight into all the problems they might face in the event of a community-wide crisis and will help school efforts.

Consider existing efforts. Before jumping in to develop your crisis plan, investigate existing plans, such as those of the district and local government. How do other agencies' plans integrate with yours? Are there conflicts? Does the comprehensive school safety plan include a crisis plan? What information from the district's crisis plan can be used in the school's crisis plan?

If the school recently completed a crisis plan, efforts may be limited to revising the plan in response to environmental, staff, and student changes:

Has the building been renovated or is it currently under renovation?
Is the list of staff current?
Have there been changes in the student population?
Have other hazards revealed themselves?

Determine what crises the plan will address. Before assigning roles and responsibilities or collecting the supplies that the school will need during a crisis, define what a crisis is for your school based on your vulnerabilities, needs, and assets. (Remember this was covered in Section 2.)

Describe the types of crises the plan addresses, including local hazards and problems identified from safety audits, evaluations, and assessments conducted during the mitigation/prevention phase. Consider incidents that may occur during community use of the school facility and prepare for incidents that occur while students are off-site (e.g., during a field trip).

Define roles and responsibilities. How will the school operate during a crisis? Define what should happen, when, and at whose direction—that is, create an organizational system. This should involve many of the school staff. Important tasks will be neglected if one person is responsible for more than one function. School staff should be assigned to the following roles:

School commander
Liaison to emergency responders
Student caregivers
Security officers
Medical staff
Spokesperson

During the planning process, both individuals and backups should be assigned to fill these roles. If the district has not already appointed a public information officer (PIO), it should do so right away. Some large school districts have staff dedicated solely to this function. Many smaller districts use the superintendent, school security officers, or a school principal as their PIO.

Work with law enforcement officers and emergency responders to identify crises that require an outside agency to manage the scene (fire, bomb threat, hostage situations). Learn what roles these outsiders will play, what responsibilities they will take on, and how they will interact with school staff. Especially important is determining who will communicate with families and the community during an incident.

Many schools and emergency responders use the Incident Command System (ICS) to manage incidents. ICS provides a structured way for delegating responsibilities among school officials and all emergency responders during crisis response. An ICS and/or other management plan needs to be created with all emergency responders and school officials before a crisis occurs.

Develop methods for communicating with the staff, students, families, and the media. Address how the school will communicate with all of the individuals who are directly or indirectly involved in the crisis. One of the first steps in planning for communication is to develop a mechanism to notify students and staff that an incident is occurring and to instruct them on what to do. It is critical that schools and emergency responders use the same definitions for the same terms. Don't create more confusion because terms do not mean the same things to everyone involved in responding to a crisis.

It is important to determine how to convey information to staff and students by using codes for evacuation and lockdown, or simply by stating the facts. FEMA recommends simply using plain language rather than codes. If students are evacuated from the school building, will staff use cell phones, radios, intercoms, or runners to get information to the staff supervising them? Be sure to discuss the safest means of communication with law enforcement and emergency responders. For example, some electronic devices can trigger bombs.

Plan how to communicate with families, community members, and the media. Consider writing template letters and press releases in advance so staff will not have to compose them during the confusion and chaos of the event. It's easier to tweak smaller changes than to begin from scratch.

Often the media can be very helpful in providing information to families and others in the community. Be sure to work with local media before a crisis occurs to help them understand school needs during an incident.

Obtain necessary equipment and supplies. Provide staff with the necessary equipment to respond to a crisis. Consider whether there are enough master keys for emergency responders so that they have complete access to the school. Get the phones or radios necessary for communication. Ask for contact information for families. Maintain a cache of first aid supplies. What about food and water for students and staff during the incident?

Prepare response kits for secretaries, nurses, and teachers so they have easy access to the supplies. For example, a nurse's kit might include student and emergency medicines ("anaphylaxis kits," which may require physician's orders, for use in breathing emergencies, such as severe, sudden allergic reactions), as well as first aid supplies. A teacher's kit might include a crisis management reference guide, as well as an updated student roster.

Prepare for immediate response. When a crisis occurs, quickly determine whether students and staff need to be evacuated from the building, returned to the building, or locked down in the building. Plan action steps for each of these scenarios.

- Evacuation requires all students and staff to leave the building. While evacuating to the school's field makes sense for a fire drill that only lasts a few minutes, it may not be an appropriate location for a longer period of time. The evacuation plan should include backup buildings to serve as emergency shelters, such as nearby community centers, religious institutions, businesses, or other schools. Agreements for using these spaces should be negotiated or reconfirmed prior to the beginning of each school year. Evacuation plans should include contingencies for weather conditions, such as rain, snow, and extreme cold and heat. While most students will be able to walk to a nearby community center, students with disabilities may have more restricted mobility. Your plan should include transportation options for these students.
- If an incident occurs while students are outside, you will need to return them to the building quickly. This is a reverse evacuation. Once staff and students are safely in the building, you may find the situation calls for a lockdown.
- Lockdowns are called for when a crisis occurs outside of the school and an evacuation would be dangerous. A lockdown may also be called for when there is a crisis inside, and movement within the school will put students in jeopardy. All exterior doors are locked and students and staff stay in their classrooms. Windows may need to be covered.
- Shelter-in-place is used when there is not time to evacuate or when it may be harmful to leave the building. Shelter-in-place is commonly used during hazardous material spills. Students and staff are held in the building, and windows and doors are sealed. There can be limited movement within the building.

Create maps and facilities information. In a crisis, emergency responders need to know the location of everything in a school. Create site maps that include information about classrooms, hallways and stairwells, the location of utility shutoffs, and potential staging sites. Emergency responders need copies of this information in advance. During a crisis designate locations—staging sites—for emergency responders to organize, for medical personnel to treat the injured, for the public information officer to brief the media, and for families to be reunited with their children. Student reunification sites should be as far away from the media staging area as possible. Law enforcement will help determine the plans needed to facilitate access of emergency responders and to restrict access of well-wishers and the curious.

Develop accountability and student release procedures. As soon as a crisis is recognized, account for all students, staff, and visitors. Emergency responders treat a situation very differently when people are missing. For example, when a bomb threat occurs, the stakes are substantially higher if firefighters do not know whether students are in the school when they are trying to locate and disarm a bomb.

Be sure to inform families of release procedures before a crisis occurs. In many crises, families have flocked to schools wanting to collect their children immediately. A method should be in place for tracking student release and ensuring that students are only released to authorized individuals.

Practice. Preparedness includes emergency drills and crisis exercises for staff, students, and emergency responders. Many schools have found tabletop exercises very useful in practicing and testing the procedures specified in their crisis plan. Tabletop exercises involve school staff and emergency responders sitting around a table discussing the steps they would take to respond to a crisis. Often, training and drills identify issues that need to be addressed in the crisis plan and problems with plans for communication and response. Teachers also need training in how to manage students during a crisis, especially those experiencing panic reactions. Careful consideration of these issues will improve your crisis plan and better prepare you to respond to an actual crisis.

Address liability issues. Consideration of liability issues is necessary before crisis planning can be completed and may protect you and your staff from a lawsuit. Situations where there is a foreseeable danger can hold liability if the school does not make every reasonable effort to intervene or remedy the situation. A careful assessment of the hazards faced by the school is critical.

Response

ACTION CHECKLIST

- Determine if a crisis is occurring.
- Identify the type of crisis that is occurring and determine the appropriate response.
- Activate the incident management system.
- Ascertain whether an evacuation, reverse evacuation, lockdown, or shelter-in-place needs to be implemented.
- Maintain communication among all relevant staff at officially designated locations.
- Establish what information needs to be communicated to staff, students, families, and the community.
- Monitor how emergency first aid is being administered to the injured.
- Decide if more equipment and supplies are needed.

Expect to be surprised, regardless of how much time and effort was spent on crisis planning. The members of the crisis team should know that there always will be an element of surprise and accompanying confusion when a school is confronted with a crisis.

Assess the situation and choose the appropriate response. Following the plan requires a very quick but careful assessment of the situation. Determine whether a crisis exists and, if so, the type of crisis, the location, and the magnitude. Because the team has practiced the plan, the leaders are ready to make these decisions. After basic protective steps are in place, more information can be gathered to adjust later responses.

Respond within seconds. When a crisis actually happens, make the basic decisions about what type of action is needed and respond within seconds. An immediate, appropriate response depends on a plan with clearly articulated roles and responsibilities, as well as training and practice. With proper training, district and school staff and students will respond appropriately within seconds.

Notify appropriate emergency responders and the school crisis response team. One common mistake is to delay calling emergency responders, such as the police or fire department. In the midst of a crisis, people often believe that the situation can be handled in-house. It is better to have emergency responders on the scene as soon as possible, even if the incident has been resolved by the time they arrive, than to delay calling and risk further injury and damage. For instance, it is better to have emergency responders arrive at a school to find a fire put out than to arrive too late to prevent loss of life or serious property damage.

Notifying a district or school crisis team allows them to begin the necessary measures to protect the safety of all persons involved. Unless informed otherwise by the incident commander, school crisis team members should proceed with their responsibilities.

Evacuate or lock down the school as appropriate. This step is crucial and should be one of the first decisions made, regardless of the order in which initial decisions are implemented.

Triage injuries and provide emergency first aid to those who need it. The plan should assign emergency medical services personnel and school staff with relevant qualifications to determine who needs emergency first aid. Designate a location for EMS to treat the seriously injured on the scene.

Keep supplies nearby and organized at all times. If you move to another location, remember to take your supplies with you. Monitor the amount of supplies and replace them as needed.

Trust leadership. Trust the internal crisis team members and external emergency responders who have been trained to deal with crises. Trust will help calm the situation and minimize the chaos that may occur during a crisis.

During a crisis, leaders need to project a calm, confident, and serious attitude to assure people of the seriousness of the situation and the wisdom of the directions being given. This leadership style will help all involved to respond in a similarly calm and confident manner, as well as helping to mitigate the reactions of anyone who might deny that a crisis has occurred.

In certain situations it may be necessary to yield leadership to others in the plan's designated command structure. In some jurisdictions laws state the protocol for the command structure. This structure may vary from state to state and even from community to community within a state. For instance, in a fire, the expertise of firefighters should lead the way, with others filling designated roles, such as manager of family-student reunification.

Communicate accurate and appropriate information. During a crisis, districts and schools will communicate with the school community, as well as the community at large. Use the channels of communication identified in the plan. For instance, all information released to the media and public should be funneled through a single public information officer or appointed spokesperson. This will maximize the likelihood of presenting consistent and accurate information to the public.

The crisis team should communicate regularly with staff managing the students. A school's most important responsibility, the safety of the students entrusted to the school by their families, cannot be fulfilled during a crisis without timely and accurate information to those caring for students.

At a minimum, families need to know that a crisis has occurred and that all possible steps are being taken to see to the safety of their children. Additional details about assembly and shelter procedures may also be provided, as determined by the plan or those managing the crisis. At some point, families will also need to know when and where their children will be released.

Activate the student release system. Always keep in mind that the earliest possible safe release of students is a desired goal. Often student release will be accomplished before complete resolution of a crisis.

Allow for flexibility in implementing the crisis plan. It is impossible for any crisis plan, no matter how complete, to address every situation that may arise during a crisis. With proper training and practice, emergency responders and staff will be able to respond appropriately and to adapt the school crisis plans to the situation.

Documentation. Write down every action taken during the response. This will provide a record of appropriate implementation of the crisis plan. Also necessary is recording damage for insurance purposes and tracking financial expenditures related to the incident. Keep all original notes and records. These are legal documents.

RECOVERY

The goal of recovery is to return to learning and restore the infrastructure of the school as quickly as possible. Focus on students and the physical plant, and take as much time as needed for recovery. School staff can be trained to deal with the emotional impact of the crisis, as well as to initially assess the emotional needs of students, staff, and responders. One of the major goals of recovery is to provide a caring and supportive school environment.

Action Checklist

- Strive to return to learning as quickly as possible.
- Restore the physical plant, as well as the school community.
- Monitor how staff is assessing students for the emotional impact of the crisis.
- Identify what follow-up interventions are available to students, staff, and first responders.
- Conduct debriefings with staff and first responders.
- Assess curricular activities that address the crisis.
- Allocate appropriate time for recovery.
- Plan how anniversaries of events will be commemorated.
- Capture "lessons learned" and incorporate them into revisions and trainings.

Plan for recovery in the preparedness phase. Determine the roles and responsibilities of staff and others who will assist in recovery during the planning phase. District-level counselors may want to train school staff to assess the emotional needs of students and colleagues to determine intervention needs. Experience shows that after a crisis many unsolicited offers of assistance from outside the school community are made. During planning, you may want to review the credentials of service providers and certify those that will be used during recovery.

Assemble the Crisis Intervention Team. A Crisis Intervention Team (CIT) is composed of individuals at either the district or school level involved in recovery. A review of the literature shows that there are different models for organizing a CIT. In one model, there is a centralized CIT at the district level, which serves all schools in that district. In another model, the district trains school-based CITs. Even when crisis intervention teams exist within individual schools, it may be necessary for the superintendent to allocate additional resources on an as-needed basis.

Service providers in the community may want to assist after a crisis. With prior planning, those with appropriate skills and certifications may be tapped to assist in recovery. This will help district and school personnel coordinate activities of the community service providers and see that district procedures and intervention goals are followed.

Return to the "business of learning" as quickly as possible. Experts agree that the first order of business following a crisis is to return students to learning as quickly as possible. This may involve helping students and families cope with separations from one another with the reopening of school after a crisis.

Schools and districts need to keep students, families, and the media informed. Be clear about what steps have been taken to attend to student safety. Let families and other community members know what support services the school and district are providing or what other community resources are available. Messages to students should be age appropriate. It may be necessary to translate letters and other forms of communication into languages other than English depending on the composition of the communities feeding the affected school(s). Be sure to consider cultural differences when preparing these materials.

Focus on the building, as well as people, during recovery. Following a crisis, buildings and their grounds may need repairing or repainting/re-landscaping. Conduct safety audits and determine the parts of the building that can be used, and plan for repairing those that are damaged.

Provide assessment of emotional needs of staff, students, families, and responders. Assess the emotional needs of all students and staff, and determine those who need intervention by a school counselor, social worker, school psychologist, or other mental health professional. Arrange for appropriate interventions by school or community-based service providers. In addition, available services need to be identified for families who may want to seek treatment for their children or themselves. Appropriate group intervention may be beneficial to students and staff experiencing less severe reactions to the crisis. Group interventions should be age appropriate.

Provide stress management during class time. Trauma experts emphasize the need to create a caring, warm, and trusting environment for students following a crisis. Allow students to talk about what they felt and experienced during the traumatic event. Younger children who may not be able to fully express their feelings verbally will benefit from creative activities such as drawing or painting. They can also be encouraged to tell their stories to teachers or parents who can then write them down.

Young adolescents benefit from group discussions in which they are encouraged to talk about their feelings, as well as from writing plays or stories about their experiences. Engage older adolescents in group discussions and address any issues of guilt ("I could have taken some action to change the outcome of the crisis").

Conduct daily debriefings for staff, responders, and others assisting in recovery. Mental health workers who have provided services after crises stress the importance of ensuring that those who are providing "psychological first aid" are supported with daily critical incident stress debriefings. Debriefings help staff cope with their own feelings of vulnerability.

Take as much time as needed for recovery. An individual recovers from a crisis at his or her own pace. Recovery is not linear. After a crisis, healing is a process filled with ups and downs. Depending on the traumatic event and the individual, recovery may take months or even years.

Remember anniversaries of crises. Many occasions will remind staff, students, and families about crises. The anniversary of a crisis will stimulate memories and feelings about the incident. In addition, other occasions may remind the school community about the crisis, including holidays, returning to school after vacations and other breaks, as well as events or occasions that seemingly do not have a connection with the incident. This underscores the notion that recovery may take a longer time than anticipated.

Staff members need to be sensitive to their own as well as the students' reactions in such situations and provide support when necessary. School crisis planning guides suggest holding appropriate memorial services or other activities, such as planting a tree in memory of victims of the crisis. Trauma experts discourage memorials for suicide victims to avoid glorifying and sensationalizing these deaths.

EVALUATE

Evaluating recovery efforts will help prepare for the next crisis. Use several methods to evaluate recovery efforts. Conduct brief interviews with emergency responders, families, teachers, students, and staff. Focus groups may also be helpful in obtaining candid information about recovery efforts. The following are examples of questions to ask:

- Which classroom-based interventions proved most successful and why?
- Which assessment and referral strategies were the most successful and why?
- What were the most positive aspects of staff debriefings and why?
- Which recovery strategies would you change and why?
- Do other professionals need to be tapped to help with future crises?
- What additional training is necessary to enable the school community and the community at large to prepare for future crises?

- What additional equipment is needed to support recovery efforts?
- What other planning actions will facilitate future recovery efforts?

WORKING WITH THE MEDIA

Though there are not many certainties in school crises, it is guaranteed that the media will be at the scene. Instead of being overwhelmed and threatened by the media, be prepared to work with them. The media can be a valuable asset during a crisis. In the event of a catastrophic event, the media may be your only outlet for communicating with families. However, as with all crisis planning, it is important to be proactive, not reactive. If members of the media feel that they are not getting a story, they will seek one out.

- Work with local media before a crisis occurs to make sure they understand your needs during an incident. The media can even help report on preparedness efforts—families and community members will appreciate knowing about a plan for dealing with the situation should a crisis arise.
- Designate one representative within your crisis team to deal with the media. This should be the PIO. The PIO may be the principal or another team member designated by the principal or the head of the response team. There also may be media specialists at the district level. Investigate this and make sure that the school-level representative immediately contacts the district-level media representative in the event of a crisis.
- Emphasize that only the designated representative will give information to the media. In order to be proactive, only one PIO/spokesperson should speak with the media, even if there is nothing yet available to share. It is helpful for the representative to introduce himself or herself as the spokesperson and say, "We don't have/ aren't able to release any information yet, but we will keep you updated as soon as we are able. We would really appreciate your cooperation with staying in the media staging area. I will be making all announcements from this area and will keep you informed."
- Designate a predetermined site for the media to congregate in event of a school crisis. If it is not possible to use the predetermined site that is away from students and staff, the principal or head of the command chain should designate an alternate site.
- Prepare staff to deal with the media trying to get live coverage pictures and interviews. Media personnel will often try to get on campus and interview staff and students. Make it clear to staff that they should direct media people to the media area and to the school spokesperson or PIO.
- Arrange for a joint press conference with emergency responders or choose one media representative to disseminate information to all other media outlets. This will give you some control over the content, flow, and timing of information that is released.
- Work with state and local emergency management agencies to have the Federal Aviation Administration restrict air space over your site. This will prevent helicopters flying over your school at a time of chaos. Media helicopters can be very frightening to children.

GOOD IDEAS

A three-ring binder detailing every aspect of response, complete with floor plans, facilities information, and roles and responsibilities is not the only product you'll need to be able to respond to a crisis. Teachers should have abbreviated guides, principals should have crisis response boxes, and emergency responders should have floor plans and facilities information. Some school districts have found the following products useful.

TEACHER QUICK REFERENCE GUIDES

The director of school safety in Bulloch County, Georgia, discovered that teachers found having copies of the district's safety plan inadequate for crisis response. Using the master plan, they were unable to quickly identify their roles and responsibilities in a crisis. Teachers recommended that the district develop something they could hold in their hands and quickly flip through.

At one high school, staff including teachers, nurses, and media center staff, were drafted to develop such a tool. All teachers at that school piloted their Quick Guide for one year. Overall, teachers were happy with the guide but did report some bugs. Over the summer the district-level team worked to refine the guide to address the bugs and make sure the guide contained all key information from the district-level plan. The guide is a spiral-bound notebook with plastic insert pages. The pages contain district- and school-specific information. General district procedures are on the front pages and school-specific information, such as evacuation locations for fire drills, are on the back pages. The title of each incident is at the bottom of the page so staff can quickly flip to the procedures for the situation at hand.

The Quick Guide has been designed to be a dynamic document that can be updated every year. Now all faculty members, from teachers to cafeteria workers, have a copy of the guide, and only principals and members of school safety team have the big book.

CRISIS BOXES

The California Safe Schools Task Force realized school administrators should have crisis boxes so that they will immediately have the information essential for effective management of a critical incident. They created a monograph that can be found at www.cde.ca.gov/spbranch/safety/crisismgnt/crisis.asp.

The monograph contains tips on how to organize the information that should be in the crisis response box, recommendations for who should get copies of the box, and details of what should be in the box and why. Recommended contents include the following:

- Crisis response team roster and contact information
- Student attendance rosters
- Student disposition forms and emergency data cards

- Student photos
- Special needs data
- Staff roster
- Keys
- Aerial photos of campus
- Maps of the surrounding neighborhood
- Campus layout
- Evacuation sites
- Designated command post and staging areas
- Fire alarm turn-off procedures
- Sprinkler systems turn-off procedures
- Utility shutoff valves
- Gas line and utility line layout

The guide also reminds schools of the importance of having first aid supplies easily accessible from multiple locations.

TEACHER CRISIS BAGS

Many experts recommend that each classroom be equipped with a crisis bag. These can take the form of backpacks, tote bags, or even five-gallon buckets. The contents should include the following:

- Current class roster
- Copy of emergency procedures
- First aid supplies
- Flashlight and extra batteries
- Activities for students
- Paper and pens
- Clipboard

Store teacher crisis bags in easily accessible locations.

FAMILY REUNIFICATION PLANS

Staff in Bibb County School District, Georgia, has put a lot of effort into developing the family reunification procedures that are in the district crisis plan. They have worked with the Red Cross to set up evacuation/reunification sites around the county. Not only does every school have two evacuation kits that include student rosters and emergency notification/contact cards, the district has a system-wide reunification kit. This kit includes drafts of notices that can be faxed to local media outlets with information necessary to let families know both that an evacuation has occurred and where they can collect their children. Bibb County's crisis preparations included discussions with the media on how media outlets could help distribute information in the event of a crisis. The chief of Bibb County School Police noted that the media has been very cooperative in developing these protocols.

SCHOOL SITE INFORMATION

When a crisis occurs, emergency responders will immediately need a great deal of information about your school campus. They will need to know the members of your crisis response team, how various sites can be accessed, and the location of utility shutoff valves. Many schools share this information with local police and rescue agencies during the crisis planning process. Some schools give these agencies copies of floor plans that indicate shutoff information. Some school districts compile site information for all schools on a CD-ROM and distribute copies to responders; other schools post this information on a secure Web site that responders can access from laptops at the scene. The following are two examples of how this information can be assembled.

Maryland Virtual Emergency Response System (MVERS): MVERS was developed in partnership with the Maryland State Police, the Maryland Institute for Emergency Medical Services Systems, and the Maryland Emergency Management Agency. This system can be used to prepare an electronic plan that allows quick and easy access to information in order to expedite a response to a critical situation. MVERS utilizes digital floor plans with specific icons that link the viewer to photographs, panoramic pictures, or spreadsheets containing essential data. The images can include instructions for disconnecting utilities, gaining access to a certain area, and pinpointing locations of potential hazards. The combination of floor plans and associated information provides a virtual tour of the structure's interior and exterior, allowing responders to understand the building layout prior to entering. Schools can also load contact information into MVERS. The Virtual Emergency Response System Construction Kit will provide the user with a description of the MVERS, an appendix of resources, and shareware for completing the plan. The MVERS team estimates it takes about sixty hours to collect and load all information to create the digital floor plan for each school. The bulk of this time will be spent taking and editing pictures of the buildings.

Charlotte-Mecklenburg, North Carolina, Police Virtual Tour: After an incident where there were communication glitches between school staff and police, the Charlotte-Mecklenburg Police Department realized it needed to better prepare for school crises. An officer was detailed to create Virtual Tours for each school. The Virtual Tour is a combination of the school plan and the police plan. School resource officers (SROs) develop basic crisis plans around the plans their school has already developed. The SROs identify on-scene and off-scene command posts and initial roadblocks. They also collect information on crucial players at the school and district (maintenance supervisors), bell schedules, aerial photographs of the school and surrounding community, and extensive photos of the school campus.

For each school, a master Web page contains a picture of the school and links to the crisis plan, the Virtual Tour, and aerial photos of the school and surrounding neighborhood. The tour allows emergency responders to move around the school building from the safety of a laptop as they prepare to respond to the crisis. The Virtual Tour opens with a map of the school. Users can zoom in on a door or window, click on a door and go through, walk down a hallway, look left, right, up and down, and turn around. Each screen includes an orientation map that shows where you are on the site map. The program also flags potential hazards, such as closets, windows in unusual spaces, and crawl spaces. This information is loaded on police laptops and computers and updated monthly. This material is stored on a private Web site and cannot be accessed by the public.

CONSIDERATIONS OF SPECIAL NEEDS STAFF AND STUDENTS

You must give special consideration to the unique needs of staff and students with disabilities when developing the crisis plan. Evacuation and relocation procedures will need to address mental, physical, motor, developmental, and sensory limitations. For example, individuals who use wheelchairs or other auxiliary aids will not be able to traverse the front steps of a building without substantial assistance. The following issues should be addressed:

- In some cases, individuals with disabilities may have limited mobility. In an evacuation there may not be enough time to move mobility-impaired students and staff to traditional shelters. It is important to identify alternative, accessible, safe shelter locations and to communicate these locations to emergency responders.
- Individuals with hearing disabilities may not be able to communicate verbally, to read lips, or to hear fire alarms or other emergency signals. Consider providing basic sign language training to designated school staff.
- Visual impairments might impede reading signs or traversing unfamiliar or altered terrain—consider whether debris might obstruct the evacuation of such staff and students and necessitate alternative shelter locations.
- Debris may obstruct the evacuation of individuals with mobility impairments. Be sure to assign sufficient staff to assist these individuals during a crisis or consider identifying alternative shelter locations.
- Is staff trained to assist students with developmental disabilities? These students may become upset if routine patterns of activity are disrupted.
- Do any students or staff have special needs for medicines, power supplies, or medical devices that are not likely to be available in emergency shelters? Consider what alternative arrangements can be made to provide these necessities.

In addition to addressing these concerns, find out whether specific crises will require additional considerations for hazards, such as fire, severe weather, or earthquake. For example, mobility impairments might prevent some staff or students from being able to bend over to assume the protective position recommended during tornadoes. Also, during a fire, elevators will be unavailable to transport wheelchairs. As noted earlier, it is critical to identify safe and appropriate shelter areas inside school buildings that can be reached quickly and accommodate individuals with disabilities.

STUDENT RELEASE

Student release is a crucial part of crisis planning. In all school crisis planning, the safety of the students is the main priority. During a crisis, traditional student release procedures are frequently unsafe or otherwise inoperable. Accordingly, a comprehensive crisis plan needs to include certain procedures:

- **Update student rosters.** Rosters should be updated at a minimum of twice a year; some districts recommend updating rosters weekly.
- **Distribute updated rosters.** All teachers need updated rosters of all their classes. This information should be stored in their classroom so that a substitute teacher could easily find it. A copy of all rosters should also be placed in the crisis response box, as well as with the principal and any other stakeholder as advisable. It is critical to know which students are present during a crisis.
- **Create student emergency cards.** At the beginning of the school year, make sure the school has an emergency card for each student containing contact information on parents/guardians, as well as several other adults who can be contacted if the parent or guardian is not available. The card should also indicate whether the student is permitted to leave campus with any of the adults listed on the card, if necessary. Some districts recommend authorizing one or more parents of children at your child's school to pick up your child. The card should also include all pertinent medical information, such as allergies, medications, and doctor contact information. These cards should be stored in the front office, both in hard copy and electronically, if possible.
- **Create student release forms to be used in times of crisis and store them with crisis response materials.** Create a backup plan if forms are not available.
- **Designate student release areas, as well as backup options.** These areas should be predetermined and communicated to families. If necessary, changes should be communicated through the designated channels.
- **Assign roles for staff.** For example, a staff member is needed to take the emergency cards from the office to the release area, while several staff members are needed to deal with families and sign out students. These roles should be assigned before a crisis occurs. If roles change, the principal or designated leader should assign new roles.
- **Create student release procedures.** These procedures should create a flexible, yet simple, system for the release of students. Families will want immediate access to their children; emotions will be running high. Create a system that considers this, and train staff to expect it. Procedures should require proof of identity, if necessary. Wait until such proof can be ascertained. It is important not to release a student to a non-custodial guardian if custody is an issue for the family. Do not release students to people not listed on student emergency cards. A well-intentioned friend may offer to take a child home; however, school staff must be certain that students are only released to the appropriate people so students' families will know where they are.
- **Arrange for transportation for students who are not taken home by a parent or guardian.** Also arrange for shelter and provisions, if necessary.

- **Use all communication outlets to keep families, the media, and the community informed during and after the crisis.** Signal the end of the crisis as well.

FAMILIES

Many facets of school safety planning impact families. Much of the literature on school safety planning provides guidelines for communicating with families and advice for families on how to deal with their children after a crisis. Additionally, verbatim statements from families of children attending school near the World Trade Center on September 11 provide insight into crisis planning. The following sections address the school's role in communicating with families both before and immediately following a school crisis and what families can do to facilitate their children's recovery.

- **Communicating information to families before a crisis.** Families will appreciate information on crisis preparations. It is especially useful to explain family members' roles before an incident occurs. Some school districts send families letters describing the school's expectations for their response. Other school districts have found it useful to work with local media to disseminate this information. School and district staff and emergency responders need to be able to do their jobs. Families need to know that they should rely on media outlets for information during an incident, rather than telephoning schools. It is very important that families understand that during a crisis, school phones will be needed to manage the situation. Families should also know that they should wait for instructions on student release rather than rushing to the school. It is helpful to explain to families that emergency responders need the area clear to do their job. Also explain that only after emergency responders determine that a safe student release is possible will families be reunited with their children. It is also useful to remind families that in many situations, their children will be safer in the school building than outside or in a car, particularly in cases of severe weather.
- **Communicating information to families during a crisis.** It is important to have a mechanism for communicating with families in the event of a crisis. The mode of communication could be a telephone voice recording with information about welfare of the children, evacuation sites, or release of students. Arrangements could be made with TV and radio stations to release such information. In the case of an extended crisis, such as the sniper attacks on the Washington, D.C., metropolitan area, a school official may want to write a letter to families each day of the crisis to update them on safety measures devoted to the safety of their children. Schools should be sensitive to the communities they draw upon and enlist volunteers to help communicate with families who do not speak English. It is important to acknowledge cultural differences in responding to crises.
- **Contact information for students.** Schools need contact information from families, including numbers where they can be reached during the day. In addition, each child should have several alternative contacts, such as a relative or family friend who would

be able to pick up the child in the event of an emergency. One of the backup adults should live outside of the immediate area, if possible.

GUIDELINES FOR FAMILIES IN DEALING WITH THEIR CHILDREN AFTER A CRISIS

- **Remain calm.** It is important to remain calm in the aftermath of a crisis. Children are greatly influenced by their family's sense of well-being, and anything that families can do to reassure students will be helpful. At the same time, families need to be compassionate listeners when their children speak of the crisis.
- **Attend to children's reactions.** Be alert to children's emotional needs. Individuals recover from crisis at their own pace. Many children will benefit from mental health services regardless of whether they were directly or indirectly involved in the incident.
- **Return children to normal routine as quickly as possible.** Families should adhere to the schedule of the school, and if the school remains open immediately after the aftermath of a crisis, it is important to let children return to school. Adhering to a typical routine will help children in the recovery process.
- **Refer the media to the PIO.** Undoubtedly, the media will try to interview families and children during or after a crisis. Families can make a very positive contribution to the school by referring the media to the PIO.
- **Attend community meetings.** Families will receive invaluable information and support by attending community or school meetings. Community meetings often provide information to help dispel rumors and establish mechanisms of communication with parents, the media, and other affected parties.

Mitigation and Prevention Policies and Procedures

CRIME PREVENTION

The U.S. Departments of Education and Justice report that schools are safe and secure learning environments (Kaufman, P., et al., Indicators of School Crime and Safety, 2000, U.S. Department of Education [NCES 2001–017]), and this is borne out by the most recent published findings of the School Survey on Crime and Safety, which analyzed data gathered during 2003–2004 (SSOCS, 2004). Developed by the National Center for Education Statistics (NCES) and supported by the Office of Safe and Drug-Free Schools, SSOCS asks public school principals about the frequency of criminal incidents in their schools, such as physical attacks, robberies, and thefts.

The main findings are:

- High schools (96 percent) and middle schools (94 percent) were more likely than primary schools (74 percent) to report violent incidents of crime. High schools were no different than middle schools in the percentage reporting violent incidents of crime.

- High schools (44 percent) were more likely to report that students were distributing illegal drugs at school than were middle schools (27 percent) or primary schools (1 percent).
- Middle schools (42 percent) were more likely than high schools (21 percent) and primary schools (24 percent) to report that student bullying occurs at least once a week at school.
- Of the disciplinary actions administered for use or possession of a weapon other than a firearm, the percentage of out-of-school suspensions lasting five or more days but less than the remainder of the school year (37 percent) was no different from the percentage of other disciplinary actions (36 percent). Both out-of-school suspensions and other disciplinary actions were used more often than were removals with no continuing services for at least the remainder of the school year (5 percent) and transfers to specialized schools (23 percent).
- Schools with 1,000 or more students (24 percent) were less likely to have 76 to 100 percent of students with a parent or guardian who attended an open house or back-to school night than were schools with fewer than 300 students (48 percent), schools with 300 to 499 students (49 percent), or schools with 500 to 999 students (43 percent).
- City schools (95 percent) were more likely than rural schools (89 percent) to use student-to-student or adult-to-student methods of violence prevention, such as individual attention, mentoring, tutoring, or coaching of students.
- The percentage of schools that drilled students on an existing written plan for school shootings (47 percent) was lower than the percentage of schools that drilled students on an existing written plan for natural disasters (84 percent).
- Among factors that were reported to limit schools' efforts to reduce crime in a major way, three factors were more likely to be reported than others: a lack of or inadequate alternative placements or programs for disruptive students (24 percent); inadequate funds (22 percent); and federal, state, or district policies on disciplining special education students (16 percent).

STUDENT-LED CRIME PREVENTION

In the autumn of 1997, a Mississippi high school student member of a crime prevention program that encourages anonymous reporting alerted his adviser to the fact that an armed student was coming to campus intending to shoot someone. The armed student was apprehended, no one was harmed, and a potential tragedy was averted.

Student-led crime prevention can help make schools and surrounding communities safer. The concept, increasingly popular around the nation, is simple: young people given the opportunity to take the lead in making their schools safer will benefit both the school and themselves. They also strengthen the social bonds that are essential to their healthy growth as members of the larger community.

Middle school students in Iowa involved in a school-based crime prevention program decided to teach elementary school students crime prevention tips to make them safer. In addition to helping their younger colleagues, the middle school students themselves became more involved in school activities and were better students.

Elementary school students trained as playground mediators in California have greatly reduced the amount of time that administrators and faculty spend on school disputes, as well as the number of fights between students.

A report by the U.S. Department of Education's Office of Elementary and Secondary Education entitled "Crime Prevention—A Real Resource With Powerful Promise," provides examples of student-led crime prevention, outlines its variations, and describes key steps for bringing it to schools.

It has to be stated that schools are still predominantly safe places,[1] and students are about two times as likely to be victims of serious violent crime away from school as at school. However, just because young people are less likely to be victimized by crime in school does not mean that schools are crime free. Recent tragedies have raised awareness that no community can be complacent. For years, we have known that America's youths are disproportionately both victims and offenders, and that this vulnerability extends inside the schoolhouse doors.

- According to recent studies, students are victims of over one million nonfatal violent crimes each year.
- Theft is the most common crime in schools, and students are generally more likely to be victims of theft at school than in the community.
- A report in 1999 found that about 15 percent of all students in grades 9 through 12 said that they had been in a physical fight on school property in the prior twelve months. In that same year, 37 percent reported that they had been in a physical fight in any location (including on school property).[2]
- One-quarter to one-third of students report being offered drugs while at school.[3]

The challenges of dealing with crime and violence are not limited to middle and secondary schools. Though statistics are not readily available for elementary-age youths, we do know that certain behaviors (e.g., bullying, fighting, harassing, disrespecting property), as well as being victimized may predict future delinquent behavior. Several studies, for example, suggest that bullying in early childhood may be an early sign for developing violent tendencies and criminality.[4]

The presence of crime in schools and the community plays a real and damaging role in the lives of many youths. Nearly half of students change their daily routine because of the fear of violence at school or in the community.[5] As many as four in ten teenagers thought that at some point during their lifetimes someone would fire a gun at them.[6]

Crime, violence, and drugs are consistently at the top of teen concerns in national polls.[7] The good news is that, in many communities, students have worked in leadership roles, as well as in partnership with adults, to reclaim schools, parks, playgrounds, and streets. Their energy, idealism, vitality, and commitment have proved worthy antidotes to crime and its consequences. Young people may represent one of our greatest resources in making schools safer, according to some studies, in which, for example:

- Teenagers were more likely to volunteer than any other age group; more than one out of three teenagers and six out of ten volunteers started volunteering by the age of fourteen; over half of teen volunteers got involved with volunteering through school or religious institutions.[8]

- Seven out of ten young people saw themselves as capable of making positive changes in their communities; almost nine out of ten young people could name specific steps that should be taken to reduce violence among their peers and in the community.[9]
- Nearly nine in ten teens said they would volunteer for one or more kinds of activities that help prevent crime.[10]

Student-led crime prevention provides a vehicle to actively engage young people in the life of the school community, to ask for their help and guidance, and to offer them the same. It allows those close to the crime problem a means of action.

Asking students to become part of the solution is an important step toward safe and crime-free schools. The most obvious benefit of doing so is that students provide an available resource in that work. Less obvious, but no less important a benefit is that involving students builds partnership and teamwork skills, provides nontraditional roles for leadership, engages a wide range of students, and enlists students in setting and sustaining positive behavioral norms.

WHAT IS STUDENT-LED CRIME PREVENTION?

Crime prevention involves both reducing opportunities for crime to occur and addressing causes of crime. According to the Crime Prevention Coalition of America, crime prevention is about adopting a pattern of attitudes and behaviors that reduce the threat of crime to individuals and communities and enhance their sense of safety and security. Both actual crime rates and fear of crime must be addressed; criminologists have amply documented the independent influence of these factors. Social ills, such as poverty, racism, neighborhood disorganization, and youth alienation, are all part of the equation that yields crime-ridden and dangerous neighborhoods. Because crime has many causes, the arena for meaningful preventative action is large. Crime prevention initiatives can tackle issues as diverse as substance abuse, violence, vandalism, neighborhood environment, gang activity, and the participation of citizens in neighborhood organizations. Ultimately, crime prevention seeks to positively influence the quality of living and learning and helps to develop schools and communities in which crime will not flourish.

What does "student-led" add to this picture?

Student-led crime prevention means that:

- Students have real opportunities to develop, organize, and execute crime prevention programs and projects.
- Students hold appropriate responsibility and accountability for activities, but school officials' responsibilities are acknowledged and respected.
- School officials, teachers, and community members view students as collaborators and partners in school safety.
- Crime prevention and a student's role in it are viewed as an opportunity to create synergy with other strategies designed to ensure that schools are responsive to all children.

A number of independent evaluations of school-based prevention programs have shown them to have great promise.

- A curriculum-based crime prevention program involving secondary school student leadership was shown to increase students' sense of social responsibility, as well as their crime prevention knowledge.[1]
- A study of peer mediation efforts in California showed that the implementation of these efforts reduced by one-third the amount of time that administrators spent helping to resolve student conflicts.[2]
- A study of a bullying prevention program for elementary and junior high school children (in several countries including the United States) showed substantial reductions in the frequency with which students reported being bullied or bullying others.[3]
- Engaging students in structured problem solving of crime issues in their schools helped to reduce fighting among students, victimization of teachers, and fear for personal safety, compared to a similar school where students were not so trained.[4]
- A conflict resolution program focusing on empowering students to take leadership roles in resolving conflicts demonstrated positive changes in classroom climate, moderate to significant decreases in physical violence in the classroom, and reduced name-calling and verbal insults.[5]

In short, evaluations confirm that the right prevention program implemented with fidelity and incorporated into a comprehensive prevention strategy can have a real and positive impact on the safety and efficacy of a school.[6]

At its core, student-led crime prevention is about youth-adult collaboration and trusting the capacities of young people to make a real difference in an area important to them—the safety and security of themselves, their friends, their school, and their community. The actions may vary by age, by jurisdiction, and by circumstance. But the purposes are consistent:

- To reduce or prevent crime
- To engage students as active leaders in the process
- To develop pervasive support in the school community for crime prevention
- To engage adults in partnership with youth
- To enhance the sense of community in the school

High school students might volunteer with prevention programs in collaboration with school security officers to patrol hallways; middle school students might organize a forum to give students a chance to air concerns about safety; elementary school students might develop a skit that teaches their peers the importance of avoiding strangers.

Student-led crime prevention cultivates a sense of shared mission between youths and adults, a sense that can be important for conducting other school activities. According to the Hawkins and Weis social development model, meaningful participation in activities is one of the foundations upon which the elements of the social bond, that is, attachment, commitment, and belief, are generated, reinforced, and maintained.[7]

Though student-led crime prevention encourages youths to collaborate with school administrators and other community leaders, adults retain the ultimate responsibility to both higher authorities and the public for the safety of the schools.

WHY IS A SCHOOL-BASED PROGRAM SO IMPORTANT?

According to Denise Gottfredson, a University of Maryland criminologist who is among the nation's leading researchers on school crime prevention, schools have great potential as a locus for crime prevention. They provide regular access to students throughout the developmental years, and perhaps the only consistent access to large numbers of the most crime-prone young children in the early school years; they are staffed with individuals paid to help youths develop as healthy, happy, productive citizens; and the community usually supports schools' efforts to socialize youth. Many of the precursors of delinquent behavior are school-related and, therefore, likely to be amenable to change through school-based interventions.[8]

Preventing crime and promoting civil and law-abiding behavior have to be paramount goals of educators to ensure both an effective learning environment and the civic development of our youths, with which our schools are charged.

WHY THE NEED FOR SCHOOL-BASED CRIME PREVENTION?

- Schooling is a central experience in the lives of young people.
- A young person's interactions in school may significantly affect how he or she relates to peers, family members, or future employees.
- Classroom disruptions, truancy, violence, and vandalism can all compromise the efficacy of the education experience.
- School-related variables are among the strongest predictors of delinquent behavior in students.[9]
- School is one of the only formal institutions through which society can address a wide range of youths on youth-focused problems related to crime, including substance abuse, youth employment, peer and family relations, violent behavior, and truancy.[10]

ORGANIZATIONAL FRAMEWORKS

School based, student-led crime prevention can take place in a curricular, co-curricular, or extracurricular context. Curriculum-based efforts may have their origins in virtually any discipline, ranging from health to economics, although they most often relate to civics, social studies, government, or law-related education efforts in middle and high school environments. Curricular student-led crime prevention programs often take place in the classroom, where students are given the opportunity to present text material, to identify and recruit resource persons to share their expertise, and to lead classroom discussions.

Though some curricular programs emphasize instruction, others encourage students to plan their own crime prevention program or projects, usually drawn from subjects in the curriculum. These crime prevention initiatives, carried out by students, meet the needs of school, neighborhood, or community.

Middle school students may teach elementary school children tips on street safety. High school students may educate their peers on preventing and reporting date rape and sexual assault. Elementary school students may work with older residents on a neighborhood cleanup.

Community service and service-learning curricula also provide a venue for crime prevention efforts. In some schools, for example, community service credit is provided for such crime prevention activities as patrols or peer mediation centers.

Co-curricular and extracurricular programs, like curricular programs, are sanctioned and supported by a school. They may or may not possess the instructional features associated with curricular models.

Co-curricular models take place during school hours but are not part of the official school curriculum. Student patrols during school hours, a student council–organized crime prevention assembly, or student development and administration of an anonymous crime reporting system are all examples of co-curricular activity.

Extracurricular models take place outside regular school hours. Their focus can range widely.

Consider the following, for example: an after-school club may meet regularly and work to prevent drunk driving; students may organize and participate in a march against crime or attend a candlelight vigil; elementary school children may develop a bus safety program.

Various organizational settings may serve as the base for student-led crime prevention activities:

- A group focusing on an issue, such as stopping drunk driving, helping peers in crisis, or stopping bullying
- A regularly scheduled activity such as crime prevention announcements over the public address system each morning
- Part of an initiative of a school organization that has another principal interest, such as drama, public speaking, art, or writing
- A leadership project, such as a special committee of the student council
- A project as part of a regularly scheduled class, for example, health, social studies, business, or English

As with all school activities, it is important that crime prevention initiatives have home bases—that they be seen and valued as part of the school's core activity. Having an established, recognized position provides a sense of identity and a structure for the development of leaders, materials, and resources.

Finally, although these programs are connected to the school, their activities need not be limited to the school campus. Students may extend their activities to work on problems shared by the school and the neighborhood or to address a community-wide problem of concern to students. This extension may help students to recognize the links between the school and the community.

Student-led crime prevention benefits the school, the students, and the larger community.

Benefits may be immediate, such as making a particular location safer, as well as long-term, such as making crime prevention a behavioral norm.

The School: Student-led crime prevention can:

- Reduce student and staff victimization
- Reduce rule violations as well as law breaking
- Reduce fear of crime
- Help establish anticrime, pro-safety, pro-community norms among students
- Enlist the entire school community in helping to "produce" safety
- Offer multiple levels and avenues for participation in school life by diverse groups of students
- Leverage student knowledge of community situations and events that could pose a danger
- Promote positive behavior
- Develop new resources to address specific problems or concerns
- Engage students as active participants in the school's safety plan
- Help to identify issues and concerns before they become major problems
- Develop closer adult-student relationships
- Provide real-life applications for many concepts taught in the classroom
- Provide a new base for school-community links
- Develop the community's appreciation for the school and its students
- Decrease the community's fear of students
- Provide a positive means through which community members may support the school's safety and security
- Develop student leadership skills as a community resource

The Students: Student-led crime prevention can:

- Help students feel safer at school
- Give students opportunities to make decisions that improve their learning conditions
- Help students apply and be recognized for talents used in the programs
- Link instructional content to real-life issues
- Enable students to learn skills that may benefit them as adults
- Reinforce acceptable student behavior through peer expectations and support
- Give students who face major crime issues outside of school an opportunity for positive control and achievement

THE SIX Rs OF EFFECTIVE YOUTH CRIME PREVENTION PROGRAMMING

In order to reap the benefits of student-led crime prevention, it is important to adhere to the principles that underlie effectiveness. These may be stated as the six Rs.[1]

Roles

Students and adults should have clear and clearly understood roles. They must understand how these roles support and enhance each other. Roles for students must be substantive and should include key planning and leadership tasks. A school administration's sanction and support are instrumental to the implementation of a successful crime prevention initiative. Students, teachers, parents, law enforcement officials, and the school administration all have roles to play in building and sustaining an effective student-led crime prevention effort.

Responsibilities

The responsibilities of youths and adults must be well mapped out, and youths must perceive that they have meaningful levels of responsibility and authority (directly or implicitly). Youths should be responsible for reflecting upon and constructively correcting their own efforts and the overall project or program.

Relationships

Student-led crime prevention is most effective when it generates a positive web of relationships:

- Between students, between adults, and between students and adults
- Between people and institutions that can be strengthened (e.g., between students and the police)
- Between institutions that can be strengthened (e.g., between the school and the community's social service network)

Rewards

Rewards do not have to be cash. An appreciation party with pizza or cake, a certificate, or some other sincere acknowledgment can suffice. Whichever way it is done, youths and adults need recognition for their positive efforts. Beyond the thanks to each participant, rewards can include the results themselves—less fear, safer schools, and the like.

Respect

Respect is a two-way street. Youths must respect adults and adults must respect youths, including their ideas and their work. Respecting students entails recognizing their differences, realizing that each child is unique and acknowledging each student's power to contribute. Former British Prime Minister Tony Blair reminded us, "Everyone has talent, everyone has something to offer, and . . . we owe it to every child to unleash their potential."[2] Dr. Martin Luther King, Jr., once said, "Everyone can be great because everyone can serve."[3]

Reaching Out

Crime prevention activities can link people, places, and institutions to the common goal of safer schools and communities. They can help students connect with the neighborhood or larger community. Collaborations with those at the local or even state and national levels can give students a broader context for their studies and lives. Law enforcement officers can share their experience, business leaders can provide information and resources, national organizations can offer training and expertise, the prosecutor's office can provide training, community organizations can provide support for projects, restaurants can provide food for recognition events, and teachers and administrators can stay connected with students throughout these activities. The list of potential collaborators is virtually endless.

PUTTING PRINCIPLES INTO ACTION

Here are some examples of concrete ways to make student-led crime prevention a part of the school environment.

School administrators can:

- Set policies through which students can exercise leadership.
- Ensure that students are educated about crime prevention throughout their school experience.
- Set clear rules and expectations about student behaviors, with input from students themselves.
- Provide resources (space, materials, money, adult support).
- Be accessible to students and listen thoughtfully to their needs.
- Create open discussion and establish among staff a high level of respect and trust for students.
- Gain the trust and respect of students, especially in light of the need to protect anonymity where necessary.
- Place students on school decision-making bodies.
- Recognize individual and collective achievement.
- Insist that faculty, staff, and students treat each other with respect, courtesy, and thoughtfulness.

Teachers can:

- Integrate crime prevention concepts and activities involving students in the classroom.
- Support and sponsor co-curricular and extracurricular activities that emphasize student leadership in prevention.
- Set norms for behavior in the classroom with help from students.
- Encourage crime reporting.

Students can:

- Identify crime and disorder problems in and around their schools.
- Research prevention strategies to help address these problems.
- Design programs and projects to implement the strategies.
- Develop prevention education programs for peers and others.
- Use artistic, performance, and other talents to deliver prevention messages.

Parents can:

- Value and welcome the efforts of students implementing crime prevention activities.
- Support student-led crime prevention activities.
- Collaborate with students.
- Support the discipline code of the school.
- Provide resources (money, leadership, expertise, training).
- Take an active interest in school; talk regularly with teachers and staff; volunteer in a classroom or in after-school activities; collaborate with parent-teacher organizations.
- Help children learn how to find constructive solutions to problems.
- Discourage name-calling and teasing.

The community can:

- Provide space, adult support, expertise, time, information, training, and sometimes security.
- Adopt a school and/or sponsor a student-led crime prevention activity.
- Help to strengthen links between the school and the community.
- Support or sponsor competitions including speech, dance, drawing, music, and other forms of expression focused on crime prevention.

TEN STRATEGIES FOR STUDENTS (AND EXAMPLES OF ACTIVITIES)

1. Report crime and help to make crime reporting a school norm (establish a school reporting system).
2. Help other students with problems (set up a hotline, develop a peer counseling program).
3. Keep the campus physically safe (establish youth patrols or identify to the administration problem areas that need attention).
4. Incorporate crime prevention into existing school clubs or activities (place in such organizations as student council, drama club, art club).
5. Set consequences for violation of school rules or laws (establish a teen court, work to give students a voice in codes of conduct and disciplinary procedures).
6. Help resolve conflict fairly and without violence (establish peer mediation programs, provide conflict mediation/resolution training for all students).

7. Unify the student body by respecting differences and working together (hold town meetings to ensure that everyone's voice is heard, survey students to ensure their concerns are being met).
8. Educate peers and younger youths about prevention issues (establish a cross-age teaching program, encourage the use of cross-age teaching through existing school institutions, develop education programs for peers).
9. Partner with adults to conduct projects (provide presentations).
10. Use problem-solving teams (respond to specific problems, e.g., vandalism in the locker room, tension among student groups).

GETTING UNDER WAY

There is no single formula for all the ways that student-led crime prevention can be brought into your school.

Assess the Opportunities

Look at conditions in and around your school that might offer opportunities for student-led crime prevention.

- What kinds of crime prevention problems do you and the students see?
- What crime-related issues generate fear or concern among students, teachers, or staff?
- What student-led activities are already in place in your school?
- What neighborhood problems or situations affect students and staff?
- What kind of support exists from the school system? What kind of opposition?
- What kinds of student interest and concern are there with respect to crime?
- What signs suggest that students may be prepared to take action on crime-related problems?

Identify Adult Allies in the School and Community

Even with the multitude of benefits offered by student-led crime prevention, when bringing a new concept into a school, students can use all the adult support they can get. Adults should be program and project sponsors, and they should be available for students to tap into their relevant expertise. Consider reaching out to:

- School administrators, teachers, and other faculty
- Local law enforcement chiefs and officers
- Community-based organizations, including faith-based organizations
- Health, maintenance, and security staff
- Victim assistance agencies
- The local Chamber of Commerce
- Youth-serving organizations

Select a Starting Framework

You may decide to change the program's framework as your school gains experience, but it is necessary to start somewhere. There are four structural aspects of selection to consider:

Position

Curricular
Co-curricular
Extracurricular

Base

All students
Student leadership
New student organization

Scope

Individual projects
Long-term programs

Sponsorship

Single sponsor
Multiple sponsors

Recruit Local Resources

Student-led crime prevention activity can benefit from adult support, especially if that support can help students succeed. Often overlooked but valuable local resources include, but are not limited to:

School security staff
School resource officers
School health staff
Parents
Local crime prevention officers
Guidance counselors
Probation officers
Students from other schools

A major local resource, nationally generated, is the U.S. Department of Education's Office of Safe and Drug-Free Schools and the funds that it makes available to local schools. Other locally accessible national resources include:

Web sites that are invaluable and getting better
Conferences, especially those that involve both youth and adults
National organizations that work with youths and/or focus on crime prevention

PERMISSIONS, LIMITATIONS, AND LIABILITIES

It is necessary to review and secure permission or approval from school system personnel for student-led crime prevention activities. Parental permission may be required either as a general policy or for specific (usually off-site) activities.

Limitations on the program may be needed or desired for one or more reasons:

- Student safety: students should never be put into a position where they will have to confront or detain suspected criminals, whether those suspects are fellow students or strangers to the campus. This must be left to trained adults, preferably to law enforcement officials.
- Lack of training: student projects or programs should not put young people in the position of providing services that they are not qualified to offer. Counseling of victims, mediation of disputes, and counseling of peers are examples of work for which special training is needed.
- School policies: these may restrict when and where students may carry out projects in which students may take part, or what school resources may be used.
- Liability: liability issues have not been a problem in well-designed programs and projects where appropriate supervision is provided that are also consonant with student leadership.

GOALS, OBJECTIVES, AND EVALUATION

Regardless of the project or program structure, both the school program and programs or projects designed by students should have a goal or goals. Each goal should have clear, measurable objectives. The objectives form a framework for a simple but useful evaluation of the activity. Taking on these tasks offers an excellent opportunity for students to learn effective management techniques.

TRAINING AND TECHNICAL ASSISTANCE

Crime prevention information and skills are vital to effective student-led efforts. The local police department and sheriff's office are the strongest partners in your community both for training and for referrals to other training resources. However, it is important to tap into other resources, such as victim service agencies, community mediation services, local prosecutors' offices, social services providers, school security staff, and those who can teach public speaking and other skills.

CHALLENGES TO IMPLEMENTING
STUDENT-LED CRIME PREVENTION

Breaking the Ice

The first students to engage in crime prevention may need extra support for their efforts. They may have an idea for a prevention project but be reluctant to undertake it; they may have the desire to fix a problem, but lack the training, skills, or resources to do so. Here are a few strategies for helping to build a foundation for future leaders:

- Provide youths crime prevention examples from elsewhere for inspiration.
- Send students and their adult advisers outside their usual environment for a planning retreat or a relevant conference, which can break the ice, as well as build enthusiasm.
- Encourage students to select initial activities that are realistic and visible.
- Provide youths leadership training and/or crime prevention training.

FINDING AND ENLISTING THE RIGHT CHAMPION

Fostering student-led crime prevention does not imply reduced adult commitment or energy for school safety. Rather, it means more adult attention to working with youths and their issues. Finding the right adult champion who understands the potential of the program and the commitment it requires can spell the difference between a successful and an unsuccessful program.

An adult champion must believe in the value of youths' contributions, must be able to share enough authority and decision-making power for youths to exercise real influence, must have the character and communication skills to be a role model, and must be willing to take the time to make the extra effort needed to support the program, including acquiring crime prevention skills and resources if needed. An adult sponsor may need release time from classroom responsibilities, opportunities to learn more about prevention, or less tangible forms of support, such as continued encouragement and validation.

SUSTAINING THE PREVENTION EFFORT

There is an ever-present need to sustain and advance the efforts driven by those who lead the prevention effort for a very limited time. Here are a few suggestions to accomplish this.

- Consider continuing your crime prevention organization with an adult champion, someone who is recognized and valued by the administration and students alike and who has a proven record of success.
- Provide opportunities for ongoing peer recruitment and encourage continued promotion of activities.
- Ensure that incoming teachers and administrative staff know about the program's value.

- Nurture constant expectations (e.g., the tradition of student patrols, alcohol-free prom parties, crime prevention awareness weeks, etc.), but provide sufficient flexibility for students to direct the program.
- Continually and consistently educate all students about crime prevention so that the entire student body recognizes its value and values the students who lead it.

NOT ENOUGH RESOURCES

Student-led crime prevention initiatives cost surprisingly little. Prevention is principally about changing the way people think and act, such that activities are usually more human resource driven than money driven.

Raising the resources to meet your program's needs requires creativity, persistence, and a firm belief in the mission of the program, as well as its potential to create real change.

- Involve students in the planning and development of your program. Doing so will help to motivate them to find whatever resources are necessary.
- Develop a clear and compelling vision that states why the project should be done.

REACHING YOUNGER STUDENTS

Do not overlook the potential for crime prevention initiatives by elementary school students. They can do a lot. Bus and hallway patrols can help maintain order. Peer mediators can help settle disputes before they become fights. Skits and role-plays can educate peers. Involving elementary school students requires careful planning and additional guidance. Here are a few things to keep in mind:

- Motivation in this age group is strong. Often, they will have specific concerns for their safety, as well as ideas about how to deal with those concerns. Tap those resources.
- An adult-led, age-appropriate school-wide prevention education program can be a good way to introduce the concepts and practices of prevention.
- Planning carefully what students can do and providing good guidance about school priorities and crime reporting will help younger children act within the limits of their capacities and power.

Model Approaches to Student-led Crime Prevention

Student-led crime prevention programs vary a great deal with respect to the age of the students involved, their comprehensiveness, and the approaches that they take. It is important to recognize, however, that anyone or any group can work to address crime concerns in the school and community. Key Club members might work to refine the disciplinary code; the community service club may reach out to teach younger children about safety; a group of students may simply get together and work with the faculty to reduce school vandalism; an individual student may produce and distribute brochures linking students to valuable community resources.

Here are brief descriptions of school-based, student-led crime prevention programs from around the country. These programs share proven records of effectiveness, innovation, and a commitment to the development of positive social skills.

YOUTH CRIME WATCH OF AMERICA

Youth Crime Watch of America (YCWA) has more than 1,200 school sites in thirty-five U.S. states, the District of Columbia, Guam, and Brazil. The program, active in primary and secondary schools (ages five to eighteen), seeks to bring together youths of all backgrounds to identify and correct problems unique to their schools and communities. The YCWA program aims to build positive values, good citizenship, and self-esteem, and empowers youths to take an active leadership role in addressing the problems around them.

YCWA assists students in developing youth-led programs through nine components: crime reporting; youth patrols; drug, violence, and crime prevention education; bus safety; mentoring; conflict resolution; mediation; peer and cross-age teaching; and action projects. These nine components overlap, are linked, and provide a framework for structuring a youth-led crime prevention initiative within a school or community in which the youths can take ownership of their own program. A core group of students, usually five to fifteen in number, directs the program with guidance from an adult adviser.

Many program sites have shown great success. For example, crime dropped a reported 40.5 percent in YCWA's first year at Braddock High School in Dade County, Florida (the largest school in Florida, with over five thousand students). Between 1994 and 1997 the number of incidents of disruptive behavior dropped by 38 percent, narcotics possession dropped 31 percent, and the number of fights declined by 39 percent.[1] YCWA also produces positive outcomes related to delinquency prevention, safer schools, and healthy social development. A third-party evaluation of YCWA in fifteen Florida middle and high schools in the spring of 2000 found that an overwhelming majority of the students surveyed felt that YCWA was mostly or totally run by the students; well over half of the surveyed students reported an above average or extremely close relationship with other YCWA members; 100 percent reported that they made new friends as a result of YCWA; 92 percent reported that YCWA members totally or mostly look out for one another; and nine out of ten felt that YCWA helped improve student relationships with police officers.[2]

STUDENTS AGAINST VIOLENCE EVERYWHERE

In 1989, a high school student in North Carolina was shot and killed while breaking up a fight at a Friday night party. His classmates responded by forming Students Against Violence Everywhere (SAVE). Since then, SAVE has spread to locations across the United States and abroad. As of 2000, there were 957 local SAVE chapters in 35 states and Canada, with more than 89,000 registered SAVE members.

SAVE is a club-based program in middle and high schools. At the elementary school level, SAVE lessons are taught in the classroom. Students, who are responsible for the scope and focus of the program, direct each school. While features vary from chapter to chapter the key to the program is that it is student initiated and student run. S.A.V.E. members work to stop violence before it starts through the promotion of non-violence in the school and community.

Chapter meetings revolve around educating students about violence, its causes, and its consequences. They learn about alternatives to violence, and practice what they learn through school and community service projects. As they participate in SAVE activities, students learn conflict management and mediation skills and the virtues of good citizenship, civility, and nonviolence.

TEENS, CRIME, AND THE COMMUNITY

Teens, Crime, and the Community (TCC), a collaborative effort of the Office of Juvenile Justice and Delinquency Prevention, the National Crime Prevention Council, and Street Law, has grown since 1987 into a large-scale effort leveraging state and local partnerships toward making teens safer and giving them a positive stake in their communities. As of 1999, 500,000 youths in more than 40 states have participated in TCC. As of 1999, 73 percent of the TCC programs were in schools, 14 percent were in juvenile justice settings, and the remaining 13 percent were in community-based sites.

The TCC model combines education and action to reduce teen victimization and seeks to engage the strengths of young people, educating them and providing the opportunity for them to serve their communities. One cornerstone of the TCC program is the TCC curriculum used in grades 6 through 12. The TCC curriculum, which can be used independently or infused into such courses as law-related education, civics, social studies, health, or contemporary issues, focuses on building understanding of crime, crime prevention, victimization, specific crime prevention strategies, and juvenile justice issues.

In one of several independent evaluations, researchers compared TCC program students and control students in pre- and post-test evaluations in ten Iowa schools. The evaluators concluded that TCC appeared to have an impact on students' belief in ethical rules, associations with delinquent peers, self-reported delinquency, and altruism. Results also indicated that students in the program group demonstrated an increased belief in the need for laws. A 1997 study demonstrated that the increase in social responsibility of participating students was statistically significant in five of the seven categories, compared with a control group.[3]

STUDENTS AGAINST DRIVING DRUNK/STUDENTS AGAINST DESTRUCTIVE DECISIONS

Students at Wayland High School, in Wayland, Mass., founded Students Against Driving Drunk (SADD) in 1981 after two high school hockey players were killed in separate alcohol-related car crashes one week apart. In 1997, that mission expanded, with the acronym SADD now representing Students Against Destructive Decisions. The core of SADD, then and now, is the Contract for Life in which students pledge to make responsible decisions and avoid the perils of drunk driving. SADD is a chapter-based, youth-led prevention model with about ten thousand chapters in middle schools, high schools, and colleges representing 5 million students in all fifty states. SADD chapter members engage in school and community activities and campaigns responsive to the needs of their particular locations. Projects may include peer-led classes and theme-focused forums, teen workshops, conferences, rallies, prevention education, leadership training, or awareness-raising activities. SADD reports that independent studies show that students in schools with an established SADD chapter are more aware and informed about the risks of underage drinking, other drug use, and impaired driving than those in schools without SADD. Students in schools with a SADD chapter are more likely to hold attitudes reflecting positive reasons not to use alcohol.

SADD continues to endorse a firm "no use" message about alcohol and other drugs, and its signature product—the Contract for Life—has expanded to include communication between young people and adult caregivers on important issues. With its expanded focus, SADD now highlights prevention of all destructive behaviors and attitudes young people face, including underage drinking, substance abuse, impaired driving, violence, and suicide.

Notes

EXECUTIVE SUMMARY

1. Kaufman, P., Chen, X., Choy, S.P., Ruddy, S., Miller, A., Fleury, J., Chandler, K., Rand, M., Klaus, P., Planty, M. *Indicators of School Crime and Safety, 2000.* Washington, D.C.: U.S. Departments of Education and Justice. NCES 2001–017/NCJ-184176, 2000.

2. Ibid., p. 11.

3. Kann, L., et al. "Youth Risk Behavior Surveillance." *Morbidity and Morality Weekly* Report 47 (1997): SS-3.

4. Olweus, D. "Victimization by Peers: Antecedents and Long-Term Outcomes." In *Social Withdrawal, Inhibition, and Shyness.* Ed. K.H. Rubin, D.H. Crowell, I.M. Evans, and C.R. O'Donnell. New York: Plenum, 1987, pp. 249–262.

5. Louis Harris and Associates. *Between Hope and Fear: Teens Speak Out on Crime and the Community.* Washington, D.C.: National Crime Prevention Council and The National Institute for Citizen Education in the Law, 1996, p. 9.

6. *Youthviews: The Newsletter of the Gallup Youth Survey.* Vol. 4, no. 10. Princeton, N.J.: George H. Gallup International Institute, 1997.

7. Louis Harris and Associates, *Between Hope and Fear,* p. 11.

8. *America's Teenage Volunteers.* Ed. M. Hamilton and A. Hussain. Washington, D.C.: Independent Sector, 1998, pp. 2–3.

9. National Crime Prevention Council. *Are We Safe? Focus on Teens: The 2001 National Crime Prevention Survey.* Washington, D.C.: National Crime Prevention Council, 2002.

10. Louis Harris and Associates, *Between Hope and Fear,* pp. 8–9.

WHAT IS STUDENT-LED CRIME PREVENTION?

1. Hwalek, M., et al. (SPEC Associates of Detroit). *Teens, Crime, and Community: National Outcomes Study on Social Responsibility.* Washington, D.C.: National Crime Prevention Council, 1999.

2. Harder and Company Community Research. *Whole School Conflict Resolution Project: A Joint Project of San Francisco Peer Resources and The Community Board Program* (Evaluation Report, Year Three of Project). San Francisco, Calif.: The Community Board Program, August 1997, p. 36.

3. Olweus, D. "Bullying Among School Children: Intervention and Prevention." In *Aggression and Violence Throughout the Life Span.* Ed. R.D. Peters, R.J. McMahon, and V.L. Quinsey. Newbury Park, Calif.: Sage Publications, 1992, pp.100–125.

4. Kenney, D.J., and Watson, T.S. *Crime in the Schools: Reducing Conflict With Student Problem Solving.* Washington, D.C.: National Institute of Justice Research in Brief, NCJ 177618, 1999.

5. Schneider, S.J. *Resolving Conflict Creatively Program: 1988–89 Summary of Significant Findings.* New York: Metis Associates, 1990.

6. Olweus, D. "Bullying Among School Children," pp. 100–125.

7. Developmental Research and Programs, Inc. *Communities That Care: Risk-Focused Prevention Using the Social Development Strategy: An Approach to Reducing Adolescent Problem Behaviors.* Seattle, Wash.: DPR, 1993, pp.12–13. Student-led Crime Prev. Booklet 1/22/03 2:17 PM Page 45.

8. Gottfredson, Denise. "School-Based Crime Prevention." In *Preventing Crime: What Works, What Doesn't, What's Promising.* Ed. D. Mackenzie, P. Reuter, and L.W. Sherman. Washington, D.C.: Office of Justice Programs (U.S. Department of Justice) Research Report NCJ 165366, 1997, p. 1.

9. Elliott, D.S., and Voss, H. *Delinquency and Dropout.* Lexington, Mass.: Lexington Books, 1974, pp. 36, 63–103, 169–171.

10. Hawkins, J.D., and Weis, J. *The Social Development Model: An Integrated Approach to Delinquency Prevention.* Washington, D.C.: National Institute of Justice, 1980.

THE SIX Rs OF EFFECTIVE YOUTH CRIME PREVENTION PROGRAMMING

1. Adapted from "Four Rs in Making A Difference." Washington, D.C.: National Crime Prevention Council, 1985.

2. Tony Blair speaking at the Labour Party Conference, September 28, 1999, Bournemouth UK.

3. Martin Luther King, Jr., speech, April 4, 1967.

MODEL APPROACHES TO STUDENT-LED CRIME PREVENTION

1. Youth Crime Watch of America. *Site Profiles and Individual Success Stories.* Miami: Youth Crime Watch of America, 2000.

2. Lynch, C.O., Essenmacher, V., and Hwalek, M. *Youth Crime Watch of America Florida Outcomes Report.* Detroit: SPEC Associates, 2000, p. iii.

3. Hwalek, M., et al. (SPEC Associates of Detroit, Mich.). *Teens, Crime, and Community: National Outcomes Study on Social Responsibility.* Washington, D.C.: National Crime Prevention Council, 1999. Student-led Crime Prev. Booklet 1/22/03 2:17 PM, page 46.

Collecting Data

In public schools across America, students thrive and learn in an environment that is free of crime and violence. Students report that they feel safe when they perceive discipline to be fair and consistent across the school, and when teachers are caring and helpful. With consideration to several tragic, violent events that occurred in our nation's schools, ensuring the safety of students within Florida schools is as important as providing students with a quality education. Therefore, one of the goals of the Florida Department of Education (DOE) is to develop and implement safety and security measures that will help schools continue to provide safe and secure learning environments. One of the tools developed to help districts with data assessment and evaluation when planning for school safety is the publication, *Statewide Report on School Safety and Discipline Data.*

Now, more than ever, data play a pivotal role in the planning for school safety by assisting in the identification of potential or existing safety problems within schools. Since the 1995–1996 school year, DOE has annually collected data on twenty-one incidents of crime, violence, and disruptive behavior through the School Environmental Safety Incident Report (SESIR) system. SESIR, as it is commonly identified, collects incident data that occur on school grounds, school transportation, and at off-campus, school-sponsored events during any 24-hour period, 365 days per year. Incidents are reported to SESIR whether individuals are students, non-students, or if the offender is unknown. DOE also collects annual data on the types and number of discipline actions administered when students violate school or district rules. The three reported discipline actions are in-school suspensions, out-of-school suspensions, and expulsions. Data are reported statewide and by district.

Specifically, this publication summarizes the most recent three years of SESIR and discipline data that were reported to DOE by the sixty-seven school districts in Florida. Under state totals, the following are provided:

- The "SESIR Incident Summaries" includes "Time of Incidents," "Persons Involved," "Location of Incidents," and "Number and Percent of Schools Reporting No SESIR Incidents."
- "SESIR Totals" includes student population, raw totals of each of the twenty-one incidents, as well as the number of incidents per thousand students. (This provides a means of standardizing for comparisons with state average and other districts.)
- "SESIR Totals: Trends by Categories" includes a trend analysis of the SESIR data over a period of three school years for incidents grouped in categories. Discipline data includes data for the past three school years, 2002–2003, 2003–2004, and 2004–2005, and disaggregated by gender and race for each of the school levels: elementary, middle, and high. The report identifies the total number of disciplinary actions per school level, gender, and race, as well as the number and percent of individual stu-

dents who have been suspended or expelled one or more times. This allows for comparisons among levels and by gender and race for further analysis.

The student population numbers that are provided in this report are from Survey 5 Demographics that provides a cumulative count of all the students served in a given school year. The SESIR and discipline data provided and discussed are also collected in Survey 5 and are a cumulative record of all the incidents in the respective years. The SESIR data (for the 2002–2003 school year) is current as of December 2003, for 2003–2004 as of November 2004, and for 2004–2005 as of October 2005.

SESIR INCIDENTS AND RELATED ELEMENTS

As previously stated, the SESIR system collects data on twenty-one incidents of crime, violence, and disruptive behavior that occur in schools or on school grounds, during transportation, or at school-sponsored events. Below, the incidents have been divided into categories based on incident characteristics.

- Violent Acts against Persons
    1. Homicide
    2. Sexual battery
    3. Robbery
    4. Battery
    5. Kidnapping
- Alcohol, Tobacco, and Other Drugs
    6. Drugs
    7. Alcohol
    8. Tobacco
- Property
    9. Breaking/entering
    10. Larceny/theft
    11. Motor vehicle theft
    12. Arson
    13. Vandalism
- Harassment
    14. Threat/intimidation
    15. Sexual harassment
- Other Nonviolent Incidents
    16. Sexual offense
    17. Trespassing
    18. Other major
- Incidents Not Categorized
    19. Fighting
    20. Disorderly conduct
    21. Weapons possession

Following the 1998–1999 school year, the SESIR incident definitions were revised to better define the incidents and help schools correctly identify the incidents. These new definitions were effective for the 1999–2000 school year. Subsequent revisions were made in 2001 to refine the definitions and provide additional examples and non-examples of the twenty-one incidents. These definitions and guidelines may be found on the Office of Safe and Healthy Schools Web page (www.firn.edu/doe/besss/discipline.htm.).

In addition to the twenty-one incident types, SESIR also collects five data elements that may be associated with the incidents. These elements describe whether external factors from one of the following areas are related to the incident:

- Gang-related
- Alcohol-related
- Drug-related
- Hate-crime related
- Weapon-related

These related elements allow SESIR incidents to be described more comprehensively. For example, during a battery incident in which a knife was used and the student was also under the influence of alcohol, the incident would be reported as battery, weapon-related, and alcohol-related. This coding method provides a more accurate depiction of the related elements that often occurs with SESIR incidents. The weapon-related incidents also ask for schools to enter a description of the weapon. It is especially important that guns or other firearms are accurately coded, as this information is used to substantiate federal Gun-Free Schools violations for the federal Gun-Free Schools Act annual report.

The following are the weapon definitions schools use as part of the Comprehensive Management Information System:

Code	Code Definition
F	Firearm, Other
H	Handgun
R	Rifle or Shotgun
K	Knife
O	Other Weapon
U	Unknown Weapon
Z	Not Applicable

In addition to the five related elements, other specific details about SESIR incidents are also collected. These include the following:

- Type of offender—student or non-student
- Time of day—during school hours or after school hours
- Type of weapon involved—firearm, handgun, knife, other weapon, rifle or shotgun, or unknown weapon.

Collectively, these descriptive elements provide an inclusive picture of the various types of incidents that occur in schools.

SESIR DATA QUALITY

The National Center for Education Statistics has previously recognized the SESIR system as a model for school safety data collection. Although the system has been nationally recognized, the data continue to be based on subjective decisions and interpretations made by administrators at the school level. Thus, caution must be exercised in the interpretation and application of SESIR data. Threats to data validity that have been identified include the inaccurate and inconsistent application of incident definitions, over- and under-reporting of SESIR data, and variations within the formats utilized by districts to record SESIR incidents.

The Department of Education is aware of these concerns with the SESIR system and has, over the past several years, developed and delivered training courses to school district personnel throughout the state. The training courses were designed to help schools and districts become more knowledgeable of the SESIR incident definitions and to develop more accurate and consistent data reporting. In addition, DOE developed a training CD-ROM that provides interactive instruction on SESIR incident reporting requirements. The CD-ROM includes details about the SESIR incidents and definitions, examples of how and when to code SESIR incidents, video clips that illustrate incidents and proper coding procedures, and a self-assessment test that evaluates users on their knowledge of the SESIR system. This CD-ROM was disseminated to school districts before the 2000–2001 school year to assist in improving the knowledge and skills of school-level personnel who identify and report SESIR incidents. Since 2002, a revised version has been distributed as requested. A poster summarizing the incident definitions and the incidents that require reporting to law enforcement is also available as a job aid upon request to the Office of Safe and Healthy Schools.

The SESIR data and categories provided in this report will differ slightly from that which is reported in the Florida School Indicators Report (FSIR). The FSIR provides incident data for the elementary, middle, and high schools in categories only, so it is not possible to view data on individual incidents at this site (http://info.doe.state.fl.us/fsir/). Total incident numbers may differ from the *Statewide Report on School Safety and Discipline Data* because of different capture dates. These reports are based on data as of a particular date. The statewide report has historically used a November/December date to allow districts to make modifications/corrections, whereas the FSIR is based on an earlier fall date.

SESIR DATA INTERPRETATION

When examining the data contained in this report, caution should be exercised if making comparisons between school districts. Numerous social and environmental factors, such as the size of the district population, can significantly impact SESIR data between districts. The number of incidents may vary among districts due to differing interpretations of incident definitions, varying levels of consistency with which schools report incidents, and variation in the amount and level of training provided to school personnel who report SESIR incidents.

It is extremely difficult, and not recommended, to make general comparisons of SESIR data from one district to another without taking into context other social fac-

Table 3–1:   SESIR Incident Summaries

SESIR Incident Summaries

STATE OF FLORIDA	2003 - 2004		2004 - 2005		2005 - 2006	
Time of Incidents						
	%	Raw Data	%	Raw Data	%	Raw Data
During School Hours	97.40	110,680	96.57	101,153	96.04	92,447
Not During School Hours	1.80	2,045	2.77	2,901	3.07	2,954
Unknown	0.80	909	0.66	689	0.89	857
Total Number of Incidents		113,634		104,743		96,258
Persons Involved						
	%	Raw Data	%	Raw Data	%	Raw Data
Students	93.84	106,631	93.32	97,743	93.10	89,621
Non-Students	1.10	1,246	1.19	1,242	1.49	1,439
Both Students and Non-Students	1.40	1,589	1.35	1,410	1.21	1,165
Unknown	3.67	4,168	4.15	4,348	4.19	4,033
Total Number of Incidents		113,634		104,743		96,258
Location of Incidents						
	%	Raw Data	%	Raw Data	%	Raw Data
School Grounds	96.50	109,654	97.18	101,786	97.02	93,390
School Sponsored Activity	0.75	847	0.44	466	0.37	360
School Sponsored Transportation	2.76	3,133	2.38	2,491	2.61	2,508
Total Number of Incidents		113,634		104,743		96,258
Number of Schools Reporting No SESIR Incidents						
	%	Raw Data	%	Raw Data	%	Raw Data
Elementary ²	20.15	329	24.84	418	28.69	511
Middle ³	0.63	3	1.24	6	5.75	32
High ⁴	5.88	25	6.09	26	15.17	83
Combination ⁵	17.65	12	14.47	11	31.25	50
Charter ⁶	51.20	128	56.54	173	0.00	0
Total Number of Schools		497		634		676

1 Some schools may have had no SESIR incidents occur.
2 Elementary includes Kindergarten through Grade Five.
3 Middle includes Grades Six through Eight.
4 High includes Grades Nine through Twelve.
5 Combination includes schools combining elementary, middle, or high groupings or overlap grade levels, e.g., K-6, 6-12, or K-12.
6 Charter Schools no longer categorized as a separate school type.

Please note that SESIR incidents are reported by schools by incident, not by individual student.

Source: State of Florida Department of Education's School Environment Safety Incident Reporting System (SESIR) 2005–2006 Statewide Report

tors and variables that are not provided in this report. It is important to recognize that the information contained in this report should not be misconstrued to imply that districts that reported fewer incidents have safer schools. The purpose of this report is to simply provide the SESIR and discipline data that were reported to DOE by the sixty-seven Florida school districts; it is not to use the data to formulate assumptions to draw conclusions about the safety within schools. Any further interpretation regarding the safety and security of Florida schools using this report is not advised.

Table 3–1:   Continued

STATE OF FLORIDA	2003 - 2004		2004 - 2005		2005 - 2006	
Student Population:	2,705,674		2,765,032		2,818,606	
	Per 1,000	Raw Data	Per 1,000	Raw Data	Per 1,000	Raw Data
Violent Acts Against Persons	3.68	9,969	3.94	10,900	3.75	10,560
Homicide	0.00	5	0.00	0	0.00	2
Sexual Battery	0.05	123	0.03	91	0.03	89
Robbery	0.09	249	0.09	242	0.11	298
Battery	3.54	9,585	3.82	10,551	3.61	10,167
Kidnapping	0.00	7	0.01	16	0.00	4
Alcohol, Tobacco, Other Drugs	5.71	15,452	4.91	13,568	4.61	12,995
Drug	2.40	6,505	1.91	5,272	NA	NA
Drug Use**	NA	NA	NA	NA	1.71	4,821
Drug Dealing**	NA	NA	NA	NA	0.17	473
Alcohol	0.48	1,300	0.44	1,214	0.43	1,223
Tobacco	2.83	7,647	2.56	7,082	2.30	6,478
Property	3.59	9,706	3.27	9,030	2.93	8,259
Breaking/Entering	0.39	1,064	0.37	1,034	0.40	1,130
Larceny/Theft	1.75	4,747	1.65	4,576	1.48	4,179
Motor Vehicle Theft	0.04	110	0.05	129	Combined With Theft	
Arson	0.08	214	0.07	187	0.07	185
Vandalism	1.32	3,571	1.12	3,104	0.98	2,765
Harassment	3.75	10,146	3.20	8,841	3.11	8,773
Threat/Intimidation	2.80	7,582	2.39	6,596	2.32	6,545
Sexual Harassment	0.95	2,564	0.81	2,245	0.79	2,228
Other Non-Violent Incidents	2.57	6,944	2.35	6,510	2.15	6,060
Sexual Offense	0.61	1,646	0.57	1,573	0.50	1,398
Trespassing	0.46	1,247	0.42	1,152	0.39	1,105
Other Major	1.50	4,051	1.37	3,785	1.26	3,557
Fighting	18.86	51,032	16.76	46,342	14.46	40,746
Disruption on Campus	2.22	6,014	1.95	5,405	1.90	5,361
Weapons Possession	1.62	4,371	1.50	4,147	1.24	3,504
TOTAL	42.00	113,634	37.88	104,743	34.15	96,258

Note: Data for 2003-2004 as of November 2004, for 2004-2005 as of October 2005, and for 2005-2006 January 2007.

** Drugs category has been separated into two incident types, drug use and drug dealing, for 2005-2006 reporting period.

Figure 3–1:   SESIR Totals: Trends by Categories

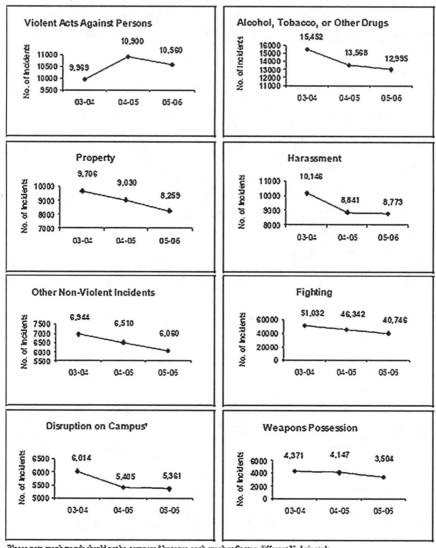

Please note graph trends should not be compared because each graph reflects a different Y-Axis scale.

Source: State of Florida Department of Education's School Environment Safety Incident Reporting
System (SESIR) 2005–2006 Statewide Report

Guns and Weapons

SUMMARY OF FINDINGS, DEPARTMENT OF EDUCATION, 2006

- Overall, fifty states, the District of Columbia (D.C.), Puerto Rico, and the four outlying areas reported data under the GFSA for the 2002–2003 school year (latest figures available). They reported that they expelled a total of 2,143 students from school for bringing a firearm to school or possessing a firearm at school.
- Fifty-eight percent of the expulsions were students in senior high school, 31 percent were in junior high, and 11 percent were in elementary school.
- Fifty-five percent of the expulsions were for bringing or possessing a handgun. Thirty-two percent were for some other type of firearm or other destructive device, such as bombs, grenades, or starter pistols, and 13 percent of the expulsions were for bringing or possessing a rifle or shotgun.
- There was a 16 percent decrease in the number of expulsions from 2001–2002 to 2002–2003.
- The number of expulsions has continued to decrease from 1996–1997 to 2002–2003.
- Forty-seven percent of expulsions were modified to less than one year.
- Eighty-one percent of modified expulsions were for students who were not considered disabled.
- Thirty-six percent of students in the reporting states were referred to an alternative placement. Among those referred, 41 percent of the expulsions were modified and 59 percent were not modified.
- All of the "states" and outlying areas reported that their Local Education Authorities (LEAs) submitted a GFSA report. Of the fifty states, D.C., Puerto Rico, and outlying areas, Alabama and the Virgin Islands had the highest percentage of LEAs that reported one or more students for an offense under the GFSA.

OVERALL YEAR-TO-YEAR CHANGES IN NUMBER OF EXPULSIONS— 2001–2002 TO 2002–2003

Overall, the reported number of expulsions decreased 16 percent from 2,554 in 2001–2002 to 2,143 in 2002–2003 (see table 3.1). Of the fifty-six "states" and outlying areas reporting expulsions, thirty showed a decrease in the number of expulsions from 2001–2002 to 2002–2003. Among these, the greatest decrease was reported in Alabama. Conversely, seventeen states showed an increase in the number of expulsions from 2001–2002 to 2002–2003 with the largest increase in Arkansas.

SCHOOL SHOOTINGS

The eighteen-year-old honor student brought guns and a homemade bomb to school. He set off the fire alarm and shot at the janitors and firefighters who responded. The boy hung himself while awaiting trial. This story sounds as current as today's media headlines, but it happened in 1974. School shootings are not a new phenomenon.

There is no one reason why school shootings occur and no one type of student who becomes a shooter, according to the *National Institute of Justice Journal* (no. 248), which summarized the results of a study by the U.S. Secret Service's National Threat Assessment Center.

Children who attack can be any age and from any ethnic group, race, or family situation. Contrary to assumptions that some of our youth "just snap," they don't. They plan.

Most official statistics show a steady decline in the rates of school violence.

Reports from the U.S. Department of Education show school to be one of the safest places for our children.[1] However, several high-profile shootings in schools over the past decade have resulted in increased fear among students, parents, and educators.

The National Institute of Justice joined forces with the U.S. Secret Service and the U.S. Department of Education to assess ways to prevent school shootings. The Secret Service has a long tradition of protecting our nation's leaders by identifying, assessing, and managing persons who might pose a threat of targeted violence.

"Targeted violence" is a term developed by the Secret Service to refer to any incident of violence where a known (or knowable) attacker selects a particular target prior to the act of violence. Because of the Secret Service's expertise in the study and prevention of targeted violence, the secretary of education asked the agency to conduct a similar operational study of school shootings.

The findings clearly emphasize the importance of paying attention and listening to America's young people. More than a handful of adults—parents, teachers, school administrators and counselors, coaches, and law enforcement—can make an important contribution to and play a key role in preventing violence on school grounds.

Young people who need help often do not keep it a secret. They may exhibit obvious warning signs either through behavior or remarks, such as voicing problems or grievances, complaining about persecution or bullying, or showing signs of depression or desperation.

The Secret Service found that when young people plan targeted violence they often tell at least one person about their plans, give out specifics before the event takes place, and obtain weapons they need—usually from their own home or a relative's home.

An important effort in prevention may be to ensure that young people have opportunities to talk and connect with caring adults.

WHAT WE KNOW

Attackers Talk About Their Plans

Prior to most incidents, the attackers told someone about their ideas or plans. In more than three-fourths of the cases examined in the Safe School Initiative, the attacker told a friend, schoolmate, or sibling about the idea for a possible attack before taking action. In one case, an attacker made comments to at least twenty-four friends and classmates about his interest in killing other students, building bombs, or carrying out an attack at the school. Some of the conversations were long enough that peers conveyed detailed information about the plans, including the date it would happen.

However, the study identified a major barrier to the prevention of targeted school violence. In nearly all of the cases, the person who was told about the impending incident was a peer, and rarely did anyone bring the information to an adult's attention. It is important, therefore, that threat assessment inquiries involve efforts to gather information from anyone who may have contact with the student in question. It also is important to decrease barriers that may prevent students who have information from coming forward. In addition, both schools and investigators need a thoughtful, effective system for handling and analyzing any information that is provided.

Although some attackers did make threats, most did not threaten their target directly. The researchers indicate it is helpful to distinguish between *making* a threat (telling people they intend to harm someone) and *posing* a threat (engaging in behaviors that indicate intent, planning, or preparation for an attack). The study notes that plans to prevent school violence should involve adults attending to concerns when someone poses a threat rather than waiting for a direct threat.

Attackers Make Plans

Incidents of targeted violence at school are rarely impulsive. In almost all incidents, the attacker developed the idea to harm the target before the attack. In many cases, the attacker formulated the idea for the attack at least two weeks in advance and planned out the incident. Targeted violence is typically the end result of an understandable, often discernible, process of thinking and behavior. For more than half of the attackers, the motive was revenge. In several cases, students made efforts to acquire firearms—often from their own home—or bomb-making equipment and solicited the assistance of friends to do so.

Because information about intent and planning was potentially knowable before the incident, the findings suggest some violent events may be preventable. Quick efforts to inquire and intervene are extremely important because the time span may be short between the attacker's decision to attack and the actual incident. An inquiry should include investigation of, and attention to, grievances and bad feelings a student may be experiencing about school or potential targets.

There Is No Stereotype or Profile

There is no accurate or useful profile of "the school shooter." The personality and social characteristics of the shooters varied substantially. They came from a variety of racial and ethnic backgrounds and varied in age from eleven to twenty-one years. Family situations ranged from intact families to foster homes. Academic performance ranged from excellent to failing. Few had been diagnosed with any mental disorder prior to the incident, and less than one-third had histories of drug or alcohol abuse.

Thus, profiling is not effective for identifying students who may pose a risk for targeted violence at school. Knowing that an individual shares characteristics, features, or traits with prior school shooters does not advance the appraisal of risk. The use of pro-files carries a risk of over-identification, and the vast majority of students who fit any given profile will not actually pose a risk. The use of these stereotypes will fail to iden-tify some students who do, in fact, pose a risk of violence, but who share few character-istics with prior attackers.

A fact-based approach may be more productive in preventing school shootings than a trait-based approach. This study indicates that an inquiry based on a student's behaviors and communications will be more productive than attempts to determine risk by attending to students' characteristics or traits. The aim should be to deter-mine if the student appears to be planning or preparing for an attack. If so, how far along are the plans, and when or where would intervention be possible?

Attackers Had Easy Access to Guns

Most attackers had used guns previously and had access to guns. In nearly two-thirds of the incidents, the attackers obtained the gun(s) used in the attack from their own home or that of a relative. In some cases, the guns were gifts from the students' parents.

While access to weapons among students may be common, when the idea of an attack exists, any effort to acquire, prepare, or use a weapon may signal an attacker's progression from idea to action. A threat assessment inquiry should include investiga-tion of weapon access and use and attention to communication about weapons. The large number of attackers who acquired their guns from home highlights the need to consider issues of safe gun storage.

School Staff Are Often First Responders

Most shooting incidents were not resolved by law enforcement intervention. More than half of the attacks ended before law enforcement responded to the scene—despite law enforcement's often prompt response. In these cases, faculty or fellow students stopped the attacker, or the attacker either stopped shooting on his own or committed suicide. Many of the incidents were over in twenty minutes or less.

Schools can make the best use of their resources by working with law enforcement on prevention efforts as well as critical incident response plans.

Attackers Are Encouraged by Others

In many cases, other students were involved in some capacity. The attackers acted alone in at least two-thirds of the cases. However, in almost half of the cases, friends or fellow students influenced or encouraged the attacker to act.

In one case, the student planned to bring a gun to school in an attempt to appear tough to other students who had been harassing him. The attacker shared his plan with two friends who convinced him to actually shoot students at the school to persuade others to leave him alone. Several days later, he did just that.

The attacker schemed to shoot fellow students in the lobby of his school at a spe-cific time in the morning. On the morning of the attack, he asked three others to meet him in the mezzanine overlooking the lobby, where only a few students could be found every morning. The students told so many others that by the time he opened fire in the lobby—killing two and injuring two—a total of twenty-four students were in the mezzanine watching the attack. One student brought a camera to record the event.

Advance knowledge among students about the planned incidents contradicts the assumption that shooters are "loners" and that they "just snap." The research suggests that an inquiry should not only include efforts to gather information from a student's friends and schoolmates, but also give attention to the influence that a student's friends or peers may have on intent, planning, and preparations.

Bullying Can Be a Factor

In a number of cases, bullying played a key role in the decision to attack. A number of attackers had experienced bullying and harassment that were longstanding and severe. In those cases, the experience of bullying appeared to play a major role in motivating the attack at school. Bullying was not a factor in every case, and clearly not every child who is bullied in school will pose a risk. However, in a number of cases, attackers described experiences of being bullied in terms that approached torment.

Attackers told of behaviors that, if they occurred in the workplace, would meet the legal definition of harassment. That bullying played a major role in a number of school shootings should strongly support ongoing efforts to combat bullying in American schools.

Two recent cases not included in the Secret Service's interim report brought the issue of bullying to the nation's attention. One boy experienced the torment of kids lighting their cigarette lighters and then pressing the hot metal against his neck. Even his friends constantly picked on him. To stop the daily taunting, he opened fire on his classmates, killing two.[2]

In the second case, a girl had been the victim of such severe harassment that she frequently skipped school; administrators threatened legal action if she did not begin to attend school regularly. Students called her names and threw stones at her as she walked home. Increasingly concerned, her parents transferred her to a small parochial school. The teasing continued. In an effort to stop the pain, the student planned to commit suicide in front of a classmate to whom she had revealed personal information. Instead of killing herself, she pointed the gun at her classmate and wounded her in the shoulder.

Warning Signs Are Common

Most attackers engaged in some behavior prior to the incident that caused concern or indicated a need for help. In more than half of the cases, the attacker's behavior caught the attention of more than one person. Behaviors that led others (e.g., school officials, police, fellow students) to be concerned included those related to the attack, such as efforts to obtain a gun. But they also included behaviors not clearly related to the attack. More than three-fourths of the attackers threatened to kill themselves, made suicidal gestures, or tried to kill themselves before their attacks. In one case, a student

For More Information

Borum, R. "Assessing Violence Risk Among Youth." *Journal of Clinical Psychology* 56 (2000): 1263–1288.

Borum, R., Fein, R., Vossekuil, B., Berglund, J. "Threat Assessment: Defining an Approach for Evaluating Risk of Targeted Violence." *Behavioral Sciences & the Law* 17 (1999): 323–337.

Fein, R.A., Vossekuil, B. *Protective Intelligence and Threat Assessment Investigations: A Guide for State and Local Law Enforcement Officials.* Washington, D.C.: U.S. Department of Justice, 1997 (NCJ 167556).

Fein, R.A., Vossekuil, B., Holden, G.A. *Threat Assessment: An Approach to Prevent Targeted Violence, Research in Action.* Washington, D.C.: U.S. Department of Justice, National Institute of Justice, September 1995 (NCJ 155000).

Reddy, M., Borum, R., Vossekuil, B., Fein, R., Berglund, J., Modzeleski, W. "Evaluating Risk for Targeted Violence in Schools: Comparing Risk Assessment, Threat Assessment, and Other Approaches." *Psychology in the Schools* 38(2) (2001): 157–171.

wrote several poems for English class that involved themes of homicide and suicide as possible solutions to feelings of hopelessness. School authorities ultimately determined that his was a family problem and did not intervene.

He later went to school and killed two people. Many attackers had a history of feeling extremely depressed or desperate. A significant problem in preventing targeted violence is determining how best to respond to students who are already known to be in trouble. This study indicates the importance of giving attention to students who are having difficulty coping with major losses or perceived failures, particularly when feelings of desperation and hopelessness are involved.

Notes

1. Snyder, Thomas, and Charlene Hoffman. *Digest of Education Statistics, 2000.* Washington, D.C.: National Center for Education Statistics, April 2001.

2. McCarthy, Terry. "Warning." *Time* 157(11) (March 2001): 24–28.

PREVENTION PROGRAMS

The majority of youth gun violence prevention programs involve instruction carried out in schools, community-based organizations, and physicians' offices. They emphasize the prevention of weapon misuse, the risks involved with the possession of a firearm, and the need for conflict resolution and anger management skills. Educational programs often use videotapes to support their presentation of the tragic results of gun violence and may also include firearm safety instructions, public information campaigns, counseling programs, or crisis intervention hotlines. Key elements of a gun violence prevention program may include:

- Creating an interagency gun-free school committee
- Standardizing anti-weapon policies and procedures for an immediate response for gun-related incidents
- Developing a Safe and Drug-Free School Plan with a crisis response team for gun-related incidents
- Establishing an interdisciplinary review committee to examine gun-related incidents and determine offender outcomes in addition to expulsion (e.g., alternative school)
- Providing student assessment for alternative school placement and linking of services for student and family, if needed
- Developing prerelease and transition strategies for returning the student to a mainstream school
- Providing follow-up services to track the student's performance in the mainstream school
- Developing methods for communicating the requirements of the Gun-Free Schools Act and corresponding school policies through school and community newsletters, parent-teacher and parent-student associations, school resource officers, and other outlets
- Developing and implementing a gun violence prevention curriculum
- Establishing a student group against gun violence

Some examples of prevention practices are:

Classroom Strategies: The Center to Prevent Handgun Violence has developed a school-based curriculum that has been used extensively across the country and has been evaluated by the Education Development Center with positive results. The Straight Talk About Risks (STAR) program at the Center to Prevent Handgun Violence is a comprehensive school-based program designed to reduce gun injuries and deaths with prevention activities for children and their families. Through STAR, students also learn how to make better, safer decisions and resolve conflicts without violence through role-playing, goal setting, and the development of leadership skills.

Gun Buy-back Programs: Weapons Watch was organized by the mental health center of the Memphis School District, the Memphis Police Department, and Crimestoppers. Weapons Watch was implemented to get children involved in ridding their schools of weapons. A hotline was established for students to call anonymously with information about a classmate who brings a weapon to school. Students are rewarded if the information leads to the confiscation of weapons and the arrest of the classmate who brings a weapon on campus.

Public Education Campaigns: Fresno's Youth Violence Prevention Network campaign in California is unique because it directly involves young people in delivering an anti-gun violence message. Previously known as Radio Bilingue, the Network is the result of collaboration among Chicano Youth Center, House of Hope, Save Our Sons and Daughters, and End Barrio Warfare. Violence prevention activities include developing gun-free-zone programs in city parks and neighborhoods, school emergency response and mediation teams, youth conferences, and youth leadership programs.

INTERVENTION PROGRAMS

Police and sheriffs' departments have been instrumental in supporting gun violence prevention/intervention programs. As part of drug education, public safety, and violence prevention efforts, police officers and sheriffs across the nation have worked collaboratively with schools to present critical information on gun violence to young people and, simultaneously, to develop more effective and interpersonal relations with young people.

Community Law Enforcement Programs: The Illinois State Police School Security Facilitator Program identifies jurisdictions with concerns about school violence. Representatives from all community programs that play a role in addressing problems of youth crime and violence are invited to attend an intensive five-day team building and education program. Part of the curriculum deals directly with the interdiction of guns in schools. Teams return to their communities to educate others on youth violence issues and to implement specific strategies for violence reduction. While no short- or long-term evaluation of this program has been implemented, anecdotal information from prior participants indicates some degree of usefulness and success.

Gun Market Disruption and Interception: The Kansas City Weed and Seed program is a joint effort of the U.S. Department of Justice, the U.S. attorney, and the Kansas City police department. The program focuses police efforts in high-crime neighborhoods on traffic violations, curfew violations, and other infractions of the law. Despite the fact that previous police campaigns have drawn protests of discrimination, the gun intercept program in Kansas City has not. Police have involved community and religious leaders in initial planning, and neighborhoods have made requests for greater police activity.

Diversion and Treatment Programs: In Pima County, Arizona, the Juvenile Diversion Program has set up a firearms prevention course for youngsters who are not hardcore delinquents, but who have been referred to juvenile court for firing or carrying a gun, and for young people at risk for being involved with guns. At least one parent is required to attend the monthly sessions. During the course, the assistant prosecutor informs the juveniles and their parents about gun laws. Parents are given instruction on safe gun storage. By agreeing to take the course, the youth do not have their cases adjudicated and are not placed on probation; however, they do acquire a juvenile record.

Gun Courts: A special type of court called a gun court has recently been established by Providence, Rhode Island, to focus on gun crimes. All gun crimes are referred to a single judge who processes cases on a fast track. Gun courts have cut the processing time of gun crime cases in half.

Alternative Schools: The Second Chance School in Topeka, Kansas, is a voluntary half-day instructional course for students who have been expelled for possession of weapons or assaulting a staff member. Students engage in studies of math, social sciences, and language skills, participate in some recreational activities, and are required to participate in community service. Depending on the seriousness of the offense, students attend the program for one semester or one year. To date, 90 percent of the students enrolled have successfully completed the program. The program has been operating for three years and has developed partnerships with the juvenile courts, the public schools, the police department, and the recreational department.

COMPREHENSIVE INITIATIVES

In Atlanta, the Center for Injury Control at Emory University is working together with the community, state, and local governments and with Project Pulling America's Cities Together (PACT) to analyze the magnitude, extent, and characteristics of youth firearms violence and to develop a broad-based strategy for addressing the problem. The planned intervention includes a three-part strategy: (1) to reduce the demand for firearms through a comprehensive community education program; (2) to reduce supply by promoting safe storage of firearms and by increasing law enforcement efforts to interdict the illegal gun market; and (3) to provide aggressive rehabilitation to decrease recidivism among juvenile gun offenders.

In Dade County, Florida, the Youth Crime Watch program, mandated for all schools by the Miami school board, was created in 1984 to extend the Neighborhood Watch concept to schools. The Gun Safety Awareness program, a district-wide effort, began in November 1988. In addition to this comprehensive curriculum, the school board declares a week in November as Gun Safety Awareness Week. The Gun Safety Awareness program targets kindergarten through 12th grade students and their parents, examining causes of handgun violence and teaching the consequences of being arrested. Area Youth Crime Watches, school resource officers, and police officers supplement the curriculum. Parents attend training workshops on handgun safety awareness. Metal detectors are used unannounced at selected schools, and students caught with guns are referred to juvenile or adult court, and recommended for expulsion and assignment to an alternative school. Awareness levels among youth and parents about the need to prevent handgun violence have increased in Dade County as a result of this comprehensive program.

Violence and Bullying

EFFECTIVE STRATEGIES

Policy grounded in research promises to be most effective if it draws on expertise in a range of disciplines. Schools have taken steps to lower the risk of weapon-related incidents, but whether they choose techniques that have had a record of success is unknown. The following are three research papers prepared for the National Institute of Justice. While much of the research was conducted in the 1980s and 1990s the results and recommendations are still appropriate in curbing violence in schools and in the wider community.

COMMUNITY AND INSTITUTIONAL PARTNERSHIPS FOR SCHOOL VIOLENCE PREVENTION

Sheppard G. Kellam, M.D., Johns Hopkins University

It is a long-held belief among veteran public health workers that the first rule is,
"Don't get thrown out of the community." The field has many examples of this rule being followed and many examples of it being broken. One well-known example of achieving trust at the community level—being allowed to add chlorine, a potent poison, to drinking water—illustrates successful institutionalized prevention programming at the universal level (i.e., reaching all individuals in the community).

Who gives permission in the community? What are the processes of developing trust and maintaining acceptance, and even "owning" programs in the community? Our immediate concern, and the subject of this paper, is how we approach the problem of introducing a new prevention program that offers proven efficacy in a way that promotes acceptance of the program, perception of the program as in keeping with the community's values, and willingness to take up the program as part of the community's own institutions.[1]

WHY COMMUNITY PARTNERSHIPS?

The emergence of prevention science over the past three decades has made possible a growing body of prevention programs that have been rigorously tested for their impact in defined populations within specific social contexts.[2]

The nature of prevention often makes it necessary to address how specific aspects of environments help or hinder the development of individuals, given the varied capacity of individuals to adapt. For example, programs aimed at preventing mental and behavioral disorders are often based in schools and involve students' families and peers in the community as well as in other settings, such as the workplace or the context of intimate relationships.

Evidence-based prevention programs are generally guided by one or more specific prevention science strategies, each requiring community partnerships for implementation.[3] Some prevention programs address policy changes that may reduce risk or address community issues and organizational structure related to risk. For example, interventions may involve minimum age requirements for obtaining a driver's license or local practices regarding serving alcohol in bars.[4] Some programs involve the media in promoting less risky behavior. Prevention programs may also address antecedents of problem behaviors that occur in early childhood or later. These programs may, for example, involve changing family practices, schools' teaching practices and curricula, families' relationships to teachers and schools, peer group values and processes, and other highly intrusive activities that have been shown to influence developmental trajectories toward healthier, more socially efficacious outcomes. Prevention programs require great sensitivity to the power structure, values, and symbols of the local community and the broader society, and recognition that values vary dramatically from one community to the next and even within our society.[5]

Some newly tested prevention programs include how to parent, how to teach in the classroom, what children should know about sex and the availability of condoms, minimum age requirements for driving cars and purchasing cigarettes or alcohol, how to resist peer pressure about drugs, and many other intimate and value-laden issues. All of these programs, if imposed by outsiders, are very likely to bring about intense community response. How prevention program leaders relate to community concerns will dictate the fate of their efforts.

In prevention research, the field trial is an important element in the most rigorous designs.[6] Decisions about whether children or schools are to be randomly assigned to trial groups or whether control conditions are to be permitted will evolve, in large part, from the quality and structure of the relationship between the researchers and the community. After the research has been completed, questions about how to implement programs can also affect community interests, which, in turn, can aid or impede access to schools and classrooms for purposes of implementation.

Even after a program has been adopted, the quality and level of community involvement can markedly influence the fidelity with which the program is carried out. The subject of how community partnerships affect prevention program research, implementation, and subsequent administration is rarely examined thoroughly, if at all, in graduate study of health and mental health disciplines, and should be the subject of research. This paper describes how to establish partnerships with communities and their institutions—partnerships that are essential for both research and implementation of prevention programs.

RISK FACTORS AS TARGETS FOR PREVENTION

Prevention research and programming, and indeed all public health programs, are built within the cultural, social, and political structure of a defined population. From a public health perspective, the goal of such programming is to promote social adaptation and psychological and physical well-being and to prevent disorders over the life course, not only for those who are already ill but also for the total population of a community or institution. Prevention is based on the development of knowledge about risk factors, mediators of risk, and moderators of risk along the life course. Interventions can then be directed at improving specific risk factors to forestall specific mental and behavioral disorders. Such prevention interventions can also, in the same process, promote good social adaptation and psychological well-being in the population.

Risk factors may be in the environment, in the individual, or in the demand/response aspects in the environment and the individual's ability to respond. For example, a teacher may be either consistent or inconsistent in telling a child in the classroom to "sit still and pay attention," the child's response may be influenced by other classmates, or the child may or may not be cognitively or developmentally ready to respond adaptively. Such risk factors require providing teachers with methods for improving classroom management and instruction, for example.

Prevention programs directed at mental and behavioral disorders usually do not deal with individuals in isolation but rather in the context of major social fields at each life stage, such as families, classrooms, peer groups, intimate relationships, and the workplace. Because individuals must respond to social task demands within these environments, many prevention programs must be integrated within the major social fields and/or the relevant social institutions within which these fields are embedded. Therefore, partnerships involving prevention programs, institutions, and the community must support access to teachers, principals, children, parents, workplace leaders, lawmakers, and community leaders who may or may not allow such intrusive programs. Again, the key is the adequacy of these partnerships.

THE ECOLOGICAL CONTEXT FOR PREVENTION

Prevention programs can be developed within defined residential areas, elementary school catchment areas, and workplaces. The size of the population is not the issue; the focus is the totality of the population in its ecological environment, including its power structure, values, and symbols. The perspective of public health and, in recent years, of public education, is directed toward the whole population rather than the undefined individuals who may happen to come to a clinic or participate in a program. In effective public health prevention, the delivery agents are most often not clinicians who care for a few. Instead, they are the individuals who may, because of their position in an institution, improve the effectiveness of the institution by addressing risk or protective factors that may be part of the institution's structure.

Prevention programs may, for example, provide teachers with tools to develop and maintain classroom-learning environments, may improve parents' tools for teaching their children to regulate behavior, or may promote law enforcement efforts to impede the sale of tobacco to adolescents. Because such activities can alter classrooms and schools, families, business practices, laws, and media positions, the whole community has an interest and should, therefore, accept and even become the "owners" of these new ways of socializing and supporting individuals at all stages of life.

Building and maintaining such prevention and health promotion programs also involves the ethics and governance of human research and public health and education. Intimately coupled with problems of access to institutions and individuals are issues of confidentiality and of the representativeness and roles of participants in policy making and the administration of programs.

POLITICAL AND CULTURAL ANALYSIS

In the 1960s, and particularly during the "War on Poverty," several models of gaining community support were used.[7] In one model, the interagency council, social service agency leaders met periodically and discussed priorities and coordination. These meetings were based on the premise that, working together, social agencies could provide legitimacy for new community programs. As interest in citizen participation grew, the interagency council model came under attack by citizen groups that did not accept agency leaders as representing local values, priorities, or interests.

A second model, dubbed the storefront, literally implemented programs in vacant stores, posting invitations in the windows for citizen participation. Storefront programs also aroused protest, particularly from community organizations that claimed they failed to recognize, and even deliberately excluded, local leadership and organizations. A third model involved hiring local citizens as paraprofessionals, on the assumption that they would be accepted by the community for participation in decision making. All these models lacked structures for deliberately including the existing community organizations and their constituents in the planning, acceptance, and ownership of new programs.[8] Their participation from the beginning is the key to solid partnerships between programs and communities.

In developing solid partnerships, there is a three step process:

Step One

The first important step is the analysis of different groups (and their institutions and power structure) within the population, taking into account the diversity of the population and its links to the broader society. To reach all people in a potential prevention program population, leaders of constituencies that need to lend support must be identified. This analysis and identification of decision makers and their constituencies within and across subgroups of the total population may include clergymen, newspaper owners, leaders of political organizations, block club presidents, youth organization leaders, and neighborhood and business association leaders.[9]

In conducting this "power analysis," it is extremely important to understand the difference between locally based leaders of community organizations with local constituencies, and heads of public and private social service agencies. Agency heads (paid staff) have less authority to approve or not approve programs for children than do parents and leaders of their local social, religious, and political organizations. Agencies may be colleagues of prevention program staff in offering services to children and families, but they do not represent the population. Therefore, although a program may have won the support of the local family service agency, there may not be sufficient local support for a school or family prevention program. Parents, speaking through leaders of their own local organizations, may be far more effective in interpreting community concerns to program leaders and bringing reports from the program back to the community.

Step Two

The second step in developing partnerships is learning about the values, priorities, and acceptable language within the population. Such knowledge makes it possible to explain the proposed research and/or prevention activities in a way that is understandable to community members and reflects their values and priorities.[10]

Step Three

The third step is implementing population-based programs. This involves negotiating with specific leaders of community organizations whose constituencies lie within the population itself rather than within agency departments "downtown." These negotiations must begin with the process of engagement, working through trust issues and looking for mutual priorities and mutually acceptable research and service solutions. This does not imply that the community dictates the research question or the program to be adopted. The key is negotiating so that all parties' interests are served, including the values and aspirations of the community and the scientific or program missions of the professional staff.

Accomplishing the above three steps requires a thorough interviewing process in which many potential leaders answer detailed questions about the community, including how decisions are made and who makes them. Program advocates should also establish a consistent presence in the community through frequent visits to local churches, organization meetings, offices, and other places where personal engagement can begin, and information about specific community subgroups and their organizations can be learned. Such visits help researchers and/or program staff in getting to know the community, establishing credibility, and establishing and building on mutual investments in collaboration.[11] In our experience, the time required for this process of building a strong community base for a program—one that includes both community leaders and service agency colleagues—is about a year. Many investigators have found the effort to be well rewarded with the development of new and meaningful personal and professional relationships for building research and services that make it more likely that programs will be truly institutionalized and implemented with fidelity.

ESTABLISHING THE COMMUNITY AND INSTITUTIONAL BOARD

Another model, one found to be most beneficial, was introduced to the author and his colleagues[12] in the period from 1963 to 1966 by leaders of community organizations in Woodlawn (a very disadvantaged black neighborhood on Chicago's South Side) and by a centrally important mentor and highly esteemed friend, the late Saul Alinsky. Woodlawn community leaders had solicited Alinsky and the Industrial Areas Foundation to help in their struggle for local oversight of their community services and to engage in collective bargaining with city hall and other communities for Woodlawn's share of Chicago's human resources.

The approach used in Woodlawn begins with the premise that, for evidence-based prevention programs to be adopted and implemented with fidelity, local populations must participate actively in decisions and ultimately own the kind of prevention programs now being considered nationwide.[13] The second premise is that a board of local community and institutional leaders is the central structure for participation. Through it, leaders can set priorities and negotiate mutual interests across constituencies, with scientists and other professionals serving as the technicians for the community's emerging prevention programs. The third premise is that local populations can participate in decisions through leaders of their own community organizations, if these leaders constitute a local oversight and governance board. Examples of such local representatives include ministers, block club presidents, welfare union presidents, and presidents of neighborhood or business associations. Constituent organizations, reinforced by professional staff, should continually seek out citizens who are not members of any organizations and invite them to participate in decisions.

During a program's developmental phases, the scientists and program leaders represent the technical requirements of the research and the need for fidelity in implementation. The role of board members is to represent and ensure the protection of their constituents' values and priorities and to interpret to their constituents the objectives and plans of the emerging program(s). Beyond the developmental phases is the long-term goal of institutionalizing the program (i.e., building it into the structure of the community) as part of the core programs serving the community. Institutionalizing the program should be a goal from the start. The role of the board in achieving this goal is essential, first in building acceptance within the community and then in bringing the power of voting constituencies to bear in representing programs and budget requirements to government officials at the city, state, and federal levels.

BOARD MEMBERSHIP AND OVERSIGHT

Who decides on the board membership? Although professional staff can investigate organizations and leaders, they can only strongly request that the leaders become board members. In practice, the major role of the professional staff is to urge that all relevant population subgroups be represented to ensure that the community eventually owns the program and that all people who need the program can benefit from it. Guided by staff, community leaders can then identify leaders of other constituencies and organizations within the community for potential board membership and reach a consensus.[14] The professional staff is not in charge of the board but, rather, agrees to work under the oversight of the community through the board.

In the Chicago program, leaders of The Woodlawn Organization (TWO) took on the initial role of organizing a watchdog committee to ensure that the commitment to work with oversight by the community was real. TWO leaders, sometimes accompanied by professional staff, approached other community organization leaders, and the watchdog committee grew to become the board.

In the Baltimore program, Alice Pinderhughes, the highly esteemed black superintendent of Baltimore City Public Schools, provided original support for program development. She was later joined by a local veteran social-services professional, Elva Edwards, MSW, also a member of one of the leading national black sororities, who brought credentials of long residence and high community leadership status. Ms. Edwards took on the task of teaching program staff and inviting leaders of community organizations to join the board. She has played a critical role in promoting the long-term continuity and acceptance of the program.

Interaction among board members and staff is a continuous process, requiring monthly meetings, with subgroup discussions between meetings. In the beginning, the professional leader or program director should initiate communication, work through trust issues within the community, and also work to identify mutual interests. As the process moves forward, senior staff can share this vital role. To ensure the active participation of board members, project staff should maintain constant contact with them, including contact before each board meeting to emphasize the importance of their attendance.

Although this repeated contact might seem laborious, it is necessary because, in part, it confirms for members the staff's commitment to work continually with the board's oversight. As trust grows, the staff may be tempted to make decisions without board oversight.[15] Staff failure to consult with the board can lead to distancing from the community and weakening of community understanding and ownership of programs, which may ultimately jeopardize program fidelity and even survival.

BOARD MODEL VARIATIONS

The structure of the community board has evolved over the course of the work in Chicago and Baltimore, taking on three variations, described here as models 1, 2, and 3. Each was designed to fit needs identified through analysis (based on community feedback) of the political structure required to carry out the prevention program at a particular stage of its work. The first model provided a community and institutional base for work in Woodlawn from 1963 to the present.[16] The second provided a partnership for the earlier phase of the prevention work in Baltimore, which was conducted in the classroom and later involved parents in school-based programs.[17] The third model broadened the base beyond the schools, as the Baltimore children who participated in the first generation of preventive trials became young adults. (The first generation involved 2,311 first- and second-graders in 19 schools; the second generation involved nine schools and 680 first-graders, who are now entering middle school.) Their follow-up is also being conducted with the oversight of the current board. The three board models reflect shared principles but also the somewhat different political structures required for different stages of developmental epidemiological prevention research in Woodlawn and Baltimore.[18]

Model 1. The prevention program in Woodlawn was based in a Chicago Board of Health mental health center. The choice of a mental health center was a matter for intense negotiation. In 1963, Woodlawn was among the four most economically disadvantaged communities in Chicago, with infant mortality rates comparable to those in developing countries. The Chicago Board of Health had planned to establish a mental health center there, but was confronted with a militant community that saw "mental health" as another bad label and did not see the center as a priority.

After many intense discussions, three psychiatrists (including the author) and a social worker were invited to establish the Board of Health-Woodlawn Mental Health Center, with a services and research mission. The discussions involved Woodlawn community organization leaders, Chicago Board of Health officials, a State Department of Mental Health official (director Harold Visotsky, MD), and a representative of the University of Illinois Department of Psychiatry (Melvin Sabshin, MD, chair of psychiatry). The University of Chicago, an immediate neighbor of the Woodlawn community, became part of the group only when Daniel X. Freedman, MD, became board chair in 1967.

The issues: In 1963, the Woodlawn community was highly distressed over the state of its public schools and the lack of parental or community involvement. The central office led the school district with no parental participation at the local community level. Parents were not allowed in classrooms and could talk to teachers in the hall only during the twenty minutes between 8:40 a.m. and 9:00 a.m.

The community had recently been the scene of militant organizing, with a resulting confederation of more than 110 block clubs and churches banded together under the leadership of the major community organizations. As noted earlier, this group, with the consultation of Saul Alinsky and the Industrial Areas Foundation, became The Woodlawn Organization. TWO's goal was to provide a power base to fight for community participation in collective bargaining at the city and state levels and, thus, to help the community gain resources for human services and economic development, including school reform. Again, to emphasize its importance, trust issues were paramount. This was complicated by the existence of separate organizations in the more middle-class, western area of Woodlawn, which were sometimes antagonistic toward tactics employed by TWO.

During the year it took to develop trust, senior program staff attended many community meetings held by TWO and other organizations in West Woodlawn. During these meetings, community members raised tough questions about the program team's willingness to work within the community power structure and to recognize the role of the community in defining its boundaries and setting priorities. Eventually, twenty-five leaders of community organizations were appointed by both TWO and the West Woodlawn community organizations to form a board. The board would oversee and work with prevention program technical staff and would be chaired by the vice president of TWO, who lived in West Woodlawn and was acceptable to all groups. (The community board, not program staff, chose the chair.) The role of the program staff was to ensure that the science and services programs were conducted rigorously, as well as to develop study designs that were mutually acceptable, and to make certain that community values and interests were respected. Board members and program staff arrived at decisions through negotiation and collaboration. Members interpreted these decisions to their organizations and also informed program staff of community concerns.

The Woodlawn Mental Health Center board consisted entirely of community organization leaders. Not until much later did board members accept school officials as part of the collaborative process, because the officials had engaged in intensive confrontations with major segments of the Woodlawn community.

In order for prevention staff to gain access to the schools, a great deal of negotiation between the board and local school officials was necessary. At the beginning, parents and TWO members picketed the district superintendent's house until he granted the prevention program access to the schools. Later, the same district superintendent realized the importance and usefulness of having parents and community organizations as partners and became an ardent supporter of local oversight and active parental participation.

The result of board and program staff collaboration has been a thirty-five-year partnership that continues to this day, as staff (led by Margaret Ensminger, PhD) conduct follow-up studies of the total cohort of 1,243 children who were first-graders in 1966–1967. Recently, the staff also conducted a follow-up of mothers of these same first-graders, whose current ages range from fifty to seventy.

Defining boundaries and priorities: What did the board do beyond working through the trust issue? Since prevention science and programming are aimed at reducing incidence and prevalence rates, they are necessarily epidemiologically based. We can only calculate incidence and prevalence by knowing the boundaries of the community. (Public health prevention also needs to be directed toward the total population and its institutions, not just toward the individuals who participate in specific programs.) Thus, an early role of the board was to define these boundaries. In Chicago, this meant that organizations, which might eventually like to expand, would now have to define boundaries in their current position and size. The board finally endorsed the historical definitions of Woodlawn's boundaries and schools and, after much debate and expressions of concern, also endorsed the study designs (including randomization and control groups) to obtain data that would strengthen their demands for resources to establish new programs.

Priority setting was another early focus of the board. Social service agencies emphasized the need for a psychiatric professional to serve as backup to help individuals who had major mental health disorders. The board felt, however, that because the children represented the future, prevention was the highest priority. Although in 1963 prevention science in mental and behavioral disorders was a new and uncharted field, the board members wanted to give it top priority, with services for people who were ill to be developed later.

Program staff saw priority setting as an issue of community values. They agreed to assess early risk and developmental modeling in an epidemiological framework and to develop and test preventive interventions as the new data offered direction and made targets clear.

Model 2. The research base for the second model was the Department of Mental Hygiene of the Johns Hopkins University School of Hygiene and Public Health, where the author was chair in the period 1982 through 1993. After much negotiation and work on trust issues, the Baltimore Prevention Program was developed as a partnership between the Baltimore City Public Schools (BCPS) and the Department of Mental Hygiene, with funding from the National Institute of Mental Health (NIMH) Prevention Research Center and supplemental funding from the National Institute on Drug Abuse.

Lessons from Chicago: Much was learned in Woodlawn about elementary school antecedents of teenage depression, aggression, drug abuse, and other problem behaviors. The research and that of others indicated that, among vulnerable (i.e., high-risk) first-graders, failure to master reading predicted later depression, and early aggressive-disruptive behavior predicted later conduct and drug abuse disorders.[19] As a result of this research, early antecedents of problem behaviors became the focus for new prevention programs.

A first step in Baltimore was working out a partnership with the public school system that made it possible to mutually agree upon and design prevention programs directed at these early antecedents. The political base for these programs was the Board of

School Commissioners and superintendent. The first programs tested were conducted in first- and second-grade classrooms.[20] Through the principals of the original nineteen participating schools, program staff met with parents in community meetings. All decisions about program implementation were made openly, with the involvement of the school system and parents.[21] Later in the programs, a schools' committee was formed to bring all principals into active decision-making roles and to encourage mutual support. Meetings with parents continued periodically and as needed.

Convergence of community and research goals: The interest of BCPS was in developing curriculum and improving classroom behavior. The researchers' interests were the same. They wanted to test whether, working together, the program staff and the school staff could improve the targeted behavioral antecedents in first and second grades and thereby reduce the risk of later aggressive behavior, drug abuse, and depressive symptoms and disorders. All work on the design was done with school staff and under the superintendent's authority.[22] In the last generation of trials, 97 percent of the parents agreed to have their children randomly assigned to one of three intervention conditions in the nine participating elementary schools. These figures affirm the extent of mutual interest and trust among school officials, parents, and researchers.

Model 3. The current stage of prevention research in Baltimore involves following up the 2,311 children, now young people ages nineteen to twenty-one, who were the program's original first-grade participants. This first generation consisted of the entire first-grade population of the nineteen participating elementary schools in the period from 1985 through 1987. A second generation of 680 children, who are now in middle school, is also being contacted again, but it is the first generation, now beyond the public school years, that requires a broader community base for follow-up.

Community base: The community base needed for such intensive follow-up into adulthood would be an extension of the original base. An important new partner in this expanded base is Morgan State University (MSU), a historically black university with strong leadership ties to other community organizations. The community and institutional board now includes leaders from MSU, city judges, church leaders, and sorority and fraternity leaders of major black professional groups. The one problem we have not been able to solve is how to involve the young adults themselves. There appears today to be a great lack of social and political organizations among young adults. This issue itself may be important to address in the context of prevention and of the socialization of young adults.

Expanded collaboration: An outgrowth of the third model was a program for undergraduates at MSU. They developed a mutual interest with MSU to recruit top undergraduates as research assistants, interviewers, and observers, obtaining funding from the National Institutes of Health and the National Institute of Mental Health. This minority undergraduate training provided an opportunity to develop a program of advanced training for undergraduates that would prepare them for graduate education in public health and prevention science.

MSU faculty and administrative leaders constitute a strong community power structure, with ties to major branches of public institutions and government. The collaboration among MSU, the Baltimore City Public Schools Board of School Commissioners, and the Johns Hopkins School of Public Health created a strong, broad community base and also made possible a useful undergraduate training program. A community board, consisting of leaders within these institutions and overlapping with other community organizations, provides the authority for the research program to move forward with ongoing negotiation, understanding, and program support.

PROGRAM SUCCESS: PARTNERSHIPS ARE KEY

Neither prevention research nor prevention programming can be conducted in the isolated halls of academia.[23] Both are conducted within the very structure of society at all levels—from the broad societal level through the local community, the schools, and the workplace, as well as families, peers, and intimates, and down to the level of the individual.

ROLES OF THE PARTNERS

Strong community partnerships are essential for good prevention research. If children are to participate in school intervention programs, their parents need to give informed consent. A community board that can explain research goals and design (including why children are randomly assigned to classrooms) to the parents can be vital in obtaining such consent. The number of children who are allowed to participate and the number of schools that agree to participate affect the strength of a study design, including whether the study is representative of a given geographic area, whether a sufficient number of children will be available to assign to intervention groups and control groups large enough to permit meaningful comparisons, and whether the researchers are allowed to continue long enough to collect meaningful longitudinal data about the impact of interventions.

Other partners have equally important roles. Teachers who implement classroom interventions play a key role in ensuring that the program is conducted with fidelity to the design. Principals and superintendents who encourage teachers to give priority to the interventions also have a major role in ensuring fidelity. And community support is vital in showing local policy makers that successful prevention programs are a valued priority, deserving funding and institutionalization.

To conduct policy-relevant research, community partnerships are essential if researchers are to gain access to lawmakers and those who enforce laws and policy. Generally, prevention researchers may gain more credibility by demonstrating familiarity with the local situation than by showing academic expertise.[24] They may also find that community members have more accurate knowledge about communities than can be obtained from academic sources.

CENTRALITY OF THE BOARD

In building community partnerships, community boards have several functions.[25] In communities with racial and social class divisions, a local university may seem isolated from the community or even perceived as a source of inequality or discrimination.[26]

Community boards can help communities recognize that prevention programs serve both research and community interests. Oversight by the board can also make possible the cooperation of public mental health, education, and other human services agencies that might otherwise have felt threatened or territorial when presented with a prevention research proposal, or that might not have seen similarities between their priorities and those of researchers.[27]

Having representatives of diverse constituencies on the board helps elicit a variety of ideas from the community about how to define the community,[28] about the causes of complex health problems, about community health priorities,[29] and about encouraging involvement of community members.[30] Incorporating the community's self-identified health priorities and issues in the proposed program is especially likely to build trust between the community and the program and promote long-term support for it.[31] In Woodlawn, for example, the community itself chose to address mental health issues through prevention programming for its children and continues to support the program thirty-three years later.

SUSTAINING THE PARTNERSHIP

Collaborative relationships mean sharing control.[32] Designing successful program and evaluation plans may require a long process of trust building and negotiation as partnerships resolve differences in philosophies, principles, values, work histories, strategic interests, and vision.[33] The partners may need to address and correct inequities in power and should be certain to speak with one another rather than for one another.[34]

Although the commitment of program staff's time in building relationships and trust is likely to be greatest at the beginning of a project, cultivating the board's continuing commitment and support also takes patience and time. Integrating new participants (and approaches) may also involve negotiations to accommodate perspectives different from those at the project's start. However, with reciprocity and mutual respect,[35] combined with trust and long-term commitment,[36] community partnerships have a good chance of succeeding in the long run. Empowered by implementing change for their members, communities may grow in strength and effectiveness. Indeed, as Saul Alinsky suggested, community empowerment may also benefit individuals and contribute to health promotion for all.

Finally, on a personal note, the year-long process of analyzing and engaging with the political and social structure of each community we aspired to work with has produced some of the most enduring and rewarding professional and personal relationships. It is truly a powerful reward to experience the mutual respect that such work generates. On the basis of our experience, I would venture to say there seems to be no other way to conduct prevention research and programming if these efforts are to endure.

Notes

1. This work would not have been possible without the great contributions over thirty-five years of many individuals in Woodlawn (Chicago) and Baltimore, including community and

school leaders, parents, teachers, and the adults who were the participating children. My collaborators over the years in Woodlawn and Baltimore have been partners in every sense and have contributed tremendously to the development of the ideas and programs described here. Dr. Jean Oggins provided critical reading and literature background, and Natalie Keegan provided critical reading and editorial refining.

2. Center for the Study and Prevention of Violence. *Blueprints for Violence Prevention: Promoting Alternative Thinking Strategies (PATHS)*. Boulder, Colo.: Center for the Study and Prevention of Violence, 1998; Mrazek, P.J., Haggerty, R.J., eds. *Reducing Risks for Mental Disorders: Frontiers for Preventive Intervention Research*. Washington, D.C.: National Academy Press, 1994; National Institute on Drug Abuse (NIDA), *Preventing Drug Use Among Children and Adolescents—A Research-Based Guide* (NIH No. 97–4212). Bethesda, Md.: NIDA, 1997; National Institute of Mental Health (NIMH). *Prevention of Mental Disorders: A National Research Agenda*. Bethesda, Md.: NIMH, 1993; and National Institute of Mental Health (NIMH). *A Plan for Prevention Research for the National Institute of Mental Health: A Report to the National Advisory Council*. Bethesda, Md.: NIMH, 1996.

3. Kellam, S.G. "Integrating Prevention Science Strategies." Paper presented to the Society for Prevention Research, New Orleans, Louisiana, June 24–26, 1999.

4. Holder, H.D. *Alcohol and the Community: A Systems Approach to Prevention*. Cambridge: Cambridge University Press, 1998.

5. Small, S.A. "Collaborative Community-Based Research on Adolescents: Using Research for Community Change." *Journal of Research on Adolescence* 6(1) (1996): 9–22.

6. Kellam, S.G., Rebok, G.W. "Building Developmental and Etiological Theory Through Epidemiologically Based Preventive Intervention Trials." In *Preventing Antisocial Behavior: Interventions from Birth Through Adolescence*. Ed. J. McCord and R.E. Tremblay. New York: The Guilford Press, 1992.

7. Kellam, S.G., Branch, J.D. "An Approach to Community Mental Health: Analysis of Basic Problems." *Seminars in Psychiatry* 3 (1971): 207–225; and Kellam, S.G., Branch, J.D., Agrawal, K.C., Grabill, M.E. "Strategies in Urban Mental Health." In *Handbook of Community Mental Health*. Ed. S.E. Golann and C. Eisdorfer. New York: Appleton-Century-Crofts, 1972, pp. 711–727.

8. Kellam and Branch, "An Approach to Community Mental Health"; Kellam et al., "Strategies in Urban Mental Health"; and Kellam, S.G., Branch, J.D., Agrawal, K.C., Ensminger, M.E. *Mental Health and Going to School: The Woodlawn Program of Assessment, Early Intervention, and Evaluation*. Chicago: University of Chicago Press, 1975. Reprinted in paperback by same publisher, 1977.

9. Pillsuk, M. "Power: The Appropriate Target of Community Research." *Community Mental Health Journal* 11 (1975): 257–266.

10. Small, "Collaborative Community-Based Research"; and Wallerstein, N. "Power Between Evaluator and Community: Research Relationships Within New Mexico's Healthier Communities." *Social Science and Medicine* 49(1) (1999): 39–53.

11. Ebata, A.T. "Making University-Community Collaborations Work: Challenges for Institutions and Individuals." *Journal of Research on Adolescence* 6(1) (1996): 71–79; Perry, H., Robison, N., Chavez, D., Taja, O., Hilari, C., Shanklin, E., Wyon, J. "Attaining Health for All Through Community Partnerships: Principles of the Census-Based, Impact-Oriented (CBIO) Approach to Primary Health Care Developed in Bolivia, South America." *Social Science and Medicine* 48(8) (1999): 1053–1067; and Weinberg, R.A., Erickson, M.F. "Minnesota's Children, Youth and Family Consortium: A University-Community Collaboration." *Journal of Research on Adolescence* 6(1) (1996): 37–53.

12. The author's colleagues included Jeannette Branch, MSW; Edward H. Futterman, MD; and Sheldon K. Schiff, MD.

13. Saul Alinsky believed that a community achieving decision-making and collective-bargaining power over its institutions and services was itself preventive of social maladaptation and mental and behavioral disorders. This hypothesis may now be easier to test, given the generally held value of local community empowerment, and what is now known about prevention science methods, prevention programs, and the availability of economic building incentives at the community level.

14. Burrus, B.B., Liburd, L.C., Burroughs, A. "Maximizing Participation by Black Americans in Population-Based Diabetes Research: The Project DIRECT Pilot Experience." *Journal of Community Health* 23(1) (February 1998): 15–27; and Pillsuk, "Power."

15. Kupst, M.J., Reidda, P., McGee, T.F. "Community Mental Health Boards: A Comparison of Their Development, Functions, and Powers by Board Members and Mental Health Center Staff." *Community Mental Health Journal* 11 (1975): 249–256.

16. Kellam et al., *Mental Health and Going to School;* and Kellam, S.G., Brown, C.H., Rubin, B.R., Ensminger, M.E. "Paths Leading to Teenage Psychiatric Symptoms and Substance Use: Developmental Epidemiological Studies in Woodlawn." In *Childhood Psychopathology and Development.* Ed. S.B. Guze, F.J. Earls, and J.E. Barrett. New York: Raven Press, 1983, pp. 17–51.

17. Dolan, L.J., Kellam, S.G., Brown, C.H., Werthamer-Larsson, L., Rebok, G.W., Mayer, L.S., Laudolff, J., Turkkan, J., Ford, C., Wheeler, L. "The Short-Term Impact of Two Classroom Based Preventive Interventions on Aggressive and Shy Behaviors and Poor Achievement." *Journal of Applied Developmental Psychology* 14 (1993): 317–345; Kellam, S.G., Anthony, J.C. "Targeting Early Antecedents To Prevent Tobacco Smoking: Findings From an Epidemiologically Based Randomized Field Trial." *American Journal of Public Health* 88 (10) (1998): 1490–1495; Kellam, S.G., Werthamer-Larsson, L. Dolan, L.J., Brown, C.H., Mayer, L.S., Rebok, G.W., Anthony, J.C., Laudolff, J., Edelsohn, G., Wheeler, L. "Developmental Epidemiologically Based Preventive Trials: Baseline Modeling of Early Target Behaviors and Depressive Symptoms." *American Journal of Community Psychology* 19(4) (August 1991): 563–584; and Kellam, S.G., Ling, X., Merisca, R., Brown, C.H., Ialongo, N. "The Effect of the Level of Aggression in the First Grade Classroom on the Course and Malleability of Aggressive Behavior into Middle School." *Development and Psychopathology* 10(2) (1998): 165–185.

18. The prevention science paradigm developed in Chicago and used in Baltimore consisted of the integration of developmental modeling in epidemiologically defined populations, with preventive interventions directed at early antecedents (mediators and/or moderators) along developmental trajectories leading to problem outcomes, such as aggression, depression, and drug abuse. The research designs in Woodlawn and Baltimore required randomly assigning children, teachers, classrooms, and schools to either intervention or control conditions.

19. Ensminger, M.E., Kellam, S.G., Rubin, B.R. "School and Family Origins of Delinquency: Comparisons by Sex." In *Prospective Studies of Crime and Delinquency.* Ed. K.T. Van-Dusen and S.A. Mednick. Boston: Kluwer-Nijhoff, 1983, pp. 79–97; and Kellam et al., "Paths Leading to Teenage Psychiatric Symptoms and Substance Use."

20. Ialongo, N., Werthamer, L., Kellam, S.G., Brown, C.H., Wang, S., Lin, Y. "Proximal Impact of Two First-Grade Preventive Interventions on the Early Risk Behaviors for Later Substance Abuse, Depression, and Antisocial Behavior." *American Journal of Community Psychology* 27(5) (October 1999): 599–642.

21. Kellam, S.G., Hunter, R.C. "Prevention Begins in First Grade." *Principal* 70(2) (November 1990): 17–19.

22. Kellam et al., "Developmental Epidemiologically Based Preventive Trials."

23. Denner, J., Cooper, C.R., Lopez, E.M., Dunbar, N. "Beyond 'Giving Science Away': How University-Community Partnerships Inform Youth Programs, Research, and Policy." *Social Policy Report: Society for Research in Child Development* 13 (1999): 1–19; Kellam and Branch, "An Approach to Community Mental Health"; Kellam and Hunter, "Prevention Begins in First Grade"; and Kellam et al., "Strategies in Urban Mental Health."

24. McHale, S.M., Lerner, R.M. "University-Community Collaborations on Behalf of Youth." *Journal of Research on Adolescence* 6(1) (1996): 1–7.

25. Nelson, J.C., Rashid, H., Galvin, V.G., Essien, J.D.K., Levine, L.M. "Public/Private Partners: Key Factors in Creating a Strategic Alliance for Community Health." *American Journal of Preventive Medicine* 16 (3 Supp.) (April 1999): 94–102.

26. Denner et al., "Beyond Giving Science Away."

27. Lamb, S., Greenlick, M.R., McCarty, D. eds. *Bridging the Gap Between Practice and Research: Forging Partnerships with Community-Based Drug and Alcohol Treatment.* Washington, D.C.: National Academy Press, 1998; and Weinberg and Erickson, "Minnesota's Children, Youth and Family Consortium."

28. Mayo, M. "Partnerships for Regeneration and Community Development." *Critical Social Policy* 17 (1997): 3–26.

29. Perry et al., "Attaining Health for All."

30. McHale, S.M., Lerner, R.M. "University-Community Collaborations on Behalf of Youth." *Journal of Research on Adolescence* 6 (1996): 1–7.

31. Perry et al., "Attaining Health for All"; and Burrus et al., "Maximizing Participation."

32. McHale and Lerner, "University-Community Collaborations."

33. Kanter, R.M. "Collaborative Advantage: The Art of Alliances." *Harvard Business Review* (July–August 1994): 96–108; and Perry et al., "Attaining Health for All."

34. Wallerstein, "Power Between Evaluator and Community."

35. Weinberg and Erickson, "Minnesota's Children, Youth and Family Consortium."

36. Ebata, "Making University-Community Collaborations Work."

Research-based Prevention of School Violence and Youth Antisocial Behavior:

A DEVELOPMENTAL AND EDUCATIONAL PERSPECTIVE

Ron Prinz, PhD, University of South Carolina

Definitions of the term "school violence" range from very narrow—for example, relating only to the use of guns in school—to very broad, encompassing all youth misconduct and the many community and societal influences on such behavior.

This paper considers the full range of aggressive and antisocial behavior that occurs among school-age children and adolescents primarily (but not exclusively) in school settings, including bullying, hostile verbal aggression, fighting, uncontrolled rage toward others, drug dealing, stealing, vandalism, physical assault, sexual assault, gun carrying, threats with weapons, use of knives or blunt weapons, and use of guns.

UNDERSTANDING THE DEVELOPMENT OF ANTISOCIAL BEHAVIOR

During the past fifteen years, prevention science—grounded in psychology, public health, and related behavioral sciences—has grown to play an important role in understanding and preventing youth antisocial behavior. One lesson learned is that prevention must be considered from a developmental perspective, with emphasis on how youth trajectories toward violence evolve. Moreover, a successful plan of action (or intervention) must be based on specific, empirically supported theory.

DEVELOPMENTAL ANTECEDENTS AND TRAJECTORIES

Media reports about youthful perpetrators sometimes give the impression that violent acts are committed totally without warning by individuals with no apparent prior maladjustment. It is rare, however, that youths who initiate school violence have no history of problem behavior of any kind. While the youths previously may have done nothing to bring their behavior to the attention of school authorities, this does not indicate the absence of developmental precursors leading up to the egregious behavior. Invariably, youthful perpetrators have experienced difficulties, such as loneliness or minor misconduct, or they have been exposed to significant risk factors, such as family turmoil, ineffective parenting, non-stimulating educational environments, peer rejection, or witnessing of violent acts.

ROLE OF THEORY

Unfortunately, some behavioral scientists and program implementers in the violence prevention field work without a theoretical "net"—that is, programs and interventions are applied to a problem using what appears to be a logical and justifiable approach but without specific, empirically supported theory to guide the way. If the program does not live up to expectations or fails (as often occurs), the absence of theory makes it difficult for professionals in the field to proceed with the next steps in the process. Behavioral scientists may wander aimlessly in frustration, while administrators may discard the program and replace it with another offering new promise but no theoretical or empirical base.

One might reasonably ask what the role of theory is and on what foundation theory should be based. Use of theory in violence prevention is twofold. First, investigators consider the operating assumptions about how youth violence and associated antisocial behavior develop. Through a series of incremental studies, they try to establish how youth trajectories toward violence evolve and identify the variables that play a crucial role. Some theories emphasize parent-child interaction and parenting gone awry,[1] others implicate larger systems, such as neighborhoods and schools,[2] and still others combine the different domains into a composite picture.

Next, investigators consider how theory underlies the proposed intervention. Given limited time and resources, interventionists must judiciously choose the area to be targeted. Having a theory-driven intervention requires that the proposer specify the dimensions the intervention is supposed to influence and why such an effect is critical to violence prevention.

The two roles of theory—describing the development of risk for violence and identifying the specific basis for an intervention—work in tandem. Interventions are sometimes inadequate in one or both areas. For example, a program developer may articulate an elaborate theory of how families and neighborhoods influence youth development and then may propose a school conflict-management program that does not operate on family and neighborhood dimensions.

A theory of antisocial development provides an important backdrop for creating an intervention, and an intervention theory is an essential element for testing the intervention. However, scientists and evaluators may specify their intervention theory and then fall short by not assessing the specified variables.

For example, one might consider an intervention predicated on the assumption that effective parenting (close supervision, nurturing interactions, appropriate discipline) is important in preventing elementary school children from engaging in aggressive and antisocial behavior. If a controlled study showed that the intervention could reduce the incidence of aggression, but the study did not include measures of parenting changes (improvements) over time, we would not know whether intervention effects were due to the targeted variables (i.e., parenting practices) or to coincidental factors. Thus, even under apparently successful conditions, not assessing the hypothesized theoretical constructs (the previously mentioned parenting dimensions, for example) would limit the ability to draw useful conclusions.

The problem is even more obvious when an intervention or program is not successful. Scientists and evaluators do not want to bounce randomly from one unsuccessful program to another, hoping to discover the right one. Theoretical and empirical guidance, coupled with testing of both the theory itself and the derived intervention, is necessary to make progress. Implementing violence prevention programs, whether in a prevention trial or in an applied evaluation context, can be expensive, and the field cannot afford to gamble on endeavors that are not based on theory and that fail to provide schools with useful information on how to modify inadequate programs.

Theories about the causes of violence have become quite complex and multidimensional. Researchers recognize multiple causes of youth violence and other antisocial behavior, making the development and testing of interventions an even more daunting task.[4]

Prevention theories are not the sole province of social scientists—teachers, principals, parents, and youths are all sources to inform theories. Sometimes school administrators have hunches about why certain problems are occurring in their schools. Hunches can be developed into mini-theories that can be tested through the systematic collection of key data. If a hunch is correct, then an intervention can be developed and tested.

TARGETED LEVELS IN PREVENTION

Violence prevention involves many choices among the levels targeted for intervention. A basic issue in prevention science (not just in violence prevention) is how to define the population. The current prevention terminology identifies "universal," "selected," and "indicated" interventions:[5]

- Universal includes the entire group or population (such as all children in an elementary school), unselected with respect to risk for the outcome to be prevented.
- Selected refers to a subset of the population for whom there is elevated risk by virtue of exposure to environmental or organismic conditions or circumstances (such as elementary school children who live in neighborhoods where there are high rates of violent crime).
- Indicated refers to a subset of the population that is beginning to show the forerunners of the outcome to be prevented (such as first-graders engaging in more disruptive misconduct than their classmates).

These modes of prevention do not consider only the child as the unit or level of intervention. Multiple levels may be chosen as intervention targets, including larger units, such as the classroom or school, and very large contexts, such as media influences and national policy, each of which can be crossed with the three modes of prevention. For example, if teachers were the chosen level of intervention, a universal intervention would be applied with all teachers in a particular grade or school, perhaps to enhance behavioral management strategies for all classrooms; a selected intervention might involve only teachers working in schools with high rates of child misconduct; and an indicated intervention might involve only teachers who are struggling to cope with frequent misconduct in their classrooms and who have not yet mastered positive discipline and effective teaching methods (i.e., those at risk for feeding into the development of child aggression).

Levels are often nested within each other, and over time prevention researchers have moved beyond the child as the main unit of intervention and have increasingly targeted the socialization practices and influences of families, teachers, and peers.[6] Prevention research on the social climates and physical environments of schools can be expected to focus to a greater degree on the neighborhood, community, and school district as potentially important contexts for mitigating school violence.

CONCEPTS AND PRACTICES FROM PREVENTION RESEARCH

Insight gained through prevention research underscores the benefits of the following practices:

- Intervene early. A large body of research indicates that risk for aggressive and violent behavior begins in early childhood.[7] For youths exhibiting the greatest risk, waiting until adolescence to begin intensive programming is ill advised.[8] Schools and communities are much more inclined now than they were twenty years ago to recognize the need to launch interventions at school entry or earlier. Although recognizing the benefits of early intervention is not yet matched with sufficient staffing and other resources to institutionalize early prevention, policy makers seem to be moving in that direction.

- Intervene in multiple settings. Several comprehensive preventive intervention trials include programming in multiple settings. Potential settings include the classroom, school, family, peer group, and neighborhood and one-on-one interactions, such as mentoring, tutoring, or counseling.[9] Multiple-setting programs are needed for a number of reasons. First, socially determined behaviors, including aggression and violence, are shaped through interactions in many settings. Second, intervening in only one setting may not be sufficient to have a positive impact. Third, interventions across settings permit programming in one setting to compensate for less-effective programming in another setting. Fourth, children learn best when environments are more congruent with respect to message and expectations. Unfortunately, multiple-setting programs affecting any given child are the exception rather than the norm in many schools.

- Move beyond the individual child, taking into account larger contexts. As the earlier discussion about levels implies, children do not function in a vacuum. Prevention research has demonstrated that youth violence and conduct problems are socially embedded phenomena. Attempts to alter the risk for antisocial behavior and violence that have focused exclusively on processes internal to the child have met with limited success. At minimum, family, classroom, and peer contexts are integrally related to child functioning and should be considered in designing a comprehensive prevention plan.

- Motivate children, teachers, and parents. Many of the more effective preventive interventions include elaborate strategies to motivate and reinforce participants. Social reinforcement is the glue that makes programs work or the missing element in cases of failure. Good teaching, good parenting, and good management (by principals, for example) all have in common that people need frequent positive feedback to develop and sustain desirable habits.

- Set and enforce appropriate limits. An emphasis on building positive behaviors and reinforcing socially desired actions of children (as well as teachers and parents) may give the false impression that parents, teachers, and schools should not set and enforce behavioral limits. On the contrary, positively framed prevention programs can and do have limit-setting components. For example, one type of extensive programming to reduce school bullying includes several prescriptions about effective ways to label and sanction bullying behavior and, thus, to create a norm for discouraging such behavior.[10] Sometimes prevention programs do not provide enough information about how to set and enforce limits for misconduct at school, and administrators are often hungry for such guidance. However, we do know that programming that emphasizes punishment and harsh consequences (such as expulsion), in the absence of ample opportunity to earn benefits, runs the risk of backfiring or of moving misbehaving youths to other parts of the community without diminishing their misconduct.

- Use modeling as a powerful influence. Much research has demonstrated that young children will copy both positive and negative behaviors under various conditions. Some preventive interventions capitalize on modeling as an influence.[11] However, the other side of this issue is that we need to pay closer attention to how staff (including program staff, teachers, and administrators) accidentally model coercive or verbally aggressive behaviors that children might copy. Prevention programs need to build many opportunities for children to observe the pro-social behaviors of adults and other children and to diminish their opportunities to observe the antagonistic and inappropriate behaviors that should not be imitated.

- Involve the community. Two of the strongest predictors of school violence rates are neighborhood crime rate and level of local community disorganization.[12] Both schools and their surrounding communities suffer from the ill-effects of crime and violence. Neighborhood crime feeds school violence, and youths suspended or expelled from school contribute to neighborhood crime. Prevention of school violence, then, offers a challenge for schools and communities to work together to reduce violence in all settings.

- Provide adequate alternatives. There is no such thing as the absence of behavior. Human beings, including children, always are doing something. Effective programming is about building positive alternatives to aggression and violence to either prevent or supplant such behavior. Examples are plentiful in the prevention research literature. Building positive school bonding to prevent alienation and subsequent misconduct is one example.[13] Another is the Promoting Alternative Thinking Strategies (PATHS) program, which is about teaching emotion-regulation and thinking strategies that supplant more impulsive or irrational approaches to situations.[14] In addition, the Peer Coping Skills program's prevention team arms children with prosocial methods for coping with everyday challenges so that they do not have to fall back on antisocial and asocial coping.[15] All of these examples and others in prevention share the broadening of children's (or families' or teachers' or schools') positive repertoires to offset less-desirable modes of interacting. Many schools recognize the need to frequently strengthen positive alternatives to aggression.

Unfortunately, much of the effort is directed toward containing or reacting to aggression and relatively less is allocated toward building positive alternatives.

A related issue is the provision of alternative opportunities. We know that children are more likely to get in trouble after school during the afternoon and early evening. Schools and communities are painfully aware of the need to create and maintain well-supervised after-school programs offering children positive alternatives to roaming the streets and getting into problem situations.

Prevention research literature provides some guidance about the kinds of programming that can be integrated into after-school settings.[16] The physical plant is readily available, and many schools are using their facilities to good advantage after school and during evening, weekend, and summer periods. The challenge lies in how to support such programs with adequate staffing and resources.

APPLYING THE LESSONS

Policy makers, school administrators, and behavioral scientists have a broad range of issues to consider in addressing school violence. Information resource policy makers would do well to recognize that the term "violence prevention" does not adequately reflect the nature and scope of the problem. The scope of the issue needs to be broadened to address key processes. Moreover, in dealing with the problem of youth aggressive and antisocial behavior (including demonstrable violence), the community needs to consider the early trajectories of children who may be at risk not only for violence but also for other misconduct, substance abuse, academic failure, and early parenthood, all of which adversely affect youths and the community. In addition, policy makers might want to consider:

- Insisting on scientific testing and data-informed programs, resisting the temptation to promote fads or programs with great marketing but no empirical basis.
- Asking for explanations (not just outcomes) of prevention programming efforts—policy makers can benefit from guiding theory as much as scientists can.
- Helping schools increase their resources for early intervention. Assist communities by providing ways to cope with misbehaving youths other than simply by turning them loose in neighborhoods without adequate supervision.

SCHOOL ADMINISTRATORS

School administrators can choose programs and strategies that build the nonviolent and pro-social behaviors children should exhibit at school. They will want to resist the temptation to emphasize sanctions without offering opportunities to reward and strengthen appropriate and desired behaviors. In addition, administrators could consider:

- Examining and, if necessary, changing the school "climate." School personnel can make or break any preventive intervention. Effective programs usually are associated with competent staff that is well managed and content in its work.
- Resisting the temptation to stigmatize and dismiss children. Suspensions and expulsions are on the rise, but people are still victimized if misbehaving youths are simply passed around the community without adequate programming.

BEHAVIORAL SCIENTISTS

Finally, behavioral scientists will want to consider:

- Building interventions based on strategic information from teachers, parents, administrators, and children, and request their help in designing and piloting programs before adoption.
- Paying attention to larger contexts. Classroom, peer group, school, and community contexts are key to understanding school violence. Revised theories and interventions will need to better integrate these contexts in meaningful ways.
- Improving measures of settings so their impact on larger systems can be examined.

Notes

1. Patterson, G.R. *Coercive Family Process.* Eugene, Ore.: Castalia, 1982; and Patterson, G.R., Reid, J.B., Dishion, T.J. *Antisocial Boys.* Eugene, Ore.: Castalia, 1992.

2. Sampson, R.J., Raudenbush, S.W., Earls, F. "Neighborhoods and Violent Crime: A Multilevel Study of Collective Efficacy." *Science* 277 (August 1997): 918–924.

3. Blechman, E.A., Prinz, R.J., Dumas, J.E. "Coping, Competence, and Aggression Prevention." *Applied and Preventive Psychology* 4(4) (Fall 1995): 211–232.

4. American Psychological Association. *Violence and Youth: Psychology's Response, Summary Report of the American Psychological Association Commission on Violence and Youth.* Vol. I. Washington, D.C.: American Psychological Association, 1993; Elliott, D.S., Hamburg, B.A., Williams, K.R., eds., *Violence in American Schools: A New Perspective.* New York: Cambridge University Press, 1998; National Institutes of Health. *Report of the Panel on NIH Research on Antisocial, Aggressive, and Violence-Related Behaviors and Their Consequences.* Bethesda, Md.: National Institutes of Health, 1994.

5. Mrazek, P.J., Haggerty, R.J., eds. *Reducing Risks for Mental Disorders: Frontiers for Preventive Intervention Research.* Washington, D.C.: National Academy Press, 1994.

6. Prinz, R.J., Connell, C. "Prevention of Conduct Disorders and Antisocial Behavior." In *Handbook of Prevention and Treatment With Children and Adolescents: Intervention in the Real World Context.* Ed. R.T. Ammerman and M. Hersen, New York: Wiley, 1997, pp. 238–258.

7. Loeber, R., Hay, D. "Key Issues in the Development of Aggression and Violence From Childhood to Early Adulthood." *Annual Review of Psychology* 48(1) (1997): 371–410; Maughan, B., Rutter, M. "Continuities and Discontinuities in Antisocial Behavior From Childhood to Adult Life." In *Advances in Clinical Child Psychology,* vol. 20. Ed. T.H. Ollendick and R.J. Prinz. New York: Plenum Press, 1998, pp. 1–47; and Patterson, G.R., Forgatch, M.S., Yoerger, K.L., Stoolmiller, M. "Variables That Initiate and Maintain an Early-Onset Trajectory for Juvenile Offending." *Development and Psychopathology* 10(3) (1998): 531–547.

8. Kazdin, A.E. "Treatment of Antisocial Behavior in Children: Current Status and Future Directions." *Psychological Bulletin* 102 (1987): 187–203.

9. Conduct Problems Prevention Research Group. "A Developmental and Clinical Model for the Prevention of Conduct Disorder: The FAST Track Program (Conduct Problems Prevention Research Group)." *Journal of Development and Psychopathology* 4 (1992): 509–527; Dumas, J.E., Prinz, R.J., Smith, E.P., Laughlin, J. "The Early Alliance Prevention Trial: An Integrated Set of Interventions To Promote Competence and Reduce Risk for Conduct Disorder, Substance Abuse, and School Failure." *Clinical Child and Family Psychology Review* 2(1) (March 1999): 37–52; Hawkins, J.D., Weis, J.G. "The Social Development Model: An Integrated Approach to Delinquency Prevention." *Journal of Primary Prevention* 6 (1985): 73–97; Kellam, S.G., Rebok, G.W., Ialongo, N., Mayer, L.S. "The Course and Malleability of Aggressive Behavior From Early First Grade Into Middle School: Results of a Developmental Epidemiology-Based Preventive Trial." *Journal of Child Psychology and Psychiatry and Allied Disciplines* 35(2) (February 1994): 259–281; Reid, J.B. "Prevention of Conduct Disorder Before and After School Entry: Relating Interventions to Development Findings." *Journal of Development and Psychopathology* 5 (1993): 243–262; and Reid, J.B., Eddy, J.M. "The Prevention of Antisocial Behavior: Some Considerations in the Search for Effective Interventions." In *The Handbook of Antisocial Behavior.* Ed. D.M. Stoff, J. Breiling, and J.D. Maser. New York: Wiley, 1997, pp. 343–356.

10. Olweus, D. "Bullying at School: Basic Facts and Effects of a School-Based Intervention Program." *Journal of Child Psychology and Psychiatry* 35(7) (October 1994): 1171–1190;

and Olweus, D. *Bullying at School: What We Know and What We Can Do.* Oxford: Blackwell, 1994.

11. Conduct Problems Prevention Research Group, "A Developmental and Clinical Model"; Foster, S.L., Prinz, R.J., O'Leary, K.D. "Impact of Problem-Solving Communication Training and Generalization Procedures on Family Conflict." *Child and Family Behavior Therapy* 5 (1983): 1–23; Greenberg, M.T., Kusche, C.A., Cook, E.T., Quamma, J.P. "Promoting Emotional Competence in School-Aged Children: The Effects of the PATHS Curriculum." *Development and Psychopathology* 7(1) (1995): 117–136; Miller, G.E., Prinz, R.J. "The Enhancement of Social Learning Family Interventions for Childhood Conduct Disorder." *Psychological Bulletin* 108(2) (September 1990): 291–307; and Prinz, R.J., Blechman, E.A., Dumas, J.E. "An Evaluation of Peer Coping-Skills Training for Childhood Aggression." *Journal of Clinical Child Psychology* 23(2) (June 1994): 193–203.

12. Laub, J.H., Lauritsen, J.L. "The Interdependence of School Violence With Neighborhood and Family Conditions." In *Violence in American Schools: A New Perspective,* pp. 127–155.

13. Hawkins and Weis, "The Social Development Model."

14. Greenberg et al., "Promoting Emotional Competence."

15. Prinz et al., "An Evaluation of Peer Coping-Skills Training."

16. Beck, E.L. "Prevention and Intervention Programming: Lessons From an After-School Program." *Urban Review* 31 (1999): 107–124; Chaiken, M.R. "Tailoring Established After-School Programs To Meet Urban Realities." In *Violence in American Schools: A New Perspective,* pp. 348–375; Flannery, D.J., Williams, L.L. Vazsonyi, A.T. "Who Are They With and What Are They Doing? Delinquent Behavior, Substance Use, and Early Adolescents' After-School Time." *American Journal of Orthopsychiatry* 69(2) (April 1999): 247–253; and Prinz and Connell, "Prevention of Conduct Disorders," pp. 238–258.

Controlling Violence: What Schools Are Doing

Joseph F. Sheley, PhD, California State University

Recent shootings of students by peers on suburban and rural school grounds have heightened public concern about weapons in the hands of youths. Horrifying as such incidents might be, however, we must resist the temptation to conceptualize the problem of school violence around them. Episodes in which students seek to harm large numbers of their schoolmates fairly at random are not the challenges most commonly faced by the average school administrator.

Administrators are more likely to deal with students bringing weapons (primarily guns and knives) to campus to settle scores with specific individuals, to show off, or to protect themselves in an environment they perceive as hostile.

Indeed, the problem administrators most often encounter is how to address the day-to-day verbal and physical confrontations that may lead a student to carry a weapon to school or spontaneously use a weapon already brought to campus.

WHAT WE KNOW

While national trends indicate that youth violence appears to be declining, the quality of response to these trends will reflect the quality of information available to policy

Preventing Youth Antisocial Behavior and School Violence:

INFORMATION RESOURCES

Available resources on school violence include the following:

Brewer, D.D., Hawkins, J.D., Catalano, R.F., Neckerman, H.J. "Preventing Serious, Violent, and Chronic Juvenile Offending: A Review of Evaluations of Selected Strategies in Childhood, Adolescence, and the Community." In *Sourcebook on Serious, Violent, and Chronic Juvenile Offenders*. Ed. J.C. Howell, B. Krisberg, J.D. Hawkins, and J.J. Wilson. Thousand Oaks, Calif.: Sage Publications, 1995, pp. 61–141.

Catalano, R.F., Arthur, M.W., Hawkins, J.D., Berglund, L., Olson, J.J. "Comprehensive Community- and School-Based Interventions To Prevent Antisocial Behavior." In *Serious and Violent Juvenile Offenders: Risk Factors and Successful Interventions*. Ed. R. Loeber and D.P. Farrington. Thousand Oaks, Calif.: Sage Publications, 1998, pp. 248–283.

Dishion, T.J., McCord, J., Poulin, F. "When Interventions Harm: Peer Groups and Problem Behavior." *American Psychologist* 54(9) (September 1999): 755–764.

Dwyer, K., Osher, D., Warger, C. *Early Warning, Timely Response: A Guide to Safe Schools.* Washington, D.C.: U.S. Department of Education, U.S. Department of Health and Human Services, and U.S. Department of Justice, National Institute of Justice, 1998. NCJ 172880 (www.air-dc.org/cecp/).

Harvard School of Public Health (Violence Prevention Programs), Education Development Center Inc., and Prevention Institute Inc. Partnerships for Preventing Violence: Six-Part Satellite Training Forum. Sponsored by the U.S. Department of Education, Safe and Drug Free Schools Program, in conjunction with the U.S. Department of Health and Human Services (DHHS), Maternal and Child Health Bureau; DHHS, Centers for Disease Control and Prevention; DHHS, Indian Health Service, Center for Injury Prevention; and the U.S. Department of Justice, Office of Juvenile Justice and Delinquency Prevention (www.walcoff.com/partnership/).

Hawkins, J.D., Catalano, R.F., Brewer, D.D. "Preventing Serious, Violent, and Chronic Juvenile Offending: Effective Strategies From Conception to Age 6." In *Sourcebook on Serious, Violent, and Chronic Juvenile Offenders*. Ed. J.C. Howell, B. Krisberg, J.D. Hawkins, and J.J. Wilson. Thousand Oaks, Calif.: Sage Publications, 1995, pp. 47–60.

McCord, J., and Tremblay, R.E. *Preventing Antisocial Behavior.* New York: Guilford, 1992.

makers and administrators. We are just beginning to implement a systematic approach to using information about patterns of youth involvement in weapon-related activity—and other information—in our efforts to protect young people in our schools.

NATIONAL TRENDS

Even at its worst, violence in schools has paled compared with the violence occurring in the communities where students live. Violent acts have not been committed only, or even mainly, at school. Rather, most school-related violence has spilled over from the community onto the campus. After years of increases in youth attacks upon one another[1] and, especially, a surge of such violence in the late 1980s and early 1990s, we appear to be experiencing a downturn in violence generally and in youth violence in particular[2] and a decline in homicide rates across the age spectrum and especially in cities. The violent crime arrest rate for youths younger than age seventeen has declined steadily since 1994,[3] and gun-related homicides committed by youths, ages fourteen through seventeen, have declined steadily since 1993.[4]

The reasons for such declines are not fully apparent. Much of the change has been attributed to a bottoming out of the crack trade that, beginning in the mid-1980s, seemed to spawn a wave of firearm-related homicides by youths and young adults.[5] Much also has been linked to criminal justice crackdowns on serious juvenile offenders and to more sophisticated community and criminal justice efforts to address youth violence, especially as related to gangs.[6]

Others relate changes to such demographic trends as the aging (and death and jailing) of the violence-prone juveniles in the most recent cohorts of high-crime age groups.[7]

Although violence has declined, we should not be lulled into thinking that all is well—the rates of violence among youths remain appalling. The rate for homicides committed by juveniles remains about 70 percent higher than it was from 1970 to 1985. While the numbers are down from previous years, the 1996 U.S. homicide victimization rate per 100,000 black males, ages 14 to 17, was a shocking 53.3; for their white counterparts, the rate was 8.4 per 100,000, low actually only in comparison to the rate for black youths.[8]

Certainly, school administrators may not yet relax their vigilance. More information is needed, and the higher the quality of information supplied to policy makers and school administrators, the higher the potential quality of response to the youth violence problem.

WHAT RESEARCH TELLS US

Sufficient investigation has been conducted to permit us to state with confidence that certain subsets of youth, by virtue of their lifestyles, are more likely than others to be involved in weapon-related violence.[9] Ignoring for now the specific causal tracks by which these variables are linked to harmful outcomes, research results indicate, for example, that juveniles who report serious infractions of the law (such as robbery), are arrested many times, sell drugs (and, to a lesser extent, use drugs), and are gang members generally will report higher levels of gun ownership, carrying, and use.[10]

Yet involvement in illegal behaviors does not predict all weapon-related activity. For example, we have learned that if we hold constant recreational use of guns (such as hunting), problem handgun activities occur even among relatively "good boy" populations. Results of a 1996 survey indicate that three of every hundred male high school students (youths from a broad range of socioeconomic backgrounds and with little involvement in serious crime) possessed a revolver or automatic or semiautomatic handgun; in addition, six of every hundred had carried a gun (generally a handgun) outside the home (more likely in the car than on the person) during the twelve months before the survey interview.[11]

We also know that, although weapon use and transport by juveniles is a problem to some extent for all communities, including suburban and rural populations,[12] traditionally the most serious firearm-related activities have apparently occurred in less-affluent urban populations. One-third of a sample of inner-city male high school students surveyed in 1991, for example, said they had carried a gun outside the home at least occasionally—although, as important, two-thirds had not.[13] We know, however, that once we look at broader populations rather than at inner-city populations, the rates of non-recreational gun carrying (not carried for hunting purposes, for example)—though not the carrying of other types of weapons—appear to be higher in rural areas than in urban areas and higher in urban settings than in suburban settings.[14]

Finally, we know that juveniles apparently do not encounter major difficulties in obtaining firearms. Until recently, rates of gun-related crimes committed by juveniles have been at record levels,[15] amounts and quality of guns in the hands of gang members have appeared to be high,[16] and survey after survey has indicated that youths of all socioeconomic backgrounds generally believe that they can acquire a firearm with relative ease.[17]

If, through all our research, we have learned anything significant that may be applied to making schools safer, it is that most violence committed against juveniles by juveniles and most weapon-carrying by youths is not done for criminal-, drug-, or gang-related ends.[18] Status enhancement (the need for attention and respect from peers) appears to motivate some adolescents to carry firearms outside the home and, by definition, to make the social environments of other youths more dangerous.[19] However, our studies of juveniles' motivation to carry firearms—whether the subjects already are hardened criminals or "good boys," whether they are from the inner city or the farm—persistently point to fear. Juveniles carry guns and other weapons because they believe their social worlds are dangerous places and that they need protection.[20]

Are they wrong? Clearly, individuals easily can misjudge levels of threat to them. Yet, National Crime Victimization Survey data indicate that, in 1997, approximately 1 of every 100 people between ages 12 and 19 was the victim of a robbery, and about 2 of every 100 fell victim to aggravated assault.[21] In 1995, approximately 4 percent of U.S. students, ages 12 through 19, were victims of physical attacks or had property taken from them by force or threat of force on school grounds; of those victims, 12 percent reported seeing a student with a gun at school.[22] Four in 10 inner-city youths surveyed in 1991 reported they had been threatened with a gun or shots had been fired at them.

Three in 10 had been beaten up at or on the way to school, and nearly 2 in 10 had been injured with a weapon other than a gun or knife in or on the way to school.[23] Eight percent of a broader national survey of male students, conducted in 1996, had experienced firearm threats, and 13 percent had been threatened with a knife. One in 4 had a friend and 1 in 20 a family member who had been the victim of a firearm-related crime. In addition, 13 percent reported attending parties where shots had been fired.[24]

Perceptions undoubtedly matter. Nationally, 28 percent of students characterize their school as harboring street gangs, and 65 percent indicate that drugs are available on school grounds.[25] Forty-two percent of the inner-city students who took part in the 1991 survey reported that their friends carried guns, and 8 percent knew someone who had brought a gun to school.[26]

Of the broader (1996) student sample noted above, 14 percent reported that their friends carried weapons. Also, 7 percent estimated their chances of becoming the victim of a shooting as at least "somewhat likely."[27] In summary, although students' level of fear and perception of the need for protection may vary greatly across social strata, it is a mistake to dismiss such concerns as confined to the urban core. Furthermore, whether or not the perception of danger that leads a student to carry a weapon is empirically grounded, the carrying nonetheless shapes the reality of others. Research suggests that, on average, most violence among students stems from unprovoked offensive touches, interference with "personal space," perceived slights, insults, accusations, and so forth.[28] The eventual outcome of these disputes will depend significantly on the presence or absence of a lethal weapon in the hands of one or both disputants.

WHAT SCHOOLS ARE DOING TO RESPOND

The context of youth violence established, we turn to the question of measures taken by schools to address prevention and control. What seems to be a fairly simple research question is not. Until recently, relatively little information had been gathered systematically regarding safety in schools, including the large number of options and programs available to schools as they attempted to provide secure learning environments.[29] Although there would seem to be clear differences in the potential effectiveness of a range of commonly used school safety measures,[30] one of the few national-level studies of types of standard school security measures (e.g., hall monitors, visitor sign-ins) found no significant relationship between these measures and students' chances of violent victimization.[31] Now viewing the issue as more critical, government agencies are beginning to disseminate information about youth violence prevention programs throughout the nation[32] and to call for evaluations of aspects of the U.S. Safe Schools/ Healthy Students Initiative.[33] The movement to produce better-quality information inspired the research described below.

SCHOOL ANTIVIOLENCE MEASURES—SURVEY OF ADMINISTRATORS

In the course of a larger 1996 study of weapon acquisition and use by male students in fifty-three high schools, the opportunity arose to ask administrators of forty-eight of those schools about school characteristics, levels of weapon-related activity in the schools, and antiviolence strategies employed by the schools.[34]

Information from the administrators was supplemented with census data for the cities and towns in which the sampled schools were located. These data included size of city or town; racial and ethnic populations; age, gender, and educational attainment; median household and per capita income; poverty rates; labor force rates, and unemployment rates; and violent and property crime rates. The national directory, Patterson's

American Education, from which the sample of schools for the study was derived, provided information about type of school, grades taught, enrollment, and size of community.[35] These data also were integrated with the administrator survey data. Although the number of administrators who did not participate (five of fifty-three) was too small to include evaluation of statistically significant differences between them and survey participants, they were somewhat more likely to be located at smaller schools in the South and West and in cities or towns with higher than average male populations and higher than average violent crime rates.

The 53 schools themselves were part of a sample of 132 selected randomly from Patterson's American Education. Sampling probabilities were proportionate to the size of the tenth- and eleventh-grade populations enrolled in a given school. At both bivariate and multivariate levels, the 53 participating schools were compared with nonparticipating schools across several variables: region of country, grades offered (6 years, 4 years, 2 years, and so forth), size of enrollment, and public or private status.[36] In addition, they were compared in terms of numerous characteristics of the cities and towns in which they were located: population size, racial and ethnic distributions, age and gender, average educational attainment, income, unemployment rate, percentage in poverty, and crime levels. In all instances except one, no significant differences were apparent between the two samples. The exception was related to the fact that participating schools tended to be located in cities with higher percentages of the population, age sixty-five and older, but this variable ultimately proved to be unrelated to participation status.

As the findings indicate, in the aggregate, the schools ultimately participating in this project displayed considerable variation in all but a few categories. They were roughly evenly divided among regions of the country.

The majority served high school students only. More than half of the schools sampled enrolled more than 1,000 pupils, although few exceeded 2,500.

Nearly 9 of every 10 schools were public institutions, and 7 of every 10 were located in towns with populations of 10,000 or fewer, although most of these schools served regional or county populations.

The population characteristics of the cities and towns in which participating schools were located also varied considerably. In nearly 1 of every 4 cities and towns, more than 30 percent of the citizens were nonwhite, and in nearly 1 in 6 more than a third of the population was younger than 25. Male-female distributions were roughly equal; more than 51 percent of the population was male in only 4 percent of the sites, and the male population was less than 45 percent of the total population in only 2 percent. In 6 of 10 cities and towns, at least 70 percent of the population had earned a high school diploma. At least 3 of every 10 households in 51 percent of the sample cities and towns were headed by less affluent females. One in four sites had unemployment rates exceeding 8 percent, and half had median household incomes below $25,000. Finally, 1 in 3 had violent crime rates exceeding 900 per 100,000 population.

How administrators view the problems: The high school administrators surveyed in this study were asked to describe weapon-related problems in their schools and how they were confronting the problems. While 1 in 5 (19 percent) considered violence either a "somewhat serious" or "very serious" problem in their schools, far fewer saw guns (2 percent) and other weapons (8 percent) as at least "somewhat serious." Only 2 percent considered it even somewhat likely that the average male junior routinely would carry a gun while off campus. The administrators also tended to estimate as relatively low the physical threat to their students. Only 10 percent felt it at least somewhat likely that the average male junior would be physically threatened at school; 10 percent also considered the possibility that the same junior would be physically threatened while out of school as at least somewhat likely. It is also important to note that 50 percent of the administrators considered drugs at least a somewhat serious problem in their schools.

Frequency of actual incidents of violence: The administrators also reported actual experiences with the problem of weapons among students. Only 42 percent reported not recalling any incidents involving guns on school grounds during the past 3 years. Twenty-one percent recalled 3 or more such incidents. Forty-six percent recalled at least 3 incidents involving knives on school grounds during the past 3 years; only 17 percent remembered none. Twenty-eight percent indicated that 3 or more on-campus incidents had involved weapons other than guns or knives; 40 percent indicated no such incidents. Finally, 45 percent of the respondents reported that at least one of their students had been shot, on or off school grounds, during the past 3 years; in fact, 1 in 4 administrators (28 percent) reported at least 2 such shootings.

Links among perceptions, incidents and school characteristics: Not surprisingly, the level of association among most of the problem, threat, and incident variables just described was statistically significant. A sense of violence as a campus problem also suggested a view of guns and other weapons on campus as problems. To the extent that administrators viewed violence on campus as a problem, so also did they offer higher estimates of the likelihood that their students would carry guns off campus. The likelihood of threats of physical violence to students both on and off campus was related to the sense of the campus itself as violent. Finally, recollections of gun- and knife-related incidents on school grounds during the past three years were themselves related statistically significantly. Both were linked to recollections of shootings of students, on or off campus, during the same period.

Given the high level of attention to guns and violence in the urban youth culture, we had expected to find most of the above variables related to size of city or town in which the survey participant lived and the urban, suburban, or rural character of the school's neighborhood. However, administrators' perceptions of the school having a problem with violence, guns, or other weapons were unrelated to either variable. Estimates of the likelihood of gun carrying out of school and of threat in or out of school also were unrelated to either variable.

Only the numbers of gun incidents on school grounds and shootings of students in or out of school were significantly statistically associated with city size and with urban character of school neighborhood. Most of the problem, threat, and incident variables were significantly associated with the administrator's perception of drugs as a problem at his or her school; the sense of a drug problem was highly related to sense of a violence problem, for example. The administrator's estimate of the percentage of the student body whose families received public assistance also was related significantly to many of the problem, threat and incident variables—to the number of gun incidents on campus, for example. An estimate of the percentage of students who drop out of school was related to half of the variables in question—for example, to the likelihood of a threat to a student off campus.

MEASURES TO LIMIT VIOLENCE ON CAMPUS

Administrators were asked to identify which measures, from a long list, their schools had implemented to reduce violence. The more common devices included revised disciplinary codes, locker searches, conflict resolution programs, establishment of dress codes, multicultural sensitivity training, designation of schools as "gun-free" and "drug-free" zones, and suspensions for weapons violations. Relatively few schools (10 percent or fewer) used ID checks at school entrances, metal detectors at school entrances, and video monitoring of hallways and classrooms (although 31 percent used such monitors on school buses). Police patrols in hallways and on school grounds found slightly more favor (15 percent and 27 percent, respectively), as did extra police patrols around school property (21 percent). Photo ID systems for students and staff had been introduced in 33 percent of the schools.

It is important to note that obvious clustering of mechanisms to address violence generally was not apparent. First, there was no cumulative pattern in which those who used more directly security-oriented devices, such as metal detectors at entrances, also used less directly security-oriented devices, such as revised dress codes. Second, the ability to predict use of certain devices based on use of others was moderate at best. Schools that had a dress code, for example, also were statistically significantly more likely to use police patrols in hallways and on school grounds, photo ID systems, and gun-free and drug-free zone designations. They were not more likely to use revised disciplinary codes, suspensions for weapons violations, ID checks at school entrances, locker searches, conflict resolution programs, non-police monitors, extra police patrols around school property, metal detectors, or various video monitoring devices. Finally, other than sharing the use of dress and disciplinary codes, the devices chosen by schools declared gun-free zones and those declared drug-free zones were dissimilar.

LINKS AMONG CONTROL MEASURES, SCHOOL CHARACTERISTICS, AND PERCEPTIONS OF PROBLEMS

None of the violence-limiting measures discussed above was related statistically significantly to size of city or town of residence of the survey participant. Only three—suspension for weapons violations, a dress code, and a photo ID system for staff and students—were related, and one (suspension) negatively so, to degree of urban character of the neighborhood in which the school was located.

Only three—conflict resolution programs, photo IDs, and video monitoring of buses—were related, one (bus video) negatively, to perception of drugs as a problem for the school.

The percentage of students who drop out of school was the predictor of the greatest number of violence-limiting measures used. Its association with use of police on campus and in school hallways, deployment of extra police patrols around school property, use of non-police monitors at the school, use of photo IDs for staff and students, and establishment of the school as a gun-free zone was statistically significant. The administrator's estimate of the percentage of students from families receiving public assistance was linked to the use of police patrols in hallways as well as the use of video monitoring in classrooms and buses (negative association).

In sum, differing pictures of school safety emerge depending on whether we focus on administrators' estimates of the degree of danger on campus or on their recollections of weapon-related incidents on campus or those involving their pupils more generally. The latter suggest the more serious situation. While it may be that the incidents to which administrators referred were not very serious, it is also important to note that nearly half of the administrators (45 percent) recalled that at least one of their pupils had been shot during the past three years (though, again, such shootings did not necessarily occur on school grounds).[37] Neither the estimates of level of danger nor the recollections of actual weapon-related incidents were related to the urban, suburban, or rural character (city or neighborhood) of the school. However, they were related to administrators' estimates of level of campus drug problem and to school dropout rate.

Most schools had adopted some form of institutional response to the problem of violence. Generally, the measures were not extreme and, during the past decade, they have become fairly common in schools nationally. Such measures have included conflict resolution and multicultural programs, designation of the schools as gun-free and drug-free zones, revised disciplinary and dress codes, and suspensions for weapon violations. Far fewer schools had turned to law enforcement for assistance. Again, the choice of violence-limiting mechanism was not related to the urban, suburban, or rural character (city or neighborhood) of the school, although it was related to the administrator's estimate of the school's dropout rate.

THE SEARCH FOR BETTER ANSWERS

During the past several years, communities, their criminal justice systems, and their school systems have made serious strides toward preventing violence by and against children. Trends in violence are sloping downward. We know more about the patterns of youth involvement in weapon-related activity than we ever have before—not only about crime, drugs, gangs, and weaponry but also about children's perceptions of danger in their social environments and their relationship to the transport and use of firearms and other weapons. Nonetheless, we are only at the beginning of a systematic approach to using this and other information in our schools' efforts to protect their pupils.

LITTLE PATTERN IN USE OF VIOLENCE CONTROL MEASURES

Most schools are using some techniques, and many schools many techniques, to lower the risk of weapon-related violence on their premises. The most striking aspect of the study findings, however, is the general absence of patterning in which schools employ which mechanisms. No stacking or cumulative effect is apparent. There is little that is systematic in the relationship of the use of one measure to the use of another. While the dropout rate and, to a lesser extent, other variables are related to use of certain measures against violence, the underlying reason for choosing those measures is unclear. The choice of mechanisms seems unrelated to the level of an administrator's perception of violence as a problem on his or her campus and even to the urban, suburban, or rural nature of that campus.

LITTLE SYSTEMATIC SENSE OF WHAT WORKS

In trying to make sense of these findings, we need to recall that administrators do not make decisions about the prevention of violence in schools in a vacuum. The political liability of administrators and political leaders who "fail to act" before a crisis is enormous. Those who cannot show that they have introduced all or most of the available "common" preventive measures will pay dearly if a serious incident occurs on their watch, whether or not the common preventive measures would have prevented the incident. Thus, to the degree that certain mechanisms have been introduced into some schools, they likely will be introduced into others. We do not know—and we should find out—whether the choices are tied to knowledge about the record of success (or failure) of a given violence prevention technique.

We have reached a point at which enough programs are being used in enough schools to enable us to sort out the more effective programs from the less effective within subsets of school settings. It is highly unlikely that there are many generic violence prevention mechanisms. Mechanisms employed in some schools (inner-city schools, for example) may not work well in others (rural schools, for example). To discover these patterns, we need to work with a large sample of schools, all of which will share much of the same information about what they are doing and what has been happening to the children in their care. Furthermore, we need to be able to ascertain a "quality" application of a given program or mechanism; the manner in which schools introduce conflict resolution programs surely varies, for example. Only if we have this information can we judge whether a finding of "no effect" regarding the use of a measure across schools reflects lack of efficacy of the measure itself or lack of its appropriate application.

COMMUNITY TIES TO SCHOOLS

Increasingly, intervention in the cycle of youth violence is being framed, quite appropriately, less as a school project and more as a community project.[38] While communities must do what they can to remove guns from the hands of juveniles, they likely will not accomplish this goal until they have removed the structural and cultural conditions that now promote gun-related activity in the youth population. If the average community in America has not yet "crossed the line" into truly unsafe situations, then the key to warding off problems lies in discouraging the conditions that have produced them in other settings (i.e., in discouraging the development of a youth culture that defines gun possession as necessary to one's survival). Once such a culture exists, criminal justice attempts to disrupt gun sales and acquisition markets may succeed partially but will not rid communities of the problem because demand for weapons will remain. Indeed, a more organized supply likely will develop to meet demand.

The study findings suggest that most schools have adopted the fundamental elements of persuasion against a culture of violence—some combination of deterrence (locker searches, for example) and ideology (teaching conflict-avoidance skills, for example). The education system is asked to remedy yet another social problem. However, we must guard against the danger of assigning control of violence solely or even primarily to the school curriculum.

Communities may gain schools that are safe havens and permit education to occur—quite reasonable goals. Yet, schools rarely are the source of violence as much as they are the place where disputes arising in the neighborhood are acted out. To the extent that schools succeed in pushing violence off campus, it likely will be displaced back into the surrounding community.

The issue for communities, then, is how to dissuade youths from resolving disputes through violent means and, thereby, convince them that weapons are not necessary to the conduct of everyday living. Conflict resolution and multicultural sensitivity training in schools clearly are helpful, but they do not address the conditions that produce neighborhood disputes in the first place. Nor do they touch deeply, if at all, youths only marginally committed to education, those with extensive school absence records and, certainly, youths who have dropped out of school. The current findings have suggested that schools with high dropout rates appear to encounter greater weapon-related problems on campus. This, it would seem, is more a community problem than a school problem.

Communities with such problems understandably must turn to the criminal justice system for help.[39] Communities without such problems, or those that have them to a lesser degree, should be exploring policy initiatives that identify and address the antecedents of weapon-related activities among juveniles.

Notes

1. Cook, P., and Laub, J. "The Unprecedented Epidemic in Youth Violence." In *Crime and Justice: An Annual Review of Research*, vol. 24. Eds. M. Tonry and M. Moore. Chicago: University of Chicago Press, 1998.

2. Federal Bureau of Investigation. *Crime in the United States, 1997: Uniform Crime Reports.* Washington, D.C.: U.S. Department of Justice, 1998; Rand, M. *Criminal Victimization 1997: Changes 1996–97 with Trends 1993–97.* Washington, D.C.: U.S. Department of Justice, Bureau of Justice Statistics, 1998, NCJ 173385; and Rand, M., Lynch, J., Cantor, D. *Criminal Victimization, 1973–95.* Washington, D.C.: U.S. Department of Justice, Bureau of Justice Statistics, 1997, NCJ 163069.

3. Puzzanchera, C. *The Youngest Offenders, 1996.* Washington, D.C.: U.S. Department of Justice, 1998.

4. Fox, J., Zawitz, M. *Homicide Trends in the United States.* Washington, D.C.: U.S. Department of Justice, Bureau of Justice Statistics, 1999, NCJ 173956.

5. Blumstein, A. "Youth Violence, Guns, and the Illicit-Drug Industry." *Journal of Criminal Law and Criminology* 86(1) (Fall 1995): 10–36; Fagan, J., Wilkinson, D. "Firearms and Youth Violence." In *Handbook of Antisocial Behavior*. Ed. D. Stoff, J. Breiling, and J. Maser. New York: Wiley, 1997; and Sheley, J., Wright, J. *In the Line of Fire: Youth, Guns, and Violence in Urban America*. New York: Aldine de Gruyter, 1995, p. 155.

6. Curry, D., Decker, S. *Confronting Gangs: Crime and Community*. Los Angeles: Roxbury, 1998; Ingersoll, S. "National Juvenile Justice Action Plan: A Comprehensive Response to a Critical Challenge." *Juvenile Justice* 3(2) (September 1997): 11–20; Kennedy, D. "Pulling Levers: Chronic Offenders, High-Crime Settings, and Theory of Prevention." *Valparaiso University Law Review* 31(2) (Spring 1997): 449–484; Roth, J. *The Detroit Handgun Intervention Program: A Court-Based Program for Youthful Handgun Offenders*. Washington, D.C.: U.S. Department of Justice, National Institute of Justice, 1998; Sheppard, D. *Promising Strategies To Reduce Gun Violence*. Washington, D.C.: U.S. Department of Justice, Office of Juvenile Justice and Delinquency Prevention, 1999.

7. Blumstein, A. "The Context of Recent Changes in Crime Rates." In *What Can the Federal Government Do To Decrease Crime and Revitalize Communities? Research Forum, U.S. Department of Justice, National Institute of Justice*. Washington, D.C.: U.S. Department of Justice, National Institute of Justice and Executive Office for Weed and Seed, October 1998, NCJ 172210; Zimring, F. "Kids, Guns, and Homicide: Policy Notes on an Age-Specific Epidemic." *Law and Contemporary Problems* 59(1) (Winter 1996): 24–38; and Zimring, F. *American Youth Violence*. New York: Oxford University Press, 1998.

8. Fox, J. *Trends in Juvenile Violence*. Boston: Northeastern University Press, 1998.

9. Lauritsen, J., Laub, J., Sampson, R. "Conventional and Delinquent Activities: Implications for the Prevention of Violent Victimization Among Adolescents." *Violence and Victims* 7(2) (Summer 1992): 91–108; Lowry, R., Powell, K., Kann, L., Collins, J., Kolbe, L. "Weapon-Carrying, Physical Fighting, and Fight-Related Injury Among U.S. Adolescents." *American Journal of Preventive Medicine* 14(2) (February 1998): 122–129.

10. Decker, S., Pennell, S., Caldwell, A. "Arrestees and Guns: Monitoring the Illegal Firearms Market," final report submitted to the National Institute of Justice, U.S. Department of Justice, 1996, grant no. 95-IJ-R-014; Huff, R. *Comparing the Criminal Behavior of Youth Gangs and At-Risk Youths, Research in Brief*. Washington, D.C.: U.S. Department of Justice, National Institute of Justice, October 1998, NCJ 172852; Sheley and Wright, *In the Line of Fire*; and Sheley, J., Wright, J. *High School Youths, Weapons, and Violence: A National Survey, Research in Brief*. Washington, D.C.: U.S. Department of Justice, National Institute of Justice, October 1998, NCJ 172857.

11. Sheley and Wright, *High School Youths, Weapons, and Violence*.

12. Sheley, J., Brewer, V. "Possession and Carrying of Firearms Among Suburban Youth." *Public Health Reports* 110(1) (January–February 1995): 18–26; and Sheley and Wright, *High School Youths, Weapons, and Violence*.

13. Sheley and Wright, *In the Line of Fire*; Blumstein, "Youth Violence, Guns, and the Illicit-Drug Industry"; and Callahan, C., Rivara, F. "Urban High School Youth and Handguns." *Journal of the American Medical Association* 267(22) (June 1992): 3038–3042.

14. Sheley and Wright, *High School Youths, Weapons, and Violence*.

15. Greenbaum, S. "Kids and Guns: From Playgrounds to Battlegrounds." *Juvenile Justice* 3(2) (September 1997): 3–10; U.S. Department of the Treasury. *ATF Crime Gun Trace Analysis Report: Youth Crime Gun Interdiction Initiative*. Washington, D.C.: U.S. Department of the Treasury, Bureau of Alcohol, Tobacco and Firearms, 1997.

16. Huff, *Comparing the Criminal Behavior of Youth Gangs and At-Risk Youths*.

17. Callahan and Rivara, "Urban High School Youth and Handguns"; Greenbaum, "Kids and

Guns"; Decker et al., "Arrestees and Guns"; Sheley and Wright, *In the Line of Fire;* and Sheley and Wright, *High School Youths, Weapons, and Violence.*

18. Lockwood, D. *Violence Among Middle School and High School Students: Analysis and Implications for Prevention, Research in Brief.* Washington, D.C.: U.S. Department of Justice, National Institute of Justice, October 1997, NCJ 166363; Sheley and Wright, *In the Line of Fire;* Wilkinson, D., Fagan, J. "The Role of Firearms in Violence Scripts: The Dynamics of Gun Events Among Adolescent Males." *Law and Contemporary Problems* 59(1) (Winter 1996): 55–89.

19. Sheley and Wright, *High School Youths, Weapons, and Violence.*

20. Decker et al., *Arrestees and Guns;* Lizotte, A., Tesoriero, J., Thornberry, T., Krohn, M. "Patterns of Adolescent Firearms Ownership and Use." *Justice Quarterly* 11(1) (March 1994): 51–73; Lizotte, A., Howard, G., Krohn, M., Thornberry, T. "Patterns of Illegal Gun Carrying Among Young Urban Males." *Valparaiso University Law Review* 31(2) (Spring 1997): 375–393; and Sheley, J., Wright, J. "Motivations for Gun Possession and Carrying Among Serious Juvenile Offenders." *Behavioral Sciences and the Law* 11(4) (Autumn 1993): 375–388.

21. Rand, *Criminal Victimization 1997.*

22. Chandler, K., Chapman, C., Rand, M., Taylor, B. *Students' Reports of School Crime: 1989 and 1995.* Washington, D.C.: U.S. Department of Justice, 1998.

23. Sheley and Wright, *In the Line of Fire.*

24. Sheley and Wright, *High School Youths, Weapons, and Violence.*

25. Chandler et al., *Students' Reports of School Crime.*

26. Sheley and Wright, *In the Line of Fire.*

27. Sheley and Wright, *High School Youths, Weapons, and Violence.*

28. Lockwood, *Violence Among Middle School and High School Students.*

29. National School Safety Center. *School Safety Check Book.* Malibu, Calif.: National School Safety Center, Pepperdine University, 1988; and Ross, J., Einhaus, K., Hohenemser, L., Greene, B., Kann, L., Gold, R. "School Health Policies Prohibiting Tobacco Use, Alcohol and Other Drug Use, and Violence." *Journal of School Health* 65(8) (October 1995): 333–338.

30. Butterfield, G., Arnette, J. *Weapons in Schools,* NSSC Resource Paper. Malibu, Calif.: National School Safety Center, 1993; and Dwyer, K., Osher, D., Warger, C. *Early Warning, Timely Response: A Guide to Safe Schools.* Washington, D.C.: U.S. Department of Education, 1998.

31. Bastion, L.D., Taylor, B.M. *School Crime: A National Crime Victimization Survey Report.* Washington, D.C.: U.S. Department of Justice, Bureau of Justice Statistics, September 1991, p. 13, NCJ 131645.

32. Dwyer et al., *Early Warning, Timely Response;* U.S. Department of Justice, National Institute of Justice, *What Can the Federal Government Do To Decrease Crime and Revitalize Communities?;* Office of Juvenile Justice and Delinquency Prevention, Juvenile Mentoring Program. *1998 Report to Congress.* Washington, D.C.: U.S. Department of Justice, December 1998; and Sheppard, D. *Promising Strategies To Reduce Gun Violence.* Washington, D.C.: U.S. Department of Justice, Office of Juvenile Justice and Delinquency Prevention, 1999, NCJ 173950.

33. Office of Juvenile Justice and Delinquency Prevention. *National Evaluation of the Safe Schools/Healthy Students Initiative (Solicitation for Proposals).* Washington, D.C.: Office of Justice Programs, 1999.

34. Sheley and Wright, *High School Youths, Weapons, and Violence.*

35. Educational Directories, Inc. *Patterson's American Education.* Mount Prospect, Ill.: Educational Directories, Inc., 1994.

36. Studies of the topic of violence in schools are becoming increasingly difficult. The political climate of the late 1990s differed considerably from that of the early 1990s. Although only a few years before we had gained easy access to students in studies of virtually the same subject, access in 1996 often was effectively denied. Most principals (especially in the western states) who

decided against participating in this study stated that their school boards would not permit a survey of students concerning exposure to weapons and violence. The topic was deemed far too politically sensitive for the community, in the sense that it might lead to embarrassing findings (even though the schools would not be identified) or that it would introduce impressionable students to ideas they should not be considering. In many instances, principals who had pledged cooperation were ordered by their superintendents or their school boards to reverse their decision.

37. The time referent "past three years" used in the survey perhaps somehow softens the effect of the incidents in question. That is, an administrator who recalls a student having been shot three years ago may not indicate the sense of "problem" perceived by the administrator who recalls a more recent shooting.

38. U.S. Department of Justice, National Institute of Justice, *What Can the Federal Government Do To Decrease Crime and Revitalize Communities?*

39. Methods to reduce firearm-related violence among youths are now being tested in Boston. They target reductions without necessarily addressing larger community structural issues. The results have been encouraging, but considerably more research must be conducted in this area. See Kennedy, D., Piehl, A., Braga, A. "Youth Violence in Boston: Gun Markets, Serious Youth Offenders, and a Use-Reduction Strategy." *Law and Contemporary Problems* 59(1) (Winter 1996): 147–196; and Kennedy, "Pulling Levers."

The Federal Government Responds to School Violence

Acutely aware of the problem of school violence, federal government agencies are working to reduce it, both through their own initiatives and in collaboration with other agencies and with states and local communities.

Among these agencies are the Centers for Disease Control and Prevention (Department of Health and Human Services [DHHS]), Department of Education, Department of Housing and Urban Development, Department of Justice, National Institutes of Health (DHHS), Office of National Drug Control Policy, and Substance Abuse and Mental Health Services Administration (DHHS).

An inventory of their activities categorized by type and updated twice a year is at www.cdc.gov/nccdphp/dash. It consists of ongoing and recently completed activities that either directly address violence in or around schools or indirectly address school violence by focusing on its precursors, associated factors, or prevention mechanisms.

WEB BULLYING

The typical bully used to torment unlucky victims out in the open—in school hallways, for instance—spitting out insults and disparaging remarks for anyone to hear and see. But times have changed. Bullying has gone high-tech and anonymous, although it's just as humiliating.

The Internet and cell-phone text messages are the new mediums for "cyberbullies." They post nasty pictures or messages about others in blogs and on Web sites or exploit another person's online username to spread rumors about others.

A COMPREHENSIVE THREE-LEVEL APPROACH TO PREVENTION

Research on safe schools demonstrates that a comprehensive three-level approach to prevention is the most efficient and cost-effective way to reduce the risk of violence.

1. School-wide Foundation

An effective school-wide foundation is designed to improve the academic performance and behavior of all children. The school-wide foundation includes the following:

- Compassionate, caring, respectful staff who model appropriate behaviors, create a climate of emotional support, and are committed to working with all students.
- Developmentally appropriate programs for all children that teach and reinforce social and problem-solving skills.
- Teachers and staff who are trained to support positive school and classroom behaviors.
- Engaging curricula and effective teaching practices.
- Child- and family-focused, culturally competent approaches.
- Collaborative relationships with families, agencies, and community organizations.

These approaches alone are sufficient for most students' needs, but they will not address fully the needs of all students. However, an effective foundation makes it easier to identify students who require additional interventions and increases the effectiveness of all interventions—both early and intensive.

2. Early Intervention

Early intervention is necessary for those students who are at risk of academic failure or behavior problems. Early intervention, along with an appropriate foundation, is sufficient for almost all students and can be used to respond to early warning signs.

3. Intensive Interventions

Intensive interventions are necessary for those students whose needs cannot be fully addressed by early intervention. Intensive interventions should always be individualized to a student's needs and strengths. These interventions often involve multiple coordinated services, such as individualized special education services or interagency wraparound supports.

Safe Schools Combine All Three Levels

For a school to be safe for all children, all three levels must be in place. A school that builds a school-wide foundation will still fail if it ignores the needs of children at risk of severe academic or behavioral problems or children who are seriously troubled. In most schools, a school-wide foundation will meet the needs of most students, while early intervention will address the needs of most of the other students. Individualized intensive interventions will be needed for a relatively small number of students.

I-Safe America, an organization promoting Web safety, surveyed 1,500 students in fourth through grade grade, and found that 42 percent have been bullied online. And 53 percent admitted to saying something mean or hurtful to someone else online.

The Pew Internet & American Life Project reports that approximately 17 million kids ages twelve to seventeen use the Internet. Teens have embraced Instant Messaging (IM)—74 percent of teens IM, compared to only 44 percent of adults.

School officials in Lake County, Florida, have introduced a cyberbullying policy that prohibits this behavior on school computers. Parents must sign a form confirming they have read the policy and discussed it with their children. Punishment could range from a phone call home to an out-of-school suspension, depending on the offense.

"It's obviously happening all over the country, and it could be happening here," said Lynn Jones, safety coordinator for Lake schools.

School districts throughout Central Florida have adopted this policy, as have a growing number of schools across the country. The districts use filters to block the very popular MySpace.com at school, but that doesn't stop bullies who can easily access the site at home. Awareness and education are the keys to preventing cyberbullying, says the anti-bullying Web site www.cyberbullying.org. It offers this advice:

Place/keep computer(s) with Internet access in an open, commonly used space.
Never give out personal information or passwords, PIN numbers, and the like. Personal information includes your name, the names of friends or family, your address, phone number, and school name (or team name if you play sports). Personal info also includes pictures of yourself and your e-mail address. Ask permission before sharing any information with a Web site or a "chat buddy" and even when registering a product purchased for your computer (like a game). Passwords are secrets. Never tell anyone your password, except your parents or guardian.
Don't believe everything you see or read. Just because someone online tells you that they are fifteen doesn't mean they are telling the truth. Even adults can't tell when a male pretends to be a female or a fifty-year-old pretends to be a fifteen-year-old.
Use Netiquette. Be polite to others online just as you would off-line. If someone treats you rudely or meanly—do not respond. Online bullies are just like off-line ones— they WANT you to answer (don't give them the satisfaction).

Don't send a message to someone else when you are angry. Wait until you have calmed down and had time to think. Do your best to make sure that your messages are calmly and factually written. You will usually regret sending a "Flame" (angry) to someone else later on. Once you've sent a message, it is VERY hard to undo the damage that such "flames" can do.

Don't open a message from someone you don't know. If in doubt ask your parents, guardian, or another adult.

If it doesn't look or feel right, it probably isn't. Trust your instincts and teach your kids to trust theirs. While surfing the Internet, if you find something that you don't like, makes you feel uncomfortable, or scares you, turn off the computer and tell an adult.

You don't have to be "Always On"—turn off, disconnect, unplug, try actual reality instead of virtual reality! Give yourself a break. Don't stay online or connected for too long. Spend time with your family and friends off line.

Sign on the dotted line. Make and print out an online contract with your parents or guardians. Ask your parents to read the information for them on this Web site, so they will be informed about cyberbullying and Internet safety issues.

ADVICE TO THE VICTIM

Don't reply to messages from cyberbullies. Even though you may really want to, this is exactly what cyberbullies want. They want to know that they've got you worried and upset. They are trying to mess with your mind and control you, to put fear into you. Don't give them that pleasure.

Do not keep this to yourself! You are NOT alone and you did NOT do anything to deserve this! Tell an adult you know and trust!

Inform your Internet Service Provider (ISP) or cell phone/pager service provider.

Do not erase or delete messages from cyberbullies. You don't have to read it, but keep it; it is your evidence. You may unfortunately get similar messages again, perhaps from other accounts. The police and your ISP and/or your telephone company can use these messages to help you. You might notice certain words or phrases that are also used by people you know. These messages may reveal certain clues as to whom is doing this to you, but don't try and solve this on your own. Remember, tell an adult you know and trust. GET HELP!

Protect yourself. Never arrange to meet with someone you met online unless your parents go with you. If you are meeting them make sure it is in a public place. You may need to delete your current e-mail accounts and/or cell phone/pager accounts and set up new ones. If your cyberbullying problems persist, do this as soon as possible, unless you are working with the police and your telecommunications provider to keep the account(s) active to try and catch the cyberbully.

If you are more technically inclined, you can do a little cyber-sleuthing of your own to provide the police and your telecommunications provider with more information, but NEVER try to meet someone personally whom you suspect might be the cyberbully. This is best left in the hands of the legal authorities.

If you receive an unsolicited harassing e-mail message from a cyberbully, you can often use your mouse to right-click on the header of the offending message and choose the "Options" section of the menu. This will often reveal greater details about the message. You can then do a "**WHOIS**" search with Internic.com. This Web site was established to provide the public information regarding Internet domain name registration services and is updated frequently. The "WHOIS" search will often provide information as to who owns the domain name and their contact information. Share this information with your local police and your telecommunications or Internet service provider.

You can also use software to help protect and/or find out who is sending you harassing messages.

If you are receiving harassing messages from cyberbullies through Web-based mail services, such as Hotmail, Yahoo Mail, and the like, it becomes very difficult to trace such accounts as cyber-bully@hotmail.com. You may have to delete your current e-mail account and start a new one. Tell only a select few people you trust about your new e-mail account when, and if, you choose to reestablish one. If you are receiving harassing messages from cyberbullies through Instant Messaging (IM), software, such as ICQ, MSN Messenger, AOL Instant Messenger, and the like, such programs usually have a "Block," "Ignore," or "Ban" feature. Use this feature to try to "Block," "Ignore," or "Ban" the cyberbullies.

If you are the victim of a cyberbully who has set up a Web site that is defaming or mocking you, contact the Internet service provider and inform them about what is happening; also inform the police. Use the "WHOIS" search tool to help you in the manner described above.

If this is a large Web hosting company, it may take a long time to get a response and a promise of action. ISPs are often very reluctant to act in such cases. Unfortunately, some people have only received a response, or seen such cyberbullying Web sites taken down after the threat of legal action. For more information go to www.cyberbullying.org.

Sexual Harassment

OVERVIEW

Sexual harassment of students is a real and serious problem in education at all levels, including elementary and secondary schools, as well as colleges and universities. It can affect any student, regardless of sex, race, or age. Sexual harassment can threaten a student's physical or emotional well-being, influence how well a student does in school, and make it difficult for a student to achieve his or her career goals. Moreover, sexual harassment is illegal—Title IX of the Education Amendments of 1972 (Title IX) prohibits sex discrimination, including sexual harassment. Preventing and remedying sexual harassment in schools is essential to ensure nondiscriminatory, safe environments in which students can learn.

> A . . . student should feel safe and comfortable walking down the halls of his
> or her school. School is a place for learning and growing. Sexual harassment
> stops that process.

School officials should read "Sexual Harassment Guidance: Harassment of Students by School Employees, Other Students, or Third Parties" to ensure a full understanding of the law. These guidelines were produced by the Office of Civil Rights (OCR), U.S. Department of Education, and published in 1997. More information can be obtained about this and other civil rights issues from their online reading room at www.ed.gov/about/offices/list/ocr/publications.html.

Sexual harassment can occur at any school activity and can take place in classrooms, halls, cafeterias, dormitories, and other areas. Too often, the behavior is allowed to continue simply because students and employees are not informed about what sexual harassment is or how to stop it. Students, parents, and school staff must be able to recognize sexual harassment, and understand what they can do to prevent it from occurring and how to stop it if it does occur.

Harassing behavior, if ignored or not reported, is likely to continue and become worse, rather than go away. The impact of sexual harassment on a student's educational progress and attainment of future goals can be significant and should not be underestimated. As a result of sexual harassment, a student may, for example, have trouble learning, drop a class, or drop out of school altogether, lose trust in school officials, become isolated, fear for personal safety, or lose self-esteem.

For these reasons, a school should not accept, tolerate, or overlook sexual harassment. A school should not excuse the harassment with an attitude of "that's just emerging adolescent sexuality" or "boys will be boys," or ignore it for fear of damaging a professor's reputation. This does nothing to stop the sexual harassment and can even send a message that such conduct is accepted or tolerated by the school. When a school makes it clear that sexual harassment will not be tolerated, trains its staff, and appropriately responds when harassment occurs, students will see the school as a safe place where everyone can learn.

QUESTIONS AND ANSWERS

Q: What are some examples of sexual conduct?

A: Some examples of sexual conduct are:

- Sexual advances
- Touching of a sexual nature
- Graffiti of a sexual nature
- Displaying or distributing sexually explicit drawings, pictures, and written materials
- Sexual gestures
- Sexual or "dirty" jokes
- Pressure for sexual favors

- Touching oneself sexually or talking about one's sexual activity in front of others
- Spreading rumors about or rating other students as to sexual activity or performance

Not all types of physical conduct would be considered sexual in nature. Some examples are a high school athletic coach hugging a student who made a goal, a kindergarten teacher's consoling hug for a child with a skinned knee, or one student's demonstration of a sports move requiring contact with another student.

Q: Must sexual conduct be unwelcome in order to be sexual harassment?

A: Yes. Conduct is unwelcome if the student does not request or invite the conduct and views it as offensive or undesirable. However, just because a student does not immediately speak out or complain does not mean that the sexual conduct was welcome. A student might feel that objecting would only result in increasing the harassing conduct. Sometimes, students feel intimidated by the conduct and/or feel too embarrassed, confused, or fearful to complain or resist. Also, a student who willingly participates in conduct on one occasion may later decide that the same conduct on a subsequent occasion has become unwelcome.

Both parents and school officials should encourage students to speak out and complain about unwelcome sexual conduct—to the harasser, to a school employee, or to a parent. Using age-appropriate methods, parents and school officials should let students know that they should not tolerate unwanted sexual conduct.

Q: Does all sexual conduct create a sexually hostile environment?

A: No. Although even one incident of quid pro quo harassment (e.g., threatening to fail a student) is unlawful, generally, a hostile environment may be created by a series of incidents. So, for example, a sexual joke, even if offensive to the student to whom it was told, will not by itself create a sexually hostile environment. However, a sexual assault or other severe single incident can create a hostile environment.

Q: When does sexual conduct create a sexually hostile environment?

A: In order to answer this question several factors must be considered. Did the student view the environment as hostile? Was it reasonable for the student to view the environment as hostile? All relevant circumstances should be considered, including the following:

- The nature of the conduct
- How often the conduct occurred
- How long the conduct continued
- The age and sex of the student
- Whether the conduct adversely affected the student's education or educational environment
- Whether the alleged harasser was in a position of power over the student subjected to the harassment

- The number of alleged harassers
- The age of the alleged harasser
- Where the harassment occurred
- Other incidents of sexual harassment at the school involving the same or other students

Q: What steps can a school take to prevent sexual harassment?

A: OCR's experience shows that the best way for a school to deal with sexual harassment is to prevent it from occurring. A school may take a number of steps to prevent harassment:

- Develop and publicize a sexual harassment policy that clearly states sexual harassment will not be tolerated and that explains what types of conduct will be considered sexual harassment.
- Develop and publicize a specific grievance procedure for resolving complaints of sexual harassment.
- Develop methods to inform new administrators, teachers, guidance counselors, staff, and students of the school's sexual harassment policy and grievance procedure.
- Conduct periodic sexual harassment awareness training for all school staff, including administrators, teachers, and guidance counselors.
- Conduct periodic age-appropriate sexual harassment awareness training for students.
- Establish discussion groups for both male and female students where students can talk about what sexual harassment is and how to respond to it in the school setting.
- Survey students to find out whether any sexual harassment is occurring at the school.
- Conduct periodic sexual harassment awareness training for parents of elementary and secondary students.
- Work together with parents and students to develop and implement age-appropriate, effective measures for addressing sexual harassment.

Adoption of strong preventive measures is often the best way to confront the serious problem of sexual harassment. In addition, the steps described above may also be useful in responding to sexual harassment once it has occurred to ensure that it does not happen again.

Q: What can a student do if he or she is confronted with sexual harassment?

A: A student who believes he or she has been sexually harassed (or a parent who believes that his or her child has been harassed) should immediately report it to a responsible school official. This could be a teacher, principal, faculty member, administrator, campus security officer, affirmative action officer, staff in the office of student affairs, or the school's Title IX coordinator. If the student feels comfortable doing so, the student should let the harasser know that he or she does not welcome the conduct and wants it to stop. A student may also file a complaint with the school or with OCR, as explained below.

Q: How should a school respond to information about alleged sexual harassment?

A: If a school receives information that sexual harassment may have occurred, the school should move quickly to determine what happened. When a student or parent reports sexual harassment, the school should explain how its grievance procedures work and offer the student or parent the opportunity to use them.

This does not mean that every school employee who learns that harassment may have occurred is directly responsible for finding out what happened, or for taking steps to end any harassment and prevent its recurrence. However, the school should have procedures in place that clearly define each employee's responsibilities. For example, a school could decide that certain employees are only required to report evidence or claims of possible harassment to other school officials (e.g., a principal, dean or Title IX coordinator) who have the responsibility to take appropriate action. The important thing is that something be done and that the school takes steps to find out the facts.

Sometimes a school may need to take interim measures before the investigation is concluded. These steps may include reporting the incident to law enforcement officials, separating the students, or allowing the person claiming harassment to transfer to another class.

Regardless of how a school finds out about possible harassment, it should make every effort to prevent public disclosure of the names of all parties involved, except to the extent necessary to find out what happened. When looking into the matter, particularly where a grievance is filed, the school should pay attention to any due process or other rights the accused student or teacher might have. However, the school should make sure that doing so does not interfere with the protections provided to the complainant by Title IX.

Finally, it is extremely important for a school to make certain to the best of its ability that no harm comes to a student for reporting incidents of sexual harassment. The school should take steps to prevent any retaliation by the alleged harasser or anyone else at the school. The school should tell the student that Title IX prohibits retaliation and reassure the student that the school will take strong responsive actions if it occurs.

Q: What if the student who was harassed insists on confidentiality or asks that the matter not be pursued?

A: Sometimes, a student complaining of harassment may ask the school not to use his or her name in its investigation. Similarly, a student may even ask that the school take no action. In these situations, a school's ability to deal with the alleged harassment may be limited. However, a school may still be able to take some steps to address the matter. For example, a school should, at a minimum, report a sexual assault or other possible criminal activities to the police, even without a complaint from the student. Indeed, state or local laws may require this. In other, less-severe cases, the school should at least keep track of the incident so that it can identify and take action against repeat offenders. However, when faced with a request for confidentiality or to take no action, the school must consider whether the alleged harassment may affect other students. If so, the school may need to take action to prevent those students from being harassed.

Q: What should a school do if it determines that there has been sexual harassment?

A: If a school finds out that there has been sexual harassment, it has an obligation to stop it and make sure that it does not happen again. This includes ending any quid pro quo harassment, eliminating a hostile environment if one has been created, preventing the harassment from occurring again, and, when appropriate, correcting its effects on the student who had been harassed. The judgment and common sense of teachers and school administrators are very important elements of any response to sexual harassment, especially when dealing with very young children. For example, an appropriate response to unwanted sexual touching of an older student by another might be suspension. Where very young children are involved, however, a teacher or administrator may decide that the best way to deal with the situation would be through a discussion of respect for others, including not touching them inappropriately.

Q: What should be included in a school's grievance procedures?

A: The regulations issued by OCR under Title IX require schools to have grievance procedures applying to all forms of sex discrimination. While a school does not have to have procedures specifically addressing sexual harassment, such procedures are often the most effective way of preventing and dealing with this unique problem.

In any event, a school's grievance procedures should:

- Give notice of the procedure, including where complaints can be filed, to students, parents of elementary and secondary students, and employees.
- Assign an impartial investigator to the complainant, and give the parties involved the opportunity to present witnesses and other evidence.
- Set time frames for the major stages of the complaint process.
- Give notice to the parties of the outcome of the complaint.
- Give an assurance that the school will take steps to prevent recurrence of any harassment and that it will correct its discriminatory effects on the complainant and others, where appropriate.

Although not required by Title IX, many schools find that their grievance procedures can be more effective if the procedures:

- Provide an opportunity to appeal the findings and/or remedy.
- Prohibit retaliation for filing a complaint or participating in an investigation or inquiry.
- Include a voluntary and informal means for resolving complaints.
- Keep students informed of the status of their complaints.

Q: What should a school do to publicize its policy against sex discrimination and its grievance procedures?

A: The school should make sure that its policy and grievance procedures are widely distributed and easily understood by students, parents of elementary and secondary students, and employees. Steps a school can take are:

- Publish the policy and grievance procedures as separate documents and make copies available at various locations throughout the school.
- Include the policy and a summary of the procedures in the school's major publications.
- Identify individuals who can explain how the procedures work.
- Designate an employee with in-depth knowledge of sexual harassment and the school's grievance procedures as the Title IX coordinator.

Q: How does a student file an OCR complaint?

A: If a student or a student's parent or other representative decides to file a complaint with OCR, the complaint should be filed with the OCR enforcement office responsible for the state in which the school is located. Generally, the complaint should be filed within 180 days of the last act of alleged discrimination.

The student should give OCR his or her name, address, and daytime phone number, and provide the date(s) and enough information about the alleged incident(s) so that OCR can understand the nature of the complaint.

OCR may extend the time for filing a complaint in certain circumstances. Because OCR encourages the use of school grievance procedures, OCR will generally accept a complaint raising the same allegations up to sixty days after the end of the procedure. OCR case resolution would usually then be limited to the allegations raised in the grievance.

Conclusion

OCR is the federal agency that ensures that schools comply with Title IX. Students should contact one of the OCR offices to receive information about filing a complaint. Schools should also contact one of these offices for technical assistance.

THE LATEST POSITION

In the last few years the Supreme Court has issued several important decisions in sexual harassment cases, including two decisions specifically addressing sexual harassment of students under Title IX: *Gebser v. Lago Vista Independent School District,* 524 U.S. 274 (1998), and *Davis v. Monroe County Board of Education,* 526 U.S. 629 (1999). The Court held in *Gebser* that a school can be liable for monetary damages if a teacher sexually harasses a student, an official who has authority to address the harassment has actual knowledge of the harassment and that official is deliberately indifferent in responding to the harassment. In *Davis,* the Court announced that a school also may be liable for monetary damages if one student sexually harasses another student in the school's program and the conditions of *Gebser* are met.

The Court was explicit in *Gebser* and *Davis* that the liability standards established in those cases are limited to private actions for monetary damages. See, for example, Gebser, 524 U.S. 283, and *Davis,* 526 U.S. at 639. The Court acknowledged, by contrast, the power of federal agencies, such as the Department, to "promulgate and enforce requirements that effectuate [Title IX's] nondiscrimination mandate," even in circumstances that would not give rise to a claim for money damages. See *Gebser,* 524 U.S. at 292.

In an August 1998 letter to school superintendents and a January 1999 letter to college and university presidents, the secretary of education informed school officials that the *Gebser* decision did not change a school's obligations to take reasonable steps under Title IX and the regulations to prevent and eliminate sexual harassment as a condition of its receipt of federal funding.

Detailed Guidelines

It continues to be the case that a significant number of students, both male and female, have experienced sexual harassment, which can interfere with a student's academic performance and emotional and physical well-being. Preventing and remedying sexual harassment in schools is essential to ensuring a safe environment in which students can learn. The guidance applies to students at every level of education. School personnel, who understand their obligations under Title IX, for example, understand that sexual harassment can be sex discrimination in violation of Title IX, are in the best position to prevent harassment and to lessen the harm to students if, despite their best efforts, harassment occurs.

In addressing allegations of sexual harassment, the good judgment and common sense of teachers and school administrators are important elements of a response that meets the requirements of Title IX. A critical issue under Title IX is whether the school recognized that sexual harassment had occurred and took prompt and effective action calculated to end the harassment, prevent its recurrence, and, as appropriate, remedy its effects. If harassment has occurred, doing nothing is always the wrong response. However, depending on the circumstances, there may be more than one right way to respond. The important thing is for school employees or officials to pay attention to the school environment and not to hesitate to respond to sexual harassment in the same reasonable, commonsense manner as they would to other types of serious misconduct.

It is also important that schools not overreact to behavior that does not rise to the level of sexual harassment. As the Department stated in the 1997 guidance, a kiss on the cheek by a first-grader does not constitute sexual harassment. School personnel should consider the age and maturity of students in responding to allegations of sexual harassment.

You must have well-publicized and effective grievance procedures in place to handle complaints of sex discrimination, including sexual harassment complaints. Nondiscrimination policies and procedures are required by the Title IX regulations. In fact, the Supreme Court in *Gebser* specifically affirmed the Department's authority to enforce this requirement administratively in order to carry out Title IX's nondiscrimination mandate, 524 U.S. at 292. Strong policies and effective grievance procedures are essential to let students and employees know that sexual harassment will not be tolerated and to ensure that they know how to report it.

Sexual Harassment Guidance: Harassment of Students by School Employees, Other Students, or Third Parties

I. INTRODUCTION

Title IX of the Education Amendments of 1972 and the Department of Education's implementing regulations[1] prohibit discrimination on the basis of sex in federally assisted education programs and activities.[2] The Supreme Court, Congress, and federal executive departments and agencies, including the Department, have recognized that sexual harassment of students can constitute discrimination prohibited by Title IX.[3] This guidance focuses on a school's[4] fundamental compliance responsibilities under Title IX and the Title IX regulations to address sexual harassment of students as a condition of continued receipt of federal funding. It describes the regulatory basis for a school's compliance responsibilities under Title IX, outlines the circumstances under which sexual harassment may constitute discrimination prohibited by the statute and regulations, and provides information about actions that schools should take to prevent sexual harassment or to address it effectively if it does occur.[5]

II. SEXUAL HARASSMENT

Sexual harassment is unwelcome conduct of a sexual nature. Sexual harassment can include unwelcome sexual advances, requests for sexual favors, and other verbal, non-verbal, or physical conduct of a sexual nature.[6] Sexual harassment of a student can deny or limit, on the basis of sex, the student's ability to participate in or to receive benefits, services, or opportunities in the school's program. Sexual harassment of students is, therefore, a form of sex discrimination prohibited by Title IX under the circumstances described in this guidance.

It is important to recognize that Title IX's prohibition against sexual harassment does not extend to legitimate nonsexual touching or other nonsexual conduct. For example, a high school athletic coach hugging a student who made a goal or a kindergarten teacher's consoling hug for a child with a skinned knee will not be considered sexual harassment.[7] Similarly, one student's demonstration of a sports maneuver or technique requiring contact with another student will not be considered sexual harassment. However, in some circumstances, nonsexual conduct may take on sexual connotations and rise to the level of sexual harassment. For example, a teacher's repeatedly hugging and putting his or her arms around students under inappropriate circumstances could create a hostile environment.

III. APPLICABILITY OF TITLE IX

Title IX applies to all public and private educational institutions that receive federal funds, that is, recipients, including, but not limited to, elementary and secondary schools, school districts, proprietary schools, colleges, and universities. The guidance uses the terms "recipients" and "schools" interchangeably to refer to all of those institutions. The "education program or activity" of a school includes all of the school's operations.[8] This means that Title IX protects students in connection with all academic, educational, extracurricular, athletic, and other programs of the school, whether they take place in the facilities of the school, on a school bus, at a class or training program sponsored by the school at another location, or elsewhere.

A student may be sexually harassed by a school employee,[9] another student, or a non-employee third party (e.g., a visiting speaker or visiting athletes). Title IX protects any "person" from sex discrimination. Accordingly, both male and female students are protected from sexual harassment[10] engaged in by a school's employees, other students, or third parties. Moreover, Title IX prohibits sexual harassment regardless of the sex of the harasser, that is, even if the harasser and the person being harassed are members of the same sex.[11] An example would be a campaign of sexually explicit graffiti directed at a particular girl by other girls.[12]

Although Title IX does not prohibit discrimination on the basis of sexual orientation,[13] sexual harassment directed at gay or lesbian students that is sufficiently serious to limit or deny a student's ability to participate in or benefit from the school's program constitutes sexual harassment prohibited by Title IX under the circumstances described in this guidance.[14] For example, if a male student or a group of male students target a gay student for physical sexual advances, serious enough to deny or limit the victim's ability to participate in or benefit from the school's program, the school would need to respond promptly and effectively, as described in this guidance, just as it would if the victim were heterosexual. On the other hand, if students heckle another student with comments based on the student's sexual orientation (e.g., "gay students are not welcome at this table in the cafeteria"), but their actions do not involve conduct of a sexual nature, their actions would not be sexual harassment covered by Title IX.[15]

Though beyond the scope of this guidance, gender-based harassment, which may include acts of verbal, nonverbal, or physical aggression, intimidation, or hostility based on sex or sex-stereotyping,[16] but not involving conduct of a sexual nature, is also a form of sex discrimination to which a school must respond, if it rises to a level that denies or limits a student's ability to participate in or benefit from the educational program.[17] For example, the repeated sabotaging of female graduate students' laboratory experiments by male students in the class could be the basis of a violation of Title IX. A school must respond to such harassment in accordance with the standards and procedures described in this guidance.[18] In assessing all related circumstances to determine whether a hostile environment exists, incidents of gender-based harassment combined with incidents of sexual harassment could create a hostile environment, even if neither the gender-based harassment alone nor the sexual harassment alone would be sufficient to do so.[19]

IV. TITLE IX REGULATORY COMPLIANCE RESPONSIBILITIES

As a condition of receiving funds from the Department, a school is required to comply with Title IX and the Department's Title IX regulations, which spell out prohibitions against sex discrimination. The law is clear that sexual harassment may constitute sex discrimination under Title IX.[20]

Recipients specifically agree, as a condition for receiving federal financial assistance from the Department, to comply with Title IX and the Department's Title IX regulations. The regulatory provision requiring this agreement, known as an assurance of compliance, specifies that recipients must agree that education programs or activities operated by the recipient will be operated in compliance with the Title IX regulations, including taking any action necessary to remedy its discrimination or the effects of its discrimination in its programs.[21]

The regulations set out the basic Title IX responsibilities a recipient undertakes when it accepts federal financial assistance, including the following specific obligations.[22] A recipient agrees that, in providing any aid, benefit, or service to students, it will not, on the basis of sex—

- Treat one student differently from another in determining whether the student satisfies any requirement or condition for the provision of any aid, benefit, or service;[23]
- Provide different aid, benefits, or services or provide aid, benefits, or services in a different manner;[24]
- Deny any student any such aid, benefit, or service;[25]
- Subject students to separate or different rules of behavior, sanctions, or other treatment;[26]
- Aid or perpetuate discrimination against a student by providing significant assistance to any agency, organization, or person that discriminates on the basis of sex in providing any aid, benefit, or service to students;[27] and
- Otherwise limit any student in the enjoyment of any right, privilege, advantage, or opportunity.[28]

For the purposes of brevity and clarity, this guidance generally summarizes this comprehensive list by referring to a school's obligation to ensure that a student is not denied or limited in the ability to participate in or benefit from the school's program on the basis of sex. The regulations also specify that, if a recipient discriminates on the basis of sex, the school must take remedial action to overcome the effects of the discrimination.[29]

In addition, the regulations establish procedural requirements that are important for the prevention or correction of sex discrimination, including sexual harassment. These requirements include issuance of a policy against sex discrimination[30] and adoption and publication of grievance procedures providing for prompt and equitable resolution of complaints of sex discrimination.[31] The regulations also require that recipients designate at least one employee to coordinate compliance with the regulations, including coordination of investigations of complaints alleging noncompliance.[32]

To comply with these regulatory requirements, schools need to recognize and respond to sexual harassment of students by teachers and other employees, by other students, and by third parties. This guidance explains how the requirements of the Title IX regulations apply to situations involving sexual harassment of a student and outlines measures that schools should take to ensure compliance.

V. DETERMINING A SCHOOL'S RESPONSIBILITIES

In assessing sexually harassing conduct, it is important for schools to recognize that two distinct issues are considered. The first issue is whether, considering the types of harassment discussed in the following section, the conduct denies or limits a student's ability to participate in or benefit from the program based on sex. If it does, the second issue is the nature of the school's responsibility to address that conduct. As discussed in a following section, this issue depends in part on the identity of the harasser and the context in which the harassment occurred.

A. Harassment That Denies or Limits a Student's Ability to Participate in or Benefit from the Education Program

This guidance moves away from specific labels for types of sexual harassment.[33] In each case, the issue is whether the harassment rises to a level that it denies or limits a student's ability to participate in or benefit from the school's program based on sex. However, an understanding of the different types of sexual harassment can help schools determine whether or not harassment has occurred that triggers a school's responsibilities under, or violates, Title IX or its regulations.

The type of harassment traditionally referred to as *quid pro quo* harassment occurs if a teacher or other employee conditions an educational decision or benefit on the student's submission to unwelcome sexual conduct.[34] Whether the student resists and suffers the threatened harm or submits and avoids the threatened harm, the student has been treated differently, or the student's ability to participate in or benefit from the school's program has been denied or limited, on the basis of sex in violation of the Title IX regulations.[35]

By contrast, sexual harassment can occur that does not explicitly or implicitly condition a decision or benefit on submission to sexual conduct. Harassment of this type is generally referred to as hostile environment harassment.[36] This type of harassing conduct requires a further assessment of whether or not the conduct is sufficiently serious to deny or limit a student's ability to participate in or benefit from the school's program based on sex.[37]

Teachers and other employees can engage in either type of harassment. Students and third parties are not generally given responsibility over other students and, thus, generally can only engage in hostile environment harassment.

1. Factors Used to Evaluate Hostile Environment Sexual Harassment

As outlined in the following paragraphs, OCR considers a variety of related factors to determine if a hostile environment has been created, that is, if sexually harassing conduct by an employee, another student, or a third party is sufficiently serious that it denies or limits a student's ability to participate in or benefit from the school's program based on sex. OCR considers the conduct from both a subjective[38] and objective[39] perspective. In evaluating the severity and pervasiveness of the conduct, OCR considers all relevant circumstances, that is, "the constellation of surrounding circumstances, expectations and relationships."[40] Schools should also use these factors to evaluate conduct in order to draw commonsense distinctions between conduct that constitutes sexual harassment and conduct that does not rise to that level. Relevant factors include the following:

- *The degree to which the conduct affected one or more students' education.* OCR assesses the effect of the harassment on the student to determine whether it has denied or limited the student's ability to participate in or benefit from the school's program. For example, a student's grades may go down or the student may be forced to withdraw from school because of the harassing behavior.[41] A student may also suffer physical injuries or mental or emotional distress.[42] In another situation, a student may have been able to keep up his or her grades and continue to attend school, even though it was very difficult for him or her to do so because of the teacher's repeated sexual advances. Similarly, a student may be able to remain on a sports team, despite experiencing great difficulty performing at practices and games from the humiliation and anger caused by repeated sexual advances and intimidation by several team members that create a hostile environment. Harassing conduct in these examples would alter a reasonable student's educational environment and adversely affect the student's ability to participate in or benefit from the school's program on the basis of sex.

    A hostile environment can occur even if the harassment is not targeted specifically at the individual complainant.[43] For example, if a student, group of students, or a teacher regularly directs sexual comments toward a particular student, a hostile environment may be created not only for the targeted student, but also for others who witness the conduct.

- *The type, frequency, and duration of the conduct.* In most cases, a hostile environment will exist if there is a pattern or practice of harassment, or if the harassment is sustained and nontrivial.[44] For instance, if a young woman is taunted by one or more young men about her breasts or genital area or both, OCR may find that a hostile environment has been created, particularly if the conduct has gone on for some time, or takes place throughout the school, or if the taunts are made by a number of students. The more severe the conduct, the less the need to show a repetitive series of incidents; this is particularly true if the harassment is physical. For instance, if the conduct is more severe, for example, attempts to grab a female student's breasts or attempts to grab any student's genital area or buttocks, it need not be as persistent to create a hostile environment. Indeed, a single or isolated incident of sexual harassment may, if sufficiently severe, create a hostile environment.[45] On the other hand, conduct that is not severe will not create a hostile environment, for example, a comment by one student to another student that she has a nice figure. Indeed, depending on the circumstances, this may not even be conduct of a sexual nature.[46] Similarly, because students date one another, a request for a date or a gift of flowers, even if unwelcome, would not create a hostile environment. However, there may be circumstances in which repeated, unwelcome requests for dates or similar conduct could create a hostile environment. For example, a person, who has been refused previously, may request dates in an intimidating or threatening manner.

- *The identity of and relationship between the alleged harasser and the subject or subjects of the harassment.* A factor to be considered, especially in cases involving allegations of sexual harassment of a student by a school employee, is the identity of and relationship between the alleged harasser and the subject or subjects of the harassment. For example, due to the power a professor or teacher has over a student, sexually based conduct by that person toward a student is more likely to create a hostile environment than similar conduct by another student.[47]

- *The number of individuals involved.* Sexual harassment may be committed by an individual or a group. In some cases, verbal comments or other conduct from one person might not be sufficient to create a hostile environment, but could be if done by a group. Similarly, while harassment can be directed toward an individual or a group,[48] the effect of the conduct toward a group may vary, depending on the type of conduct and the context. For certain types of conduct, there may be "safety in numbers." For example, following an individual student and making sexual taunts to him or her may be very intimidating to that student, but, in certain circumstances, less so to a group of students. On the other hand, persistent unwelcome sexual conduct still may create a hostile environment if directed toward a group.

- *The age and sex of the alleged harasser and the subject or subjects of the harassment.* For example, in the case of younger students, sexually harassing conduct is more likely to be intimidating if coming from an older student.[49]

- *The size of the school, location of the incidents, and context in which they occurred.* Depending on the circumstances of a particular case, fewer incidents may have a greater effect at a small college than at a large university campus. Harassing conduct occurring on a school bus may be more intimidating than similar conduct on a school playground because the restricted area makes it impossible for students to avoid their harassers.[50] Harassing conduct in a personal or secluded area, such as a dormitory room or residence hall, can have a greater effect (e.g., be seen as more threatening) than would similar conduct in a more public area. On the other hand, harassing conduct in a public place may be more humiliating. Each incident must be judged individually.

- *Other incidents at the school.* A series of incidents at the school, not involving the same students, could taken together create a hostile environment, even if each by itself would not be sufficient.[51]

- *Incidents of gender-based, but nonsexual harassment.* Acts of verbal, nonverbal, or physical aggression, intimidation, or hostility based on sex, but not involving sexual activity or language, can be combined with incidents of sexual harassment to determine if the incidents of sexual harassment are sufficiently serious to create a sexually hostile environment.[52]

It is the totality of the circumstances in which the behavior occurs that is critical in determining whether a hostile environment exists. Consequently, in using the factors discussed previously to evaluate incidents of alleged harassment, it is always important to use common sense and reasonable judgment in determining whether a sexually hostile environment has been created.

2. Welcomeness

The section entitled "Sexual Harassment" explains that in order for conduct of a sexual nature to be sexual harassment, it must be unwelcome. Conduct is unwelcome if the student did not request or invite it and "regarded the conduct as undesirable or offensive."[53] Acquiescence in the conduct or the failure to complain does not always mean that the conduct was welcome.[54] For example, a student may decide not to resist sexual advances of another student or may not file a complaint out of fear. In addition, a student may not object to a pattern of demeaning comments directed at him or her by a group of students out of a concern that objections might cause the harassers to make more comments. The fact that a student may have accepted the conduct does not mean that he or she welcomed it.[55] Also, the fact that a student willingly participated in conduct on one occasion does not prevent him or her from indicating that the same conduct has become unwelcome on a subsequent occasion. On the other hand, if a student actively participates in sexual banter and discussions and gives no indication that he or she objects, then the evidence generally will not support a conclusion that the conduct was unwelcome.[56]

If younger children are involved, it may be necessary to determine the degree to which they are able to recognize that certain sexual conduct is conduct to which they can or should reasonably object and the degree to which they can articulate an objection. Accordingly, OCR will consider the age of the student, the nature of the conduct involved, and other relevant factors in determining whether a student had the capacity to welcome sexual conduct.

Schools should be particularly concerned about the issue of welcomeness if the harasser is in a position of authority. For instance, because students may be encouraged to believe that a teacher has absolute authority over the operation of his or her classroom, a student may not object to a teacher's sexually harassing comments during class; however, this does not necessarily mean that the conduct was welcome. Instead, the student may believe that any objections would be ineffective in stopping the harassment or may fear that by making objections he or she will be singled out for harassing comments or other retaliation.

In addition, OCR must consider particular issues of welcomeness if the alleged harassment relates to alleged "consensual" sexual relationships between a school's adult employees and its students. If elementary students are involved, welcomeness will not be an issue: OCR will never view sexual conduct between an adult school employee and an elementary school student as consensual. In cases involving secondary students, there will be a strong presumption that sexual conduct between an adult school employee and a student is not consensual. In cases involving older secondary students, subject to the presumption,[57] OCR will consider a number of factors in determining whether a school employee's sexual advances or other sexual conduct could be considered welcome.[58] In addition, OCR will consider these factors in all cases involving postsecondary students in making those determinations.[59] The factors include the following:

- The nature of the conduct and the relationship of the school employee to the student, including the degree of influence (which could, at least in part, be affected by the student's age), authority, or control the employee has over the student.
- Whether the student was legally or practically unable to consent to the sexual conduct in question. For example, a student's age could affect his or her ability to do so. Similarly, certain types of disabilities could affect a student's ability to do so.

If there is a dispute about whether harassment occurred or whether it was welcome in a case in which it is appropriate to consider whether the conduct would be welcome, determinations should be made based on the totality of the circumstances. The following types of information may be helpful in resolving the dispute:

- Statements by any witnesses to the alleged incident.
- Evidence about the relative credibility of the allegedly harassed student and the alleged harasser. For example, the level of detail and consistency of each person's account should be compared in an attempt to determine who is telling the truth. Another way to assess credibility is to see if corroborative evidence is lacking where it should logically exist. However, the absence of witnesses may indicate only the unwillingness of others to step forward, perhaps due to fear of the harasser or a desire not to get involved.
- Evidence that the alleged harasser has harassed others may support the credibility of the student claiming the harassment; conversely, the student's claim will be weakened if he or she has made false allegations against other individuals.
- Evidence of the allegedly harassed student's reaction or behavior after the alleged harassment. For example, were there witnesses who saw the student immediately after the alleged incident who say that the student appeared to be upset? However, it is important to note that some students may respond to harassment in ways that do not manifest themselves right away, but may surface several days or weeks after the harassment. For example, a student may initially show no signs of having been harassed, but several weeks after the harassment, there may be significant changes in the student's behavior, including difficulty concentrating on academic work, symptoms of depression, and a desire to avoid certain individuals and places at school.
- Evidence about whether the student claiming harassment filed a complaint or took other action to protest the conduct soon after the alleged incident occurred. However, failure to immediately complain may merely reflect a fear of retaliation or a fear that the complainant may not be believed rather than that the alleged harassment did not occur.
- Other contemporaneous evidence. For example, did the student claiming harassment write about the conduct and his or her reaction to it soon after it occurred (e.g., in a diary or letter)? Did the student tell others (friends, parents) about the conduct (and his or her reaction to it) soon after it occurred?

B. Nature of the School's Responsibility to Address Sexual Harassment

A school has a responsibility to respond promptly and effectively to sexual harassment. In the case of harassment by teachers or other employees, the nature of this responsibility depends in part on whether the harassment occurred in the context of the employee's provision of aid, benefits, or services to students.

1. Harassment by Teachers and Other Employees

Sexual harassment of a student by a teacher or other school employee can be discrimination in violation of Title IX.[60] Schools are responsible for taking prompt and effective action to stop the harassment and prevent its recurrence. A school also may be responsible for remedying the effects of the harassment on the student who was harassed. The extent of a recipient's responsibilities if an employee sexually harasses a student is determined by whether or not the harassment occurred in the context of the employee's provision of aid, benefits, or services to students.

A recipient is responsible under the Title IX regulations for the nondiscriminatory provision of aid, benefits, and services to students. Recipients generally provide aid, benefits, and services to students through the responsibilities they give to employees. If an employee who is acting (or who reasonably appears to be acting) in the context of carrying out these responsibilities over students engages in sexual harassment, generally this means harassment that is carried out during an employee's performance of his or her responsibilities in relation to students, including teaching, counseling, supervising, advising, or transporting students, and the harassment denies or limits a student's ability to participate in or benefit from a school program on the basis of sex,[61] the recipient is responsible for the discriminatory conduct.[62] The recipient is, therefore, also responsible for remedying any effects of the harassment on the victim, as well as for ending the harassment and preventing its recurrence. This is true whether or not the recipient has "notice" of the harassment. (As explained in the section on "Notice of Employee, Peer, or Third Party Harassment," for purposes of this guidance, a school has notice of harassment if a responsible school employee actually knew or, in the exercise of reasonable care, should have known about the harassment.) Of course, under OCR's administrative enforcement, recipients always receive actual notice and the opportunity to take appropriate corrective action before any finding of violation or possible loss of federal funds.

Whether or not sexual harassment of a student occurred within the context of an employee's responsibilities for providing aid, benefits, or services is determined on a case-by-case basis, taking into account a variety of factors. If an employee conditions the provision of an aid, benefit, or service that the employee is responsible for providing on a student's submission to sexual conduct, that is, conduct traditionally referred to as *quid pro quo* harassment, the harassment is clearly taking place in the context of the employee's responsibilities to provide aid, benefits, or services." In other situations, that is, when an employee has created a hostile environment, OCR will consider the following factors in determining whether or not the harassment has taken place in this context, including:

- The type and degree of responsibility given to the employee, including both formal and informal authority, to provide aids, benefits, or services to students, to direct and control student conduct, or to discipline students generally.
- The degree of influence the employee has over the particular student involved, including in the circumstances in which the harassment took place.

- Where and when the harassment occurred.
- The age and educational level of the student involved.
- As applicable, whether, in light of the student's age and educational level and the way the school is run, it would be reasonable for the student to believe that the employee was in a position of responsibility over the student, even if the employee was not.

These factors are applicable to all recipient educational institutions, including elementary and secondary schools, colleges, and universities. Elementary and secondary schools, however, are typically run in a way that gives teachers, school officials, and other school employees a substantial degree of supervision, control, and disciplinary authority over the conduct of students.[63] Therefore, in cases involving allegations of harassment of elementary and secondary school-age students by a teacher or school administrator during any school activity,[64] consideration of these factors will generally lead to a conclusion that the harassment occurred in the context of the employee's provision of aid, benefits, or services.

For example, a teacher sexually harasses an eighth-grade student in a school hallway. Even if the student is not in any of the teacher's classes and even if the teacher is not designated as a hall monitor, given the age and educational level of the student and the status and degree of influence of teachers in elementary and secondary schools, it would be reasonable for the student to believe that the teacher had at least informal disciplinary authority over students in the hallways. Thus, OCR would consider this an example of conduct that is occurring in the context of the employee's responsibilities to provide aid, benefits, or services.

Other examples of sexual harassment of a student occurring in the context of an employee's responsibilities for providing aid, benefits, or services include, but are not limited to—a faculty member at a university's medical school conditions an intern's evaluation on submission to his sexual advances and then gives her a poor evaluation for rejecting the advances; a high school drama instructor does not give a student a part in a play because she has not responded to sexual overtures from the instructor; a faculty member withdraws approval of research funds for her assistant because he has rebuffed her advances; a journalism professor who supervises a college newspaper continually and inappropriately touches a student editor in a sexual manner, causing the student to resign from the newspaper staff; and a teacher repeatedly asks a ninth-grade student to stay after class and attempts to engage her in discussions about sex and her personal experiences while they are alone in the classroom, causing the student to stop coming to class. In each of these cases, the school is responsible for the discriminatory conduct, including taking prompt and effective action to end the harassment, prevent it from recurring, and remedy the effects of the harassment on the victim.

Sometimes harassment of a student by an employee in the school's program does not take place in the context of the employee's provision of aid, benefits, or services, but nevertheless is sufficiently serious to create a hostile educational environment. An example of this conduct might occur if a faculty member in the history department at a university, over the course of several weeks, repeatedly touches and makes sexually suggestive remarks to a graduate engineering student while waiting at a stop for the university shuttle bus, riding on the bus, and upon exiting the bus. As a result, the student stops using the campus shuttle and walks the very long distances between her classes. In this case, the school is not directly responsible for the harassing conduct because it did not occur in the context of the employee's responsibilities for the provision of aid, benefits, or services to students. However, the conduct is sufficiently serious to deny or limit the student in her ability to participate in or benefit from the recipient's program. Thus, the school has a duty, upon notice of the harassment,[65] to take prompt and effective action to stop the harassment and prevent its recurrence.

If the school takes these steps, it has avoided violating Title IX. If the school fails to take the necessary steps, however, its failure to act has allowed the student to continue to be subjected to a hostile environment that denies or limits the student's ability to participate in or benefit from the school's program. The school, therefore, has engaged in its own discrimination. It then becomes responsible, not just for stopping the conduct and preventing it from happening again, but for remedying the effects of the harassment on the student that could reasonably have been prevented if the school had responded promptly and effectively. (For related issues, see the sections on "OCR Case Resolution" and "Recipient's Response.")

2. Harassment by Other Students or Third Parties

If a student sexually harasses another student and the harassing conduct is sufficiently serious to deny or limit the student's ability to participate in or benefit from the program, and if the school knows or reasonably should know[66] about the harassment, the school is responsible for taking immediate effective action to eliminate the hostile environment and prevent its recurrence.[67] As long as the school, upon notice of the harassment, responds by taking prompt and effective action to end the harassment and prevent its recurrence, the school has carried out its responsibility under the Title IX regulations. On the other hand, if, upon notice, the school fails to take prompt, effective action, its own inaction has permitted the student to be subjected to a hostile environment that denies or limits the student's ability to participate in or benefit from the school's program on the basis of sex.[68] In this case, the school is responsible for taking effective corrective actions to stop the harassment, prevent its recurrence, and remedy the effects on the victim that could reasonably have been prevented had it responded promptly and effectively.

Similarly, sexually harassing conduct by third parties, who are not employees or students at the school (e.g., a visiting speaker or members of a visiting athletic team), may also be of a sufficiently serious nature to deny or limit a student's ability to participate in or benefit from the education program. As previously outlined in connection with peer harassment, if the school knows or should know[69] of the harassment, the school is responsible for taking prompt and effective action to eliminate the hostile environment and prevent its recurrence.

The type of appropriate steps that the school should take will differ depending on the level of control that the school has over the third party harasser.[70] For example, if athletes from a visiting team harass the home school's students, the home school may not be able to discipline the athletes. However, it could encourage the other school to take appropriate action to prevent further incidents; if necessary, the home school may choose not to invite the other school back. (This issue is discussed more fully in the section on "Recipient's Response.")

If, upon notice, the school fails to take prompt and effective corrective action, its own failure has permitted the student to be subjected to a hostile environment that limits the student's ability to participate in or benefit from the education program.[71] In this case, the school is responsible for taking corrective actions to stop the harassment, prevent its recurrence, and remedy the effects on the victim that could reasonably have been prevented had the school responded promptly and effectively.

C. Notice of Employee, Peer, or Third-Party Harassment

As described in the section on "Harassment by Teachers and Other Employees," schools may be responsible for certain types of employee harassment that occurred before the school otherwise had notice of the harassment. On the other hand, as described in that section and the section on "Harassment by Other Students or Third Parties," in situations involving certain other types of employee harassment, or harassment by peers or third parties, a school will be in violation of the Title IX regulations if the school "has notice" of a sexually hostile environment and fails to take immediate and effective corrective action.[72]

A school has notice if a responsible employee "knew, or in the exercise of reasonable care should have known," about the harassment.[73] A responsible employee would include any employee who has the authority to take action to redress the harassment, who has the duty to report sexual harassment or any other misconduct by students or employees to appropriate school officials, or an individual whom a student could reasonably believe has this authority or responsibility.[74] Accordingly, schools need to ensure that employees are trained so that those with authority to address harassment know how to respond appropriately, and other responsible employees know that they are obligated to report harassment to appropriate school officials. Training for employees should include practical information about how to identify harassment and, as applicable, the person to whom it should be reported.

A school can receive notice of harassment in many different ways. A student may have filed a grievance with the Title IX coordinator[75] or complained to a teacher or other responsible employee about fellow students harassing him or her. A student, parent, or other individual may have contacted other appropriate personnel, such as a principal, campus security, bus driver, teacher, affirmative action officer, or staff in the office of student affairs. A teacher or other responsible employee of the school may have witnessed the harassment. The school may receive notice about harassment in an indirect manner, from sources such as a member of the school staff, a member of the educational or local community, or the media. The school also may have learned about the harassment from flyers about the incident distributed at the school or posted around the school. For the purposes of compliance with the Title IX regulations, a school has a duty to respond to harassment about which it reasonably should have known, that is, if it would have learned of the harassment if it had exercised reasonable care or made a "reasonably diligent inquiry."[76]

For example, in some situations if the school knows of incidents of harassment, the exercise of reasonable care should trigger an investigation that would lead to a discovery of additional incidents.[77] In other cases, the pervasiveness of the harassment may be enough to conclude that the school should have known of the hostile environment if the harassment is widespread, openly practiced, or well-known to students and staff (such as sexual harassment occurring in the hallways, graffiti in public areas, or harassment occurring during recess under a teacher's supervision.)[78]

If a school otherwise knows or reasonably should know of a hostile environment and fails to take prompt and effective corrective action, a school has violated Title IX even if the student has failed to use the school's existing grievance procedures or otherwise inform the school of the harassment.

D. The Role of Grievance Procedures

Schools are required by the Title IX regulations to adopt and publish grievance procedures providing for prompt and equitable resolution of sex discrimination complaints, including complaints of sexual harassment, and to disseminate a policy against sex discrimination.[79] (These issues are discussed in the section on "Prompt and Equitable Grievance Procedures.") These procedures provide a school with a mechanism for discovering sexual harassment as early as possible and for effectively correcting problems, as required by the Title IX regulations. By having a strong policy against sex discrimination and accessible, effective, and fairly applied grievance procedures, a school is telling its students that it does not tolerate sexual harassment and that students can report it without fear of adverse consequences.

Without a disseminated policy and procedure, a student does not know either of the school's policy against and obligation to address this form of discrimination, or how to report harassment so that it can be remedied. If the alleged harassment is sufficiently serious to create a hostile environment and it is the school's failure to comply with the procedural requirements of the Title IX regulations that hampers early notification and intervention and permits sexual harassment to deny or limit a student's ability to participate in or benefit from the school's program on the basis of sex,[80] the school will be responsible under the Title IX regulations, once informed of the harassment, to take corrective action, including stopping the harassment, preventing its recurrence, and remedying the effects of the harassment on the victim that could reasonably have been prevented if the school's failure to comply with the procedural requirements had not hampered early notification.

VI. OCR CASE RESOLUTION

If OCR is asked to investigate or otherwise resolve incidents of sexual harassment of students, including incidents caused by employees, other students, or third parties, OCR will consider whether (1) the school has a disseminated policy prohibiting sex discrimination under Title IX[81] and effective grievance procedures;[82] (2) the school appropriately investigated or otherwise responded to allegations of sexual harassment;[83] and (3) the school has taken immediate and effective corrective action responsive to the harassment, including effective actions to end the harassment, prevent its recurrence, and, as appropriate, remedy its effects.[84] (Issues related to appropriate investigative and corrective actions are discussed in detail in the section on "Recipient's Response.")

If the school has taken, or agrees to take, each of these steps, OCR will consider the case against the school resolved and will take no further action, other than monitoring compliance with an agreement, if any, between the school and OCR. This is true in cases in which the school was in violation of the Title IX regulations (e.g., a teacher sexually harassed a student in the context of providing aid, benefits, or services to students), as well as those in which there has been no violation of the regulations (e.g., in a peer sexual harassment situation in which the school took immediate, reasonable steps to end the harassment and prevent its recurrence). This is because, even if OCR identifies a violation, Title IX requires OCR to attempt to secure voluntary compliance.[85] Thus, because a school will have the opportunity to take reasonable corrective action before OCR issues a formal finding of violation, a school does not risk losing its federal funding solely because discrimination occurred.

VII. RECIPIENT'S RESPONSE

Once a school has notice of possible sexual harassment of students, whether carried out by employees, other students, or third parties, it should take immediate and appropriate steps to investigate or otherwise determine what occurred and take prompt and effective steps reasonably calculated to end any harassment, eliminate a hostile environment if one has been created, and prevent harassment from occurring again. These steps are the school's responsibility whether or not the student who was harassed makes a complaint or otherwise asks the school to take action.[86] As described in the following section, in appropriate circumstances the school will also be responsible for taking steps to remedy the effects of the harassment on the individual student or students who were harassed. What constitutes a reasonable response to information about possible sexual harassment will differ depending upon the circumstances.

A. Response to Student or Parent Reports of Harassment; Response to Direct Observation of Harassment by a Responsible Employee

If a student or the parent of an elementary or secondary student provides information or complains about sexual harassment of the student, the school should initially discuss what actions the student or parent is seeking in response to the harassment. The school should explain the avenues for informal and formal action, including a description of the grievance procedure that is available for sexual harassment complaints and an explanation of how the procedure works. If a responsible school employee has directly observed sexual harassment of a student, the school should contact the student who was harassed (or the parent, depending upon the age of the student),[87] explain that the school is responsible for taking steps to correct the harassment, and provide the same information described in the previous sentence.

Regardless of whether the student who was harassed, or his or her parent, decides to file a formal complaint or otherwise request action on the student's behalf (including in cases involving direct observation by a responsible employee), the school must promptly investigate to determine what occurred and then take appropriate steps to resolve the situation. The specific steps in an investigation will vary depending upon the nature of the allegations, the source of the complaint, the age of the student or students involved, the size and administrative structure of the school, and other factors. However, in all cases the inquiry must be prompt, thorough, and impartial. (Requests by the student who was harassed for confidentiality or for no action to be taken, responding to notice of harassment from other sources, and the components of a prompt and equitable grievance procedure are discussed in subsequent sections of this guidance.)

It may be appropriate for a school to take interim measures during the investigation of a complaint. For instance, if a student alleges that he or she has been sexually assaulted by another student, the school may decide to place the students immediately in separate classes or in different housing arrangements on a campus, pending the results of the school's investigation. Similarly, if the alleged harasser is a teacher, allowing the student to transfer to a different class may be appropriate. In cases involving potential criminal conduct, school personnel should determine whether appropriate law enforcement authorities should be notified. In all cases, schools should make every effort to prevent disclosure of the names of all parties involved—the complainant, the witnesses, and the accused—except to the extent necessary to carry out an investigation.

If a school determines that sexual harassment has occurred, it should take reasonable, timely, age-appropriate, and effective corrective action, including steps tailored to the specific situation.[88] Appropriate steps should be taken to end the harassment. For example, school personnel may need to counsel, warn, or take disciplinary action against the harasser, based on the severity of the harassment or any record of prior incidents or both.[89] A series of escalating consequences may be necessary if the initial steps are ineffective in stopping the harassment.[90] In some cases, it may be appropriate to further separate the harassed student and the harasser, for example, by changing housing arrangements[91] or directing the harasser to have no further contact with the harassed student. Responsive measures of this type should be designed to minimize, as much as possible, the burden on the student who was harassed. If the alleged harasser is not a student or employee of the recipient, OCR will consider the level of control the school has over the harasser in determining what response would be appropriate.[92]

Steps should also be taken to eliminate any hostile environment that has been created. For example, if a female student has been subjected to harassment by a group of other students in a class, the school may need to deliver special training or other interventions for that class to repair the educational environment. If the school offers the student the option of withdrawing from a class in which a hostile environment occurred, the school should assist the student in making program or schedule changes and ensure that none of the changes adversely affect the student's academic record. Other measures may include, if appropriate, directing a harasser to apologize to the harassed student. If a hostile environment has affected an entire school or campus, an effective response may need to include dissemination of information, the issuance of new policy statements, or other steps that are designed to clearly communicate the message that the school does not tolerate harassment and will be responsive to any student who reports that conduct.

In some situations, a school may be required to provide other services to the student who was harassed, if necessary, to address the effects of the harassment on that student.[93] For example, if an instructor gives a student a low grade because the student failed to respond to his sexual advances, the school may be required to make arrangements for an independent reassessment of the student's work, if feasible, and change the grade accordingly; make arrangements for the student to take the course again with a different instructor; provide tutoring; make tuition adjustments; offer reimbursement for professional counseling; or take other measures that are appropriate to the circumstances. As another example, if a school delays responding or responds inappropriately to information about harassment, such as a case in which the school ignores complaints by a student that he or she is being sexually harassed by a classmate, the school will be required to remedy the effects of the harassment that could have been prevented had the school responded promptly and effectively.

Finally, a school should take steps to prevent any further harassment[94] and to prevent any retaliation against the student who made the complaint (or was the subject of the harassment), against the person who filed a complaint on behalf of a student or against those who provided information as witnesses.[95] At a minimum, this includes making sure that the harassed students and their parents know how to report any subsequent problems and making follow-up inquiries to see if there have been any new incidents or any retaliation. To prevent recurrences, counseling for the harasser may be appropriate to ensure that he or she understands what constitutes harassment and the effects it can have. In addition, depending on how widespread the harassment was and whether there have been any prior incidents, the school may need to provide training for the larger school community to ensure that students, parents, and teachers can recognize harassment if it recurs and know how to respond.[96]

B. Confidentiality

The scope of a reasonable response also may depend upon whether a student, or parent of a minor student, reporting harassment asks that the student's name not be disclosed to the harasser or that nothing be done about the alleged harassment. In all cases, a school should discuss confidentiality standards and concerns with the complainant initially. The school should inform the student that a confidentiality request might limit the school's ability to respond. The school also should tell the student that Title IX prohibits retaliation and that, if he or she is afraid of reprisals from the alleged harasser, the school will take steps to prevent retaliation and will take strong responsive actions if retaliation occurs. If the student continues to ask that his or her name not be revealed, the school should take all reasonable steps to investigate and respond to the complaint consistent with the student's request as long as doing so does not prevent the school from responding effectively to the harassment and preventing harassment of other students.

OCR enforces Title IX consistent with the federally protected due process rights of public school students and employees. Thus, for example, if a student, who was the only student harassed, insists that his or her name not be revealed, and the alleged harasser could not respond to the charges of sexual harassment without that information, in evaluating the school's response, OCR would not expect disciplinary action against an alleged harasser.

At the same time, a school should evaluate the confidentiality request in the context of its responsibility to provide a safe and nondiscriminatory environment for all students. The factors that a school may consider in this regard include the seriousness of the alleged harassment, the age of the student harassed, whether there have been other complaints or reports of harassment against the alleged harasser, and the rights of the accused individual to receive information about the accuser and the allegations if a formal proceeding with sanctions may result.[97]

Similarly, a school should be aware of the confidentiality concerns of an accused employee or student. Publicized accusations of sexual harassment, if ultimately found to be false, may nevertheless irreparably damage the reputation of the accused. The accused individual's need for confidentiality must, of course, also be evaluated based on the factors discussed in the preceding paragraph in the context of the school's responsibility to ensure a safe environment for students.

Although a student's request to have his or her name withheld may limit the school's ability to respond fully to an individual complaint of harassment, other means may be available to address the harassment. There are steps a recipient can take to limit the effects of the alleged harassment and prevent its recurrence without initiating formal action against the alleged harasser or revealing the identity of the complainant. Examples include conducting sexual harassment training for the school site or academic department where the problem occurred, taking a student survey concerning any problems with harassment, or implementing other systemic measures at the site or department where the alleged harassment has occurred.

In addition, by investigating the complaint to the extent possible including by reporting it to the Title IX coordinator or other responsible school employee designated pursuant to Title IX the school may learn about or be able to confirm a pattern of harassment based on claims by different students that the same individual harassed them. In some situations, there may be prior reports by former students who now might be willing to come forward and be identified, thus providing a basis for further corrective action. In instances affecting a number of students (e.g., a report from a student that an instructor has repeatedly made sexually explicit remarks about his or her personal life in front of an entire class), an individual can be put on notice of allegations of harassing behavior and counseled appropriately without revealing, even indirectly, the identity of the student who notified the school. Those steps can be very effective in preventing further harassment.

C. Response to Other Types of Notice

The previous two sections deal with situations in which a student or parent of a student who was harassed reports or complains of harassment or in which a responsible school employee directly observes sexual harassment of a student. If a school learns of harassment through other means, for example, if information about harassment is received from a third party (such as from a witness to an incident or an anonymous letter or telephone call), different factors will affect the school's response. These factors include the source and nature of the information; the seriousness of the alleged incident; the specificity of the information; the objectivity and credibility of the source of the report; whether any individuals can be identified who were subjected to the alleged harassment; and whether those individuals want to pursue the matter. If, based on these factors, it is reasonable for the school to investigate and it can confirm the allegations, the considerations described in the previous sections concerning interim measures and appropriate responsive action will apply.

For example, if a parent visiting a school observes a student repeatedly harassing a group of female students and reports this to school officials, school personnel can speak with the female students to confirm whether that conduct has occurred and whether they view it as unwelcome. If the school determines that the conduct created a hostile environment, it can take reasonable, age-appropriate steps to address the situation. If, on the other hand, the students in this example were to ask that their names not be disclosed or indicate that they do not want to pursue the matter, the considerations described in the previous section related to requests for confidentiality will shape the school's response.

In a contrasting example, a student newspaper at a large university may print an anonymous letter claiming that a professor is sexually harassing students in class on a daily basis, but the letter provides no clue as to the identity of the professor or the department in which the conduct is allegedly taking place. Due to the anonymous source and lack of specificity of the information, a school would not reasonably be able to investigate and confirm these allegations. However, in response to the anonymous letter, the school could submit a letter or article to the newspaper reiterating its policy against sexual harassment, encouraging persons who believe that they have been sexually harassed to come forward and explaining how its grievance procedures work.

VIII. PREVENTION

A policy specifically prohibiting sexual harassment and separate grievance procedures for violations of that policy can help ensure that all students and employees understand the nature of sexual harassment and that the school will not tolerate it. Indeed, they might even bring conduct of a sexual nature to the school's attention so that the school can address it before it becomes sufficiently serious as to create a hostile environment. Further, training for administrators, teachers, and staff and age-appropriate classroom information for students can help to ensure that they understand what types of conduct can cause sexual harassment and that they know how to respond.

IX. PROMPT AND EQUITABLE GRIEVANCE PROCEDURES

Schools are required by the Title IX regulations to adopt and publish a policy against sex discrimination and grievance procedures providing for prompt and equitable resolution of complaints of discrimination on the basis of sex.[98] Accordingly, regardless of whether harassment occurred, a school violates this requirement of the Title IX regulations if it does not have those procedures and policy in place.[99]

A school's sex discrimination grievance procedures must apply to complaints of sex discrimination in the school's education programs and activities filed by students against school employees, other students, or third parties.[100] Title IX does not require a school to adopt a policy specifically prohibiting sexual harassment or to provide separate grievance procedures for sexual harassment complaints. However, its nondiscrimination policy and grievance procedures for handling discrimination complaints must provide effective means for preventing and responding to sexual harassment. Thus, if, because of the lack of a policy or procedure specifically addressing sexual harassment, students are unaware of what kind of conduct constitutes sexual harassment or that such conduct is prohibited sex discrimination, a school's general policy and procedures relating to sex discrimination complaints will not be considered effective.[101]

OCR has identified a number of elements in evaluating whether a school's grievance procedures are prompt and equitable, including whether the procedures provide for:

- Notice to students, parents of elementary and secondary students, and employees of the procedure, including where complaints may be filed.
- Application of the procedure to complaints alleging harassment carried out by employees, other students, or third parties.
- Adequate, reliable, and impartial investigation of complaints, including the opportunity to present witnesses and other evidence.
- Designated and reasonably prompt time frames for the major stages of the complaint process.
- Notice to the parties of the outcome of the complaint.[102]
- An assurance that the school will take steps to prevent recurrence of any harassment and to correct its discriminatory effects on the complainant and others, if appropriate.[103]

Many schools also provide an opportunity to appeal the findings or remedy, or both. In addition, because Title IX prohibits retaliation, schools may want to include a provision in their procedures prohibiting retaliation against any individual who files a complaint or participates in a harassment inquiry.

Procedures adopted by schools will vary considerably in detail, specificity, and components, reflecting differences in audiences, school sizes, and administrative structures, state or local legal requirements, and past experience. In addition, whether complaint resolutions are timely will vary depending on the complexity of the investigation and the severity and extent of the harassment. During the investigation it is a good practice for schools to inform students, who have alleged harassment, about the status of the investigation on a periodic basis.

A grievance procedure applicable to sexual harassment complaints cannot be prompt or equitable unless students know it exists, how it works, and how to file a complaint. Thus, the procedures should be written in language appropriate to the age of the school's students, easily understood, and widely disseminated. Distributing the procedures to administrators, or including them in the school's administrative or policy manual, may not by itself be an effective way of providing notice, as these publications are usually not widely circulated to and understood by all members of the school community. Many schools ensure adequate notice to students by having copies of the procedures available at various locations throughout the school or campus; publishing the procedures as a separate document; including a summary of the procedures in major publications issued by the school, such as handbooks and catalogs for students, parents of elementary and secondary students, faculty, and staff; and identifying individuals who can explain how the procedures work.

A school must designate at least one employee to coordinate its efforts to comply with and carry out its Title IX responsibilities.[104] The school must notify all of its students and employees of the name, office address, and telephone number of the employee or employees designated.[105] Because it is possible that an employee designated to handle Title IX complaints may himself or herself engage in harassment, a school may want to designate more than one employee to be responsible for handling complaints, in order to ensure that students have an effective means of reporting harassment.[106] While a school may choose to have a number of employees responsible for Title IX matters, it is also advisable to give one official responsibility for overall coordination and oversight of all sexual harassment complaints to ensure consistent practices and standards in handling complaints. Coordination of recordkeeping (for instance, in a confidential log maintained by the Title IX coordinator) will also ensure that the school can and will resolve recurring problems and identify students or employees who have multiple complaints filed against them.[107] Finally, the school must make sure that all designated employees have adequate training as to what conduct constitutes sexual harassment and are able to explain how the grievance procedure operates.[108]

Grievance procedures may include informal mechanisms for resolving sexual harassment complaints to be used if the parties agree to do so.[109] OCR has frequently advised schools, however, that it is not appropriate for a student who is complaining of harassment to be required to work out the problem directly with the individual alleged to be harassing him or her, and certainly not without appropriate involvement by the school (e.g., participation by a counselor, trained mediator, or, if appropriate, a teacher or administrator). In addition, the complainant must be notified of the right to end the informal process at any time and begin the formal stage of the complaint process. In some cases, such as alleged sexual assaults, mediation will not be appropriate even on a voluntary basis. Title IX also permits the use of a student disciplinary procedure not designed specifically for Title IX grievances to resolve sex discrimination complaints, as long as the procedure meets the requirement of affording a complainant a "prompt and equitable" resolution of the complaint.

In some instances, a complainant may allege harassing conduct that constitutes both sex discrimination and possible criminal conduct. Police investigations or reports may be useful in terms of fact gathering. However, because legal standards for criminal investigations are different, police investigations or reports may not be determinative of whether harassment occurred under Title IX and do not relieve the school of its duty to respond promptly and effectively.[110] Similarly, schools are cautioned about using the results of insurance company investigations of sexual harassment allegations. The purpose of an insurance investigation is to assess liability under the insurance policy, and the applicable standards may well be different from those under Title IX. In addition, a school is not relieved of its responsibility to respond to a sexual harassment complaint filed under its grievance procedure by the fact that a complaint has been filed with OCR.[111]

X. DUE PROCESS RIGHTS OF THE ACCUSED

A public school's employees have certain due process rights under the U.S. Constitution. The Constitution also guarantees due process to students in public and state-supported schools who are accused of certain types of infractions. The rights established under Title IX must be interpreted consistent with any federally guaranteed due process rights involved in a complaint proceeding. Furthermore, the Family Educational Rights and Privacy Act (FERPA) does not override federally protected due process rights of persons accused of sexual harassment. Procedures that ensure the Title IX rights of the complainant, while at the same time according due process to both parties involved, will lead to sound and supportable decisions. Of course, schools should ensure that steps to accord due process rights do not restrict or unnecessarily delay the protections provided by Title IX to the complainant. In both public and private schools, additional or separate rights may be created for employees or students by state law, institutional regulations, and policies, such as faculty or student handbooks and collective bargaining agreements. Schools should be aware of these rights and their legal responsibilities to individuals accused of harassment.

XI. FIRST AMENDMENT

In cases of alleged harassment, the protections of the First Amendment must be considered if issues of speech or expression are involved.[112] Free speech rights apply in the classroom (e.g., classroom lectures and discussions)[113] and in all other education programs and activities of public schools (e.g., public meetings and speakers on campus; campus debates, school plays, and other cultural events[114]; and student newspapers, journals, and other publications[115]). In addition, First Amendment rights apply to the speech of students and teachers.[116]

Title IX is intended to protect students from sex discrimination, not to regulate the content of speech. OCR recognizes that the offensiveness of a particular expression as perceived by some students, standing alone, is not a legally sufficient basis to establish a sexually hostile environment under Title IX.[117] In order to establish a violation of Title IX, the harassment must be sufficiently serious to deny or limit a student's ability to participate in or benefit from the education program.[118]

Moreover, in regulating the conduct of its students and its faculty to prevent or redress discrimination prohibited by Title IX (e.g., in responding to harassment that is sufficiently serious as to create a hostile environment), a school must formulate, interpret, and apply its rules so as to protect academic freedom and free speech rights. For instance, while the First Amendment may prohibit a school from restricting the right of students to express opinions about one sex that may be considered derogatory, the school can take steps to denounce those opinions and ensure that competing views are heard. The age of the students involved and the location or forum may affect how the school can respond consistently with the First Amendment.[119] As an example of the application of free speech rights to allegations of sexual harassment, consider the following:

Example 1: In a college-level creative writing class, a professor's required reading list includes excerpts from literary classics that contain descriptions of explicit sexual conduct, including scenes that depict women in submissive and demeaning roles. The professor also assigns students to write their own materials, which are read in class. Some of the student essays contain sexually derogatory themes about women. Several female students complain to the dean of students that the materials and related classroom discussion have created a sexually hostile environment for women in the class. What must the school do in response?

Answer: Academic discourse in this example is protected by the First Amendment even if it is offensive to individuals. Thus, Title IX would not require the school to discipline the professor or to censor the reading list or related class discussion.

Example 2: A group of male students repeatedly targets a female student for harassment during the bus ride home from school, including making explicit sexual comments about her body, passing around drawings that depict her engaging in sexual conduct, and, on several occasions, attempting to follow her home off the bus. The female student and her parents complain to the principal that the male students' conduct has created a hostile environment for girls on the bus and that they fear for their daughter's safety. What must a school do in response?

Answer: The First Amendment does not protect against threatening and intimidating actions targeted at a particular student or group of students, even though they contain elements of speech. The school must take prompt and effective actions, including disciplinary action if necessary, to stop the harassment and prevent future harassment.

Notes

1. This guidance does not address sexual harassment of employees, although that conduct may be prohibited by Title IX. 20 U.S.C. 1681 *et seq.;* 34 CFR part 106, subpart E. If employees file Title IX sexual harassment complaints with OCR, the complaints will be processed pursuant to the Procedures for Complaints of Employment Discrimination Filed Against Recipients of Federal Financial Assistance, 28 CFR 42.604. Employees are also protected from discrimination on the basis of sex, including sexual harassment, by Title VII of the Civil Rights Act of 1964. For information about Title VII and sexual harassment, see the Equal Employment Opportunity Commission's (EEOC's) Guidelines on Sexual Harassment, 29 CFR 1604.11; for information about filing a Title VII charge with the EEOC, see 29 CFR 1601.71607.13, or see the EEOC's Web site at www.eeoc.gov.

2. 20 U.S.C. 1681; 34 CFR part 106.

3. See, e.g., *Davis v. Monroe County Bd. of Educ.,* 526 U.S. 629, 649–50 (1999); *Gebser v. Lago Vista Ind. Sch. Dist.,* 524 U.S. 274, 281 (1998); *Franklin v. Gwinnett County Pub. Sch.,* 503 U.S. 60, 75 (1992); S. REP. NO. 100–64, 100th Cong., 1st Sess. 14 (1987); *Sexual Harassment Guidance: Harassment of Students by School Employees, Other Students, or Third Parties* (1997 guidance), 62 FR 12034 (1997).

4. As described in the section on "Applicability," this guidance applies to all levels of education.

5. For practical information about steps that schools can take to prevent and remedy all types of harassment, including sexual harassment, see "Protecting Students from Harassment and Hate Crime, A Guide for Schools," which we issued jointly with the National Association of Attorneys General. This Guide is available at our Web site at: www.ed.gov/pubs/Harassment.

6. See, e.g., *Davis,* 526 U.S. at 653 (alleged conduct of a sexual nature that would support a sexual harassment claim included verbal harassment and "numerous acts of objectively offensive touching"); *Franklin,* 503 U.S. at 63 (conduct of a sexual nature found to support a sexual harassment claim under Title IX included kissing, sexual intercourse); *Meritor Savings Bank, FSB v. Vinson,* 477 U.S. 57, 60–61 (1986) (demands for sexual favors, sexual advances, fondling, indecent exposure, sexual intercourse, rape, sufficient to raise hostile environment claim under Title VII); *Ellison v. Brady,* 924 F.2d 872, 873–74, 880 (9th Cir. 1991) (allegations sufficient to state sexual harassment claim under Title VII included repeated requests for dates, letters making explicit references to sex and describing the harasser's feelings for plaintiff); *Lipsett v. University of Puerto Rico,* 864 F.2d 881, 904–5 (1stCir. 1988) (sexually derogatory comments, posting of sexually explicit drawing of plaintiff, sexual advances may support sexual harassment claim); *Kadiki v. Virginia Commonwealth University,* 892 F.Supp. 746, 751 (E.D. Va. 1995) (professor's spanking of university student may constitute sexual conduct under Title IX); *Doe v. Petaluma,* 830 F.Supp. 1560, 1564–65 (N.D. Cal. 1996) (sexually derogatory taunts and innuendo can be the basis of a harassment claim); *Denver School Dist. #2,* OCR Case No. 08–92–1007 (same to allegations of vulgar language and obscenities, pictures of nude women on office walls and desks, unwelcome touching, sexually offensive jokes, bribery to perform sexual acts, indecent exposure); *Nashoba Regional High School,* OCR Case No. 01–92–1377 (same as to year-long campaign of derogatory, sexually explicit graffiti and remarks directed at one student.)

7. See also *Shoreline School Dist.,* OCR Case No. 10–92–1002 (a teacher's patting a student on the arm, shoulder, and back, and restraining the student when he was out of control, not conduct of a sexual nature); *Dartmouth Public Schools,* OCR Case No. 01–90–1058 (same as to contact between high school coach and students); *San Francisco State University,* OCR Case No. 09–94–2038 (same as to faculty adviser placing her arm around a graduate student's shoulder in posing for a picture); *Analy Union High School Dist.,* OCR Case No. 09–92–1249 (same as to drama instructor who put his arms around both male and female students who confided in him).

8. 20 U.S.C. 1687 (codification of the amendment to Title IX regarding scope of jurisdiction, enacted by the Civil Rights Restoration Act of 1987). See 65 FR 68049 (November 13, 2000) (Department's amendment of the Title IX regulations to incorporate the statutory definition of "program or activity").

9. If a school contracts with persons or organizations to provide benefits, services, or opportunities to students as part of the school's program, and those persons or employees of those organizations sexually harass students, OCR will consider the harassing individual in the same manner that it considers the school's employees, as described in this guidance. (See section on "Harassment by Teachers and Other Employees.") See *Brown v. Hot, Sexy, and Safer Products, Inc.,* 68 F.3d 525, 529 (1st Cir. 1995) (Title IX sexual harassment claim brought for school's role in permitting contract consultant hired by it to create allegedly hostile environment).

In addition, if a student engages in sexual harassment as an employee of the school, OCR will consider the harassment under the standards described for employees. (See section on "Harassment by Teachers and Other Employees.") For example, OCR would consider it harassment by an employee if a student teaching assistant who is responsible for assigning grades in a course, that is, for providing aid, benefits, or services to students under the recipient's program, required a student in his or her class to submit to sexual advances in order to obtain a certain grade in the class.

10. Cf. *John Does 1 v. Covington County Sch. Bd.*, 884 F.Supp. 462, 464–65 (M.D. Ala. 1995) (male students alleging that a teacher sexually harassed and abused them stated cause of action under Title IX).

11. Title IX and the regulations implementing it prohibit discrimination "on the basis of sex"; they do not restrict protection from sexual harassment to those circumstances in which the harasser only harasses members of the opposite sex. See 34 CFR 106.31. In *Oncale v. Sundowner Offshore Services, Inc.* the Supreme Court held unanimously that sex discrimination consisting of same-sex sexual harassment could violate Title VII's prohibition against discrimination because of sex. 523 U.S. 75, 82 (1998). The Supreme Court's holding in *Oncale* is consistent with OCR policy, originally stated in its 1997 guidance, that Title IX prohibits sexual harassment regardless of whether the harasser and the person being harassed are members of the same sex. 62 FR 12039. See also *Kinman v. Omaha Public School Dist.*, 94 F.3d 463, 468 (8th Cir. 1996), *rev'd on other grounds*, 171 F.3d 607 (1999) (female student's allegation of sexual harassment by female teacher sufficient to raise a claim under Title IX); *Doe v. Petaluma*, 830 F.Supp. 1560, 1564–65, 1575 (N.D. Cal. 1996) (female junior high student alleging sexual harassment by other students, including both boys and girls, sufficient to raise a claim under Title IX*); John Does 1*, 884 F.Supp. at 465 (same as to male student's allegations of sexual harassment and abuse by a male teacher). It can also occur in certain situations if the harassment is directed at students of both sexes. *Chiapuzo v. BLT Operating Corp.*, 826 F.Supp. 1334, 1337 (D.Wyo. 1993) (court found that if males and females were subject to harassment, but harassment was based on sex, it could violate Title VII); but see *Holman v. Indiana*, 211 F.3d 399, 405 (7th Cir. 2000) (if male and female both subjected to requests for sex, court found it could not violate Title VII).

In many circumstances, harassing conduct will be on the basis of sex because the student would not have been subjected to it at all had he or she been a member of the opposite sex; for example, if a female student is repeatedly propositioned by a male student or employee (or, for that matter, if a male student is repeatedly propositioned by a male student or employee). In other circumstances, harassing conduct will be on the basis of sex if the student would not have been affected by it in the same way or to the same extent had he or she been a member of the opposite sex; for example, pornography and sexually explicit jokes in a mostly male shop class are likely to affect the few girls in the class more than it will most of the boys.

In yet other circumstances, the conduct will be on the basis of sex in that the student's sex was a factor in or affected the nature of the harasser's conduct or both. Thus, in *Chiapuzo*, a supervisor made demeaning remarks to both partners of a married couple working for him, for example, as to sexual acts he wanted to engage in with the wife and how he would be a better lover than the husband. In both cases, according to the court, the remarks were based on sex in that they were made with an intent to demean each member of the couple because of his or her respective sex. 826 F.Supp. at 1337. See also *Steiner v. Showboat Operating Co.*, 25 F.3d 1459, 1463–64 (9th Cir. 1994), *cert. denied*, 115 S.Ct. 733 (1995); but see *Holman*, 211 F.3d at 405 (finding that if male and female both subjected to requests for sex, Title VII could not be violated).

12. *Nashoba Regional High School*, OCR Case No. 01–92–1397. In *Conejo Valley School Dist.*, OCR Case No. 09–93–1305, female students allegedly taunted another female student about engaging in sexual activity; OCR found that the alleged comments were sexually explicit and, if true, would be sufficiently severe, persistent, and pervasive to create a hostile environment.

13. See *Williamson v. A.G. Edwards & Sons, Inc.*, 876 F2d 69, 70 (8th Cir. 1989, *cert. denied* 493 U.S. 1089 (1990); *DeSantis v. Pacific Tel. & Tel. Co., Inc.*, 608 F.2d 327, 329–30 (9th Cir. 1979)(same); *Blum v. Gulf Oil Corp.*, 597 F.2d 936, 938 (5th Cir. 1979)(same).

14. It should be noted that some state and local laws might prohibit discrimination on the basis of sexual orientation. Also, under certain circumstances, courts may permit redress for harassment on the basis of sexual orientation under other federal legal authority. See *Nabozny v.*

Podlesny, 92 F.3d 446, 460 (7th Cir. 1996) (holding that a gay student could maintain claims alleging discrimination based on both gender and sexual orientation under the Equal Protection Clause of the U.S. Constitution in a case in which a school district failed to protect the student to the same extent that other students were protected from harassment and harm by other students due to the student's gender and sexual orientation).

15. However, sufficiently serious sexual harassment is covered by Title IX even if the hostile environment also includes taunts based on sexual orientation.

16. See also *Price Waterhouse v. Hopkins,* 490 U.S. 228, 251 (1989) (plurality opinion) (where an accounting firm denied partnership to a female candidate, the Supreme Court found Title VII prohibits an employer from evaluating employees by assuming or insisting that they match the stereotype associated with their sex).

17. See generally *Gebser; Davis;* see also *Meritor Savings Bank, FSB v. Vinson,* 477 U.S. 57, 65–66 (1986); *Harris v. Forklift Systems Inc.,* 510 U.S. 14, 22 (1993); see also *Hicks v. Gates Rubber Co.,* 833 F.2d 1406, 1415 (10th Cir. 1987) (concluding that harassment based on sex may be discrimination whether or not it is sexual in nature); *McKinney v. Dole,* 765 F.2d 1129, 1138 (D.C. Cir. 1985) (physical, but nonsexual, assault could be sex-based harassment if shown to be unequal treatment that would not have taken place but for the employee's sex); *Cline v. General Electric Capital Auto Lease, Inc.,* 757 F.Supp. 923, 932–33 (N.D. Ill. 1991).

18. See, e.g., sections on "Harassment by Teachers and Other Employees," "Harassment by Other Students or Third Parties," "Notice of Employee, Peer, or Third-Party Harassment," "Factors Used to Evaluate a Hostile Environment," "Recipient's Response," and "Prompt and Equitable Grievance Procedures."

19. See *Lipsett,* 864 F.2d at 903–905 (general antagonism toward women, including stated goal of eliminating women from surgical program, statements that women shouldn't be in the program, and assignment of menial tasks, combined with overt sexual harassment); *Harris,* 510 U.S. at 23; *Andrews v. City of Philadelphia,* 895 F.2d 1469, 1485–86 (3rd Cir. 1990) (court directed trial court to consider sexual conduct as well as theft of female employee's files and work, destruction of property, and anonymous phone calls in determining if there had been sex discrimination); see *also Hall v. Gus Construction Co.,* 842 F.2d 1010, 1014 (8th Cir. 1988) (affirming that harassment due to the employee's sex may be actionable even if the harassment is not sexual in nature); *Hicks,* 833 F.2d at 1415; *Eden Prairie Schools, Dist. #272,* OCR Case No. 05–92–1174 (the boys made lewd comments about male anatomy and tormented the girls by pretending to stab them with rubber knives; while the stabbing was not sexual conduct, it was directed at them because of their sex, i.e., because they were girls).

20. *Davis,* 526 U.S. at 650 ("Having previously determined that 'sexual harassment' is 'discrimination' in the school context under Title IX, we are constrained to conclude that student-on-student sexual harassment, if sufficiently severe, can likewise rise to the level of discrimination actionable under the statute"); *Franklin,* 503 U.S. at 75 ("Unquestionably, Title IX placed on the [school] the duty not to discriminate on the basis of sex, and 'when a supervisor sexually harasses a subordinate because of the subordinate's sex, that supervisor "discriminate[s]" on the basis of sex' . . . We believe the same rule should apply when a teacher sexually harasses and abuses a student" (citation omitted).

OCR's longstanding interpretation of its regulations is that sexual harassment may constitute a violation. 34 CFR 106.31; See *Sexual Harassment Guidance,* 62 FR 12034 (1997). When Congress enacted the Civil Rights Restoration Act of 1987 to amend Title IX to restore institution-wide coverage over federally assisted education programs and activities, the legislative history indicated not only that Congress was aware that OCR interpreted its Title IX regulations to prohibit sexual harassment, but also that one of the reasons for passing the Restoration Act was to enable OCR to investigate and resolve cases involving allegations of sexual harassment. S. REP.

NO. 64, 100th Cong., 1st Sess. at 12 (1987). The examples of discrimination that Congress intended to be remedied by its statutory change included sexual harassment of students by professors, *id.* at 14, and these examples demonstrate congressional recognition that discrimination in violation of Title IX can be carried out by school employees who are providing aid, benefits, or services to students. Congress also intended that if discrimination occurred, recipients needed to implement effective remedies. S. REP. NO. 64 at 5.

21. 34 CFR 106.4.

22. These are the basic regulatory requirements. 34 CFR 106.31(a)(b). Depending upon the facts, sexual harassment may also be prohibited by more specific regulatory prohibitions. For example, if a college financial aid director told a student that she would not get the student financial assistance for which she qualified unless she slept with him, that also would be covered by the regulatory provision prohibiting discrimination on the basis of sex in financial assistance, 34 CFR 106.37(a).

23. 34 CFR 106.31(b)(1).

24. 34 CFR 106.31(b)(2).

25. 34 CFR 106.31(b)(3).

26. 34 CFR 106.31(b)(4).

27. 34 CFR 106.31(b)(6).

28. 34 CFR 106.31(b)(7).

29. 34 CFR 106.3(a).

30. 34 CFR 106.9.

31. 34 CFR 106.8(b).

32. 34 CFR 106.8(a).

33. The 1997 guidance referred to *quid pro quo* harassment and hostile environment harassment. 62 FR 1203840.

34. See *Alexander v. Yale University,* 459 F.Supp. 1, 4 (D.Conn. 1977), *aff'd,* 631 F.2d 178 (2nd Cir. 1980)(stating that a claim "that academic advancement was conditioned upon submission to sexual demands constitutes [a claim of] sex discrimination in education"); *Crandell v. New York College, Osteopathic Medicine,* 87 F.Supp.2d 304, 318 (S.D.N.Y. 2000) (finding that allegations that a supervisory physician demanded that a student physician spend time with him and have lunch with him or receive a poor evaluation, in light of the totality of his alleged sexual comments and other inappropriate behavior, constituted a claim of *quid pro quo* harassment); *Kadiki,* 892 F.Supp. at 752 (reexamination in a course conditioned on college student's agreeing to be spanked should she not attain a certain grade may constitute *quid pro quo* harassment).

35. 34 CFR 106.31(b).

36. *Davis,* 526 U.S. at 651, confirming, by citing approvingly two Title VII cases (*Meritor Savings Bank, FSB v. Vinson,* 477 U.S. 57,67 (1986) (finding that hostile environment claims are cognizable under Title VII), and *Oncale v. Sundowner Offshore Services, Inc.,* 523 U.S. 75, 82 (1998)) and OCR's 1997 guidance, 62 FR at 12041–42, that determinations under Title IX as to what conduct constitutes hostile environment sexual harassment may continue to rely on Title VII case law).

37. 34 CFR 106.31(b). See *Davis,* 526 U.S. at 650 (concluding that allegations of student-on-student sexual harassment that is "so severe, pervasive and objectively offensive that it can be said to deprive the victims of access to the educational opportunities or benefits" supports a claim for money damages in an implied right of action).

38. In *Harris,* the Supreme Court explained the requirement for considering the "subjective perspective" when determining the existence of a hostile environment. The Court stated, " if the victim does not subjectively perceive the environment to be abusive, the conduct has not actu-

ally altered the conditions of the victim's employment, and there is no Title VII violation." 510 U.S. at 21–22.

39. See *Davis*, 526 U.S. at 650 (conduct must be "objectively offensive" to trigger liability for money damages); *Elgamil v. Syracuse University*, 2000 U.S. Dist. LEXIS 12598 at 17 (N.D.N.Y. 2000) (citing *Harris*); *Booher v. Board of Regents*, 1998 U.S. Dist. LEXIS 11404 at 25 (E.D. Ky. 1998) (same). See *Oncale*, 523 U.S. at 81, in which the Court "emphasized . . . that the objective severity of harassment should be judged from the perspective of a reasonable person in the [victim's] position, considering 'all the circumstances,'" and citing *Harris*, 510 U.S. at 20, in which the Court indicated that a "reasonable person" standard should be used to determine whether sexual conduct constituted harassment. This standard has been applied under Title VII to take into account the sex of the subject of the harassment, see, e.g., *Ellison*, 924 F.2d at 878–79 (applying a "reasonable woman" standard to sexual harassment), and has been adapted to sexual harassment in education under Title IX, *Patricia H. v. Berkeley Unified School Dist.*, 830 F.Supp. 1288, 1296 (N.D. Cal. 1993) (adopting a "reasonable victim" standard and referring to OCR's use of it).

40. See *Davis*, 526 U.S. at 651, citing both *Oncale*, 523 U.S. at 82, and OCR's 1997 guidance (62 FR 12041–12042).

41. See, e.g., *Davis*, 526 U.S. at 634 (as a result of the harassment, student's grades dropped and she wrote a suicide note); *Doe v. Petaluma*, 830 F. Supp. at 1566 (student so upset about harassment by other students that she was forced to transfer several times, including finally to a private school); *Modesto City Schools*, OCR Case No. 09–93–1391 (evidence showed that one girl's grades dropped while the harassment was occurring); *Weaverville Elementary School*, OCR Case No. 09–91–1116 (students left school due to the harassment). Compare with *College of Alameda*, OCR Case No. 09–90–2104 (student not in instructor's class and no evidence of any effect on student's educational benefits or service, so no hostile environment).

42. *Doe v. Petaluma*, 830 F.Supp. at 1566.

43. See *Waltman v. Int'l Paper Co.*, 875 F.2d 468, 477 (5th Cir. 1989) (holding that although not specifically directed at the plaintiff, sexually explicit graffiti on the walls was "relevant to her claim"); *Monteiro v. Tempe Union High School*, 158 F.3d 1022, 1033–34 (9th Cir. 1998) (Title VI racial harassment case, citing *Waltman*; see also *Hall*, 842 F. 2d at 1015 (evidence of sexual harassment directed at others is relevant to show hostile environment under Title VII).

44. See, e.g., *Elgmil* 2000 U.S. Dist. LEXIS at 19 ("in order to be actionable, the incidents of harassment must occur in concert or with a regularity that can reasonably be termed pervasive"); *Andrews*, 895 F.2d at 1484 ("Harassment is pervasive when 'incidents of harassment occur either in concert or with regularity'"); *Moylan v. Maries County*, 792 F.2d 746, 749 (8th Cir. 1986).

45. 34 CFR 106.31(b). See *Vance v. Spencer County Public School District*, 231 F.3d 253 (6th Cir. 2000); *Doe v. School Admin. Dist. No. 19*, 66 F.Supp.2d 57, 62 (D. Me. 1999). See also statement of the U.S. Equal Employment Opportunity Commission (EEOC): "The Commission will presume that the unwelcome, intentional touching of [an employee's] intimate body areas is sufficiently offensive to alter the conditions of her working environment and constitute a violation of Title VII. More so than in the case of verbal advances or remarks, a single unwelcome physical advance can seriously poison the victim's working environment." EEOC Policy Guidance on Current Issues of Sexual Harassment, 17. *Barrett v. Omaha National Bank*, 584 F. Supp. 22, 30 (D. Neb. 1983), *aff'd*, 726 F. 2d 424 (8th Cir. 1984) (finding that hostile environment was created under Title VII by isolated events, i.e., occurring while traveling to and during a two-day conference, including the co-worker's talking to plaintiff about sexual activities and touching her in an offensive manner while they were inside a vehicle from which she could not escape).

46. See also *Ursuline College,* OCR Case No. 05–91–2068 (a single incident of comments on a male student's muscles arguably not sexual; however, assuming they were, not severe enough to create a hostile environment).

47. *Davis,* 526 U.S. at 653 ("The relationship between the harasser and the victim necessarily affects the extent to which the misconduct can be said to breach Title IX's guarantee of equal access to educational benefits and to have a systemic effect on a program or activity. Peer harassment, in particular, is less likely to satisfy these requirements than is teacher student harassment"); *Patricia H.,* 830 F. Supp. at 1297 (stating that the "grave disparity in age and power" between teacher and student contributed to the creation of a hostile environment); *Summerfield Schools,* OCR Case No. 15–92–1929 ("impact of the . . . remarks was heightened by the fact that the coach is an adult in a position of authority"); cf. *Doe v. Taylor I.S.D.,* 15 F.3d 443, 460 (5th Cir. 1994) (Sec. 1983 case; taking into consideration the influence that the teacher had over the student by virtue of his position of authority to find that a sexual relationship between a high school teacher and a student was unlawful).

48. See, e.g., *McKinney,* 765 F.2d at 1138–49; *Robinson v. Jacksonville Shipyards,* 760 F. Supp. 1486, 1522 (M.D. Fla. 1991).

49. Cf. *Patricia H.,* 830 F. Supp. at 1297.

50. See, e.g., *Barrett,* 584 F. Supp. at 30 (finding harassment occurring in a car from which the victim could not escape; particularly severe).

51. See *Hall,* 842 F. 2d at 1015 (stating that "evidence of sexual harassment directed at employees other than the plaintiff is relevant to show a hostile environment") (citing *Hicks,* 833 F. 2d, 1415–16). Cf. *Midwest City-Del City Public Schools,* OCR Case No. 06–92–1012 (finding of racially hostile environment based in part on several racial incidents at school shortly before incidents in complaint, a number of which involved the same student involved in the complaint).

52. In addition, incidents of racial or national origin harassment directed at a particular individual may also be aggregated with incidents of sexual or gender harassment directed at that individual in determining the existence of a hostile environment. *Hicks,* 833 F.2d at 1416; *Jefferies v. Harris County Community Action Ass'n,* 615 F.2d 1025, 1032 (5th Cir. 1980).

53. *Does v. Covington Sch. Bd. of Educ.,* 930 F.Supp. 554, 569 (M.D. Ala. 1996); *Henson v. City of Dundee,* 682 F.2d 897, 903 (11th Cir. 1982).

54. See *Meritor Savings Bank,* 477 U.S. at 68. "(The fact that sex-related conduct was 'voluntary,' in the sense that the complainant was not forced to participate against her will, is not a defense to a sexual harassment suit brought under Title VII . . . The correct inquiry is whether [the subject of the harassment] by her conduct indicated that the alleged sexual advances were unwelcome, not whether her actual participation in sexual intercourse was voluntary").

55. *Lipsett,* 864 F.2d at 898 (while, in some instances, a person may have the responsibility for telling the harasser "directly" that the conduct is unwelcome, in other cases a "consistent failure to respond to suggestive comments or gestures may be sufficient"); *Danna v. New York Tel. Co.,* 752 F.Supp. 594, 612 (despite a female employee's own foul language and participation in graffiti writing, her complaints to management indicated that the harassment was not welcome); see also *Carr v. Allison Gas Turbine Div. GMC.,* 32 F.3d 1007, 1011 (7th Cir. 1994) (finding that cursing and dirty jokes by a female employee did not show that she welcomed the sexual harassment, given her frequent complaints about it: "Even if . . . [the employee's] testimony that she talked and acted as she did [only] in an effort to be one of the boys is . . . discounted, her words and conduct cannot be compared to those of the men and used to justify their conduct . . . The asymmetry of positions must be considered. She was one woman; they were many men. Her use of [vulgar] terms . . . could not be deeply threatening").

56. See *Reed v. Shepard,* 939 F.2d 484, 486–87, 491–92 (7th Cir. 1991) (no harassment

found under Title VII in a case in which a female employee not only tolerated, but also insti-gated the suggestive joking activities about which she was now complaining); *Weinsheimer v. Rockwell Int'l Corp.*, 754 F.Supp. 1559, 1563–64 (M.D. Fla. 1990) (same, in case in which general shop banter was full of vulgarity and sexual innuendo by men and women alike, and plaintiff contributed her share to this atmosphere). However, even if a student participates in the sexual banter, OCR may in certain circumstances find that the conduct was nevertheless unwelcome if, for example, a teacher took an active role in the sexual banter and a student reasonably perceived that the teacher expected him or her to participate.

57. The school bears the burden of rebutting the presumption.

58. Of course, nothing in Title IX would prohibit a school from implementing policies pro-hibiting sexual conduct or sexual relationships between students and adult employees.

59. See note 58.

60. *Gebser*, 524 U.S. at 281 ("*Franklin* . . . establishes that a school district can be held liable in damages [in an implied action under Title IX] in cases involving a teacher's sexual harassment of a student"; 34 CFR 106.31; See *1997 Sexual Harassment Guidance*, 62 FR 12034.

61. See *Davis*, 526 U.S. at 653 (stating that harassment of a student by a teacher is more likely than harassment by a fellow student to constitute the type of effective denial of equal access to educational benefits that can breach the requirements of Title IX).

62. 34 CFR 106.31(b). Cf. *Gebser*, 524 U.S. at 283–84 (Court recognized in an implied right of action for money damages for teacher sexual harassment of a student that the question of whether a violation of Title IX occurred is a separate question from the scope of appropriate remedies for a violation).

63. *Davis*, 526 U.S. at 646.

64. See section on "Applicability of Title IX" for scope of coverage.

65. See section on "Notice of Employee, Peer, or Third-Party Harassment."

66. See section on "Notice of Employee, Peer, or Third-Party Harassment."

67. 34 CFR 106.31(b).

68. 34 CFR 106.31(b).

69. See section on "Notice of Employee, Peer, or Third-Party Harassment."

70. Cf. *Davis*, 526 U.S. at 646.

71. 34 CFR 106.31(b).

72. 34 CFR 106.31(b).

73. Consistent with its obligation under Title IX to protect students, cf. *Gebser*, 524 U.S. at 287, OCR interprets its regulations to ensure that recipients take reasonable action to address, rather than neglect, reasonably obvious discrimination. Cf. *Gebser*, 524 U.S. at 287–88; *Davis*, 526 U.S. at 650 (actual notice standard for obtaining money damages in private lawsuit).

74. Whether an employee is a responsible employee or whether it would be reasonable for a student to believe the employee is, even if the employee is not, will vary depending on factors, such as the age and education level of the student, the type of position held by the employee, and school practices and procedures, both formal and informal. The Supreme Court held that a school will only be liable for money damages in a private lawsuit where there is actual notice to a school official with the authority to address the alleged discrimination and take corrective action. *Gebser*, 524 U.S. at 290, and *Davis*, 526 U.S. at 642. The concept of a "responsible employee" under our guidance is broader. That is, even if a responsible employee does not have the authority to address the discrimination and take corrective action, he or she does have the obligation to report it to appropriate school officials.

75. The Title IX regulations require that recipients designate at least one employee to coordi-nate its efforts to comply with and carry out its responsibilities under the regulations, including complaint investigations. 34 CFR 106.8(a).

76. 34 CFR 106.31. See *Yates v. Avco Corp.*, 819 F.2d 630, 636 (6th Cir. 1987); *Katz v. Dole*, 709 F.2d 251, 256 (4th Cir. 1983).

77. For example, a substantiated report indicating that a high school coach has engaged in inappropriate physical conduct of a sexual nature in several instances with different students may suggest a pattern of conduct that should trigger an inquiry as to whether other students have been sexually harassed by that coach. See also *Doe v. School Administrative Dist. No. 19*, 66 F.Supp.2d 57, 63–64 and n.6 (D.Me. 1999) (in a private lawsuit for money damages under Title IX in which a high school principal had notice that a teacher may be engaging in a sexual relationship with one underage student and did not investigate, and then the same teacher allegedly engaged in sexual intercourse with another student, who did not report the incident, the court indicated that the school's knowledge of the first relationship may be sufficient to serve as actual notice of the second incident).

78. Cf. *Katz*, 709 F.2d at 256 (finding that the employer "should have been aware of the problem both because of its pervasive character and because of [the employee's] specific complaints"); *Smolsky v. Consolidated Rail Corp.*, 780 F.Supp. 283, 293 (E.D. Pa. 1991), *reconsideration denied*, 785 F.Supp. 71 (E.D. Pa. 1992) (where the harassment is apparent to all others in the workplace, supervisors and coworkers, this may be sufficient to put the employer on notice of the sexual harassment" under Title VII); *Jensen v. Eveleth Taconite Co.*, 824 F.Supp. 847, 887 (D.Minn. 1993); ("sexual harassment . . . was so pervasive that an inference of knowledge arises . . . The acts of sexual harassment detailed herein were too common and continuous to have escaped Eveleth Mines had its management been reasonably alert"); *Cummings v. Walsh Construction Co.*, 561 F.Supp. 872, 878 (S.D. Ga. 1983) ("allegations not only of the [employee] registering her complaints with her foreman . . . but also that sexual harassment was so widespread that defendant had constructive notice of it" under Title VII); but see *Murray v. New York Univ. College of Dentistry*, 57 F.3d 243, 250–51 (2nd Cir. 1995) (concluding that other students' knowledge of the conduct was not enough to charge the school with notice, particularly because these students may not have been aware that the conduct was offensive or abusive).

79. 34 CFR 106.9 and 106.8(b).

80. 34 CFR 106.8(b) and 106.31(b).

81. 34 CFR 106.9.

82. 34 CFR 106.8(b).

83. 34 CFR 106.31.

84. 34 CFR 106.31 and 106.3. *Gebser*, 524 U.S. at 288 ("In the event of a violation, [under OCR's administrative enforcement scheme] a funding recipient may be required to take 'such remedial action as [is] deem[ed] necessary to overcome the effects of [the] discrimination.' §106.3.").

85. 20 U.S.C. 1682. In the event that OCR determines that voluntary compliance cannot be secured, OCR may take steps that may result in termination of federal funding through administrative enforcement, or, alternatively, OCR may refer the case to the Department of Justice for judicial enforcement.

86. Schools have an obligation to ensure that the educational environment is free of discrimination and cannot fulfill this obligation without determining if sexual harassment complaints have merit.

87. In some situations, for example, if a playground supervisor observes a young student repeatedly engaging in conduct toward other students that is clearly unacceptable under the school's policies, it may be appropriate for the school to intervene without contacting the other students. It still may be necessary for the school to talk with the students (and parents of elementary and secondary students) afterwards, for example, to determine the extent of the harassment and how it affected them.

88. *Gebser,* 524 U.S. at 288; *Bundy v. Jackson,* 641 F.2d 934, 947 (D.C. Cir. 1981) (employers should take corrective and preventive measures under Title VII); *accord, Jones v. Flagship Int'l,* 793 F.2d 714, 719–720 (5th Cir. 1986) (employer should take prompt remedial action under Title VII).

89. See *Doe ex rel. Doe v. Dallas Indep. Sch. Dist.,* 220 F.3d 380 (5th Cir. 2000) (citing *Waltman*); *Waltman,* 875 F.2d at 479 (appropriateness of employers remedial action under Title VII will depend on the "severity and persistence of the harassment and the effectiveness of any initial remedial steps"); *Dornhecker v. Malibu Grand Prix Corp.,* 828 F.2d 307, 309–10 (5th Cir. 1987); holding that a company's quick decision to remove the harasser from the victim was adequate remedial action).

90. See *Intlekofer v. Turnage,* 973 F.2d 773, 779–780 (9th Cir. 1992) (holding that the employer's response was insufficient and that more severe disciplinary action was necessary in situations in which counseling, separating the parties, and warnings of possible discipline were ineffective in ending the harassing behavior).

91. Offering assistance in changing living arrangements is one of the actions required of colleges and universities by the Campus Security Act in cases of rape and sexual assault. See 20 U.S.C. 1092(f).

92. See section on "Harassment by Other Students or Third Parties."

93. *University of California at Santa Cruz,* OCR Case No. 09–93–2141 (extensive individual and group counseling); *Eden Prairie Schools, Dist. #272,* OCR Case No. 05–92–1174 (counseling).

94. Even if the harassment stops without the school's involvement, the school may still need to take steps to prevent or deter any future harassment—to inform the school community that harassment will not be tolerated. *Wills v. Brown University,* 184 F.3d 20, 28 (1st Cir. 1999) (difficult problems are posed in balancing a student's request for anonymity or limited disclosure against the need to prevent future harassment); *Fuller v. City of Oakland,* 47 F.3d 1522, 1528–29 (9th Cir. 1995) (Title VII case).

95. 34 CFR 106.8(b) and 106.71, incorporating by reference 34 CFR 100.7(e). The Title IX regulations prohibit intimidation, threats, coercion, or discrimination against any individual for the purpose of interfering with any right or privilege secured by Title IX.

96. *Tacoma School Dist. No. 10,* OCR Case No. 10–94–1079 (due to the large number of students harassed by an employee, the extended period of time over which the harassment occurred, and the failure of several of the students to report the harassment, the school committed as part of corrective action plan to providing training for students); *Los Medanos College,* OCR Case No. 09–84–2092 (as part of corrective action plan, school committed to providing sexual harassment seminar for campus employees); *Sacramento City Unified School Dist.,* OCR Case No. 09–83–1063 (same as to workshops for management and administrative personnel and in-service training for non-management personnel).

97. In addition, if information about the incident is contained in an "education record" of the student alleging the harassment, as defined in the Family Educational Rights and Privacy Act (FERPA), 20 U.S.C. 1232g, the school should consider whether FERPA would prohibit the school from disclosing information without the student's consent. *Id.* In evaluating whether FERPA would limit disclosure, the Department does not interpret FERPA to override any federally protected due process rights of a school employee accused of harassment.

98. 34 CFR 106.8(b). This requirement has been part of the Title IX regulations since their inception in 1975. Thus, schools have been required to have these procedures in place since that time. At the elementary and secondary levels, this responsibility generally lies with the school district. At the postsecondary level, there may be a procedure for a particular campus or college or for an entire university system.

99. *Fenton Community High School Dist. #100,* OCR Case 05–92–1104.

100. While a school is required to have a grievance procedure under which complaints of sex discrimination (including sexual harassment) can be filed, the same procedure may also be used to address other forms of discrimination.

101. See generally *Meritor,* 477 U.S. at 72–73 (holding that "mere existence of a grievance procedure" for discrimination does not shield an employer from a sexual harassment claim).

102. The Family Educational Rights and Privacy Act (FERPA) does not prohibit a student from learning the outcome of her complaint, that is, whether the complaint was found to be credible and whether harassment was found to have occurred. It is the Department's current position under FERPA that a school cannot release information to a complainant regarding disciplinary action imposed on a student found guilty of harassment if that information is contained in a student's education record unless—(1) the information directly relates to the complainant (e.g., an order requiring the student harasser not to have contact with the complainant); or (2) the harassment involves a crime of violence or a sex offense in a postsecondary institution. See note 97. If the alleged harasser is a teacher, administrator, or other non-student employee, FERPA would not limit the school's ability to inform the complainant of any disciplinary action taken.

103. The section in the guidance on "Recipient's Response" provides examples of reasonable and appropriate corrective action.

104. 34 CFR 106.8(a).

105. *Id.*

106. See *Meritor,* 477 U.S. at 72–73.

107. *University of California, Santa Cruz,* OCR Case No. 09–93–2131. This is true for formal as well as informal complaints. See *University of Maine at Machias,* OCR Case No. 01–94–6001 (school's new procedures not found in violation of Title IX in part because they require written records for informal as well as formal resolutions). These records need not be kept in a student or employee's individual file, but instead may be kept in a central confidential location.

108. For example, in *Cape Cod Community College,* OCR Case No. 01–93–2047, the college was found to have violated Title IX in part because the person identified by the school as the Title IX coordinator was unfamiliar with Title IX, had no training, and did not even realize he was the coordinator.

109. Indeed, in *University of Maine at Machias,* OCR Case No. 01–94–6001, OCR found the school's procedures to be inadequate because only formal complaints were investigated. While a school isn't required to have an established procedure for resolving informal complaints, they nevertheless must be addressed in some way. However, if there are indications that the same individual may be harassing others, then it may not be appropriate to resolve an informal complaint without taking steps to address the entire situation.

110. *Academy School Dist. No 20,* OCR Case No. 08–93–1023 (school's response determined to be insufficient in a case in which it stopped its investigation after complaint filed with police); *Mills Public School Dist.,* OCR Case No. 01–93–1123, (not sufficient for school to wait until end of police investigation).

111. Cf. *EEOC v. Board of Governors of State Colleges and Universities,* 957 F.2d 424 (7th Cir. 1992), cert. denied, 506 U.S. 906 (1992).

112. The First Amendment applies to entities and individuals that are state actors. The receipt of federal funds by private schools does not directly subject those schools to the U.S. Constitution. See *Rendell-Baker v. Kohn,* 457 U.S. 830, 840 (1982). However, all actions taken by OCR must comport with First Amendment principles, even in cases involving private schools that are not directly subject to the First Amendment.

113. See, for example, *George Mason University,* OCR Case No. 03–94–2086 (law professor's use of a racially derogatory word, as part of an instructional hypothetical regarding verbal torts,

did not constitute racial harassment); *Portland School Dist. 1J,* OCR Case No. 10–94–1117 (reading teacher's choice to substitute a less offensive term for a racial slur when reading an historical novel aloud in class constituted an academic decision on presentation of curriculum, not racial harassment).

114. See *Iota Xi Chapter of Sigma Chi Fraternity v. George Mason University,* 993 F.2d 386 (4th Cir. 1993) (fraternity skit in which white male student dressed as an offensive caricature of a black female constituted student expression).

115. See *Florida Agricultural and Mechanical University,* OCR Case No. 04–92–2054 (no discrimination in case in which campus newspaper, which welcomed individual opinions of all sorts, printed article expressing one student's viewpoint on white students on campus).

116. *Tinker v. Des Moines Indep. Community Sch. Dist.,* 393 U.S. 503, 506 (1969) (neither students nor teachers shed their constitutional rights to freedom of expression at the schoolhouse gates); cf. *Cohen v. San Bernardino Valley College,* 92 F.3d 968, 972 (9th Cir. 1996) (holding that a college professor could not be punished for his longstanding teaching methods, which included discussion of controversial subjects, such as obscenity and consensual sex with children, under an unconstitutionally vague sexual harassment policy); *George Mason University,* OCR Case No. 03–94–2086 (law professor's use of a racially derogatory word, as part of an instructional hypothetical regarding verbal torts, did not constitute racial harassment).

117. See, for example, *University of Illinois,* OCR Case No. 05–94–2104 (fact that university's use of Native American symbols was offensive to some Native American students and employees was not dispositive, in and of itself, in assessing a racially hostile environment claim under Title VI).

118. See *Meritor,* 477 U.S. at 67 (the "mere utterance of an ethnic or racial epithet which engenders offensive feelings in an employee" would not affect the conditions of employment to a sufficient degree to violate Title VII), quoting *Henson,* 682 F.2d at 904; cf. *R.A.V. v. City of St. Paul,* 505 U.S. 377, 389 (1992) (citing with approval EEOC's sexual harassment guidelines); *Monteiro,* 158 F.3d at 1032–34 (9th Cir. 1998) (citing with approval OCR's racial harassment investigative guidance).

119. Cf. *Bethel School Dist. No. 403 v. Fraser,* 478 U.S. 675, 685 (1986) (Court upheld discipline of high school student for making lewd speech to student assembly, noting that "the undoubted freedom to advocate unpopular and controversial issues in schools must be balanced against the society's countervailing interest in teaching students the boundaries of socially appropriate behavior."), with *Iota Xi,* 993 F.2d 386 (holding that, notwithstanding a university's mission to create a culturally diverse learning environment and its substantial interest in maintaining a campus free of discrimination, it could not punish students who engaged in an offensive skit with racist and sexist overtones).

Hate Crimes

Various federal and state laws define the term "hate crime." In its broadest sense, the term refers to an attack on an individual or his or her property (e.g., vandalism, arson, assault, murder) in which the victim is intentionally selected because of his or her race, color, religion, national origin, gender, disability, or sexual orientation.

Every year, thousands of Americans are victims of such hate crimes. Each one of these crimes has a ripple effect in our communities. The pain and injustice of such crimes tear at the fabric of our democratic society, creating fear and tensions that ultimately affect us all.

Checklist for a Comprehensive Approach to Addressing Harassment

- Board members, district administrators, and the superintendent recognize the urgency of the problem of unlawful harassment and hate crime, identify people and agencies that can help them develop effective prevention and response strategies, and compile a library of useful materials.
- School officials select personnel to work on creating an effective anti-harassment program in consultation with parents, students, and community groups.
- Compliance coordinators are appointed and trained.
- School personnel assess the school climate to determine the prevalence and types of harassment that may exist and the potential for hate-motivated violence.
- School district adopts a written anti-harassment policy or reviews and revises existing policies for accuracy, clarity, and legal compliance; the policy is clearly communicated to all members of the school community; and school personnel and students are held accountable for their actions.
- School district develops a formal grievance procedure and takes steps to make sure it is working properly.
- Instructional personnel use or supplement the district's curriculum and pedagogical strategies to foster respect and appreciation for diversity.
- School sites institute, improve, or expand age-appropriate student activities to prevent or reduce prejudice and conflict.
- School district and individual school sites institute specific measures to respond immediately and effectively when harassment occurs to stop the harassment and prevent recurrence.
- School officials flexibly apply response mechanisms to both the victim and the perpetrator, taking into account the parties' ages and the context of the behavior.
- School personnel continually monitor the school climate and promptly address problems that could lead to harassment or violence or that indicate that harassment could be occurring.
- Appropriate school officials become familiar with pertinent civil and criminal laws at the state, local, and federal levels, so that they are able to recognize possible civil rights violations, hate crimes, and other criminal acts.
- Schools develop guidelines and procedures for collaboration with law enforcement officials, make appropriate referrals to outside agencies, and designate liaison personnel.
- Crisis intervention plans are in place to minimize the possibility of violence or disruption of the educational process.
- District-level personnel and individual school sites form continuing partnerships with parents and the community to prevent hate crimes and harassing behaviors.

- Staff training and professional development programs support the district's anti-harassment efforts.
- All harassment incidents are carefully documented and incidents are reported to outside authorities as required.
- District regularly assesses the effectiveness of its anti-harassment efforts.

Source: Protecting Students from Harassment and Hate Crime, A Guide for Schools, January 1999.

Schools are not immune from such intolerance and violence. Teenagers and young adults account for a significant proportion of the country's hate crimes both as perpetrators and as victims. Hate-motivated behavior, whether in the form of ethnic conflict, harassment, intimidation, or graffiti, is often apparent on school grounds. Hate violence is also perpetrated by hate groups, which actively work to recruit young people to their ranks.

The good news is that children are not born with such attitudes; they are learned. It is possible for schools, families, law enforcement, and communities to work together to prevent the development of the prejudiced attitudes and violent behavior that lead to hate crimes. Prejudice and the resulting violence can be reduced or even eliminated by instilling in children an appreciation and respect for each other's differences, and by helping them to develop empathy, conflict resolution, and critical thinking skills. By teaching children that even subtle forms of hate are inherently wrong, we can hope to prevent more extreme acts of hate in the future.

Educators have a tremendous opportunity to reduce or eliminate hate-motivated crime and violence. A number of school districts and individual schools have already taken action to create comprehensive anti-hate policies and programs that involve every facet of the school community: students, parents, teachers, staff, and administrators. These schools have worked to create a school climate where hateful acts are not tolerated, and to provide an equitable, supportive, and safe environment for all students.

By understanding what hate-motivated behavior is and how best to respond to it, schools can become a powerful force in bringing such incidents to an end.

ELEMENTS OF EFFECTIVE SCHOOL-BASED HATE PREVENTION PROGRAMS

A comprehensive hate prevention program will involve all school personnel in creating a school climate in which prejudice and hate-motivated behavior are not acceptable, but which also permits the expression of diverse viewpoints. Hate prevention, as used in this manual, means prevention of hate-motivated behavior and crimes.

1. Provide hate prevention training to all staff, including teachers, administrators, school security personnel, and support staff. All school employees, including teachers, administrators, support staff, bus drivers, and security staff, should be aware of the various manifestations of hate and be competent to address hate incidents. Training should include anti-bias and conflict resolution methods; procedures for identifying and reporting incidents of racial, religious, and sexual harassment, discrimination and hate crime; strategies for preventing such incidents from occurring; and resources available to assist in dealing with these incidents.

2. Ensure that all students receive hate prevention training through age-appropriate classroom activities, assemblies, and other school-related activities. Prejudice and discrimination are learned attitudes and behaviors. Neither is uncontrollable or inevitable. Teaching children that, even, subtle forms of hate, such as ethnic slurs or epithets, negative or offensive name-calling, stereotyping, and exclusion are hurtful and inherently wrong can help to prevent more extreme, violent manifestations of hate. Through structured classroom activities and programs, children can begin to develop empathy, while practicing the critical thinking and conflict resolution skills needed to recognize and respond to various manifestations of hate behavior.

3. Develop partnerships with families, community organizations, and law enforcement agencies. Hate crime prevention cannot be accomplished by schools alone. School districts are encouraged to develop partnerships with parent groups, youth-serving organizations, criminal justice agencies, victim assistance organizations, businesses, advocacy groups, and religious organizations. These partnerships can help identify resources available to school personnel to address hate incidents, raise community awareness of the issue, ensure appropriate responses to hate incidents, and make certain that youth receive a consistent message that hate-motivated behavior will not be tolerated.

4. Develop a hate prevention policy to distribute to every student, every student's family, and every employee of the school district. An effective hate prevention policy will promote a school climate in which racial, religious, ethnic, gender, and other differences, as well as freedom of thought and expression, are respected and appreciated. The policy should be developed with the input of parents, students, teachers, community members, and school administrators. It should include a description of the types of behavior prohibited under the policy; the roles and responsibilities of students and staff in preventing and reporting hate incidents or crimes; the range of possible consequences for engaging in this type of behavior; and locations of resources in the school and community where students can go for help. It should respect diverse viewpoints, freedom of thought, and freedom of expression. Every student should be informed of the contents of the school district's policy on hate crime on an annual basis. School districts are advised to consult with an attorney in the course of developing such a policy.

5. Develop a range of corrective actions for those who violate school hate prevention policies. School districts are encouraged to take a firm position against all injurious manifestations of hate, from ethnic slurs, racial epithets, and taunts, to graffiti, vandalism, discrimination, harassment, intimidation, and violence. School districts can

develop a wide range of non-disciplinary corrective actions to respond to incidents, including counseling, parent conferences, community service, awareness training, or completion of a research paper on an issue related to hate, as well as disciplinary actions, such as in-school suspension or expulsion. School officials should be prepared to contact local, state, or federal civil rights officials to respond to more serious incidents and, in cases involving criminal activity or threat of criminal activity, should call the police.

6. Collect and use data to focus district-wide hate prevention efforts. Collection of data on the occurrence of school-based hate incidents or crimes will assist administrators and teachers to identify patterns and to more effectively implement hate prevention policies and programs. To obtain such data, school districts may include questions regarding hate crime on surveys they conduct related to school crime and discipline, as well as collect and analyze incident-based data on specific hate incidents and crimes. In the latter case, school districts are encouraged to work closely with local law enforcement personnel to collect uniform and consistent data on hate crime.

7. Provide structured opportunities for integration. Young people can begin to interact across racial and ethnic lines through school-supported organizations and activities. Multiethnic teams of students can work together on community service projects, to organize extracurricular events, or to complete class projects. High school students can participate in service-learning projects in which they tutor, coach, or otherwise assist younger students from diverse backgrounds.

WHICH HATE CRIME AND CIVIL RIGHTS LAWS APPLY?

A number of federal and state laws prohibit acts or threats of violence, as well as harassment and discrimination, based on race, color, religion, national origin, sexual orientation, gender, and/or disability. It is important to check with an attorney to ascertain the extent to which federal and state hate crime and civil rights laws may also apply in the school context. The applicable federal laws include the following:

18 U.S.C. Section 245. Section 245, the principal federal hate crime statute, prohibits intentional use of force or threat of force against a person because of his or her race, color, religion, or national origin, and because he or she was engaged in a federally protected activity, such as enrolling in or attending any public school or college. Legislation has been introduced that would amend Section 245 to include crimes committed because of the victim's sexual orientation, gender, or disability and to eliminate the federally protected activity requirement.

Title VI of the Civil Rights Act of 1964. Title VI and regulations promulgated under Title VI prohibit discrimination by institutions that receive federal funding, including harassment on the basis of race, color, and national origin.

Title IX of the Education Amendments of 1972. Title IX and regulations promulgated under Title IX prohibit discrimination by institutions that receive federal funding, including harassment based on sex.

Section 504 of the Rehabilitation Act of 1973. Section 504 and regulations promulgated under Section 504 prohibit discrimination by institutions that receive federal funding, including harassment based on disability.

CLASSROOM ACTIVITIES AND DISCUSSION TOPICS

The following activities illustrate the sort of classroom projects that can help students
develop empathy, critical thinking skills, and an awareness and appreciation for diversity. A number of anti-bias curricula have been developed by various organizations,
which contain additional activities; these curricula are listed in the bibliography at the
end of this manual.

In order to be most effective, such classroom activities should be part of a comprehensive hate prevention strategy that involves all members of the school community,
including the student body, parents, school administration, law enforcement, and community organizations. Issues, such as prejudice, discrimination, and hate crime, cannot
be effectively addressed in the classroom alone. Rather, classroom lessons must be reinforced by the school community and beyond.

It can sometimes be difficult for teachers and students to discuss issues, such as
prejudice and discrimination, particularly in a multicultural setting. Therefore, prior to
engaging in these or other anti-bias teaching activities, teachers may wish to receive
diversity or conflict resolution training.

ELEMENTARY SCHOOL ACTIVITIES

- Reading books aloud is an excellent way to prompt classroom discussions about the
  diversity of cultures, traditions, and lifestyles in our society. Books also help children
  to develop empathy by helping them to understand the points of view of other
  people. An annotated bibliography of multicultural children's literature is available
  from A WORLD OF DIFFERENCE Institute, Anti-Defamation League, 823 United
  Nations Plaza, New York, NY 10017. 212/885–7800; or 800/343–5540.
- Encouraging children's critical thinking ability may be one of the best antidotes to
  prejudice. Help children recognize instances of prejudice, discrimination, and stereotyping, and discuss appropriate responses to such attitudes and behaviors when they
  encounter them. Newspapers, magazines, movies, and television news and entertainment shows can provide opportunities for classroom discussion.

  A Web site that introduces children to concepts of prejudice and discrimination
  in an interactive, age-appropriate format, Hateful Acts Hurt Kids, can be found at
  www.usdoj.gov/kidspage. This Web site helps children learn empathy, an appreciation for diversity, and coping skills should they become victims of prejudice.

  A free pamphlet on talking to young children about prejudice and discrimination is available from the National PTA, 300 North Wabash Avenue, Suite 2100,
  Chicago, IL 60611. 312/670–6782.
- Young children can work together to create positive change through community-
  oriented projects. Class projects, such as painting over graffiti, or working together

to develop a classroom code of conduct (e.g., "No child shall be teased or excluded because of his or her race, religion, accent, ethnicity, disability, gender, or appearance") all affirm children's ability to take a stand against prejudiced thinking.

Additional hate prevention activities for elementary grades can be found in "Teacher, They Called Me A _____!" available for $12.50 from the Anti-Defamation League, 22D Hollywood Avenue, Hohokus, NJ 07423. 800/343–5540, or 212/885–7951; *Starting Small: Teaching Tolerance in Preschool and the Early Grades,* available free of charge from Teaching Tolerance, 400 Washington Avenue, Montgomery, AL 36104. 334/264–0286; and *Actions Speak Louder Than Words,* available free of charge from the National Conference, 71 Fifth Avenue, New York, NY 10003. 800/352–6225. Middle and Secondary School Activities.

- By learning what youth and communities can do to reduce or prevent hate violence, students learn that their choices and actions can have an impact. People working together to stop hate violence across the nation have made a big difference. The movement against hate groups and hate violence includes hundreds of national, regional, and local organizations. In particular, young people can bring to a community an increased awareness of the problems of prejudice.

  To convey the power of community mobilization against hate crime, you might show the award-winning video *Not In Our Town,* which documents community resistance to anti-Semitic and other hate crimes in Billings, Montana. You may wish to ask questions, such as: Who are the victims, bystanders, and perpetrators in this film? What form of resistance did the community initiate? How did the organized hate group members react to the union of Jews and non-Jews in the community? Do you think it is true that the community "found a weapon more powerful than [the KKK's]"? What was that weapon, and what made it more powerful? Has this, or another, type of bigotry ever occurred in your community? What, if any, forms of community action were used to combat it?

  Not In Our Town is available with a teaching guide from The Working Group, 510/268–9675, ext. 317. More on community mobilization projects can be found in *Teaching Tolerance Magazine,* a free semiannual magazine providing educators with resources for promoting interracial and intercultural understanding. Teachers and other educators can subscribe free of charge using official school letterhead. Teaching Tolerance, 400 Washington Avenue, Montgomery, AL 36104. 334/264–0286. Fax: 334/264–7310.

- By understanding the various manifestations of hate throughout our nation's history, students learn to recognize it in contemporary society. Members of racial or religious groups, immigrants, women, the disabled, and gays and lesbians have been the targets of bigotry at various times in our country's history. Regardless of the specific identity or characteristics of the victims or perpetrators, however, there are elements common to all forms of intolerance and persecution.

  You might have students research historical incidents of bigotry against particular groups, and present their reports to the class. Students can discuss what these reports show about why some people do not accept individuals who are different from them, and what individuals, groups, and our nation have done to respond to acts of intolerance (e.g., civil rights laws, hate crime laws, the United Nations Manifesto on Human Rights).

Additional activities on the historical role of hate are suggested in *Free At Last: A History of the Civil Rights Movement and Those Who Died in the Struggle,* available free of charge from Teaching Tolerance, 400 Washington Avenue, Montgomery AL, 36104. 334/264–0286; and in *Facing History and Ourselves,* from Facing History and Ourselves National Foundation, Inc., 16 Hurd Road, Brookline, MA 02146. 617/232–1595.

- Students can learn critical thinking skills to identify stereotyping that they encounter in their own lives, as well as in the media, literature, music, movies, and elsewhere.

Drugs and Alcohol

- According to the National Institute on Alcohol Abuse and Alcoholism (NIAAA), alcohol is the drug of choice among youth. "A higher percentage of youth 12–17 use alcohol (28.7%) than use tobacco (11.9%), or illicit drugs (10.6%)" (National Survey on Drug Use and Health, 2004 (NSDUH).
- Equally disturbing is the fact that tobacco and drug use for this age group is declining, while alcohol use is staying fairly constant (NSDUH, 2004).
- Many young people are experiencing the consequences of drinking too much, at too early an age. As a result, underage drinking is now a leading public health problem in this country.
- Annually, six thousand youth under age twenty-one die from alcohol-related injuries, homicides, and suicides.
- About half (50.3 percent) of Americans age twelve or older reported being current drinkers of alcohol in 2004. This translates to an estimated 121 million people and is similar to the 2002 and 2003 estimates (NSDUH, 2004).
- More than three-fourths of twelfth-graders, two-thirds of tenth-graders, and nearly half of eighth-graders have drunk alcohol at some point in their lives (Monitoring the Future Study, University of Michigan, 2004).
- In 2004, the rate of current illicit drug use was approximately eight times higher among youths, ages twelve to seventeen, who smoked cigarettes (47.5 percent) than it was among youths who did not smoke cigarettes (5.6 percent) (NSDUH, 2004).
- Illicit drug use also was associated with the level of alcohol use. Among youths, ages 12 to 17, who were heavy drinkers (i.e., drank 5 or more drinks on the same occasion on at least 5 different days in the past 30 days), 65.6 percent also were current illicit drug users, whereas among nondrinkers, the rate was only 5.0 percent (NSDUH, 2004).

Underage drinking is widespread throughout the United States. More than 13 million underage youth drink each year. In fact, according to recent research conducted by the Institute of Medicine (IOM), actual drinking patterns in the United States suggest that "almost all young people use alcohol before they are 21" (*Reducing Underage Drinking: A Collective Responsibility,* 2004). The average age of first alcohol use has generally decreased since 1965. This in itself is troubling, because the age of the youth at the onset of drinking strongly predicts the development of alcohol dependence over the

Based on the latest mortality data available, motor vehicle crashes are the leading cause of death for people from 15 to 20 years old . . . 19 percent of drivers, ages 15 to 20, who were killed in motor vehicle crashes . . . had been drinking alcohol.

NHTSA, 2003

course of an individual's lifetime (*Reducing Underage Drinking: A Collective Responsibility,* 2004).

This early onset of alcohol use has triggered tragic health, social, and economic problems for youths and their families: homicide, suicide, traumatic injury, drowning, burns, violent and property crime, high risk sex, fetal alcohol syndrome, alcohol poisoning, and a need for treatment for alcohol abuse and dependence (*Understanding Underage Drinking, National Institute on Alcohol Abuse and Alcoholism,* 2002).

It is likely that many members of your school community are not well versed on the topic of alcohol prevention. As you address the issue of underage drinking in your schools, it is important to keep in mind that many people have only just begun to understand that underage drinking is not just a matter of kids being kids—but that underage drinking actually can lead to serious and enduring problems. These problems may include academic failure, attendance issues, behavioral problems including social and emotional issues, suspension and incarceration, and even school violence (Dwyer, Osher, & Warger, 1998).

THE ROLE OF THE PREVENTION COORDINATOR

Like other forms of substance abuse, alcohol use and abuse contributes to academic problems for students, and discipline and safety problems for schools. Fortunately, schools clearly play a key role in preventing underage alcohol use and should be included in all comprehensive, community-based efforts to reduce underage drinking. There is a wide range of activities that schools can undertake to prevent underage drinking that include policy development, implementing alcohol prevention curricula, creating a safe and supportive school environment, developing after-school programs, and working in partnership with the community on alcohol prevention.

As a prevention coordinator, one of your primary roles is to continually "make the case" to administrators, teachers, parents, and community members, that a safe and drug-free school will enhance effective learning and teaching. You must identify concrete ways that prevention programming will provide students with the knowledge and skills they need to succeed. By highlighting the intrinsic connections between healthy behavior, academic achievement, and school safety, you will be better able to garner the programmatic support you need to implement and sustain your prevention programs.

PROCEDURES

The following are procedures to be followed if a teacher or administrator suspects that a student is under the influence. They are similar to those adopted by many school boards and districts.

- The staff shall immediately notify the building principal, or in his or her absence, an administrator designated by the principal and the nurse. The principal or designee shall immediately notify the superintendent of schools.
- The principal shall arrange for a staff member to escort the student to the nurse or principal's office. The transfer of the student shall be made in an orderly and tactful fashion and in as a discrete a manner as possible. No staff member other than the school nurse or medical inspector shall conduct any independent medical examination of the student. Physical restraint or force shall only be used as reasonable and necessary to:
  —Quell a disturbance threatening physical injury to self or others
  —Obtain possession of weapons or other dangerous objects upon the student or within the control of the student
  —For the purpose of self-defense
  —For the protection of persons or property
- The principal will consult with the school nurse, the student assistance counselor, and any other staff member necessary to determine if there are health-related causes for the student's behavior. When health-related causes can be substantiated, the nurse will follow the procedure for first aid and emergency care.
- If health-related causes for the student's behavior can be ruled out, the principal shall take the following steps:
  Notify the parent/guardian and the chief school administrator and arrange for an examination of the student to be completed immediately following parental/guardian contact. This examination must include a urine and/or blood collection for drug/alcohol screening and/or anabolic steroids.
  The medical examination will occur in the following order of preference:
  a. By the school physician
  b. By the student's private physician
  c. If such physician is not immediately available, the student shall be taken to the nearest hospital for examination, accompanied by the student's parent or guardian, if available, or by a member of the school staff designated by the principal. If the student is uncooperative, and/or if it appears that the student will be difficult to transport, then the local police and/or emergency squad will be called and asked to transport the student to the hospital.
- When necessary, arrange for the student to be taken to his or her home as soon as possible following the examination, after it has been verified that a parent

or guardian will be home to receive the student. The student is to remain at home for up to twenty-four hours, at which time a written report of the medical examination including an urinalysis/blood analysis for drug/alcohol and/or anabolic steroids shall be furnished to the parent/guardian, principal, and chief school administrator by the examining physician within this twenty-four-hour time period.

- If the written report of the medical examination, including a report of the urinalysis/blood analysis, is not submitted to the parent or guardian, principal, and chief school administrator within twenty-four hours, the pupil shall be allowed to return to school pending a receipt of a positive diagnosis of alcohol or other drugs.

- If there is a positive diagnosis from the medical examination indicating that the pupil is under the influence of alcoholic beverages or other drugs excluding anabolic steroids, the pupil shall be returned to the care of parent or guardian as soon as possible. Attendance at school shall not resume until a written report has been submitted to the parent or guardian of the pupil, the principal, and the chief school administrator from a physician who has examined the pupil to diagnose alcohol or other drug use. The report shall certify that substance abuse no longer interferes with the pupil's physical and mental ability to perform in school. In addition, the staff member shall complete the Violence, Vandalism, and Substance Abuse Incident Report. In the case of a positive diagnosis, the parent/guardian will be responsible for all screening costs.

THE NATIONAL PLAN

The plan to prevent and reduce underage drinking developed through the Interagency Coordinating Committee on the Prevention of Underage Drinking (ICCPUD) and described below can be characterized as comprehensive, goal-driven, evidence-based, long-term, and coordinated. The plan takes a multifaceted, balanced approach to reducing both the demand for alcohol and its availability to the young. It involves all levels of government, as well as individuals and private-sector organizations and institutions, including faith-based organizations. Prevention, education, increasing public awareness of underage drinking and its consequences, treatment opportunities, school and workplace prevention programs, research, and legal enforcement are all components of the plan.

The plan is built around the following three goals:

Goal 1: Strengthen a national commitment to address the problem of underage drinking.

This goal will be achieved by increasing national awareness of the extent of underage drinking and its negative consequences, enhancing broad-based support for the prevention and reduction of underage drinking, and strengthening leadership at all levels of government and in all sectors of society aimed at addressing the problem; increasing cooperation, coordination, and collaboration among private entities, including faith-based organizations and all levels of government; and encouraging public- and private-sector participation in, and providing support for, programs and projects that address the prevention and reduction of underage drinking.

Goal 2: Reduce demand for, the availability of, and access to alcohol by persons under the age of twenty-one.

This goal will be achieved by providing developmentally and culturally appropriate information to adults on underage drinking and its consequences, especially to parents and caregivers of those under the age of twenty-one, emphasizing their responsibility to help prevent underage drinking; providing youth under the age of twenty-one in the workforce and in kindergarten through college with developmentally and culturally appropriate information and resistance skills training to enhance protective factors and to change attitudes toward underage drinking; informing states and local communities about effective policies and procedures for reducing access to alcohol by those under the age of twenty-one; assisting states and local communities in enforcing underage drinking laws through compliance training in retail establishments and by crafting laws that prevent or reduce underage drinking; promoting partnerships at the state and local levels, including partnerships between enforcement agencies and other justice agencies, as well as those responses to underage drinking and improved adjudication and programs that dissuade adults from providing alcohol to those under twenty-one; and providing opportunities for early identification of alcohol abuse and brief interventions or treatment as appropriate.

Goal 3: Utilize research, evaluation, and surveillance to improve the effectiveness of policies and programs designed to prevent and reduce underage drinking.

This goal will be achieved by analyzing the current knowledge base on preventing and reducing underage drinking and its consequences; supporting research to address gaps in knowledge; continually monitoring the extent of the problem, contributing factors, consequences, and trends through increased surveillance; expanding the use of evidence-based programs in prevention and reduction efforts; creating a federal registry of effective programs for use by states and communities; encouraging and supporting the rigorous evaluation of innovative and promising programs; implementing funding guidelines that require the use of evidence-based programs or rigorously evaluated programs that are innovative and promising; and requiring evaluation of all programs to correct problems in design and/or implementation.

The plan establishes five-year annual performance measures in the form of numeric targets that will be used to evaluate progress. These targets are as follows:

- Target 1: By 2009, reduce the prevalence of past month alcohol use by those ages 12 through 20 by 10 percent as measured against the 2004 baseline of 28.7 percent.

- Target 2: By 2009, reduce the prevalence of those ages 12 through 20 reporting binge alcohol use in the past 30 days by 10 percent as measured against the 2004 baseline of 19.6 percent.
- Target 3: By 2009, achieve an increase of average age of first use among those who initiate before age 21 to 16.5 years of age as compared to the 2004 baseline.

1. Comprehensive: Any successful plan to reduce the widespread prevalence of alcohol consumption by persons under twenty-one must be comprehensive, by which is meant a multifaceted, balanced approach to reducing both the demand for alcohol and its availability to the young that includes the participation of all levels of government, as well as individuals and private-sector organizations and institutions, including faith-based organizations.

Such an approach promotes integration of multiple interventions, creates synergy among them, and increases the likelihood of overall success. Prevention, education, increasing public awareness of underage drinking and its consequences, treatment opportunities, school and workplace prevention programs, research, and legal enforcement are all essential components of a comprehensive plan.

2. Goal-Driven: A broad strategic initiative must be directed by a clear set of goals that determine objectives and guide the actions to be taken in the pursuit of those goals and objectives. The plan proposes three specific goals with related objectives and recommends interventions to protect young people from the immediate and long-term adverse consequences of alcohol use that threaten their health, safety, and development.

3. Evidence-Based: Underage alcohol consumption is a complex phenomenon that requires additional scientific research to address questions that cannot be answered from the current knowledge base and to confirm the efficacy of proposed policies and interventions. Without policies and interventions formulated on the basis of scientific evidence, there can be no assurance of their effectiveness. For example, root causes of underage alcohol use have to be identified and potential interventions developed; psychosocial factors that play an important role in moderating or exacerbating underage alcohol use must be investigated; epidemiological and natural-history studies should be conducted to shed light on understanding how and why alcohol-related problems develop among underage college students; and minority groups that appear to respond differently to alcohol than does the general population should be researched. In addition, since underage drinking encompasses an age range that spans childhood, through adolescence, to early adulthood, it is essential to ensure that interventions are developmentally appropriate. Finally, programs, strategies and interventions should be evaluated after implementation.

4. Long-Term: There is no quick fix for the problem of underage drinking in America.

It is deeply embedded in the American culture, is often viewed as a rite of passage, is frequently facilitated by adults, and has proven stubbornly resistant to change. A long-term effort will be required to solve it. The plan provides a structure for planning over the long term while implementing short- and medium-term initiatives that work together toward the achievement of the plan's targets.

5. Coordinated: The plan works to ensure that the national effort to reduce alcohol consumption by underage individuals is coordinated, by which is meant that each agency in the federal government with an appropriate role to play is both engaged in the effort and involved in the strategic coordination of agency activities. Furthermore, to the extent possible, the ICCPUD agencies will seek to avoid unnecessary overlap, duplication, or wasted resources. At the same time, the federal government will continue to work with the states, local communities, individuals, and nongovernmental institutions and organizations in a collaborative effort to prevent and reduce underage drinking.

Underage alcohol use is a national problem, but the ultimate implementation of prevention and reduction efforts must occur at the community and even family levels.

6. Measurable: The plan will rely on data to evaluate its success in reducing underage drinking. Specific numeric targets will be established so that progress can be measured from year to year through performance measurements developed for that purpose.

The Florida Approach

Early in his first administration, Governor Jeb Bush of Florida set as a priority the reduction of substance abuse in Florida. Despite the ambitious nature of his goal—reduction by 50 percent—Florida has made great strides toward achieving it in virtually every area. The vast majority of use rates for individual substances of abuse by children is down by significant amounts: LSD by 47 percent, ecstasy by 46 percent, heroin by 50 percent, cocaine by 40 percent, and crack cocaine by 25 percent. Youth tobacco use, after several years of concerted effort, has dropped from 18.4 percent to 11.5 percent.

Florida has led the nation in leading its children away from substance abuse. One area, however, where Florida remains locked with the rest of the nation is on youth alcohol abuse. For decades, alcohol has been the most widespread substance of abuse by youth. It far outstrips any other drug of abuse; marijuana and tobacco use is slightly more than one-third the rate of drinking among youth. While many other individual drugs and tobacco have fallen off in use by as much as 50 percent or more, alcohol use has moved down only 10 percent among children in grades 6 through 12. Moreover, binge drinking is high among this group, as are all the unsafe and unhealthy practices that go along with adolescent drinking. Current use rates (defined as one or more drinks in the past thirty days,) remain around 30 percent. However, after five years of effort and much attendant success, Florida has built a prevention system of best practices that gives the state a high probability of effectiveness wherever it focuses its efforts. The resources and infrastructure, by and large, are already in place. They need to be brought to bear on youth alcohol use.

FLORIDA'S DRUG CONTROL STRATEGY

"Florida Drug Control Strategy has but one purpose—to protect our citizens from the dangers posed by illegal drugs. It presents a balanced plan that aims to bring down both the demand for and supply of illegal drugs in Florida by advancing policies and pro-grams that support prevention and education, treatment, and law enforcement. Over the long term, its intent is to cut substance abuse in Florida by half."

The first goal in the Florida Drug Control Strategy is to "protect Florida's youth from substance abuse." That goal continues to be the first priority among Florida's prevention leaders. As it relates to underage alcohol use, the target of the strategy is to reduce alcohol use by Florida's sixth- through twelfth-graders to 20 percent or less and to reduce illegal sales of alcohol to minors to eight percent or less. Underage drinking is a serious threat to Florida's youth. In order to achieve this goal, Florida's prevention community, treatment agencies, and enforcement agencies have partnered to provide a more holistic approach to reducing underage drinking.

"Since no single approach will prevent young people from drinking illegally, we must rigorously and deliberately integrate the best practices and proven-effective programs to eliminate underage drinking into an effective strategy," states the strategy document.

An integrated, long-term approach is essential to successfully reducing youth alcohol use in Florida to 20 percent or less. The Changing Alcohol Norms Workgroup (CAN) that was established in June 2003 focused on public information efforts, education, law enforcement, collaboration, legislation, and treatment to develop a comprehensive strategy to reduce underage drinking. This multi-agency collaboration represented uni-fied leadership in promoting model programs and initiatives that are aggressively aimed at curtailing and progressively eliminating alcohol use by underage youth.

The workgroup benefited from the National Academy of Sciences (NAS) Institute of Medicine report, "Reducing Underage Drinking, A Collective Responsibility." Per-tinent recommendations from the NAS report were incorporated into the working group's white paper, with specific application at the state and local levels. The white paper, which will continually reassess itself, as the environment in which it operates is modified by its very application, is aimed at bringing youth drinking—at elementary, middle, high school, and college—down to less than 20 percent. This is not a new approach or focus for Florida and coalitions and partnerships on the local level have been a major influence in all prevention efforts.

Neighborhoods, communities, and campuses are encouraged to develop programs that offer a consistent and non-conflicted message that underage drinking is unhealthy, risky, and outside the accepted standard of behavior.

Findings from the 2003 Monitoring the Future study, a national drug use survey annually administered by the University of Michigan, highlight the pervasiveness of alcohol in middle and high schools today. Alcohol is the drug used most often by youth. This is true not only on a national level, but also on a state level in Florida. Florida's youth are using alcohol at a higher rate. In order to collect baseline data and track annual progress, Florida instituted the Florida Youth Substance Abuse Survey (FYSAS). According to the 2003 FYSAS results, underage alcohol use by Florida's sixth- through twelfth-graders was as follows:

- 55.1 percent have consumed alcohol in their lifetime
- 30.9 percent have consumed alcohol in the past thirty days with grade level results ranging from 11.2 percent for sixth-graders to 52.4 percent for twelfth-graders

- 16.0 percent reported binge drinking (consuming five or more drinks in one sitting) averaging 8.3 percent for middle school students and 22.3 percent for high school students.

If underage usage rates are not sufficient evidence that alcohol is a problem for Florida's youth, other startling statistics only reinforce the view. According to the Department of Business and Professional Regulation, Division of Alcoholic Beverages and Tobacco, the noncompliance rate for the sale of alcohol to youth is at 11 percent. This far outstrips the rate for noncompliance for the illegal sale of tobacco to minors, which is at 7 percent. According to the NIAAA, the rate of alcohol use more than doubles in young people who start drinking before age 15 compared to those who wait until age 21. The NIAAA also found that the rate of fatal crashes among alcohol-involved drivers between 16 and 20 years old is more than twice the rate for alcohol-involved drivers 21 and older.

Such compelling evidence confirms the urgent need to focus sharper attention on youth alcohol use prevention strategies. While noteworthy strides have been made in this arena, much work remains to be done. Since no single approach will prevent young people from drinking illegally, we must rigorously and deliberately combine the best ways to eliminate underage drinking into an effective strategy.

FLORIDA DRUG CONTROL STRATEGY

The first goal in the Florida Drug Control Strategy asserts a commitment to "protect Florida's youth from substance abuse." That goal continues to be the first priority among Florida's prevention leaders. As it relates to underage alcohol use, the target of the strategy is to reduce alcohol use by Florida's sixth- through twelfth-graders to 20 percent or less and to reduce illegal sales of alcohol to minors to 8 percent or less. As previously noted, Florida's progress to reaching this goal is measured each year in the Florida Youth Substance Abuse Survey. Currently, youth alcohol use is at 30.9 percent and the illegal sale of alcohol to minors is at 11 percent. In order to achieve the strategy's goal, Florida's prevention and enforcement agencies are partnering to provide a more holistic approach to reducing underage drinking.

Florida's progress in reducing youth substance abuse is evident by looking at the results of the Florida Youth Substance Abuse Survey. Under Governor Bush's leadership, the vast majority of use rates for individual substances of abuse by children is down by significant amounts: LSD by 47 percent, ecstasy by 46 percent, heroin by 50 percent, cocaine by 40 percent, and crack cocaine by 25 percent. Youth tobacco use, after several years of concerted effort, has dropped from 18.4 percent to 11.5 percent. Unfortunately, the reduction of youth alcohol use is slow. This challenge necessitates that Florida increase its efforts to reduce youth alcohol use. In order to make a change and meet the goal to reduce youth alcohol use to 20 percent and the illegal sale of alcohol to underage youth to eight percent or less, Florida must implement proven strategies using existing resources.

Without neglecting continued emphasis on further reducing youth drug use, it is time to earmark a greater share of resources, organization, and activities toward reducing the youth alcohol usage rate. By emphasizing prevention and law enforcement efforts in the areas, we believe we can do both—keep suppressing all youth drug and tobacco use and breaking the youth proclivities to consume alcohol.

The Working Group's recommendations can form the basis of an action plan for any community and at local and state levels.

RECOMMENDATIONS:

1. Public Information Effort

The Office of Drug Control, in collaboration with Clear Channel Communications, the Department of Children and Families, and local anti-drug coalitions, is heading up a statewide media campaign to raise awareness about substance abuse. The goal of the campaign is to prevent an additional fifty thousand youth in Florida from beginning illegal drug use or misuse of legal drugs. Consistently over the past four years, Florida's youth have shown decreasing rates of substance abuse. We believe this media campaign can reduce the numbers yet again by up to 2 percent, or approximately fifty thousand children in the target group of twelve- to eighteen-year-olds. The messages and the campaign are developed in conjunction with and linked to local coalition prevention efforts. The correlated messages remind youth and adults to "Think About It," a theme indicating that there are severe negative consequences to youth substance abuse. One-third of the ads target youth and underage drinking. Results of the media campaign are analyzed using random telephone surveys in four major markets. So far, the results have exceeded the original goal for 21 percent of youth being aware of the dangers associated with substance abuse and 21 percent of parents being more aware of the importance of talking to their families about the risks associated with substance abuse.

National:

Recommendation 1–1: The federal government should fund and actively support the development of a national media effort, as a major component of an adult-oriented campaign to reduce underage drinking.

Recommendation 1–2: Intensive research and development of a youth-focused media campaign relating to underage drinking should be initiated at the national level.

State:

Recommendation 1–3: Expand the existing statewide media campaign highlighting the effects of underage drinking to include the following:

- A combination of print, television, billboards, and radio public service announcements focusing on both youth and adults complementing the national campaign

- Youth involvement in the development of the campaign much like the tobacco TRUTH campaign
- Ads with high-profile sports and entertainment stars to convey the prevention message to youth
- Ads targeted to adults including information on liability; ads highlighting increased enforcement of underage drinking laws
- Education on risk and protective factors related to adolescent alcohol use. The campaign should empower adults to reduce the risks and increase the protection for Florida's youth
- Web banners on youth-oriented Web sites that link to accurate alcohol prevention information on age-appropriate Web sites, such as MADD and SADD
- Video games and computer games that further communicate the dangers of underage drinking with youth
- The Florida Education Channel broadcasting public service announcements on the dangers of youth alcohol use.

Local:

Recommendation 1–4: Monitor activities and the impact of the media campaign in order to refine/adjust the campaign as needed and use materials from the state media campaign to distribute to local media outlets including:

- Letters to the editor
- Press conferences
- Community forums
- Radio, television, and billboard public service announcements.

Recommendation 1–5: Local coalitions should serve as the information source for members of the media to contact for information on local underage drinking efforts and to provide feedback to the state campaign.

2. Education

Courtesy of the Department of Education Safe and Drug Free Schools funding and a result of centrally condensed, but locally expended programs, Florida school districts are leading the nation in using proven effective programs and strategies targeted at preventing substance abuse. Sixty-four of the 67 school districts in Florida are using evidence-based programs in their schools. Through the comprehensive school health program, school health nurses and social workers provided education on the dangers of alcohol use to 67,955 students during the 2001–2002 year. These programs are credited with playing a vital role in the overall reduction of substance abuse in the state of Florida over the past 4 years.

High-risk and illegal alcohol consumption by underage college students is also a concern in Florida. In July 2000, prevention professionals from colleges and universities from around the state created the statewide coalition known as the Florida Higher

Education: Alliance for Substance Abuse Prevention (FHE: ASAP). FHE: ASAP members include public and private, large and small, two- and four-year institutions. The coalition is committed to increasing the coordination of prevention efforts in higher education and throughout the state; encouraging the use of research-based prevention strategies; and developing campus community partnerships to begin to change environmental and cultural factors that contribute to underage drinking. Since college-age students do not live in isolation from the community at large, it is important to include a broad range of community partners. Parents, employers, local media, health care providers, treatment providers and faculty, staff, and students all have a role in Florida's prevention efforts. Ongoing collaboration from all of these partners can ensure the success of a comprehensive and effective statewide prevention strategy.

Another alcohol-related problem facing Florida is the prenatal exposure to alcohol resulting in fetal alcohol syndrome (FAS). FAS is one of the leading preventable causes of birth defects, mental retardation, and neurodevelopment disorders in the United States. Of the two hundred thousand babies born in Florida each year, approximately two thousand have FAS or fetal alcohol exposure (FAE). There is no cure for FAS or FAE; however, its incidence can be totally prevented by abstinence from alcohol during pregnancy.

Teens are especially at high risk for prenatal alcohol consumption. Education must be targeted toward teens to prevent the birth of children with FAS or FAE. The Fetal Alcohol Syndrome Interagency Action Group was established in 2001 to improve the system of care for individuals with FAS and their families. In 2002, the action group developed a strategic plan. A strong emphasis of the plan involves preventing FAS among the children of adolescent mothers.

Recommendation 1–5: Local coalitions should serve as the information source for members of the media to contact for information on local underage drinking efforts and to provide feedback to the state campaign.

National:

Recommendation 2–1: The U.S. Department of Health and Human Services and the U.S. Department of Education should focus on funding evidence-based education interventions, with priority given both to those that incorporate elements known to be effective and those that are part of comprehensive community programs.

Recommendation 2–2: The National Institute on Alcohol Abuse and Alcoholism and the Substance Abuse and Mental Health Services Administration should continue to fund evaluations of college-based interventions, with a particular emphasis on targeting of interventions to specific college characteristics, and should maintain a list of evidence-based programs.

State:

Recommendation 2–3: Support development of a research-based, positive school climate framework; continue developing school cultures that promote alcohol prevention and intervention strategies.

Recommendation 2–4: Increase state and local funding for evidence-based prevention education in schools and colleges.

Recommendation 2–5: Facilitate regional focus groups with superintendents and higher education senior administrators to delineate the effects of underage drinking in their respective school districts and communities in order to build consensus on what must be done to reduce the problem.

Recommendation 2–6: Ensure colleges and universities adopt comprehensive prevention approaches including evidence-based screening, intervention strategies, consistent policy enforcement, and environmental changes that limit underage access to alcohol. Adopt universal education interventions, as well as selective and indicated approaches with relevant populations.

Recommendation 2–7: Strongly encourage servers be certified to serve alcoholic beverages. This license would require a background check and training for the server about identifying fake identification, the effects of alcohol on an underage youth, and liability education.

Recommendation 2–8: Promote education at both the high school and college levels relating to FAS disorders.

Local:

Due to the large nature of this section, recommendations are divided into the following groups: K–12 schools, higher education, parents, businesses, community, and enforcement.

A. K–12 Schools:

Recommendation 2–9: Identify Florida prevention programs proven successful in reducing alcohol use and replicate the most commendable research-based alcohol prevention programs in Florida schools where appropriate. Programs should include peer-to-peer education, risk and protective factors, youth-developed programs, and media literacy education.

Recommendation 2–10: Provide training to teachers, school nurses, guidance counselors, and school resource officers on how to identify problem drinkers and how to make referrals to the proper authorities. Education should also include the adverse impact of alcohol on a child's developing brain. School personnel should also be aware of the risk and protective factors associated with healthy development.

Recommendation 2–11: Promote rewarding alcohol-free activities including sober spring break opportunities, alcohol-free homecoming, "Project Graduation," weekend events, and public service options.

Recommendation 2–12: Address the void in fetal alcohol spectrum disorder (FASD) awareness among teens by presenting educational information to classes including parenting classes in Teen Parent Programs throughout the state. The presentation will provide age-appropriate information regarding cognitive, behavioral, and physical disabilities caused by prenatal alcohol exposure with a focus on brain development, facial abnormalities, and other birth defects associated with FASD. In addition, presenters will facilitate a dialogue with the teens to identify reasons teens drink during pregnancy and to strategize viable alternatives.

Recommendation 2–13: Implement a systemic approach to educating middle school and high school students about the dangers of drinking alcohol.

Recommendation 2–14: Ensure that all health class curricula include information about FASD.

Recommendation 2–15: Screen (and include as criteria for text book selection) all middle and high school health texts to ensure that information regarding FASD is included.

B. Higher Education:

Recommendation 2–16: Support a concerted effort by colleges and universities to help mobilize campus/community coalitions to change the environment that supports high-risk underage use of alcohol.

Recommendation 2–18: Enlist involvement and support of college and university senior leadership for prevention of high-risk underage use of alcohol by college students on campus and in the community.

Recommendation 2–19: Identify and/or develop comprehensive campus/community coalitions and prevention programs that: Provide brief screening and intervention strategies including evidence-based motivational and skills-based interventions; Promote rewarding alcohol-free activities including sober spring break opportunities, weekend and late-night events, and public service options; Create health-promoting normative environments; Prohibit alcohol availability to underage students; Restrict the marketing and promotion of alcoholic beverages to underage students; Increase the development and enforcement of campus policies and state and local laws that help reduce high-risk underage drinking; Include prevention program evaluation and support research.

Recommendation 2–20: Provide prevention education to first-year students, student athletes, and Greek organizations that discourage high-risk underage use of alcohol and promote college success strategies both in and outside the classroom.

Recommendation 2–21: Provide education to members of the campus/community including parents and faculty and staff on signs and symptoms of alcohol abuse, on appropriate counseling and self-help referral information, underage drinking laws and policies, and nonjudgmental ways to talk to college students about alcohol use and abuse.

Recommendation 2–22: Conduct an annual statewide assessment of underage alcohol consumption by college students. The assessment will estimate the prevalence and frequency of high-risk drinking, as well as student perceptions of social norms related to high-risk drinking. An anonymous, self report, student survey will be used in the statewide assessment. The Florida Higher Education: Alliance for Substance Abuse Prevention can provide support in gathering data for the assessment.

Recommendation 2–23: Secure federal research funding for a state university to conduct a periodic survey of environmental risk and protective factors at the county and state levels.

Recommendation 2–24: Include information regarding FASD in appropriate undergraduate-level college course curricula.

C. Parents:

Recommendation 2–25: Develop parent peer groups that would offer the following resources: Presentations to parents (and to children where appropriate) by parents of teens killed or injured in alcohol-related crashes; Information on civil and criminal liability when supplying alcohol to youth; Tools to use when talking to children about the effects of alcohol; Education on the adverse impact of alcohol on a child's developing brain; Brochures describing the signs and symptoms of a child abusing alcohol; Education on risk and protective factors associated with alcohol use; and Parenting skills directed at youth alcohol use.

D. Businesses:

Recommendation 2–26: Implement evidence-based alcohol education (such as Team Awareness) for employees at alcohol serving businesses, including specialized training programs for high-risk business locations.

Recommendation 2–27: Improve server training on reading identification, including tools and easy-to-use age calendars. Provide a similar training for cashiers where alcoholic beverages are sold.

Recommendation 2–28: Provide training to retailers that include information on retailer liability for sales to underage persons and enforcement of license suspension/revocation laws.

E. Community:

Recommendation 2–29: Provide literature for landlords (especially landlords in college communities) about liability and ramifications of negligence to underage drinking on their property.

Recommendation 2–30: Ensure local coalition representation engages all aspects of the community including health care providers, businesses, parents, schools, colleges and universities, and law enforcement to achieve a holistic approach to reducing underage drinking.

Recommendation 2–31: Provide give-away items to youth and their parents and mentors that have poignant messages on the dangers of underage drinking.

Recommendation 2–32: Provide underage drinking education information to members of the religious community who, in turn, may provide education to church/synagogue/mosque members both to recognize alcohol-involved youth and to provide alcohol warning signs and referral information to parents and youth members.

Recommendation 2–34: Partner with local colleges and universities to develop strategies to change the drinking culture both on and off campus that contributes to underage and high-risk drinking.

F. Law Enforcement:

Recommendation 2–35: Provide ongoing training for all law enforcement agencies to include the following: Develop an Alcohol Enforcement Specialist training program and a designation for specifically trained officers serving as resources within their agencies; Provide training on responding to large youth gatherings where alcohol may be present; Develop guidance documents for party patrol/house party enforcement; Develop a list of "Best Practices in Youth Law Enforcement" to serve as a resource to agencies throughout the state; Assist in the development of underage drinking roll-call training videos to be distributed to law enforcement agencies in the state; Update the alcohol-related component of the police academy curriculum.

Recommendation 2–36: Provide training opportunities for judges and prosecutors who work with offenders and law enforcement agencies.

3. Enforcement of Underage Drinking Laws

The Florida Department of Business and Professional Regulation, Division of Alcoholic Beverages and Tobacco (AB&T), has statewide responsibilities for reducing underage and binge drinking among Florida's youth. Its partnership with local sheriffs' offices and police departments has reinforced the effort to prevent sales of alcohol to those underage. AB&T leadership teams around the state educate local authorities concerning beverage laws, conduct surveys to ensure compliance, and provide 1–866–540–7837(SUDS) for citizens to call in with violations of alcohol and tobacco laws. The ultimate goal of AB&T's effort to ensure adherence to local laws is to achieve a 92 percent (and working to exceed to 95 percent) compliance rate by businesses statewide regarding alcohol and tobacco sales to minors. In addition to this effort, AB&T provides funding through the Florida Office of Drug Control to fund nine law enforcement agencies around the state to assist with preventing underage alcohol use.

In conjunction with the Office of Juvenile Justice and Delinquency Prevention (OJJDP), Florida has been chosen to be one of five states to participate in the Enforcing the Underage Drinking Laws (EUDL) Discretionary Program. This community trials project implements research-based "best" and "most promising" practices to reduce the availability of alcoholic beverages to and the consumption of alcoholic beverages by underage persons. These funds will ultimately go to seven Florida communities and their law enforcement counterparts to develop a community program primarily focused on enforcing underage drinking laws. Seven other Florida communities will serve as control sites.

National:

Recommendation 3–1: The federal government should require states to achieve designated rates of retailer compliance with youth access prohibitions as a condition of receiving block grant funding, similar to the Synar Amendment's requirements for youth tobacco sales (NAS, Recommendation 9–3).

State:

Recommendation 3–2: Strengthen Florida's compliance check programs in retail outlets, using media campaigns and license revocation to increase deterrence. Communities and states should undertake regular and comprehensive compliance check programs, including notification of retailers concerning the program and follow-up communication to them about the outcome (sale/no sale) for their outlet. Enforcement agencies should issue citations for violations of underage sales laws, with substantial fines and temporary suspension of license for first offense and increasingly stronger penalties thereafter, leading to permanent revocation of license after three offenses. Communities and states should implement media campaigns in conjunction with compliance check programs detailing the program, its purpose, and outcomes (NAS, Recommendation 9–2).

Recommendation 3–3: Establish and implement a system requiring registration of beer kegs that records information on the identity of purchasers (NAS, Recommendation 9–8).

Recommendation 3–4: Mete out consistent penalties for selling alcohol to a minor or possession of alcohol by an underage person. Alcohol education should be mandated for the offender with other deterrents, including community service and fines.

Local:

Recommendation 3–5: Adopt and announce policies by local police (working with community leaders) for detecting and terminating underage drinking parties, including routinely responding to complaints from the public about noisy teenage and college student parties and entering the premises when there is probable cause to suspect underage drinking is taking place; notification to parents of offending minors should also be used.

Routinely checking, as a part of regular weekend patrols, opens areas where teenage drinking parties are known to occur and routinely citing underage drinkers and, if possible, the person who supplied the alcohol when underage drinking is observed at parties (NAS, Recommendation 9–12). During events that draw large crowds of underage persons, publicize that there is a zero-tolerance for underage drinking and have law enforcement at the event.

4. Collaboration

At the close of a site visit in September 2003, the U.S. Department of Education's representative noted how well Florida's various agencies and organizations collaborated on reducing substance abuse. Florida is modeling the ways collaboration can make a difference in reducing youth alcohol use. This White Paper is one of the products of that collaboration.

More evidence of Florida's collaboration is the number of community anti-drug coalitions. Through the results of the Florida Youth Substance Abuse Survey, the Office of Drug Control discovered that substance abuse rates were lowest in areas where community anti-drug coalitions were present. In an attempt to increase the number of coalitions and consequently decrease the rate of youth substance abuse, the Governor's Office of Drug Control, in collaboration with the Florida Alcohol and Drug Abuse Association, the Department of Children and Families, and the Florida National Guard, began a statewide initiative to increase the number of anti-drug coalitions. In 2000, only nineteen counties had anti-drug coalitions. Through the coalition expansion project (and including nine counties that have just started coalitions), sixty-five of sixty-seven counties currently have anti-drug coalitions. Using these community anti-drug coalitions and enhancing existing relationships with grassroots, prevention providers, and state agencies, Florida can use existing resources to focus on underage drinking. An established and proven system is already in place.

Florida youth substance abuse has decreased in large part because of key collaborations with community organizations throughout the state. A concentrated focus on reducing underage drinking is a logical next step to lowering youth alcohol use.

National:

Recommendation 4–1: A federal interagency coordinating committee on prevention of underage drinking should be established, chaired by the secretary of the U.S. Department of Health and Human Services, the surgeon general, or the undersecretary of education for safe and drug free schools (NAS, Recommendation 12–1).

Recommendation 4–2: We endorse the NAS Recommendation 7–1 that all segments of the alcohol industry that profit from underage drinking, inadvertently or otherwise, should join with other private and public partners to establish and fund an independent nonprofit foundation with the sole mission of preventing and reducing underage drinking (NAS, Recommendation 7–1).

Recommendation 4–3: Public and private funding sources should support community mobilization to reduce underage drinking. Federal funding for reducing and preventing underage drinking should be made available under a national program dedicated to community-level approaches to reducing underage drinking, similar to the Drug Free Communities Act, which supports communities in addressing substance abuse with targeted, evidence-based prevention strategies (NAS, Recommendation 11–2).

State:

Recommendation 4–4: Step up meaningful collaboration among state agencies and other stakeholders to engage shared responsibility in addressing widespread underage drinking in the state of Florida.

Recommendation 4–5: Ensure statewide data collection of college-age use and abuse of alcohol and other drugs.

Local:

Recommendation 4–6: Assess the underage drinking problem in communities and consider effective approaches—such as community organizing, coalition building, and the strategic use of the mass media—to reduce drinking among underage youth (NAS, Recommendation 11–1).

Recommendation 4–7: Ensure representation in local coalitions and engagement of all aspects of the community, including health care providers, local businesses, parents, schools, colleges and universities, and law enforcement to achieve a more holistic approach to reducing underage drinking.

5. Legislation

Florida has worked to protect youth from alcohol and other drugs for many years. As early as 1939, lawmakers were concerned about underage drinking and other substance abuse as evidenced by one of the first laws that implied the hazards of drug use. The passage of several anti-alcohol laws over time is a strong testament of the state's commitment to keeping young people free of alcohol and other drugs. In 1998, Governor Jeb Bush included as a major plank in his election campaign a vow to reinvigorate the state's commitment to bringing down drug abuse. That vow was acted upon almost immediately when the executive and legislative leadership of Florida convened a Drug Summit in February 1999 in Tallahassee. This two-day meeting brought together leading Floridians from all walks of life affected by, and in turn affecting, Florida's drug abuse experience. The principles produced at that summit for countering illegal drugs in Florida were the beginning steps to making changes in substance abuse rates. These principles were later codified (by September 1999) in the Florida Drug Control Strategy.

Since then, laws relating to substance abuse have been added to strengthen the penalties for illegal use. As it relates to alcohol, Section 2(c) was added to Florida Statute 562.11 in order to penalize underage persons attempting to purchase alcohol by facing the loss or delay of their driver's license and privileges.

National:

Recommendation 5–1: Encourage and support congressional hearings to address the issue of underage drinking as outlined in the NAS Report.

Recommendation 5–2: Support federal legislation to fund and actively support the development of a national media effort, as a major component of an adult-oriented campaign to reduce underage drinking (NAS, Recommendation 6–1). Note: This is already in the Media Campaign section as a national recommendation.

Recommendation 5–3: Support federal legislation that would provide the necessary funding for the U.S. Department of Health and Human Services to monitor underage exposure to alcohol advertising on a continuing basis (NAS, Recommendation 7–4).

State:

Recommendation 5–4: Amend Florida Statute 562.111 to include consumption as illegal by an underage youth. Currently, the law only includes possession of alcohol.

Recommendation 5–5: Enact and enforce graduated driver licensing laws (NAS, Recommendation 9–10).

Recommendation 5–6: Strengthen and enforce the laws to revoke or suspend alcohol licenses from businesses engaged in repeated sales to underage persons.

Recommendation 5–7: Support legislation to establish and implement a system requiring registration of beer kegs that records information on the identity of purchasers (NAS, Recommendation 9–8).

Recommendation 5–8: Strengthen Florida's current dram shop liability statute to enhance liability for commercial establishments that knowingly sell alcohol to minors who subsequently causes injury to others (NAS, Recommendation 9–5).

Local:

Recommendation 5–9: Review existing county and city ordinances related to underage drinking and strengthen the ordinances accordingly, including an environmental focus on zoning, outlet density, and related issues, such as parking, bathrooms, street setback, minors present at establishments whose principal business is serving alcoholic drinks, and irresponsible drink specials.

6. Treatment

Adolescents rarely seek help for problems related to alcohol and other drug use. Many parents are also often reluctant to seek such help, hoping that substance abuse is "just a phase," or otherwise minimize their perceptions of the negative effects drinking has on their children. Referrals by juvenile courts are, too often, the first intervention. By this time, substance abuse is likely to have contributed to delinquent behavior, violence, and high-risk activities, such as unprotected sex and driving while intoxicated. The misuse of alcohol is deadly, and youth dependent on alcohol must receive treatment. An alcohol-dependent youth may also be dealing with the addiction of a family member. In this case, a more holistic approach must be taken to ensure full recovery.

National:

Recommendation 6–1: Continue to provide funding to state agencies to provide treatment to youth and their families. Investigate and implement effective science-based models that have been validated in research studies.

State:

Recommendation 6–2: Explore issues of access to quality comprehensive assessment and treatment services for youth and implement policy changes to improve access for youth and their families. Stakeholders should work in partnership with existing community treatment providers providing assessments and treatment recommendations at Florida's Juvenile Assessment Centers to enhance and expand access to youth and their families.

Recommendation 6–3: Continue examination of the effectiveness of substance abuse screening tools and assessment in identifying and referring youth with substance abuse problems to appropriate treatment. Substance abuse screening tools and assessment instruments should be scientifically valid and reliable in order to ensure consistent quality of the assessment and treatment recommendations.

Recommendation 6–4: Encourage the use of evidence-based treatment for adolescent alcohol abuse.

Recommendation 6–5: Provide increased training on alcohol-specific intervention for adolescent addiction counselors.

Recommendation 6–6: Provide training to pediatricians, adolescent medical specialists, and other health service providers on screening for signs of alcohol abuse and on the adverse effects of alcohol on the developing adolescent brain.

Recommendation 6–7: Improve accessibility to substance abuse treatment for parents who abuse alcohol or other drugs.

Local:

Recommendation 6–8: Expand treatment services to children with special needs (e.g., family involvement with substance abuse, co-occurring mental illness, disabilities, extreme poverty, etc.).

Recommendation 6–9: Involve the entire family along with the individual in treatment. Lifestyle changes necessary to break the cycle of addiction must incorporate the family. Affected family members should be encouraged to utilize appropriate support groups.

Recommendation 6–10: Work closely with school officials to provide school-based referral and assessment services. Provide opportunities in the school for counseling and coordination of treatment.

Recommendation 6–11: Expand and fund drug courts.

Recommendation 6–12: Work with doctors, pharmacists, medical examiners, and other public and medical officials to identify and curtail prescription drug abuse and provide treatment services and referrals when patients are in danger of becoming addicted.

Recommendation 6–13: Funding should be expanded to include adequate resources to ensure rural-based populations are reached, assessed, and engaged into treatment based on the results of the assessment.

Should Schools Test Children for Illegal Drugs?

It is an important question, and ultimately one best left to parents, teachers, and school administrators. There is no single right or wrong answer, no "one size fits all" solution. A decision in June 2002 by the U.S. Supreme Court expands the authority of public schools to test students for drugs. Still, it is up to individual communities and schools to decide if drugs are a significant threat, and if testing is an appropriate response.

The question of whether to test students for drugs or alcohol should never be taken lightly. It involves myriad complex issues that must be fully understood and carefully weighed before testing begins. The Office of National Drug Control Policy has put together *What You Need To Know About Drug Testing in Schools* to shed light and offer perspective on this multifaceted and sometimes controversial topic. Its aim is to provide anyone who is considering a drug-testing program in his or her community with a broad understanding of the issue and solid, up-to-date information on which to base a decision.

Included in this booklet are answers to questions that students, parents, school officials, and other concerned individuals might have about the process. It explains, generally, what drug testing is all about, who pays for it, who does the testing, what it tells you about an individual's drug use, and, equally important, what it does not tell you. The booklet describes what services should be in place for communities to deal effectively with students who test positive for drugs, and it also offers case histories showing how several schools used testing to address their drug problems. Their experiences may help others determine whether testing is right for their communities.

WHY TEST?

Thanks to advances in medical technology, researchers are now able to capture pictures of the human brain under the influence of drugs. As these images clearly show, the pleasurable sensations produced by some drugs are due to actual physical changes in the brain. Many of these changes are long lasting and some are irreversible. Scientists have recently discovered that the brain is not fully developed in early childhood, as was once believed, but is, in fact, still growing even in adolescence. Introducing chemical changes in the brain through the use of illegal drugs can, therefore, have far more serious adverse effects on adolescents than on adults.

Even so-called soft drugs can take a heavy toll. Marijuana's effects, for example, are not confined to the "high." The drug can also cause serious problems with memory and learning, as well as difficulty in thinking and problem solving. Use of methamphetamine or Ecstasy (MDMA) may cause long-lasting damage to brain areas that are critical for thought and memory. In animal studies, researchers found that four days of exposure to Ecstasy caused damage that persisted for as long as six or seven years. Kids on drugs cannot perform as well in school as their drug-free peers of equal ability. So if testing reduces students' use of illicit drugs, it will remove a significant barrier to academic achievement.

Substance abuse should be recognized for what it is—a major health issue—and dealt with accordingly. Like vision and hearing tests, drug testing can alert parents to potential problems that continued drug use might cause, such as liver or lung damage, memory impairment, addiction, overdose, and even death. Once the drug problem has been identified, intervention and then treatment, if appropriate, can begin.

Testing can also be an effective way to prevent drug use. The expectation that they may be randomly tested is enough to make some students stop using drugs—or never start in the first place.

That kind of deterrence has been demonstrated many times over in the American workplace. Employees in many national security and safety-sensitive positions—airline

Case History

A REWARD FOR STAYING CLEAN

Autauga County School System

In rural Autauga County, Alabama, students have a special incentive to stay off drugs. As part of a voluntary drug-testing program, participating students who test negative for drugs in random screenings receive discounts and other perks from scores of area businesses.

Community leaders and school officials, prompted by a growing concern about the use of drugs, alcohol, and cigarettes among students, launched the program in 2000 with the help of a local drug-free coalition called Peers Are Staying Straight (PASS). "Our community was awakening to the fact that we needed to do something," says PASS Executive Director Martha Ellis.

The Independent Decision program began with just the seventh grade but will expand each year to include all grade levels. In the 2001–2002 school year, more than half of all seventh- and eighth-graders at public and private schools participated.

To enter the program, kids take a urine test for nicotine, cocaine, amphetamines, opiates, PCP, and marijuana. Those who test negative get a picture ID that entitles them to special deals at more than fifty-five participating restaurants and stores. Students keep the ID as long as they test negative in twice-yearly random drug tests.

Those who test positive (there have been only three) must relinquish their cards and any special privileges. The school counselor notifies the parents and, if appropriate, offers advice about where to find help. At that point, the matter is strictly in the parents' hands. If the child tests negative in a subsequent random test, his or her card is returned. "Our whole purpose," says Ellis, "is to reward kids who stay clean and help them see the benefits of a drug-free lifestyle."

Surveys taken by PRIDE (the National Parents' Resource Institute for Drug Education) before the program began, and again in 2002, showed significant reductions in drug use among Autauga County's eighth-graders: from 35.9 percent to 24.4 percent for nicotine, 39.9 percent to 30 percent for alcohol, and 18.5 percent to 11.8 percent for marijuana. For more information about Autauga's Independent Decision program, call (334) 358–4900.

pilots, commercial truck drivers, school bus drivers, to name a few—are subject to pre-employment and random drug tests to ensure public safety.

Employers who have followed the federal model have seen a 67 percent drop in positive drug tests. Along with significant declines in absenteeism, accidents, and health care costs, they've also experienced dramatic increases in worker productivity.

While some students resist the idea of drug testing, many endorse it. For one thing, it gives them a good excuse to say "no" to drugs. Peer pressure among young people can be a powerful and persuasive force. Knowing they may have to submit to a drug test can help kids overcome the pressure to take drugs by giving them a convenient "out." This could serve them well in years to come. Students represent the workforce of tomorrow, and eventually many will need to pass a drug test to get a job.

It is important to understand that the goal of school-based drug testing is not to punish students who use drugs. Although consequences for illegal drug use should be part of any testing program—suspension from an athletic activity or revoked parking privileges, for example—the primary purpose is to deter use and guide those who test positive into counseling or treatment. In addition, drug testing in schools should never be undertaken as a stand-alone response to the drug problem. Rather, it should be one component of a broader program designed to reduce students' use of illegal drugs.

BENEFITS

Drug use can quickly turn to dependence and addiction, trapping users in a vicious cycle that destroys families and ruins lives. Students who use drugs or alcohol are statistically more likely to drop out of school than their peers who don't. Dropouts, in turn, are more likely to be unemployed, to depend on the welfare system, and to commit crimes. If drug testing deters drug use, everyone benefits—students, their families, their schools, and their communities.

Drug and alcohol abuse not only interferes with a student's ability to learn, it also disrupts the orderly environment necessary for all students to succeed.

Studies have shown that students who use drugs are more likely to bring guns and knives to school, and that the more marijuana a student smokes, the greater the chances he or she will be involved in physical attacks, property destruction, stealing, and cutting classes. Just as parents and students can expect schools to offer protection from violence, racism, and other forms of abuse, they have the right to expect a learning environment free from the influence of illegal drugs.

WHAT ARE THE RISKS?

Schools should proceed with caution before testing students for drugs. Screenings are not 100 percent accurate, so every positive screen should be followed by a laboratory-based confirming test. Before going ahead with tests, schools should also have a good idea of precisely what drugs their students are using. Testing for just one set of illegal drugs, when others pose an equal or greater threat, would do little to address a school's drug problem.

Confidentiality is a major concern with students and their parents. Schools have a responsibility to respect students' privacy, so it is vital that only the people who need to know the test results see them—parents and school administrators, for example. The results should not be shared with anyone else, not even teachers.

DEVELOPING A TESTING PROGRAM

What should you do before you begin testing?

The decision on whether to implement a drug-testing program should not be left to one individual, or even to a school board. It should involve the entire community. In fact, by making the effort to include everyone, a school can greatly increase its chances of adopting a successful testing program. It is not enough to have a general sense that student drug testing sounds like a good idea. Schools must first determine whether there is a real need for testing. Such a need can be determined from student drug-use surveys, reports by teachers and other school staff about student drug use, reports about drug use from parents and others in the community, and from discoveries of drug paraphernalia or drug residue at school.

If student drug use is found to be a significant problem, schools will want to consult early in their deliberations with an attorney familiar with laws regarding student drug testing. They should seek the advice of drug prevention and treatment professionals, and also contact officials at schools that already have drug-testing programs to learn what works and what doesn't.

Schools considering testing will want plenty of public input. They should bring together members of the board of education, school administrators and staff, parents, community leaders, local health care agencies, local businesses, students, and anyone else who has an interest in reducing student drug use—even those who are against the idea. Listening to opponents and including their views can strengthen the testing program and improve its chances of success.

ELEMENTS OF A DRUG-TESTING PROGRAM

Many workplaces have had drug-testing programs in place for years, and recently some school districts have implemented programs for testing their athletes. Successful programs typically share a number of common elements, beginning with a clear written policy. Parents and teachers sign a statement declaring that they understand the policy, which is announced at least ninety days before testing begins. An effective policy addresses questions, such as:

- Which students can be tested for drug use?
- What is the process for selecting students for testing?
- Who will conduct the test?
- What are the consequences of a positive drug test?
- Are steps clearly articulated for helping students who test positive for drugs?
- Will a second confirming test be done?
- Who pays for the test?
- Will subsequent positive tests result in suspension or expulsion from extracurricular activities?
- Are test results cumulative throughout a student's tenure at the school, or is the slate wiped clean each year?

- What happens if a student refuses to take the test? Will refusal be construed as a drug-positive test?
- Who will see the test results, and how will confidentiality be maintained?
- How will parents be informed about positive test results?
- How does a student contest the results of a positive test result?
- What mechanism is in place for students whose prescription medication triggers a positive reading?

WHAT KINDS OF TESTS ARE AVAILABLE?

Urinalysis, the most common drug testing method, has been studied exhaustively and used extensively, has undergone rigorous challenge in the courts, and has proved to be accurate and reliable. As a result, urinalysis currently is the only technique approved for drug testing in the federal workforce. Some employers, however, have already begun using other types of drug tests—on hair, sweat, and oral fluids. Each of these new tests has benefits as well as drawbacks.

What Does Each Test Measure?

Drug tests are used to determine whether a person has used alcohol or illegal drugs. Some tests show recent use only, while others indicate use over a longer period. Each type of test has different applications and is used to detect a specific drug or group of drugs. The Federal Drug-Free Workplace program, which serves as a model for accuracy and quality assurance in drug testing, relies on a urine test designed to detect the use of marijuana, opiates, cocaine, amphetamines, and phencyclidine (PCP). Urine tests can also be used to detect alcohol, LSD, and cotenine, the major metabolite of nicotine.

Following are summaries of the most commonly used tests:

Urine

Results of a urine test show the presence or absence of specific drugs or drug metabolites in the urine. Metabolites are drug residues that remain in the system for some time after the effects of the drug have worn off. A positive urine test does not necessarily mean the subject was under the influence of drugs at the time of the test. Rather, it detects and measures use of a particular drug within the previous few days.

Hair

Analysis of hair may provide a much longer "testing window" for the presence of drugs and drug metabolites, giving a more complete drug-use history that goes back as far as ninety days. Like urine testing, hair testing does not provide evidence of current impairment, only past use of a specific drug. Hair testing cannot be used to detect alcohol.

Table 3–2: Pros and Cons of the Various Drug Testing Methods

Type of Test	Pros	Cons	Window of Detection
Urine	• Highest assurance of reliable results • Least expensive • Most flexible in testing different drugs, including alcohol and nicotine • Most likely of all drug-testing methods to withstand legal challenge	• Specimen can be adulterated, substituted, or diluted • Limited window of detection • Test sometimes viewed as invasive or embarrassing • Biological hazards for specimen handling and shipping to lab	Typically one to five days
Hair	• Longer window of detection • Greater stability (does not deteriorate) • Can measure chronic drug use • Convenient shipping and storage (no need to refrigerate) • Collection procedure not considered invasive or embarrassing • More difficult to adulterate than urine • Detects alcohol/cocaine combination use	• More expensive • Test usually limited to basic five-drug panel • Cannot detect alcohol use • Will not detect very recent drug use (one to seven days prior to test)	Depends on the length of hair in the sample. Hair grows about a half-inch per month, so a $1\frac{1}{2}$-inch specimen would show a three-month history.
Oral Fluids	• Sample obtained under direct observation • Minimal risk of tampering • Noninvasive • Samples can be collected easily in virtually any environment • Can detect alcohol use • Reflects recent drug use	• Drugs and drug metabolites do not remain in oral fluids as long as they do in urine. • Less efficient than other testing methods in detecting marijuana use.	Approximately ten to twenty-four hours.
Sweat Patch	• Noninvasive • Variable removal date (generally one to seven days) • Quick application and removal • Longer window of detection than urine • No sample substitution possible	• Limited number of labs able to process results. • People with skin eruptions, excessive hair, or cuts and abrasions cannot wear the patch. • Passive exposure to drugs may contaminate patch and affect results.	Patch retains evidence of drug use for at least seven days, and can detect even low levels of drugs two to five hours after use.

Source: Office of National Drug Policy, National Criminal Justice Reference Service NCJ 195522, July 2002.

Sweat Patch

Another type of drug test consists of a skin patch that measures drugs and drug metabolites in perspiration. The patch, which looks like a large adhesive bandage, is applied to the skin and worn for some length of time. A gas-permeable membrane on the patch protects the tested area from dirt and other contaminants. The sweat patch is sometimes used in the criminal justice system to monitor drug use by parolees and probationers, but so far it has not been widely used in workplaces or schools.

Oral Fluids

Traces of drugs, drug metabolites, and alcohol can be detected in oral fluids, the generic term for saliva and other material collected from the mouth. Oral fluids are easy to collect—a swab of the inner cheek is the most common way. They are harder to adulterate or substitute, and collection is less invasive than with urine or hair testing. Because drugs and drug metabolites do not remain in oral fluids as long as they do in urine, this method shows more promise in determining current use and impairment.

Breath Alcohol

Unlike urine tests, breath-alcohol tests do detect and measure current alcohol levels. The subject blows into a breath-alcohol test device, and the results are given as a number, known as the Blood Alcohol Concentration, which shows the level of alcohol in the blood at the time the test was taken. In the U.S. Department of Transportation regulations, an alcohol level of 0.04 is high enough to stop someone from performing a safety-sensitive task for that day.

What Do Drug Tests NOT Measure?

The five-drug urine test used in the Federal Drug-Free Workplace Program does not detect all drugs used by young people. For example, it does not detect so-called "club" drugs, such as gamma hydroxybutyrate (GHB) and Ecstasy, although other urine tests can determine use of these drugs and hair tests can easily detect Ecstasy use. No standard test, however, can detect inhalant abuse, a problem that can have serious, even fatal, consequences. (Inhalant abuse refers to the deliberate inhalation or sniffing of common household products—gasoline, correction fluid, felt-tip markers, spray paint, air freshener, and cooking spray, to name a few—with the purpose of "getting high.")

ADMINISTERING THE TEST

Drug testing is commonly a four-step process: collection, screening, confirmation, and review. When called in to take a drug test, the student sees a trained "collector," or test administrator, who gives instructions and receives the specimen. It is also the collector's job to complete the chain-of-custody form, which keeps track of where the specimen has been and who has handled it throughout the process. The form ensures that the specimen was handled properly and in such a way that does not call its source or the test results into question.

If the student is providing a urine sample, a temperature strip is put on the collection container to guard against a substitute sample. A tamper-evident tape is put over the specimen container, and then the student is asked to initial it and verify the chain-of-custody form.

Next, the specimen is screened for drugs or drug metabolites. If the screening test is positive, the test will be confirmed by a second, more exacting test. To rule out legitimate prescription drug use, a physician or nurse with knowledge of substance-abuse disorders reviews all confirmed positive tests.

Some specimens are screened at the collection site, and the initial results are known within minutes; others are screened at a laboratory. All negative screens—those that show no drugs or drug metabolites—are eliminated from further consideration. Specimens that test positive for drugs in the initial screen are examined further in the laboratory through a second analytic technique called gas chromatography/mass spectrometry (GC/MS), which is actually a combination of two specialized techniques. Technicians use gas chromatography to separate the various substances in the specimen, and then they make a positive identification through mass spectrometry.

Alcohol-specific tests may be performed entirely at the collection location if appropriate breath-alcohol testing equipment and procedures are used. Some oral fluid tests can also be used to obtain an immediate initial test result, with the positive screen going on to a laboratory for confirmation.

A positive test result does not automatically mean the student uses illegal drugs. In fact, other, legal substances sometimes trigger positive results. Certain over-the-counter medications, for example, can cause a positive reading for amphetamines. So when the GC/MS confirmation test comes back positive, it is important for a doctor, nurse, or other specialist to review the results and determine if illicit drugs are indeed the culprits. In the Federal Drug-Free Workplace Program, a medical review officer is required to go over positive test results with the donor and determine if there could be a legitimate explanation. Everything is done confidentially, and safeguards are in place to make sure workers are not falsely labeled drug users when their positive test results are found to have a legitimate cause.

Schools should also take care that a student's confidentiality and privacy are not violated, and that students who test positive because they are taking prescription medications are not wrongly branded as drug users. It bears repeating that the purpose of drug testing is to keep students from using drugs, and to help or refer to treatment those who may be drug dependent.

WHAT HAPPENS IF THE TEST IS POSITIVE?

Results of a positive drug test should not be used merely to punish a student. Drug and alcohol use can lead to addiction, and punishment alone may not necessarily halt this progression. However, the road to addiction can be blocked by timely intervention and appropriate treatment.

When a positive test result has been reviewed and confirmed for illegal drug use, the school's crucial next step is to contact the parents and help them stop their child's drug use. Parents play a key role in drug abuse prevention, so they need lots of guidance and support. They also need to know that anger, accusations, and harsh punishment could make the situation worse. The best approach for parents is usually to stay firm and to treat their child with respect as they work together as a family to change his or her behavior.

After involving the parents, school officials may refer the student to a trained substance-abuse counselor, who can perform a drug assessment and determine whether the child needs treatment or other specialized help. For young people who use drugs occasionally, a few words from the counselor or parents—coupled with the prospect of future drug tests—may be enough to put an end to the drug use. For frequent users or those in danger of becoming drug dependent, treatment will likely be necessary.

Many schools require drug-positive students to enroll in a drug education course or activity. Some also offer Student Assistance Programs, whose trained counselors are linked to resources in the greater community and can help students cope with a variety of problems, including substance abuse. In any case, the school will want to perform follow-up drug tests on students with positive results to make sure they stay drug free.

CAN STUDENTS "BEAT" THE TESTS?

Many drug-using students are aware of techniques that supposedly detoxify their systems or mask their drug use. Some drink large amounts of water just before the test to dilute their urine; others add salt, bleach, or vinegar to their sample. In some cases, users call on their drug-free friends to leave bottles of clean urine in the bathroom stalls.

Popular magazines and Internet sites give advice on how to dilute urine samples, and there are even companies that sell clean urine or products designed to distort test results. A number of techniques and products are focused on urine tests for marijuana, but masking products increasingly are becoming available for tests of hair, oral fluids, and multiple drugs.

Most of these masking products do not work, cost a lot of money, and are almost always easily identified in the testing process. But even if the specific drug is successfully masked, the product itself can be detected, in which case the student using it would become an obvious candidate for additional screening and attention.

WHO DOES THE TESTING?

Laboratories all over the country perform drug tests, but not all of them produce consistently accurate and reliable results. Many schools choose labs from among those certified by the Substance Abuse and Mental Health Services Administration (SAMHSA) to perform urine testing for federal agencies. A list of SAMHSA-certified labs is available on the Internet at http://workplace.samh—sa.gov/ResourceCenter/lablist.htm.

Before deciding on a laboratory, school officials should carefully assess the drug problem in their community. The standard federal workplace test screens for the presence of marijuana, cocaine, opiates, amphetamines, and PCP. But if a school faces a significant threat from Ecstasy, methamphetamine, ketamine, GHB, or some other drug, administrators will need to be sure that any laboratory they are considering is also capable of testing for these drugs.

HOW MUCH DO DRUG TESTS COST?

The price of drug testing varies according to the type of test and the drugs involved, but generally the cost is between $10 and $30 per test, with hair testing somewhat higher. The price for onsite alcohol tests usually ranges from $1 to $10 per test. Some schools have paid for drug tests through federal grants from SAMHSA or the U.S. Department of Education's Safe and Drug-Free Schools Program. Others get money for testing from private foundations. When school-based programs begin to expand, testing providers will likely start offering volume price incentives.

CONCLUSION

Again, the aim of drug testing is not to trap and punish students who use drugs. It is, in fact, counterproductive simply to punish them without trying to alter their behavior. If drug-using students are suspended or expelled without any attempt to change their ways, the community will be faced with drug-using dropouts, an even bigger problem in the long run. The purpose of testing, then, is to prevent drug dependence and to help drug-dependent students become drug free. Before implementing a drug-testing program, parents and communities must make sure appropriate resources are in place to deal with students who test positive. For example, substance-abuse specialists should be available to determine the nature and extent of the drug use, and there should be comprehensive treatment services for students with potentially serious drug problems.

Schools need to educate parents about exactly what the drug tests are measuring and what to do if their child tests positive. It is vital for parents to know that resources are available to help them gauge the extent of their child's drug use and, if necessary, find drug treatment.

For those who worry about the "Big Brother" dimension of drug testing, it is worth pointing out that test results are generally required by law to remain confidential, and in no case are they turned over to the police.

Vandalism

The causes of vandalism are often are complex, calling for careful study by parents/guardians, school staff, and appropriate community officials. Pupils should respect property and take pride in their schools.

When vandalism is discovered, there should be a clear procedure for dealing with it. For instance, the Somerset Hills Board of Education in New Jersey stipulates that the administration should take such steps as are necessary to identify the vandals. If pupils have taken part in the vandalism, the appropriate administrator should:

- Identify the pupils involved.
- Call together persons, including the parents/guardians, needed to study the causes.
- Decide upon disciplinary and/or legal action, possibly including suspension.
- Should parents/guardians fail to cooperate in the discussions, the administration may charge the pupil with being delinquent by a petition stating the offense and requesting appearance in juvenile court.
- Take any constructive actions needed to try to guard against further such pupil misbehavior.
- Seek appropriate restitution.

VIOLENCE AND VANDALISM DECREASES REPORTED AT NEW JERSEY SCHOOLS

More than 70 percent of New Jersey school districts reported five or fewer instances of violence, vandalism, and substance abuse in 2004–2005, and 38 percent of the districts reported no instances at all, according to the annual report on school violence released by the New Jersey Department of Education.

The annual report, which is required by statute, is compiled from data that DOE collects from schools through the Electronic Violence and Vandalism Reporting System (EVVRS) and is submitted to the education committees of the legislature.

It provides detailed information on a wide range of incidents, from fighting, trespassing, theft, and fireworks possession to major behavioral problems, such as assault, extortion, and possession of firearms and drugs at New Jersey's approximately 2,400 public and charter schools.

"As we've seen in past years, the vast majority of New Jersey's schools are safe places for students and teachers, and very few schools have persistent problems," said acting Commissioner of Education Lucille E. Davy. "In addition, DOE's ongoing collection and use of this data allows us to target changing areas of need. We can then adapt our regulations and policies and create programs to address emerging problems."

The total number of incidents reported by school districts in 2004–05 was 18,409, down 1,798 (nine percent) from the 20,207 incidents reported in the 2003–2004 school year and down 3,777 (17 percent) from the 22,186 reported during the 02–03 school year.

The decrease is reflected primarily in declines in two of the major reporting categories: violence and vandalism.

Instances of violence declined by 21 percent, driven mainly by a 37-percent reduction in the number of simple assaults, an 18-percent reduction in the number of fights and a 35-percent decline in the number of threats reported.

Overall, the number of vandalism incidents decreased by 18 percent. This included a 19 percent decrease in the number of incidents that involved damage to property and a 13 percent decline in the number of thefts reported. The number of weapons possession incidents was down 4 percent and the number of substance abuse incidents declined by 1 percent.

Acting Commissioner Davy said that while the report reflects positive trends, direct year-to-year statistical comparisons must be interpreted with caution. "Thanks to the support of the Legislature and federal funding, DOE has been able to institute many programs to reduce the incidence of violence and vandalism in schools. We have also worked hard over the past few years to bring consistency to the self-reporting process that is the basis for this report," she said. "But the decline in the number of instances during this three-year period is unusual, and we feel we have to dig a little deeper in order to make valid conclusions."

In reviewing the data, DOE officials noted that the decline of nearly four thousand incidents in the major category of violence between 2002–2003 and 2004–2005 was concentrated in fifty-one districts. Eight districts reporting at least a hundred fewer incidents of violence were associated with 58 percent of the net decline in overall school violence over the three-year period.

DOE surveyed a subgroup of nineteen of the fifty-one districts to ascertain the factors that contributed to sizable declines in the number of incidents, including successful strategies the districts may have implemented over the past few years to reduce violence and vandalism.

The districts have also been asked to confirm that the EVVRS reports and categorizations of incidents are consistent with their written records, ensure that all incidents were entered into the system, and interview appropriate staff to determine whether the proper reporting requirements were met.

The department is currently reviewing this information. Site visits and other verification activities will be conducted once the new school year begins so that DOE can assess the need for direct technical assistance in incident reporting and the general need for further clarification on reporting criteria and disseminate information on the strategies and actions taken by the various districts that influenced the decline.

The annual report also describes the many programs and initiatives that DOE, the Attorney General's Office, other state agencies, education organizations, and the districts and schools themselves have undertaken or plan to undertake to foster safety within the schools, including the promotion of student health and character education.

"Due to the Safe Schools Initiative and the cooperation of many different agencies, we are able to work with the school districts at all levels, from prevention, through crises response to recovery," Acting Commissioner Davy said.

Initiatives undertaken in recent years have included:

- Resource manuals and guidance documents for the creation of school safety plans, accessing intervention and referral services, and providing community service programs for expelled and suspended students.
- Numerous new violence-related regulatory changes, including those relating to codes of student conduct, suspensions, expulsions, conduct away from school grounds, staff

responsibilities, attendance, intimidation, harassment, bullying, and student records and confidentiality.

- New requirements for staff training in school safety and security.
- Revised model policies prohibiting harassment, intimidation, and bullying.
- New laws requiring annual public hearings on school violence, the annual observance of School Violence Awareness Week, and the imposition of penalties for the falsification of reports of violence.
- The development of an Unsafe School Choice Policy in accordance with federal law.
- The distribution of approximately $8 million annually in federal Safe and Drug-Free Schools and Communities Act funds to local school districts. Numerous initiatives related to safe schools, including *Developing Safe and Civil Schools: A Social Emotional Learning Initiative,* the Positive Student Discipline Reform Demonstration Project, the Social Norms Project, the Youth Gang Initiative, the Intervention and Referral Services Initiative, the Safe Schools and Communities Violence Prevention and Response Plan Initiative, the Character Education Initiative, the Title IV-A and USCO Training and Technical Assistance Project, and the Peer Transitions Project.
- New Core Curriculum Content Standards focusing on bullying and violence prevention strategies, with a clear emphasis on character education.
- A coordinated effort with the Domestic Security Preparedness Task Force to develop best practices for school safety and security and conduct school security audits in all buildings.
- Violence prevention programs created in collaboration with the Attorney General's Office, the departments of Human Services and Health and Senior Services, counseling and mental health organizations, the courts, and the University of Medicine and Dentistry of New Jersey.

RESPONSES TO THE PROBLEM OF SCHOOL VANDALISM AND BREAK-INS

Your analysis of your local problem should give you a better understanding of the factors contributing to it. Once you have analyzed your local problem and established a baseline for measuring effectiveness, you should consider possible responses to address the problem.

The following response strategies provide a foundation of ideas for addressing your particular problem. These strategies are drawn from a variety of research studies and police reports. Several of these strategies may apply to your community's problem. It is critical that you tailor responses to local circumstances and that you can justify each response based on reliable analysis. In most cases, an effective strategy will involve implementing several different responses. Law enforcement responses alone are seldom effective in reducing or solving the problem. Do not limit yourself to considering what police can do. Give careful consideration to who else in your community shares responsibility for the problem and can help police better respond to it.

GENERAL CONSIDERATIONS FOR AN EFFECTIVE RESPONSE STRATEGY

- Recognizing the person-environment interaction. School vandalism and break-ins are the combined results of the offenders' characteristics and those of the physical and social environment in which the behavior occurs. This means that responses must focus on both the person and the environment. Focusing on one but not on the other will prove ineffective.
- Physical measures to improve building security have great appeal. Their use is already widespread in many places, is easy to understand, and usually involves a one-time outlay of funds. In contrast, measures focused on offenders, new administrative practices, or policies and community involvement appear to be more complex and difficult to implement. It may be difficult to gain group consensus on more complex responses; however, the initiative's overall balance depends on it.
- The large number of possible responses can be overwhelming. For this reason, they are categorized into four main sections: those that impact the physical environment, those that impact the offender, those that focus on school administrative practices, and those that enlist the community's help. The overall initiative should include a balance of responses in each category and should use the most potent combinations.
- Finally, responses should be implemented with great sensitivity to the goal of creating schools that are inviting public institutions. The cumulative effect of multiple responses can make schools appear fortress-like.

Establishing a task force. While police clearly have a role in preventing and responding to school vandalism and break-ins, these problems are shared by school administrators and community residents who, as taxpayers, indirectly pay for repairs and replacements. Task forces should include broad representation from all groups who can help to define the problem, particularly students, teachers, custodians, and school security officers, and those who will be instrumental in crafting and implementing responses, including local and district-level school administrators, counselors, architects, security consultants, crime prevention officers, firefighters, maintenance contractors, and community representatives.

It is vital that students be involved in the problem-solving effort, including school leaders and more-marginalized students. A coordinator is often needed to organize the various stakeholders' efforts and to ensure that all of the selected responses are implemented according to design.

Using the media wisely. News stories, advertising, slogans, and posters are all effective ways to transmit information to the community about the impact of school vandalism and break-ins. Using student-based information sources, such as school newspapers, student councils, athletic events, and parent newsletters, can also help to ensure that the messages reach the intended audiences. However, there is a risk that media attention might promote the concept of achieving notoriety through high-profile crimes against school property. Thus, journalists should avoid sensationalizing the events, and focus instead on the resources being squandered and the loss experienced by students, as well as the consequences faced by offenders.

Setting priorities. It is impossible to address every vulnerability at a school. Examining the relationship between the monetary and social costs of specific instances of vandalism, burglary, or arson can be useful in setting strategic priorities among your responses. In general, protecting high-value items, administrative areas, computer and technology labs, computer system hubs, clinics, libraries, and band rooms will mitigate the risk of events with high financial and social costs.

Operating at the district level. Public schools are administered at a district level, and district administrators may hesitate to grant individual schools the autonomy to implement the suggested responses on their own. Instead, districts may choose to resolve problems on a large scale, while individual schools fine-tune responses to address their particular conditions. A district-wide approach may be more efficient than individual schools' efforts to address the problem.

SPECIFIC RESPONSES TO SCHOOL VANDALISM AND BREAK-INS

Controlling access to deter unauthorized entry. Gates, deadbolt locks on doors and windows, door and window shutters, and doors that open only from the inside are effective means of securing school buildings. Access can also be deterred by limiting the number of entry points in school buildings, and by planting thorny bushes and unclimbable trees near entry points. Movable gates can be used indoors to secure sections of the building, while also permitting community use of facilities after hours.

Such measures can also delay intruders' efforts to get away. The potential effectiveness of this response decreases with inconsistent or improper use of the hardware. Some jurisdictions assign a teacher or other staff member to check all locks and gates at the end of each day.

Intruder alarms, motion sensors, heat sensors, and glass-break sensors are useful for quickly detecting unauthorized entry. Because putting alarms and sensors throughout the school is likely to be cost-prohibitive, focusing on passageways to different parts of the building and on areas where valuable equipment and records are stored is most effective. Alarm signals should be sent to police, on-campus security posts, and the school principal. However, alarm systems are prone to high rates of false alarms, which not only cost the school if a fine is imposed, but also waste police resources. Faulty or inappropriately selected equipment, poor installation, and user error are the main causes of false alarms.

CHANGES TO THE PHYSICAL ENVIRONMENT

Posting of warning signs. Access-control signs are an important part of "rule setting" in that they establish the types of activities prohibited both during and after school, and notify potential intruders that they are under surveillance. School territory and permitted uses can also be established through the strategic use of gardens, designated picnic areas, and student artwork. These features indicate that the school buildings and grounds are both cared for and controlled.

Storing valuables in secure areas. Storing high-value audiovisual equipment and computers in rooms equipped with high-quality locks in the inner section of the building makes them harder to access. Further, using carts to move expensive equipment to a central storage room can reduce the number of rooms that need to be secured. Bolting computers to lab and office desks makes their removal more difficult and time-consuming. Equipping storage areas with smoke detectors linked to the fire department ensures a quick response in case of fire. Removing signs indicating the location of expensive equipment (e.g., A-V Storage Room or Computer Lab) is also advisable.

Reducing the availability of combustibles. Most arson fires are started with materials found on-site. For this reason, indoor and outdoor trash cans should be emptied regularly, and any flammable chemicals in science labs and maintenance storage areas should always be properly secured.

Inscribing valuables with identifying marks. It is harder to sell stolen goods that have permanent identifying marks on them. Engraving, stenciling, or using permanent marker to imprint the school's name, logo, or seal on all computers, televisions, VCRs, DVD players, cameras, and the like, can deter intruders who intend to sell the equipment.

Adjusting indoor or outdoor lighting. There is no consensus on whether well-lit school campuses and building interiors or "dark" campuses are superior in terms of crime prevention. Obviously, lighting adjustments alone are not effective deterrents, but in combination with other responses, both approaches have shown positive results. Well-lit campuses and buildings make suspicious activity more visible to observers, and also may offer some protection to custodial staff and others who may legitimately be on campus after dark. On the other hand, a "lights out" policy makes it more difficult for potential intruders to manipulate locks and hinges at entry points, and if intruders *do* enter the building, observers can easily spot any lights that should not be on. Not only have some schools benefited from decreased vandalism-related costs, but they have also realized significant energy savings.

Obstructing vandals through physical barriers. Target-hardening measures, such as using stronger finishes and materials, or placing objects out of reach or in an enclosure, make it harder to damage property. These can also include toughened glass or glass substitutes, fire-retardant paint, graffiti-repellent paint or coatings, concrete or steel outdoor furniture, tamperproof hardware out of reach from the ground, and door hinges with non-removable pins.

Repairing damage quickly and improving the appearance of school grounds. Clean, well-maintained buildings free of debris or garbage and with attractively landscaped grounds are less at risk for vandalism and break-ins. Consistent maintenance may serve as an "occupation proxy," giving the appearance that the school is under steady surveillance by those concerned about keeping it safe. Thus, it follows that any damage incurred, either through vandalism or normal wear and tear, should be repaired quickly.

Removing ground-floor glass windows and other vandalism targets. Vandalism to building exteriors can be thwarted by removing hardware fixtures and altering surfaces that are easily vandalized. Smooth, uniform surfaces are attractive graffiti targets, but can be protected by applying textured or patterned surfaces.

OFFENDER-FOCUSED RESPONSES

Increasing the frequency of security staff patrols. Increasing the frequency with which security staff patrols school grounds and buildings increases the likelihood that a potential intruder will be seen. While it can be useful for police to make sporadic checks of school grounds while on their normal patrol, continually patrolling school property is an inefficient use of police resources. Instead, police should conduct risk assessments and respond to and investigate vandalism incidents.

Using closed circuit television. The strategic placement of closed circuit television (CCTV) may deter potential offenders. When vandalism and break-ins occur, CCTV footage can be used to identify the perpetrators. Though the initial financial outlay may be significant, over the long term, CCTV may be less expensive than funding a full-time security patrol.

Improving opportunities for natural surveillance. The likelihood that school staff, residents, and pedestrians going about their daily activities will spot an intruder depends on the visibility of the school grounds from nearby houses, sidewalks, and streets. Clear sight lines in key locations, such as entrances, parking lots, hallways, and playgrounds, maximize the ability of residents and passersby to observe activity in vulnerable areas. Opportunities for natural surveillance are enhanced when staff offices are located throughout the school building, and staff should be vigilant as they move around the school.

Providing a caretaker or "school sitter" housing on school grounds. The continuous presence of a caretaker or "school sitter" on school grounds can deter potential intruders. An apartment in the school itself or a mobile home on the school grounds can provide rent-free housing to a responsible adult in exchange for a designated number of hours patrolling the property. An alternative to having an on-site residence is to stagger custodial shifts for twenty-four-hour coverage. In either arrangement, it is important that the caretaker or custodian is instructed not to intervene in suspicious activity, but rather to alert security staff or the police.

Holding offenders accountable. Very few perpetrators of school vandalism are identified and apprehended, and even fewer are prosecuted. Courts are generally lenient with offenders and, in most cases, the damage from an individual incident is minor and does not warrant harsh penalties. However, creative and well-publicized interventions to hold offenders accountable can have both specific and a general deterrence effect.

The most traditional approach to offender accountability involves either individual or group counseling to address the underlying motivations for the behavior. There has been some success with juvenile arsonists using this approach, and counseling that entails behavior modification (token economy, contingency contracts, incentives, and rewards) has had some success.

Restitution programs include a set of administrative and legal procedures to get money from offenders to pay for repair or replacement of damaged property. Publicizing the results of these efforts is important to maintain their deterrent effect. Obviously, these programs are effective only to the extent that offenders are identified and apprehended.

One of the more promising approaches to encouraging offender accountability is to bring together all of the stakeholders in the issue to develop a resolution collectively.

The goal is for the offender to make up for the offense, either by paying restitution or by repairing the damaged property.

Diverting offenders to alternative activities. Believing that involvement in school vandalism and break-ins arises from an excess of unstructured time, many jurisdictions develop alternative activities for students during after-school and evening hours. In addition to structured events, graffiti boards and mural programs may attract offenders to prosocial activities. Programs that foster a sense of ownership and school pride may make some students more apt to report vandalism and encourage others to respect school property, but they are unlikely to affect students whose involvement in vandalism is a result of alienation from the larger school social environment.

SCHOOL MANAGEMENT PRACTICES

Educating school staff. Not only should school staff be familiar with fire safety procedures, but they should also be aware of the various strategies enacted to protect school property. The strategies should be discussed regularly at staff meetings, and police and fire departments should be included in pre-school-year and pre-summer in-service training. Creating a manual containing important safety information, procedures for handling emergencies, and telephone numbers of those to be contacted when suspicious activity is observed ensures that teachers will have ready access to those details.

Controlling building and room keys. Intruders sometimes enter school buildings by using duplicate keys. The distribution of keys to building entrances and equipment storage rooms should be limited, and periodic key checks can be used to ensure that the owners of keys have control of them. Stamping "Do Not Duplicate" on keys and warning key holders of the dangers of students obtaining keys can prevent unauthorized access. Some jurisdictions use computer access cards, rather than keys, for rooms where valuables are stored. These cards permit access only at certain times of the day, and records can show which card was used to access any particular room.

Maintaining an inventory of valuable equipment. Missing equipment sometimes goes unreported because school officials do not know what they have and, therefore, do not know when it has been stolen. Diligent inventory checks can not only help in maintaining control of school assets, but can also help in preparing loss estimates if property is stolen. Sound inventory procedures include:

1. Taking stock of all valuables.
2. Keeping both paper and computerized inventory lists.
3. Supplementing inventory lists with serial numbers, physical descriptions, and video images.
4. Securing inventory lists and videotapes off-site.
5. Updating inventory lists each year.

Creating a "vandalism account." To provide incentives to students for acceptable conduct, school districts can allocate a specific amount of money from the maintenance account that covers the costs of all vandalism-related repairs. Any funds that remain at the end of the semester are allocated to students to pay for something of their choice (e.g., a pizza party, new equipment). Programs involving rewards are most effective with younger students, but older students often respond to the opportunity for shared administrative authority and responsibility. Some jurisdictions do not deduct repair costs if the perpetrator is identified and restitution is made, which gives students an incentive to provide information.

Changing the organizational climate. Social measures are not generally effective forms of crime prevention. However, because schools have closely structured social systems and clear authority systems, responses that affect the social environment can be effective. In particular, schools can seek to make the environment more positively reinforcing, reduce the misuse of disciplinary procedures, and work to improve administrator-teacher, teacher-student, and custodian-student relations.

COMMUNITY-FOCUSED RESPONSES

Providing rewards for information concerning vandalism or break-ins. Offender-focused responses require that vandals and intruders be identified and apprehended. Police investigations of vandalism incidents can be enhanced by high-quality information provided by students and community residents. As seen with traditional "Crime-stoppers" programs, setting up telephone or Internet-based tip-lines, offering rewards for information, and guaranteeing anonymity encourage students and residents to come forward with specific information. The most effective programs actively involve students in collecting and synthesizing information for police, and in determining pay-out amounts in the event of apprehension.

Creating "School Watch" programs. Similar to "Neighborhood Watch" efforts, community residents can conduct citizen patrols of school property during evenings and weekends. Membership and regular participation in voluntary patrols increase when some form of prestige is offered to volunteers.

Effective practices include:

- Patrolling regularly, but at unpredictable times.
- Equipping volunteers with cell phones for prompt communication with police or other emergency services.
- Engaging in passive surveillance only, and not interacting with potential vandals or intruders in any way.
- Publicizing activities and outcomes among students and residents through school-based and local media outlets.

In response to a specific problem or rash of incidents, School Watch has produced short-term reductions in vandalism. However, community watch programs are difficult to sustain, have not been shown to reduce crime over the long term, and may actually increase the fear of crime.

Evaluating public use of school facilities after hours. There is no consensus on how effective after-hours use of school facilities is in deterring vandalism and break-ins.

On the one hand, making facilities and amenities available to residents increases the opportunities for natural surveillance to protect school buildings and property. Such access is also in keeping with the spirit of schools as hubs of community activity. However, residents who use the facilities after hours may not always have innocent intentions. If this response is adopted, rules and boundaries should be made very clear to participants, and only those areas required for the activities should be accessible, with other areas of the school secured by movable gates and locking partitions.

RESPONSES WITH LIMITED EFFECTIVENESS

Controlling the sale of vandalism tools. Some jurisdictions have attempted to control the various implements used for vandalism—for graffiti, in particular. Age-specific bans on the sale of spray paint or wide-tipped markers are designed to limit youth access to them. These bans are particularly difficult to implement and enforce because they require extensive cooperation from merchants.

   Increasing penalties. Responding to school vandalism and break-ins with excessively punitive criminal justice sanctions or harsh administrative punishments (e.g., expulsion) has been found to increase the incidence of vandalism. Further, legal deterrents are generally ineffective when victim reporting and offender apprehension are not consistent, as is the case with school vandalism. Finally, most acts of vandalism are relatively minor and, thus, are not serious enough to warrant severe consequences.

The Terrorist Threat

PLANNING FOR CHEMICAL, BIOLOGICAL, AND RADIOLOGICAL AND EXPLOSIVES ATTACK

The Threat

Those responsible for developing emergency plans and procedures should recognize that there are fundamental differences between chemical, biological, and radiological (CBR) agents. In general, chemical agents will show a rapid onset of symptoms, while the response to biological and radiological agents will be delayed. Issues, such as designated areas and procedures for chemical storage, HVAC control or shutdown, and communications with school occupants and emergency responders, should all be addressed. The plans should be as comprehensive as possible, but protected by limited and controlled access. When appropriately developed, these plans, policies, and procedures can have a major impact upon school occupant survivability in the event of a CBR release.

   Staff training, particularly for those with specific responsibilities during an event, is essential and should cover both internal and external events. Holding regularly scheduled practice drills, similar to the common fire drill, allows for plan testing, as well as student and key staff rehearsal of the plan, and increases the likelihood for success in an actual event. School officials should ensure that training is provided to staff that operate and maintain the school's HVAC system. This training should include the procedures to be followed in the event of a suspected CBR agent release. Development of current, accurate HVAC diagrams and HVAC system labeling protocols should be addressed. These documents can be of great value in the event of a CBR release.

Measures

This section is based on guidance from the Centers for Disease Control and Protection (CDC)/National Institute for Occupational Safety and Health (NIOSH) and the Department of Defense (DoD) and presents protective measures and actions to safeguard the occupants of a school building from CBR threats. Evacuation, sheltering-in-place, personal protective equipment, air filtration and pressurization, and exhausting and purging will be discussed, as well as CBR detection. *FEMA 426 Reference Manual to Mitigate Potential Terrorist Attacks Against Buildings* contains detailed information on CBR threats.

Although the likelihood of a direct attack against a school is very low, recent terrorist events have increased interest in the vulnerability of all types of buildings to CBR threats. Of particular concern are building HVAC systems, because they can become an entry point and distribution system for airborne hazardous contaminants. Even without special protective systems, buildings can provide protection in varying degrees against airborne hazards that originate outdoors. Conversely, the hazards produced by a release inside a building can be much more severe than a similar release outdoors. Because buildings allow only a limited exchange of air between indoors and outdoors, not only can higher concentrations occur when there is a release inside, hazards may persist longer indoors.

Airborne hazardous contaminants can be gases, vapors, or aerosols (small solid and liquid particles). Most biological and radiological agents are aerosols, whereas most chemical warfare agents are gaseous.

After the presence of an airborne hazard is detected, there are five possible protective actions for a building and its occupants. In increasing order of complexity and cost, these actions are:

1. Evacuation
2. Sheltering-in-place
3. Personal protective equipment
4. Filtering and pressurization
5. Exhausting and purging

These actions are implemented, singly or in combination, when a hazard is present or known to be imminent. To ensure these actions will be effective, a school safety emergency plan specific to each school, as well as training and familiarization for occupants, is required. Exhausting and purging is listed last because it is usually the final action after any airborne hazard incident.

Evacuation

Evacuation is the most common protective action taken when an airborne hazard, such as smoke or an unusual odor, is perceived in a building. In most cases, existing plans for fire evacuation apply. Orderly evacuation is the simplest and most reliable action for an internal airborne hazard, but may not be the best action in all situations, especially in the case of an external CBR release or plume, particularly one that is widespread. If the area covered by the plume is too large to rapidly and safely exit, sheltering-in-place should be considered. If a CBR agent has infiltrated the building and evacuation is deemed not to be safe, the use of protective hoods may be appropriate. Two considerations in non-fire evacuation are: (1) to determine if the source of the airborne hazard is internal or external to the building; and (2) to determine if evacuation may lead to other risks. Also, evacuation and assembly of occupants should be on the upwind side of the building and at least a hundred feet away, because any airborne hazard escaping the structure will be carried downwind.

Sheltering-in-Place

Typically, buildings offer little protection to occupants from airborne hazards outside the structure because outdoor air must be continuously introduced to provide a comfortable, healthy indoor environment. However, a school can provide substantial protection against agents released outdoors if the flow of fresh air is filtered/cleaned, or temporarily interrupted or reduced. Interrupting the flow of fresh air is the principle applied in the protective action known as sheltering-in-place.

The need for schools to consider sheltering-in-place is important because if there was a nearby chemical explosion with a cloud of poisonous gas, students could be exposed if allowed to go outdoors.

The advantage of sheltering-in-place is that it can be implemented rapidly. The disadvantage is that its protection is variable and diminishes with the duration of the hazard. Sheltering requires that two distinct actions be taken without delay to maximize the passive protection a school building provides:

- First, reduce the indoor-outdoor air exchange rate before the hazardous plume arrives. This is achieved by closing all windows and doors, and turning off all fans, air conditioners, and combustion heaters.
- Second, increase the indoor-outdoor air exchange rate as soon as the hazardous plume has passed by opening all windows and doors, and turning on all fans to ventilate the building.

The level of protection that can be attained by sheltering-in-place is substantial, but it is less than can be provided by high-efficiency filtration of the fresh air introduced into the building. The amount of protection varies with:

- The building's air exchange rate. The tighter the school building (i.e., the lower the air exchange rate), the greater the protection it provides. In most cases, air conditioners and combustion heaters cannot be operated while sheltering-in-place because operating them increases the indoor-outdoor exchange of air.

- The duration of exposure. Protection varies with time, diminishing as the time of exposure increases. Sheltering-in-place is, therefore, suitable only for exposures of short duration, roughly two hours or less, depending on conditions.
- Purging or period of occupancy. How long students, faculty, and staff remain in the building after the hazardous plume has passed also affects the level of protection. Because the school building slowly purges contaminants that have entered it, at some point during plume passage, the concentration inside exceeds the concentration outside. Maximum protection is attained by increasing the air exchange rate after plume passage or by exiting into clean air.
- Natural filtering. Some filtering occurs when the agent is deposited in the school shell or upon interior surfaces as air passes into and out of the building. The tighter the school building, the greater the effect of this natural filtering.

In a home, taking the actions required for sheltering (i.e., closing windows and doors, and turning off all air conditioners, fans, and combustion heaters) is relatively simple. Doing so in a school may require more time and planning. All air-handling units must be turned off and any dampers for outside air must be closed. Procedures for a protective action plan, therefore, should include:

- Identifying all air-handling units, fans, and the switches needed to deactivate them.
- Identifying cracks, seams, joints, and pores in the building shell to be temporarily sealed to further reduce outside air infiltration. Keeping emergency supplies, such as duct tape and polyethylene sheeting, on hand.
- Identifying procedures for purging after an internal release (i.e., opening windows and doors, turning on smoke fans, air handlers, and fans that were turned off) to exhaust and purge the building.
- Identifying school safe rooms (i.e., interior rooms having a lower air exchange rate that may provide a higher level of passive protection). It may be desirable to go to a predetermined sheltering room (or rooms).
- Shut and lock all windows and doors.
- Seal any windows and vents with plastic sheeting and duct tape.
- Seal the door(s) with duct tape around the top, bottom, and sides.
- Firmly pack dampened towels along the bottom of each door.
- Turn on a TV or radio that can be heard within the shelter and listen for further instructions.
- When the "all clear" is announced, open windows and doors.

Although sheltering is for protection against an external release, it is possible, but more complex, to shelter-in-place on one or more floors of a multistory school building after an internal release has occurred on a single floor. Important considerations for use of sheltering-in-place are that stairwells must be isolated by closed fire doors, elevators must not be used, and clear evacuation routes must remain open if evacuation is required. Escape hoods may be needed if the only evacuation routes are through contaminated areas.

One final consideration for sheltering-in-place is that students, faculty, and staff cannot be forced to participate. During an event, some building emergency plans call for making a concise information announcement and then giving occupants three to five minutes to proceed to the sheltering area or evacuate the building before it is sealed. It is important to develop a plan in cooperation with likely participants and awareness training programs that include discussions of sheltering-in-place and events (CBR attacks, hazardous material releases, or natural disasters) that might make sheltering preferable to evacuation. Training programs and information announcements during an event should be tailored to help students, faculty, and staff to make informed decisions.

Personal Protective Equipment

A wide range of individual protection equipment is available, including respirators, protective hoods, protective suits, CBR detectors, and decontamination equipment.

Of particular note, new models of universal-fit escape hoods have been developed for short-duration "escape-only" wear to protect against chemical agents, aerosols (including biological agents), and some toxic industrial chemicals. These hoods are compact enough to be stored in desks or to be carried on belts. They should be stored in their sealed pouches and opened only when needed. Most of these hoods form protective seals at the neck and do not require special fitting techniques or multiple sizes to fit a large portion of the population. Training is required to use the hoods properly. Depending on hood design, the wearer must bite on and breathe through a mouth bit or use straps to tighten a nose cup around the nose and mouth. Escape hoods should be considered, but may not be an effective or efficient proposed solution for use in schools, under current threats.

There are no government standards for hoods intended for protection against the malicious use of chemical or biological agents. In selecting an escape hood, a purchaser should, therefore, require information on laboratory verification testing. Plans should be made for training, fitting, storing, and maintaining records relative to storage life, and there should be procedures for instructing building occupants about when to put on the hoods. Wearing a hood can cause physiological strain and may cause panic or stress that could lead to respiratory problems in some people. Finally, it should be recognized that no single selection of personal protective equipment is effective against every possible threat. Selection must be tied to specific threat/hazard characteristics.

Air Filtration and Pressurization

Among the various protective measures for school buildings, high-efficiency air filtration/cleaning provides the highest level of protection against an outdoor release of hazardous materials. It can also provide continuous protection, unlike other approaches for which protective measures are initiated upon detecting an airborne hazard. *FEMA 426 Reference Manual to Mitigate Potential Terrorist Attacks Against Buildings* discusses air filtration in detail.

Two basic methods of applying air filtration to buildings are external filtration and internal filtration. External filtration involves drawing air from outside, filtering and/or cleaning it, and discharging the air inside the building or protected zone. This provides a higher level of protection, but involves substantially higher costs. Internal filtration involves drawing air from inside the building, filtering and/or cleaning it, and discharging the air back inside the building.

The relative levels of protection of the two methods can be illustrated in terms of protection factor, and the ratio of external dose and internal dose (concentration integrated over time). External filtration systems with high-efficiency filters can yield protection factors greater than 100,000. For internal filtration, the protection factors are likely to be less and are highly variable. The protection of internal filtration varies with a number of factors, the efficiency of the filter, flow rate of the filter unit, and size of the room or building in which the filter unit operates.

Exhausting and Purging

Turning on building ventilation fans and smoke-purge fans is a protective action for purging airborne hazards from the building and reducing the hazard to which school occupants are exposed, but it is mainly useful when the source of the hazard is indoors.

Purging must be carefully applied with regard to the location of the source and the time of the release. It must be clear that the source of the hazard is inside the school building and, if not, purging should not be attempted. If the hazardous material has been identified before release or immediately upon release, purging should not be employed, because it may spread the hazardous material throughout the school building or HVAC zone. In this case, all air-handling units should be turned off to isolate the hazard while evacuating or temporarily sheltering-in-place.

Additionally, the ventilation system and smoke-purge fans can be used to purge the building following an external release after the hazard outdoors has dissipated and it has been confirmed that the agent is no longer present near the school building.

CBR Detection

Most strategies for protecting students, faculty, staff, and visitors from airborne hazards will require a means of detection (i.e., determining that a hazard exists). Although effective and inexpensive devices are widely available to detect, for example, smoke and carbon monoxide, there are no detectors that can rapidly alert occupants to a broad range of chemical and biological hazards.

Chemical detection technology has improved vastly since Operation Desert Storm, where many military detection systems experienced high false alarm rates, but biological detection technology has not matured as fast. Biological signatures are not as distinctive as chemical signatures and can take thirty minutes or more to detect. Biological detection systems are expensive and generally require trained specialists to operate. Current chemical detectors work in approximately ten seconds; furthermore, wide varieties of efficient radiological detectors have been developed for the nuclear industry and are commercially available.

Chemical Detectors

Driven largely by a desire to protect workers from toxic vapors in industrial environments, considerable information is known on the toxicity of chemical warfare agents, which often have dual uses in industry. A variety of detection technologies exist, ranging from inexpensive manual point detection devices (e.g., paper strips and calorimetric tubes) utilizing basic chemical reactions to trigger color changes, to sophisticated detection systems utilizing advanced technologies.

Chemical agents do not possess universal properties that permit detection by any single method. Therefore, most chemical detectors are designed to detect specific agents or a group of related agents. Most broad-range detection systems actually combine several different sensors utilizing different technologies and can be very expensive and complex. Nevertheless, today there are numerous commercially available chemical detectors. The most capable detectors utilize ion mobility spectrometry (IMS), surface acoustic wave (SAW), or gas chromatograph/mass spectrometer (GC/MS) technologies to detect chemical agents and toxic industrial materials (TIMs).

Today, there are commercially available IMS detection systems that will detect most chemical agents and many TIMs. They are suitable for integration into a building ventilation system, can interface with HVAC control systems, have reasonable maintenance requirements (every three months), have low false alarm rates, and can be programmed to detect specific chemical agents.

Biological Detectors

The current state of biological detection technology is very different from that of chemical agent detection technology. In general, most biological detection systems are currently in the research and early development stages. There are some commercially available devices that have limited utility (responding only to a small number of agents) and are generally high-cost items. Because commercially available biological warfare (BW) detection systems and/or components exhibit limited utility in detecting and identifying BW agents and are also costly, it is strongly recommended that purchasers be very careful when considering any device that claims to detect BW agents.

Indications of CBR Contamination

Most hazardous chemicals have warning properties that provide a practical means for detecting a hazard and initiating protective actions. Such warning properties make chemicals perceptible; for example, vapors or gases can be perceived by the human senses (i.e., smell, sight, taste, or irritation of the eyes, skin, or respiratory tract) before serious effects occur. The distinction between perceptible and imperceptible agents is not an exact one. The concentrations at which a person can detect an odor vary from person to person, and these thresholds also vary relative to the concentration that can produce immediate, injurious effects.

Most of the industrial chemicals and chemical-warfare agents are readily detectable by smell. Soldiers in World Wars I and II were taught to identify, by smell, such agents as mustard, phosgene, and chlorine, and this detection method proved effective for determining when to put on and take off a gas mask. An exception is the chemical warfare agent Sarin, which is odorless and colorless in its pure form and, therefore, imperceptible. Among the most common toxic industrial chemicals, carbon monoxide is one of the few that is imperceptible. Because it is odorless and colorless, it causes many deaths in buildings each year.

Biological agents are also imperceptible and there are no detection devices that can determine their presence in the air in real time. Current methods for detecting bacterial spores, such as anthrax, require a trained operator and expensive equipment. It is not currently possible to base protective responses to biological agents on detection.

Researchers are working on a prototype device to automatically and continuously monitor the air for the presence of bacterial spores. The device would continuously sample the air and use microwaves to trigger a chemical reaction, the intensity of which would correspond to the concentration of bacterial spores in the sample. If an increase in spore concentration is detected, an alarm similar to a smoke detector would sound and a technician would respond and use traditional sampling and analysis to confirm the presence of anthrax spores. Researchers hope the device response time will be fast enough to help prevent widespread contamination.

In the absence of a warning property, people can be alerted to some airborne hazards by observing symptoms or effects in others. This provides a practical means for initiating emergency plans, because the susceptibility to hazardous materials varies from person to person. The concentrations of airborne materials may also vary substantially within a given building or room, producing a hazard that may be greater to some occupants than to others.

Other warning signs of a hazard may involve seeing and hearing something out of the ordinary, such as the hiss of a rapid release from a pressurized cylinder. Awareness of warning properties, signs, and symptoms in other people is the basis of an emergency plan. Such a plan should apply four possible protective actions: evacuating, sheltering-in-place, using protective masks, and exhausting and purging, as already discussed in this chapter.

For protection against imperceptible agents, the only practical protective measures are those that are continuously in place, such as filtering all air brought into the building on a continuous basis and using automatic, real-time sensors that are capable of detecting the imperceptible agents.

CBR materials, as well as industrial agents, may travel in the air as a gas or on surfaces we physically contact. Dispersion methods may be as simple as placing a container in a heavily used area, opening a container, or using conventional (garden)/commercial spray devices, or as elaborate as detonating an aerosol. Most chemical warfare agents are gaseous, and biological and radiological agents are largely aerosols.

Chemical incidents are characterized by the rapid onset (minutes to hours) of medical symptoms and easily observed indicators (e.g., colored residue, dead foliage, pungent odor, and dead animals, birds, fish, or insects.) (See Table 3–3.)

In the case of a biological incident, the onset of symptoms takes days to weeks and, typically, there will be no characteristic indicators. Because of the delayed onset of symptoms in a biological incident, the area affected may be greater due to the migration of infected individuals.

In the case of a radiological incident, the onset of symptoms also takes days to weeks to occur and typically there will be no characteristic indicators. Radiological materials are not recognizable by the senses because they are colorless and odorless.

Table 3–3

Dead animals, birds, fish	Not just an occasional roadkill, but numerous animals (wild and domestic, small and large), birds, and fish in the same area.
Lack of insect life	If normal insect activity (ground, air, and/or water) is missing, check the ground/water surface/shoreline for dead insects. If near water, check for dead fish/aquatic birds.
Physical symptoms	Numerous individuals experiencing unexplained water-like blisters, wheals (like bee stings), pinpointed pupils, choking, respiratory ailments, and/or rashes.
Mass casualties	Numerous individuals exhibiting unexplained serious health problems ranging from nausea to disorientation to difficulty in breathing to convulsions to death.
Definite pattern of casualties	Casualties distributed in a pattern that may be associated with possible agent dissemination methods.
Illness associated with confined geographic area	Lower attack rates for people working indoors than those working outdoors, or vice versa.

Source: FEMA

Specialized equipment is required to determine the size of the affected area and if the level of radioactivity presents an immediate or long-term health hazard. Because of the delayed onset of symptoms in a radiological incident, the affected area may be greater due to the migration of contaminated individuals.

Safe Rooms

It is important to note that the probability of either a CBR or terrorist explosive event occurring in the United States is small. This is evidenced by the relatively few domestic buildings that have been targeted by intentional CBR or explosive events compared to the vast number of buildings that might be considered vulnerable. To date, two incidents of biological terrorism have been recorded and acknowledged to have had significant impacts on coincident populations in the United States: the 2001 anthrax mailings and the 1984 contamination of restaurants with Salmonella bacteria. If a localized CBR event were to occur, the potential for contamination to spread and cause collateral illnesses and fatalities up to four or more kilometers (approximately two-and-a-half miles) from the target site would be likely. Unpredictable meteorological conditions would play a key role in the spread of such CBR contamination. Similarly, if an explosive event were to occur, there would be a significant potential for injuries resulting from debris impact and structural collapse.

Therefore, in consideration of the proximity of some schools with respect to higher-profile potential targets in the United States, school board members and administrators may determine that their select facilities require the design and construction of safe rooms. Because there are so many different types of school buildings, with so many different types of construction and materials, it is not possible to relate all the following issues to specific building types; nevertheless, an attempt was made to relate the relevant threats and the general principles of protective design to the development of safe rooms within schools.

TYPES OF CBR HAZARDS

Chemical contaminants of concern are the chemical warfare agents (CWAs) and toxic industrial chemicals (TICs). Key attributes of CWAs and TICs are their toxicity, volatility, and availability. The most toxic CWAs are the nerve agent liquids, which include VX with high toxicity and low volatility, and Sarin with high toxicity and moderate volatility. The measured volatility of a chemical represents the ease with which the quantity of liquid chemical leaves the liquid state and becomes a gas in equilibrium with its volumetric surroundings. So, an occupant of a room where Sarin liquid is naturally evaporating is at much greater risk than the same individual being in the same room with the same or (to a degree greater) quantity of a naturally evaporating VX agent. The lethality of VX exceeds the lethality of Sarin by dose, but Sarin is much more volatile than VX.

Toxic Industrial Chemicals

Though of lower toxicity than nerve agents, TICs are widely available, and some can be easily obtained or produced without sophisticated equipment. Among the hundreds of TICs produced worldwide are several that have been used as CWAs (e.g., arsine, chlorine, hydrogen cyanide, phosgene, hydrogen sulfide, acrolein, and cyanogen chloride). Those that have been used in warfare are considered second-rate CWAs because their toxicity and vapor pressure make them less effective than other agents for open-air battlefield use.

Incapacitating and Tear-producing Agents

Although incapacitating and tear-producing agents are considered non-lethal, indoor releases can, under certain conditions, produce lethal concentrations. In addition to the tear-producing agents, there are commercially available agents containing oleoresin capsicum (OC), the natural oil of chili peppers. The malicious or accidental release of pepper spray has caused many disruptive incidents in recent years. In contact with the eyes, nose, or mouth, OC causes immediate pain and inflammation. Inhaled, its aerosol causes choking and gasping for breath. Of low vapor pressure, OC is easily filtered.

Biological Agents

Biological agents include bacteria, viruses, and rickettsia. Toxins, which are poisons of biological origin and not living organisms, are sometimes grouped with biological agents and sometimes with chemical agents. Although there are hundreds of microorganisms that could be used as biological agents, the likely number is much smaller when the agents' effectiveness, reliability, availability, ease of manufacture, and stability in storage and dissemination are considered. When disseminated as aerosols, biological agents are most effective in the size range of one to five microns, because they can remain suspended for long periods. Smaller particles are less likely to survive as aerosols, and larger particles settle rapidly, making them less likely to enter the lungs. The settling time in still air for an anthrax spore (one micron by 0.7 micron in size) is approximately six inches per hour. Particles of this size are readily filtered from an air stream with high-efficiency particulate air (HEPA) filters. Toxins, which may be in crystalline or liquid form, are also filterable with HEPA when disseminated as aerosols.

Radiological Agents

Radiological agents are radioactive materials. Explosive release is the most likely means of disseminating such agents in a terrorist attack (e.g., a "dirty" bomb consisting of radioactive material packaged with a conventional explosive). The likely radioactive ingredients are those used for industrial and medical purposes (e.g., isotopes of cesium, cobalt, and iridium). They are commonly found in hospitals and labs, often with few safeguards. Given the availability of nuclear reactors for research or energy production by universities, research facilities, or private industries, the threat associated with radiological materials is significant. Radiological contaminants are very persistent, in that their decay rate is extremely slow. Unlike chemical or biological agents, decontamination involves only removal, not neutralization. Radiological aerosols present a health hazard if ingested or inhaled, but are easily filtered from an air stream with HEPA filters.

Most Likely Delivery Methods for CBR Agents

For purpose of vulnerability assessments, delivery methods are divided into four types of releases: internal, external proximate, remote, and remote with forewarning.

Internal Release

This involves transporting a container of agent into a building and releasing the contents manually, automatically, or remotely. Such a device may rely simply upon natural evaporation (as in the Tokyo subway Sarin attack), with the rate of evaporation proportional to the surface area that develops as liquid agent spills from its container. Aerosolization may occur with movement of an open package or letter containing a biological agent. A sprayer powered by batteries or compressed air can produce an effective dose of an agent quite rapidly. An agent can be released in any area served by return ducts/plenums or in a mechanical room, with dissemination through an air-handling unit. Biological agents can also be placed into certain types of humidifier systems.

External Proximate Release

This involves introducing an agent or a dissemination device from outside the building directly through a penetration in the building shell, such as a fresh-air intake. Vulnerability to this type of release is highest when air intakes are at accessible, unsecured locations at ground level. Agents can also be delivered through other penetrations, but potential effectiveness is less in the absence of a driving force (a fan) to introduce and distribute air within the building. A documented example of an attack through a ground-level penetration is the release of a toxic industrial gas from a pressurized cylinder through a dryer vent. External proximate release also includes forcing open or breaking windows and doors to introduce agents from pressurized cylinders or tossing a grenade or container of an agent into the building.

Remote Release

If directed at a specific facility, this type of attack involves a plume, puff, or line source generated so that the wind carries the agent to the target building; the facility may be the target or collaterally in the direction of the attack. The most efficient type of remote attack is a directed-plume attack with a ground-level source placed upwind of a building's fresh-air intakes or open windows. A ground-level, directed-plume attack was conducted with the nerve agent Sarin from a distance of 60 yards in Matsumoto, Japan, in 1994, killing 7 and injuring 264 in a zone 500 yards deep and 100 yards wide. A remote attack can also involve an aerial release. Release from an aircraft is much less likely to affect a specific, targeted building, however, because the vertical rate of transport, governed by settling time and atmospheric stability, is extremely difficult to judge.

Remote Release with Forewarning

This type of attack differs from other remote releases because protective actions other than those for no-warning attacks can be applied. This type involves warning in the form of an explosion or an event, such as an accidental or intentional release of an agent from a chemical transport or storage tank. Scenarios involving forewarning include sabotage of toxic industrial storage tanks/trucks, transport accidents, fires, or the impending release of a chemical agent from a point upwind of the building. Quantities of agent that could be released from a single 3,000-gallon tanker truck are approximately 34,000 pounds for phosgene, 35,000 pounds for chlorine, and 17,000 pounds for hydrogen cyanide.

Vulnerability to Remote CBR Collapse

In the absence of a secure perimeter around the building and a real-time detection system, vulnerability to a remote release is determined by: (1) the efficiency of the school building's filtration system in removing aerosols and gases, (2) the unfiltered component of air exchange, and (3) the configuration of the school building and elevation of air intakes. These vulnerabilities can be characterized as follows.

- Efficiency of gas filtration. Generally, if adsorbers are found in buildings, they are for the purpose of improving indoor air quality by removing both outdoor and indoor air pollutants, particularly corrosive gases such as sulfur dioxide, nitrogen dioxide, and ozone, and are used, where appropriate, for protecting against the deleterious effects of these gases. Although not intended for protecting people from toxic chemical agents, these gas adsorbers do reduce the vulnerability to an attack with certain chemical agents. With a one-inch bed thickness of coarse (4 × 6 mesh) sorbent granules and a short residence time of these indoor air quality filters, the efficiency is about 99 percent initially, and it diminishes with time in service, typically to about 25 percent in a year. There is also an initial bypass of roughly one percent through the bed and additional bypasses among filter modules' holding frames. The bypasses may increase with time in service, dropping the net efficiency below the initial level. This compares with an efficiency of greater than 99.999 percent for gas adsorbers designed for protection of people in military applications. Removal efficiency for these indoor air-quality adsorbers is relatively low and uncertain for some of the threat agents (the capacity for arsine is low, for example). Thus, the efficiency and capacity are highly variable. Manufacturers provide surveillance testing to determine when to change filters and recommend that they be changed when reactive capacity has dropped to 25 percent of the initial value. The typical service life for single stage, one-inch beds is approximately one year.

- Particulate filtration. Significant particulate filtration can be accomplished by using a 35 percent pre-filter and a 95 percent filter in series. The efficiency of this filter train is in the range of 95 to 99 percent for one-micron particles in the new condition, and this efficiency increases as the filters load.

- Unfiltered air exchange. Typical of schools, a substantial portion of the air exchanged between indoors and outdoors may not pass through the filters of any air-handling units. When this occurs, the level of protection the building structure provides is, therefore, governed not by the efficiency of the filters but rather by that portion of makeup air bypassing the filters. There are several paths by which air exchange is driven by fans, buoyancy, and/or wind pressures. They include operable windows; doorways with flows driven by buoyancy, particularly in summer and winter when indoor-outdoor temperature differentials are highest; and unintentional openings in the building shell. When internal resistance is minimal, less dense (buoyant) warm air rises and flows out of a school building near its top in winter, drawing in cool air at the lower levels. Conversely, in summer, cool air falls and flows out of the building's base. The buoyancy effect tends to be less pronounced in spring and fall because of smaller indoor and outdoor temperature differences. With the standard draw-through configuration of the air-handling units, leakage paths at the access doors and panels are subject to inward pressure; these leakage paths increase as the gaskets age. Typically, access doors also fail to seal well with filter frames, allowing bypass that increases with age.

- Typical protection factors achievable. In terms of protection factor, protection against aerosols (biological/radiological agents and others, such as tear gas) provided by the best (standard) filtration systems available in air-handling units is substantial, but relatively low (in the range of approximately 5 to 50). Protection factor is a ratio of dose (concentration integrated over time) of an agent outside divided by the resulting dose of agent inside a building). This level of place or an active detection-based system that responds by de-energizing fans and closing dampers. The higher value in this range is estimated by taking the inverse of the penetration factor for one-micron particles through the filters, including an initial bypass of approximately one percent. The lower value in the protection factor range is estimated for both particulate and gas filters by using 20 percent as an estimate of the unfiltered air exchange; the inverse of the penetration factor (0.2) is 5. With an indoor air-quality filter unit having a gas adsorber, the protection factor for gases can be as high as 50, but only when filters are new and only with gas adsorbers. The protection drops to a low value as the filter efficiency decreases with time in service. This may be less than 2 if the efficiency drops below 50 percent after one year in service. The protection factor against gases is also reduced by the portion of outside air (which could be at least 80 percent) that does not flow through gas adsorbers. With a penetration of 80 percent, the protection factor for gases for the whole building is less than 2.

Vulnerability to Remote Release

A typical building would have high vulnerability to a remote release of aerosols (biological and radiological agents) and a high vulnerability to a remote release of gases (chemical agents). The basis for this rating is:

- Estimated protection factors are in the range of 5 to 50 for aerosols, based on a substantial volume of unfiltered air exchange.
- Use of gas adsorbers is atypical of building air-handling ventilation systems.
- Outside air intakes in building construction are often located near ground level, making them especially vulnerable.

    Vulnerability can be reduced by:

- Application of gas adsorbers to all air-handling units.
- Employing particulate filters of higher efficiency (e.g., 95 percent) and low bypass.

Vulnerability to Remote CBR Release with Forewarning

This type of attack involves release of an agent by explosion or rapid release from a tanker truck, rail car, or fixed storage tank. The potential for this type of attack is higher when the facility is near rail lines, public roads with truck traffic, or storage tanks of toxic chemicals. This type of attack may also involve an explosive release of a radiological agent (i.e., a "dirty" bomb attack at a distance from the building great enough to allow for protective actions to be taken before wind carries the agent to the building).

    The criterion for this aspect of vulnerability is the ability to rapidly assume a sheltering-in-place posture. The main requirements are plans/procedures for sheltering, controls to rapidly turn off all fans, and a communications or public address system to facilitate closing of doors and keeping them closed while an outdoor hazard is present or imminent. Protection factors vary, diminishing with time of exposure; however, scenarios of explosive release under most conditions would present a relatively short exposure to the school building.

A typical school building would have high vulnerability to a remote release with forewarning. The basis for this rating is:

- Schools should develop plans/procedures for sheltering and rapid deactivation of all fans and closing of doors and windows.
- Schools have limited filtration capabilities for gases and aerosols; therefore, the vulnerability to a remote release with forewarning is approximately the same as the vulnerability to a remote release without forewarning.

Vulnerability can be reduced by:

- Developing an emergency plan for sheltering-in-place that includes rapidly de-energizing all fans and closing doors and windows.

Vulnerability to Internal CBR Release

This is a remote possibility owing to the nature and likelihood of other vandalism and that actual targeting of a school has no historical precedence. Nevertheless, internal releases involve covert entry or covert introduction of agents in containers. Vulnerability to internal release is, therefore, determined principally by physical security measures in place. Containers of agents may be hand-carried or delivered in mail, supplies or equipment. Other factors affecting this vulnerability are internal (recirculation) filtration and how well entry zones, where any screening takes place, are isolated architecturally and mechanically.

The basis for preventing covert introduction of agents is access control and entry screening. Use of the X-ray machine for hand-carried items facilitates the detection of containers large enough to hold hazardous quantities of chemical agents; however, it requires specific operating procedures for doing so, and it may not be effective in detecting containers of hazardous quantities of biological agents. Obviously, such procedures are not recommended for schools without provocation (i.e., an actual threat) because of cost.

Vulnerability to External Proximate CBR Release

Vulnerability to external proximate release is determined mainly by the accessibility of outside air intakes to covert introduction of agent or agent-dissemination device. Unless air intakes are relocated at a higher elevation, this vulnerability would remain high.

The three strategies for protecting a school building from airborne hazards originating outdoors are air filtration, controlling air exchange, and exclusion by physical security. Options presented in this chapter focus on air filtration; however, enhanced filtration techniques discussed earlier would be applied most economically in schools to a selected safe room, such as a school gymnasium or auditorium. Without a secure exclusion zone around the school building, physical security measures are limited to those described above for external proximate release and internal release.

Controlling air exchange is most commonly employed with human detection and warning (i.e., sheltering-in-place). It can also be applied with automatic, real-time detection equipment, but with very limited effectiveness. Few agents among the full spectrum of threat agents can be detected with accuracy in real time. Protection factors vary with response time and, even with instantaneous response, protection factors are no greater than the maximum protection factors achievable with sheltering-in-place. As the response time increases, protection factors diminish. With current technology, response times are longest for biological agent detection. The response time for presumptive identification by a detector, such as the Joint Biological Point Detection System, is approximately thirty minutes and far exceeds the response time needed for effective use of sheltering-in-place. A biological detection system would not, therefore, prevent the contamination of a particular building.

CRITERIA FOR PROTECTIVE PERFORMANCE

All of the following discussion represents extreme measures applied to high-risk, high-security assets or, in general, to lesser degrees, safe rooms and, perhaps, to would-be safe rooms for schools. There is no standard requirement for protection factors. U.S. military systems are designed to achieve protection factors greater than 10,000. The criterion applied to military masks and collective protection shelters is 6,667, which is based upon specific levels for chemical agents on the battlefield and for threshold effects of the chemical agents on soldiers. There is no criterion for biological or radiological agents based upon concentrations and doses likely to be developed in an attack on a school building; however, it would be 10,000 or greater.

The selection of a CBR safe room in a school building requires an assessment of factors contributing to infiltration (or wind penetration from the outside). To prevent infiltration through the protected envelope requires an internal pressure of approximately 50 Pascals [0.2 inch, water gauge (iwg)]. This pressure does not prevent infiltration driven by buoyancy and wind pressures under all possible conditions, but it does so under wind conditions most conducive to a (standoff) plume attack. The level of safe room pressurization should exceed 95 to 99 percent of the meteorological conditions for the given school location. Note that wind does not exert a uniform pressure on a building face. The pressure varies by location on the building face and the angle of incidence. A 20-mile-per-hour (mph) wind velocity is not uncommon in the United States and, thus, a safe room pressurized to 50 Pascals would prevent infiltration from time averaged 20 mph winds.

There are several options for improving protection factors with filtration; they involve both the type/configuration of the filter system and the extent of the protective envelope.

Options for type of filter system—Four options for a dedicated type of filtration system for a safe room include:

• Improving mixed-air particulate filtration of air-handling units. Particulate filters may be upgraded to 95 percent filters, providing the potential for substantial improvement in protection against biological agent aerosols. The limit of protection factor against one-micron particles, however, is approximately 100 with pressurization of the protective envelope and reduction of bypass at the filter frames. Reduction of bypass requires sealing and gasketing existing retainers, slide-in tracks and access doors, and adding gaskets between filter frames in slide-in tracks. Pressurization can be achieved by rebalancing the air-handling units and controlling the flows through open doorways and windows. Among the options for improvement are to upgrade the filters to HEPA with leak-tight holding frames; with pressurization, this would increase the potential protection factor to about 10,000 for biological agents, but not for chemical agents. This option requires special holding fixtures for the filters and may require replacement of supply fans to accommodate higher pressure drop.

- Improving mixed-air gas filtration of the air-handling units. An option to increase protection factors of a school building for chemical agents is to install gas adsorbers in air-handling units. This would involve adding the indoor air-quality (IAQ) type adsorbers to existing air-handling units, at a cost of $0.50 per cfm. With a one-year service life, the filter replacement costs would be $0.25 per cfm. Additional energy-related operating costs would be incurred due to the pressure drop of the adsorbers (0.75 iwg). This option does not provide high efficiency against all chemical agents.

- Installing makeup-air units with HEGA and HEPA filters. A makeup air unit for both gases and aerosols includes the following components in series: pre-filter, fan, HEPA filter, HEGA filter, and heating and cooling coils. The makeup-air unit provides filtered outside air to pressurize the protective envelope. It eliminates recirculation and the internally induced infiltration associated with applying a single fan for both makeup air and recirculated air. The most cost-effective HEGA filter units currently available for protection from chemical agents employ the military-standard 200-cfm radial-flow filters per MIL-PRF-51527A, "Filter Set, Gas-particulate, 200 cfm," Type II. These contain ASZM-TEDA carbon of 12 × 30 mesh size in 2-inch-deep beds, which removes all chemical warfare agents and a substantial number of toxic industrial chemicals. These provide removal efficiency greater than 99.999 percent throughout their service life (estimated at 3 years). HEPA filters are standard components with HEGA systems. These military adsorbers cost approximately $4.50 per cfm, and their expected service life is 3 years, although service life varies with the air quality of the region and the moisture to which the filters are exposed over time. Maintenance costs run approximately $2 per year per cfm. Maintenance also includes changing HEPA filters annually and pre-filters every 90 days. With total pressure drop of 6 iwg across the adsorber and HEPA filter, energy costs for the high-efficiency filtration run approximately $0.50 per cfm per year.

- Installing makeup-air units with HEPA only. Use of only HEPA in a makeup-air unit would provide a high level of protection from biological agents, radiological agents, solid aerosols, such as tear gas, and liquid aerosols of low vapor pressure. High-level protection against biological aerosols is particularly beneficial because there is no capability for real-time detection of biological agents (all strategies that require biological detection are mitigation strategies involving decontamination and medical treatment). Use of HEPA only in a makeup-air unit would substantially reduce hardware costs, maintenance costs, and electrical costs of ventilation, as well as the space requirements for the units. Protection at a lower level would still be provided by filtration of recirculated air with gas adsorbers in air-handling units.

RECOMMENDATIONS FOR CBR PROTECTION

The following actions are recommended for CBR protection:

- To provide a substantial level of protection against an external release of CBR agents, apply any one of the filtration options summarized above to a renovated school gymnasium or auditorium safe room.
- To protect against a remote attack with a chemical or radiological agent, plans, procedures, and training for sheltering-in-place should be developed. To support this protective measure, a rapid notification system (public address system) and controls for rapid deactivation of fans and closing of dampers should be defined. A guide for developing protective action plans is available in the Army Corps of Engineers draft *Technical Instruction TI 853–01 Protecting Buildings and Their Occupants from Airborne Hazards,* dated October 2001.
- To reduce vulnerability to internal release, implement security procedures specific to entry screening for containers of unknown liquids or gases being carried into the secure area. Provide training to employees on awareness of the CBR threat and the protective action plan.

Explosive Blasts

This section discusses blast effects, potential school damage, injuries, levels of protection, standoff distance, and predicting blast effects. Explosive events have historically been a favorite tactic of terrorists for a variety of reasons, and this is likely to continue into the future. The DoD, GSA, and DOS have considerable experience with blast effects and blast mitigation. However, many architects and building designers do not have such experience. For additional information on explosive blast, see *FEMA 426 Reference Manual to Mitigate Potential Terrorist Attacks Against Buildings,* and *FEMA 427 Primer for Design of Commercial Buildings to Mitigate Terrorist Attacks.*

You have to prepare for the worst and be prepared to be on your own. Depending on the severity of an attack, communications systems could be disabled. Accurate information or direction from authorities could be delayed. Emergency response services could be critically over-burdened and not readily available. Working without assistance, schools could be called upon to provide shelter, food, medical attention, and guidance to students for extended periods of time beyond typical school hours. The physical and emotional endurance of staff members would be sorely tested as they assume parenting roles providing physical, emotional, and spiritual support to their charges.

Figure 3–2:   Explosives Environment

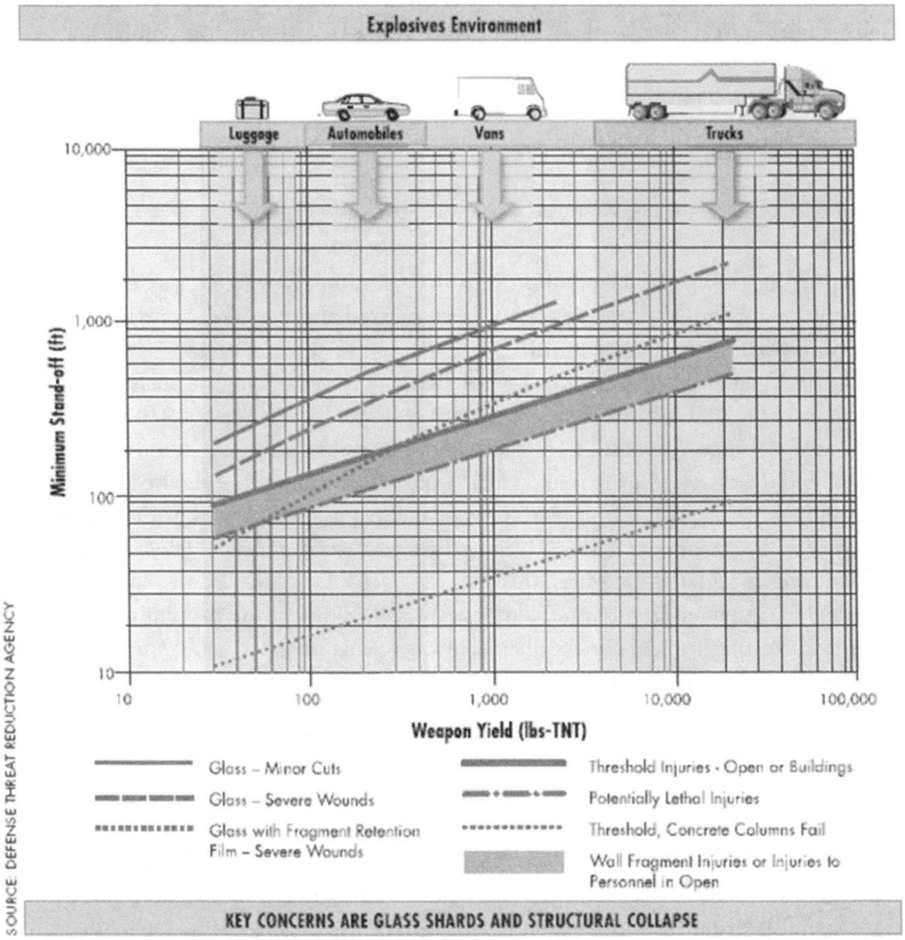

STANDOFF DISTANCE

The distance between an asset and a threat is referred to as the standoff distance. There is no ideal standoff distance, but the greater the distance between the asset and the threat the less damage that is likely. Obviously the damage will depend on the size of the explosion, the construction of the building, and the level of protection, but the most cost-effective solution for mitigating explosive effects is to ensure the explosions occur as far away from the buildings as possible. A major consideration is, of course, whether you are in an urban or rural setting because that is likely to determine how far your perimeter line is from your building.

Considerations for standoff distance are as follows:

- The first mode of site protection is to create "keep out zones" that can ensure a minimum guaranteed distance between an explosion and the target structure.
- The perimeter line is the outermost line that can be protected by the security measures incorporated during the design process. It is recommended that the perimeter line be located as far as practical from the building exterior. Many vulnerable buildings are located in urban areas where only the exterior wall of the building stands between the outside world and the building occupants. In this case, the options are obviously limited. Often, the perimeter line can be pushed out to the edge of the sidewalk by means of bollards, planters, and other obstacles. To push this line even farther outward, restricting or eliminating parking along the curb often can be coordinated with local authorities. In some extreme cases, elimination of loading zones and the closure of streets are options.
- "Keep out zones" can be achieved with perimeter barriers that cannot be compromised by vehicular ramming. A continuous line of security should be installed along the perimeter of the site to protect it from unscreened vehicles and to keep all vehicles as far away from critical assets as possible.
- When selecting a site for a new building, consider its location relative to the site perimeter. Maximize the distance between the perimeter fence and developed areas, providing as much open space as possible inside the fence along the site perimeter.
- The following critical building components should be located away from main entrances, vehicle circulation, parking, and maintenance areas. If this is not possible, harden as appropriate.
  —Emergency generator, including fuel systems, day tank, fire sprinkler, and water supply
  —Normal fuel storage
  —Telephone distribution and main switchgear
  —Fire pumps
  —Building control centers
  —Uninterruptible power-supply (UPS) systems powering critical functions
  —Main refrigeration systems if critical to building operation
  —Elevator machinery and controls
  —Shafts for stairs, elevators, and utilities
  —Critical distribution feeders for emergency power

SAFE ROOMS IN RESPONSE TO THE DOMESTIC EXPLOSIVE THREAT

The concept of safe rooms to protect against explosives has been around for quite some time. Bomb shelters were used in the United Kingdom during World War II to protect the civilian populations against aerial attack, and fall-out shelters were established in cities in the United States during the Cold War to protect against the lingering effects of a feared nuclear attack. More recently, the Israeli Defense Force (IDF) requires apartment protected spaces (APSs) or floor protected spaces (FPSs) to be constructed in every new building or to be added to existing buildings according to engineering specifications. In buildings in which no shelters exist, interior rooms may be converted to shelters by following IDF instructions. In all cases, the shelters must be accessible within two minutes of a warning siren. The protected spaces are intended to serve as a refuge when an attack is suspected, either through early warning or remote detection; however, the protected space is much less effective when the event takes place without warning. Two minutes and eleven seconds elapsed between the time the Ryder truck stopped in front of the Murrah Federal Building in Oklahoma City and the detonation of its explosives, but no one was alerted to the danger until the explosion occurred.

At Khobar Towers in Dhahran, Saudi Arabia, U.S. Air Force Security Police observers on the roof of the building overlooking the perimeter identified the attack in progress and alerted many occupants to the threat; however, evacuation was incomplete, and the explosion wounded five hundred people and killed nineteen people.

The effectiveness of the safe room in protecting occupants from the effects of an explosive detonation is, therefore, highly dependent on early detection and warning. Unless the attacker notifies authorities of a bomb threat, as often occurred in the terrorist activities in Northern Ireland, the safe room can best be used after an explosion occurs, in anticipation of a second attack. A small explosion, that drew curious embassy employees to the windows, preceded the 1998 bombing of the U.S. Embassy in Kenya; such a tactic, if repeated in the United States, would justify the relocation of school occupants to a safe room until school officials are able to determine that it is safe to disperse the students. To these limited objectives, the establishment of a safe room in schools may serve a useful purpose. Given the nature of the explosive threat, however, it may be more effective to provide debris mitigating protective measures for all exterior facade elements.

Although the patterns of past events may not predict the future, they give valuable insight to the protection against a very low-probability, but potentially high-consequence event. As previously discussed, despite a wide range of terrorist events, such as CBR contamination, an explosion remains the most insidious threat, requiring the least sophisticated materials and expertise. The principal components of an explosive device can be obtained at a variety of retail outlets, without arousing suspicion. Every year, over a thousand intentional explosive detonations are reported by the FBI Bomb Data Center. The majority of these explosives were targeted against residential properties and vehicles; however, seventy-six explosive events were detonated at educational facilities, causing a total of $28,500 in property damage. Over 70 percent of the people involved in bombing incidents were "young offenders" and less than a half of one percent were members of terrorist groups. Vandalism was the motivation in 40 percent of the intentional and accidental bombing incidents. Although two out of three attacks were perpetrated between 6:00 p.m. and 6:00 a.m., the incidents against educational facilities were more uniformly distributed throughout the day. Although each successive major domestic terrorist event exceeded the intensity of the predecessor, this is not particularly relevant to the threats to which a school structure might be subjected; if an explosive were to be detonated in or around a school building, it would most likely be a small improvised device assembled by a youth, and vandalism is most likely to be the motive.

The size of the explosive that might be considered for a protective design is limited by the maximum weight that might be transported either by hand or by vehicle. Despite the large weight of explosives that might be transported by vehicle, there have been relatively few large-scale explosive events within the United States. The 1995 explosion that collapsed portions of the Murrah Federal Building in Oklahoma City contained 4,800 pounds of ammonium nitrate and fuel oil (ANFO), and the 1993 explosion within the parking garage beneath the World Trade Center complex contained 1,200 pounds of urea nitrate. As implied by the FBI statistics, the majority of the domestic events contain significantly smaller weights of low-energy explosives. The explosive that was used in the 1996 pipe bomb attack at the Olympics in Atlanta consisted of smoke-less powder and was preceded by a warning that was called in twenty-three minutes before the detonation. Nevertheless, the protective design of structures focuses on the effects of high-energy explosives and relates the different mixtures to an equivalent weight of trinitrotoluene (TNT).

LOCATING SAFE ROOMS TO MITIGATE THREATS

The building's facade is its first real defense against the effects of a bomb and typically the weakest component that would be subjected to blast pressures. Although the re-sponse of specific glazed components is a function of the dimensions, makeup, and construction techniques, the conventionally glazed portions of the facade would shat-ter and inflict severe wounds when subjected to a 50-pound explosive detonation at a standoff distance on the order of 200 feet.

If the glazed elements are upgraded with a fragment retention film (FRF), the same facade element may be able to withstand a 50-pound explosive detonation at a stand-off distance on the order of 70 feet. Non-reinforced masonry block walls are similarly vulnerable to collapse when subjected to a 50-pound threat at a standoff distance of 50 feet; however, if these same walls are upgraded with a debris-catching system, they may be able to sustain this same intensity explosive detonation at a standoff distance on the order of 20 feet. If the weight of explosives were increased from 50 pounds to 500 pounds, the required standoff distances to prevent severe wounds increases to 500 feet for conventional window glazing, 200 feet for window glazing treated with a FRF, 250 feet for non-reinforced masonry block walls, and 60 feet for masonry walls upgraded with a debris-catching system.

Based on these dimensions, it is apparent that substantial standoff distances are required for the unprotected structure, and these distances may be significantly reduced through the use of debris mitigating retrofit systems. Furthermore, because blast loads diminish with distance and geometry of wave propagation relative to the loaded surface of the building, the larger threats at larger standoff distances are likely to damage a larger percentage of facade elements than the more localized effects of smaller threats at shorter standoff distances. Safe rooms that may be located within the school should, therefore, be located in windowless spaces or spaces in which the window glazing was upgraded with a FRF.

Although small weights of explosives are not likely to produce significant blast loads on the roof, low-rise structures may be vulnerable to blast loadings resulting from large weights of explosives at large standoff distances that may sweep over the top of the building. The blast pressures that may be applied to these roofs are likely to far exceed the conventional design loads and, unless the roof is a concrete deck or concrete slab structure, it may be expected to fail.

The building's lateral load resisting system, the structural frame or shear walls that resist wind and seismic loads, will be required to receive the blast loads that are applied to the exterior facade and transfer them to the building's foundation. This load path is typically through the floor slabs that act as diaphragms and interconnect the different lateral resisting elements. The lateral load resisting system for a school building depends, to a great extent, on the type of construction and region.

In many cases, low-rise buildings do not receive substantial wind and seismic forces and, therefore, do not require substantial lateral load resisting systems. Because blast loads diminish with distance, a package-sized explosive threat is likely to locally overwhelm the facade, thereby limiting the force that may be transferred to the lateral load resisting system. However, the intensity of the blast loads that may be applied to the building could exceed the design limits for most conventional school construction. As a result, the building is likely to be subjected to large inelastic deformations that may produce severe cracks to the structural and nonstructural partitions. There is little that can be done to upgrade the existing school structure to make it more flexible in response to a blast loading that doesn't require extensive renovation of the building. Safe rooms should, therefore, be located close to the interior shear walls or reinforced masonry walls in order to provide maximum structural support in response to these uncharacteristically large lateral loads.

In addition to the hazard of impact by facade debris propelled into the building or roof damage that may rain down, the occupants may also be vulnerable to much heavier debris resulting from structural damage. Progressive collapse occurs when an initiating localized failure causes adjoining members to be overloaded and fail, resulting in an extent of damage that is disproportionate to the originating region of localized failure. The initiating localized failure may result from a sufficiently sized parcel bomb that is in contact with a critical structural element or from a vehicle-sized bomb that is located at a short distance from the structure. However, a large explosive device at a large standoff distance is not likely to selectively cause a single structural member to fail; any damage that results from this scenario is more likely to be widespread and the ensuing collapse cannot be considered progressive. Although progressive collapse is not typically an issue for buildings three stories or shorter, transfer girders or pre-cast construction may produce structural systems that are not tolerant of localized damage conditions.

The columns that support transfer girders and the transfer girders themselves may be critical to the stability of a large area of floor space. Similarly, pre-cast construction that relies on individual structural panels may not be sufficiently tied together to resist the localized damage or large structural deformations that may result from an explosive detonation. As a result, safe rooms should not be located on a structure that is either supported by or underneath a structure that is supported by transfer girders unless a licensed professional engineer evaluates the building. The connection details for multistory pre-cast structures should also be evaluated before the building is used to house a safe room.

Nonstructural building components (e.g., piping, ducts, lighting units, and conduits) that are located within safe rooms must be sufficiently tied back to a competent structure to prevent failure of the services and the hazard of falling debris. To mitigate the effects of in-structure shock that may result from the infilling of blast pressures through damaged windows, the nonstructural systems should be located below the raised floors or tied to the ceiling slabs with seismic restraints.

FRAGMENT MITIGATING UPGRADES

The conversion of existing construction to provide blast-resistant protection requires upgrades to the most fragile or brittle elements enclosing the safe room. Failure of the glazed portion of the facade represents the greatest hazard to the occupants. Therefore, the exterior glazed elements of the school facade and, in particular, the glazed elements of the designated safe rooms should be protected with an FRF, also commonly known as anti-shatter film (ASF), "shatter-resistant window film" (SRWF), or "security film." These materials consist of a laminate that will improve post-damage performance of existing windows. Applied to the interior face of glass, ASF holds the fragments of broken glass together in one sheet, thus reducing the projectile hazard of flying glass fragments. See *FEMA 426 Reference Manual to Mitigate Potential Terrorist Attacks Against Buildings* for more information.

Most ASFs are made from polyester-based materials and coated with adhesives. They are available as clear, with minimal effects to the optical characteristics of the glass, and tinted, which provide a variety of aesthetic and optical enhancements and can increase the effectiveness of existing heating/cooling systems. Most films are designed with solar inhibitors to screen out ultraviolet (UV) rays and are available treated with an abrasion-resistant coating that can prolong the life of tempered glass. However, over time, the UV absorption damages the film and degrades its effectiveness.

According to published reports, testing has shown that a 7-mil thick film, or specially manufactured 4-mil thick film, is the minimum thickness that is required to provide hazard mitigation from blast. Therefore, a 4-mil thick ASF should be utilized only if it has demonstrated, through explosive testing, that it is capable of providing the desired hazard level response.

The application of security film must, at a minimum, cover the clear area of the window. The clear area is defined as the portion of the glass unobstructed by the frame. This minimum application, termed "daylight installation," is commonly used for retrofitting windows. By this method, the film is applied to the exposed glass without any means of attachment or capture within the frame. Application of the film to the edge of the glass panel, thereby extending the film to cover the glass within the bite, is called an edge-to-edge installation and is often used in dry-glazing installations. Other methods of retrofit application may improve the film performance, thereby reducing the hazard; however, these are typically more expensive to install, especially in a retrofit situation.

Although a film may be effective in keeping glass fragments together, it may not be particularly effective in retaining the glass in the frame. ASF is most effective when it is used with a blast-tested anchorage system. Such a system prevents the failed glass from exiting the frame.

The wet-glazed installation, a system where the film is positively attached to the frame, offers more protection than the daylight installation. This system of attaching the film to the frame reduces glass fragmentation entering the building. The wet-glazing system utilizes a high-strength liquid sealant, such as silicone, to attach the glazing system to the frame. This method is more costly than the daylight installation.

Securing the film to the frame with a mechanically connected anchorage system further reduces the likelihood of the glazing system exiting the frame. Mechanical attachment includes anchoring methods that employ screws and/or batten strips that anchor the film to the frame along two or four sides. The mechanical attachment method can be less aesthetically pleasing when compared to wet glazing because additional framework is necessary and is more expensive than the wet-glazed installation.

Window framing systems and their anchorage must be capable of transferring the blast loads to the surrounding walls. Unless the frames and anchorages are competent, the effectiveness of the attached films will be limited. Similarly, the walls must be able to withstand the blast loads that are directly applied to them and accept the blast loads that are transferred by the windows. The strength of these walls may limit the effectiveness of the glazing upgrades.

If a major rehabilitation of the facade is required to improve the mechanical characteristics of the building envelope, a laminated glazing replacement is recommended. Laminated glass consists of two or more pieces of glass permanently bonded together by a tough plastic interlayer made of polyvinyl butyral (PVB) resin. After being sealed together, the glass "sandwich" behaves as a single unit. Annealed, heat-strengthened, tempered glass or polycarbonate glazing can be mixed and matched between layers of laminated glass in order to design the most effective lite for a given application. When fractured, fragments of laminated glass tend to adhere to the PVB interlayer, rather than falling free and potentially causing injury.

Laminated glass can be expected to last as long as ordinary glass provided it is not broken or damaged in any way. It is very important that laminated glass is correctly installed in order to ensure long life. Regardless of the degree of protection required from the window, laminated glass needs to be installed with adequate sealant to prevent water from coming in contact with the edges of the glass. A structural sealant will adhere the glazing to the frame and allow the PVB interlayer to develop its full membrane capacity. Similar to attached film upgrades, the window frames and anchorages must be capable of transferring the blast loads to the surrounding walls.

Blast curtains are made from a variety of materials, including a warp knit fabric or a polyethylene fiber. The fiber can be woven into a panel as thin as 0.029 inch that weighs less than 1.5 ounces per square foot. This fact dispels the myth that blast curtains are heavy sheets of lead that completely obstruct a window opening and eliminate all natural light from the interior of a protected building. The blast curtains are affixed to the interior frame of a window opening and essentially catch the glass fragments produced by a blast wave. The debris is then deposited on the floor at the base of the window. Therefore, the use of these curtains does not eliminate the possibility of glass fragments penetrating the interior of the occupied space, but instead limits the travel distance of the airborne debris. Overall, the hazard level to occupants is significantly reduced by the implementation of the blast curtains. However, a person sitting directly adjacent to a window outfitted with a blast curtain may still be injured by shards of glass in the event of an explosion.

The main components of any blast curtain system are the curtain itself, the attachment mechanism by which the curtain is affixed to the window frame, and either a trough or other retaining mechanism at the base of the window to hold the excess curtain material. The blast curtain, with curtain rod attachment and sill trough, differs largely from one manufacturer to the next. The curtain fabric, material properties, method of attachment, and manner of operation all vary, thereby providing many options within the overall classification of blast curtains. This fact makes blast curtains applicable in many situations.

Blast curtains differ from standard curtains in that they do not open and close in the typical manner. Although blast curtains are intended to remain in a closed position at all times, they may be pulled away from the window to allow for cleaning, blind or shade operation, or occupant egress in the case of fire. However, the curtains can be rendered ineffective if installed such that easy access would provide opportunity for occupants to defeat their operation. The color and openness factor of the fabric contributes to the amount of light that is transmitted through the curtains and the see-through visibility of the curtains. Although the color and weave of these curtains may be varied to suit the aesthetics of the interior décor, the appearance of the windows is altered by the presence of the curtains.

The curtains may either be anchored at the top and bottom of the window frame or anchored at the top only and outfitted with a weighted hem. The curtain needs to be extra long with the surplus either wound around a dynamic tension retainer or stored in a reservoir housing. When an explosion occurs, the curtain feeds out of the receptacle to absorb the force of the flying glass fragments. The effectiveness of the blast curtains relies on their use, and no protection is provided when these curtains are pulled away from the glazing.

Rigid catch bar systems have been designed and tested as a means of increasing the effectiveness of laminated window upgrades. Laminated glazing is designed to hold the glass shards together as the window is damaged; however, unless the window frames and attachments are upgraded as well to withstand the capacity of the glazing, this retrofit will not prevent the entire sheet from flying free of the window frames. The rigid catch bars intercept the laminated glass and disrupt their flight; however, they are limited in their effectiveness, tending to break the dislodged facade materials into smaller projectiles.

Rigid catch bar systems collect huge forces upon impact and require substantial anchorage into a very substantial structure to prevent failure. If either the attachments or the supporting structure are incapable of restraining the forces, the catch system will be dislodged and become part of the debris. Alternatively, the debris may be sliced by the rigid impact and the effectiveness of the catch bar will be severely reduced.

Flexible catch bars can be designed to absorb a significant amount of the energy upon impact, thereby keeping the debris intact and impeding their flight. These systems may be designed to effectively repel the debris and inhibit their flight into the occupied spaces. These systems may be designed to repel the debris from the failed glazing, as well as the walls in which the windows are mounted. The design of the debris restraint system must be strong enough to withstand the momentum transferred upon impact, and the connections must be capable of transferring the forces to the supporting slabs and spandrel beams. However, under no circumstances can the design of the restraint system add significant amounts of mass to the structure that may be dislodged and present an even greater risk to the occupants of the building.

Cables are extensively used to absorb significant amounts of energy upon impact and their flexibility makes them easily adaptable to many situations. The diameter of the cable, the spacing of the strands, and the means of attachment are all critical in designing an effective catch system. Protective design window manufacturers have used these catch cable concepts as restraints for laminated lites. The use of cable systems has long been recognized as an effective means of stopping massive objects moving at high velocity. To confirm the adequacy of the cable catch system to restrain the debris resulting from an explosive event, an analytical simulation or a physical test is required.

High-performance energy-absorbing cable catcher systems retain glass and frame fragments and limit the force transmitted to the supporting structure. These commercially available retrofit products consist of a series of ¼-inch diameter stainless steel cables connected with a shock-absorbing device to an aluminum box section, which is attached to the jambs, the underside of the header, and the topside of the sill. The energy-absorbing characteristics allow the catch systems to be attached to relatively weakly constructed walls without the need for additional costly structural reinforcement. To reduce the possibility of slicing the laminated glass, the cable may either be sheathed in a tube or an aluminum strip may be affixed to the glass directly behind the cable.

Non-reinforced CMU walls provide limited protection against air-blast due to explosions. When subjected to overload from air-blast, brittle non-reinforced CMU walls will fail and the debris will be propelled into the interior of the structure, possibly causing severe injury or death to the occupants. This wall type has been prohibited for new construction where protection against explosive threats is required. Existing non-reinforced CMU walls may be retrofitted with a sprayed-on polymer coating to improve their air-blast resistance. This innovative retrofit technique takes advantage of the toughness and resiliency of modern polymer materials to effectively deform and dissipate the blast energy while containing the shattered wall fragments. Although the sprayed walls may shatter in a blast event, the elastomer material remains intact and contains the debris.

SECTION 4

Acronyms and Abbreviations, Glossary, and Bibliography

Acronyms and Abbreviations

A

AA&E	Arms, Ammunition, and Explosives
AAR	After Action Report
ACL	Access Control List
ACP	Access control point
ACS	Access Control System
ADA	Americans with Disabilities Act
ADAAG	Americans with Disabilities Act Accessibility Guidelines
AECS	Automated Entry Control System
AFJMAN	Air Force Joint Manual, also may be known as AFMAN (I) for Air Force Manual
AFMAN	Air Force Manual
ALERT	Automated Local Evaluation in Real Time
AMS	Aerial Measuring System
ANS	Alert and Notification System
ANSI	American National Standards Institute
ANSIR	Awareness of National Security Issues and Response Program
AOR	Area of Responsibility
AP	Armor piercing
APHL	Agency for Public Health Laboratories
ARAC	Atmospheric Release Advisory Capability
ARC	American Red Cross
ARG	Accident Response Group
ARS	Agriculture Research Service
ASCE	American Society of Civil Engineers
ASHRAE	American Society of Heating, Refrigerating, and Air-Conditioning Engineers
ASTHO	Association for State and Territorial Health Officials
ASTM	American Society for Testing and Materials

ASZM-TED	A copper-silver-zinc-molybdenum-triethylenediamine
AT	Antiterrorism
ATC	Air Traffic Control
ATF	Bureau of Alcohol, Tobacco, and Firearms
ATSD(CS)	Assistant to the Secretary of Defense for Civil Support
ATSDR	Agency for Toxic Substances and Disease Registry
AWG	American wire gauge

B

BCA	Benefit/Cost Analysis
BCC	Backup Control Center
BCP	Business Continuity Plan
BDC	Bomb Data Center
BLASTOP	Blast-Resistant Window Program
BMS	Balanced magnetic switch
BW	Biological warfare

C

CAMEO	Computer-Aided Management of Emergency Operations
CB	Citizens Band
CBIAC	Chemical and Biological Defense Information and Analysis Center
CBR	Chemical, biological, or radiological
CBRNE	Chemical, biological, radiological, nuclear, or explosive
CCTV	Closed circuit television
CDC	Centers for Disease Control and Prevention
CDR	Call Detail Report
CDRG	Catastrophic Disaster Response Group
CEO	Chief Executive Officer
CEPPO	Chemical Emergency Preparedness and Prevention Office
CERCLA	Comprehensive Environmental Response, Compensation, and Liability Act
CERT	Community Emergency Response Team
CFD	Computational Fluid Dynamics
CFO	Chief Financial Officer
CFR	Code of Federal Regulations
CHEMTREC	Chemical Manufacturers' Association Chemical Transportation Emergency Center
CHPPM	Center for Health Promotion and Preventive Medicine
CIAO	Chief Infrastructure Assurance Office
CIAO	Critical Infrastructure Assurance Officer
CICG	Critical Infrastructure Coordination Group
CIO	Chief Information Officer
CIP	Critical Infrastructure Protection
CIRG	Crisis Incident Response Group
CJCS	Chairman of the Joint Chiefs of Staff

CM	Consequence Management
CM	Crisis Management
CMS	Call Management System
CMU	Concrete masonry unit
CMU	Crisis Management Unit (CIRG)
COB	Continuity of Business
COBIT™	Control Objectives for Information Technology
CO/DO	Central Office/Direct Outdial
CONEX	Container Express
CONOPS	Concept of Operations
COO	Chief Operating Officer
COOP	Continuity of Operations Plan
COR	Class of Restriction
COS	Class of Service
CPG	Civil Preparedness Guide
CPTED	Crime Prevention Through Environmental Design
CPX	Command Post Exercise
CRU	Crisis Response Unit
CSEPP	Chemical Stockpile Emergency Preparedness Program
CSI	Construction Specifications Institute
CSREES	Cooperative State Research, Education, and Extension Service
CST	Civil Support Team
CSTE	Council of State and Territorial Epidemiologists
CT	Counterterrorism
CW/CBD	Chemical Warfare/Contraband Detection
D	
DBMS	Database Management System
DBT	Design Basis Threat
DBU	Dial backup
DD	Data Dictionary
DES	Data Encryption Standard
DEST	Domestic Emergency Support Team
DFO	Disaster Field Office
DHS	Department of Homeland Security
DISA	Direct Inward System Access
DMA	Disaster Mitigation Act of 2000
DMAT	Disaster Medical Assistance Team
DMCR	Disaster Management Central Resource
DMORT	Disaster Mortuary Operational Response Team
DOC	Department of Commerce
DoD	Department of Defense
DOE	Department of Energy
DOJ	Department of Justice
DOS	Department of State

DOT	Department of Transportation
DPP	Domestic Preparedness Program
DRC	Disaster Recovery Center
DTCTPS	Domestic Terrorism/Counterterrorism Planning Section (FBI HQ)
DTIC	Defense Technical Information Center
DTM	Data-transmission media
DWI	Disaster Welfare Information

E	
EAS	Emergency Alert System
ECL	Emergency Classification Level
EECS	Electronic Entry Control System
EFR	Emergency First Responder
EM	Emergency Management
EMAC	Emergency Medical Assistance Compact
EMI	Emergency Management Institute
EMP	Electromagnetic pulse
EMS	Emergency Medical Services
EOC	Emergency Operations Center
EOD	Explosive Ordnance Disposal
EOP	Emergency Operating Plan
EOP	Emergency Operations Plan
EPA	Environmental Protection Agency
EPCRA	Emergency Planning and Community Right-to-Know Act
EPG	Emergency Planning Guide
EPI	Emergency Public Information
EP&R	Directorate of Emergency Preparedness and Response (DHS)
EPZ	Emergency Planning Zone
ERP	Emergency Response Plan
ERT	Emergency Response Team
ERT-A	Emergency Response Team Advance Element
ERT-N	Emergency Response Team National
ERTU	Evidence Response Team Unit
ESC	Expandable Shelter Container
ESF	Emergency Support Function
ESS	Electronic Security System
EST	Emergency Support Team
ETL	Engineering Technical Letter
EU	Explosives unit

F	
FAsT	Field Assessment Team
FBI	Federal Bureau of Investigation
FCC	Federal Communications Commission
FCC	Fire Control Center

FCO	Federal Coordinating Officer
FEM	Finite element
FEMA	Federal Emergency Management Agency
FEST	Foreign Emergency Support Team
FHBM	Flood Hazard Boundary Map
FIA	Federal Insurance Administration
FIPS	Federal Information Processing Standard
FIRM	Flood Insurance Rate Map
FIS	Flood Insurance Study
FISCAM	Federal Information Systems Control Audit Manual
FMFIA	Federal Manager's Financial Integrity Act
FNS	Food and Nutrition Service
FOIA	Freedom of Information Act
FOUO	For Official Use Only
FPEIS	Final Programmatic Environmental Impact Statement
FRERP	Federal Radiological Emergency Response Plan
FRF	Fragment retention film
FRL	Facility Restriction Level
FRMAC	Federal Radiological Monitoring and Assessment Center
FRP	Federal Response Plan
FS	Forest Service
FSTFS	Frame-Supported Tensioned Fabric Structure
FTP	File Transfer Protocol
FTX	Functional Training Exercise
G	
GAO	General Accounting Office
GAR	Governor's Authorized Representative
GC/MS	Gas chromatograph/mass spectrometer
GIS	Geographic Information System
GP	General Purpose
GPS	Global Positioning System
GSA	General Services Administration
H	
HazMat	Hazardous material
HAZUS	Hazards U.S.
HEPA	High efficiency particulate air
HEU	Highly enriched uranium
HF	High frequency
HHS	Department of Health and Human Services
HIRA	Hazard Identification and Risk Assessment
HMRU	Hazardous Materials Response Unit
HQ	Headquarters
HRCQ	Highway Route Controlled Quantity

HRT	Hostage Rescue Team (CIRG)
HTIS	Hazardous Technical Information Services (DoD)
HVAC	Heating, ventilation, and air conditioning

I

IC	Incident Commander
ICDDC	Interstate Civil Defense and Disaster Compact
ICP	Incident Command Post
ICS	Incident Command System
ID	Identification
IDS	Intrusion Detection System
IED	Improvised Explosive Device
IEMS	Integrated Emergency Management System
IESNA	Illuminating Engineering Society of North America
IID	Improvised Incendiary Device
IMSion	Mobility spectrometry
IND	Improvised Nuclear Device
IPL	Initial Program Load
IR	Infrared
IRZ	Immediate Response Zone
IS	Information System
ISACF	Information Systems Audit and Control Foundation
ISC	Interagency Security Committee
ISO	International Organization for Standardization
ISP	Internet Service Provider
IT	Information Technology

J

JIC	Joint Information Center
JIISE	Joint Interagency Intelligence Support Element
JIS	Joint Information System
JNACC	Joint Nuclear Accident Coordinating Center
JOC	Joint Operations Center
JSMG	Joint Service Materiel Group
JTF-CS	Joint Task Force for Civil Support
JTTF	Joint Terrorism Task Force
JTWG	Joint Terrorism Working Group

K

| kHz | kilohertz |
| kPa | kilopascal |

L

LAN	Local Area Network
LAW	Light Antitank Weapon
LBNL	Lawrence Berkley National Lab

LCM	Life-cycle Management
LED	Light-emitting diode
LEED	Leadership in Energy and Environmental Design
LEPC	Local Emergency Planning Committee
LF	Low frequency
LFA	Lead Federal Agency
LLNL	Lawrence Livermore National Laboratory
LOP	Level of protection
LOS	Line of sight
LPHA	Local Public Health Agency
LPHS	Local Public Health System

M

MAC	Moves, Adds, Changes
MEDCOM	Medical Command
MEI	Minimum Essential Infrastructure
M/E/P	Mechanical/Electrical/Plumbing
MEP	Mission Essential Process
MERV	Minimum efficiency reporting value
MMRS	Metropolitan Medical Response System
MOU/A	Memorandum of Understanding/Agreement
mph	Miles per hour
MPOP	Minimum-Points-of-Presence
Ms	Millisecond
MSCA	Military Support to Civil Authorities
MSDS	Material Safety Data Sheet
MSS	Medium Shelter System
MW	Medium wave

N

NACCHO	National Association for County and City Health Officials
NAP	Nuclear Assessment Program
NAVFAC	Naval Facilities Command
NBC	Nuclear, biological, and chemical
NCJ	National Criminal Justice
NCP	National Contingency Plan (also known as National Oil and Hazardous Substances Pollution Contingency Plan)
NDA	National Defense Area
NDMS	National Disaster Medical System
NDPO	National Domestic Preparedness Office
NEST	Nuclear Emergency Search Team
NETC	National Emergency Training Center
NFA	National Fire Academy
NFIP	National Flood Insurance Program
NFPA	National Fire Protection Association
NFPC	National Fire Protection Code

NIJ	National Institute of Justice
NIOSH	National Institute for Occupational Safety and Health
NMRT	National Medical Response Team
NMS	Network Management System
NOAA	National Oceanic and Atmospheric Administration
NRC	National Response Center
NRC	Nuclear Regulatory Commission
NRT	National Response Team
NSC	National Security Council
NTIS	National Technical Information Service
NUREG	Nuclear Regulation
NWS	National Weather Service

O

OCC	Operational Control Center
ODP	Office of Disaster Preparedness
OEP	Office of Emergency Preparedness
OES	Office of Emergency Services
OFCM	Office of the Federal Coordinator for Meteorology
OHS	Office of Homeland Security
OJP	Office of Justice Programs
O&M	Operations and maintenance
OMB	Office of Management and Budget
OPA	Oil Pollution Act
OSC	On-scene Coordinator
OSD	Office of Secretary of Defense
OSHA	Occupational Safety and Health Administration
OSLDPS	Office for State and Local Domestic Preparedness Support

P

Pa	Pascal
PA	Public address
PAZ	Protective Action Zone
PBX	Public Branch Exchange
PC	Personal computer
PCC	Policy Coordinating Committee
PCCIP	President's Commission on Critical Infrastructure Protection
PCM	Procedures Control Manual
PDA	Personal data assistant
PDA	Preliminary Damage Assessment
PDD	Presidential Decision Directive
PHS	Public Health Service
PIN	Personal Identification Number
PIO	Public Information Officer
PL	Public Law

POC	Point of Contact
POD	Probability of detection
POI	Probability of intrusion
POL	Petroleum, Oils, and Lubricants
POV	Privately owned vehicle
PPA	Performance Partnership Agreement
Ppm	Parts per million
PSE	Particle size efficiency
Psi	Pounds per square inch
PT	Preparedness, Training, and Exercises Directorate (FEMA)
PTE	Potential Threat Element
PTZ	Pan-tilt-zoom (camera)
PVB	Polyvinyl butyral
PZ	Precautionary Zone

R

RACES	Radio Amateur Civil Emergency Service
RAP	Radiological Assistance Program
RCRA	Research Conservation and Recovery Act
RDD	Radiological Dispersal Device
RDT&E	Research, Development, Test, and Evaluation
REACT	Radio Emergency Associated Communications Team
REAC/TS	Radiation Emergency Assistance Center/Training Site
REM	Roentgen Man Equivalent
REP	Radiological Emergency Preparedness Program
RF	Radio frequency
ROC	Regional Operations Center
ROD	Record of Decision
RPG	Rocket Propelled Grenade
RRIS	Rapid Response Information System (FEMA)
RRP	Regional Response Plan
RRT	Regional Response Team

S

SAA	State Administrative Agency
SAC	Special Agent in Charge (FBI)
SAFEVU	Safety Viewport Analysis Code
SAME	Specific Area Message Encoder
SARA	Superfund Amendments and Reauthorization Act
SATCOM	Satellite communications
SAW	Surface acoustic wave
SBCCOM	Soldier and Biological Chemical Command (U.S. Army)
SCADA	Supervisory, Control, and Data Acquisition
SCBA	Self-Contained Breathing Apparatus
SCC	Security Control Center

SCO	State Coordinating Officer
SDO	Single-degree-of-freedom
SEA	Southeast Asia
SEB	State Emergency Board
SEL	Standardized Equipment List
SEMA	State Emergency Management Agency
SERC	State Emergency Response Commission
SFO	Senior FEMA Official
SIOC	Strategic Information and Operations Center (FBI HQ)
SLA	Service Level Agreement
SLG	State and Local Guide
SNM	Special Nuclear Material
SOP	Standard Operating Procedure
SPCA	Society for the Prevention of Cruelty to Animals
SPSA	Super Power Small Arms
SSS	Small Shelter System
STC	Sound Transmission Class
SWAT	Special Weapons and Tactics

T

TAC	Trunk Access Codes
TDR	Transferable development right
TEA	Threat Environment Assessment
TEMPER	Tent, Extendable, Modular, Personnel
TERC	Tribal Emergency Response Commission
TIA	Terrorist Incident Appendix
TIM	toxic industrial material
TM	Technical Manual
TNT	Trinitrotoluene
TRIS	Toxic Release Inventory System
TSC	Triple-standard concertina
TSO	Time Share Option
TTG	Thermally tempered glass

U

UC	Unified Command
UCS	Unified Command System
UFAS	Uniform Federal Accessibility Standards
UFC	Unified Facilities Criteria
UL	Underwriters Laboratories
ULPA	Ultra low penetration air
UPS	Uninterrupted power supply
URV	UVGI Rating Values
U.S.	United States
USA	United States Army

USAF	United States Air Force
USC	U.S. Code
USDA	U.S. Department of Agriculture
USFA	U.S. Fire Administration
USGBC	U.S. Green Building Council
USGS	U.S. Geological Survey
US&R	Urban Search and Rescue
UV	Ultraviolet
UVGI	Ultraviolet germicidal irradiation

V

VA	Department of Veterans Affairs
VAP	Vulnerability Assessment Plan
VAV	Variable Air Volume
VDN	Vector Directory Number
VHF	Very high frequency
VRU	Voice Response Unit

W

WAN	Wide Area Network
wg	Water gauge
WINGARD	Window Glazing Analysis Response and Design
WINLAC	Window Lite Analysis Code
WMD	Weapons of Mass Destruction
WMD-CST	WMD Civil Support Tea

Glossary

A

Access control.   Any combination of barriers, gates, electronic security equipment, and/or guards that can deny entry to unauthorized personnel or vehicles.

Access-control point (ACP).   A station at an entrance to a building or a portion of a building where identification is checked, and people and hand-carried items are searched.

Access controls.   Procedures and controls that limit or detect access to minimum essential infrastructure resource elements (e.g., people, technology, applications, data, and/or facilities), thereby protecting these resources against loss of integrity, confidentiality, accountability, and/or availability.

Access-Control System (ACS).   Also referred to as an Electronic Entry Control Systems; an electronic system that controls entry and egress from a building or area.

Access-Control System elements.   Detection measures used to control vehicle or personnel entry into a protected area. Access-Control System elements include locks, Electronic Entry Control Systems, and guards.

Access group. A software configuration of an Access Control System that groups together access points or authorized users for easier arrangement and maintenance of the system.

Access road. Any roadway such as a maintenance, delivery, service, emergency, or other special limited use road that is necessary for the operation of a building or structure.

Accountability. The explicit assignment of responsibilities for oversight of areas of control to executives, managers, staff, owners, providers, and users of minimum essential infrastructure resource elements.

Acoustic eavesdropping. The use of listening devices to monitor voice communications or other audibly transmitted information with the objective to compromise information.

Active vehicle barrier. An impediment placed at an access-control point that may be manually or automatically deployed in response to detection of a threat.

Aerosol. Fine liquid or solid particles suspended in a gas (e.g., fog or smoke).

Aggressor. Any person seeking to compromise a function or structure.

Airborne contamination. Chemical or biological agents introduced into and fouling the source of supply of breathing or conditioning air.

Airlock. A building entry configuration with which airflow from the outside can be prevented from entering a toxic-free area. An airlock uses two doors, only one of which can be opened at a time, and a blower system to maintain positive air pressures and purge contaminated air from the airlock before the second door is opened.

Alarm assessment. Verification and evaluation of an alarm alert through the use of closed circuit television or human observation. Systems used for alarm assessment are designed to respond rapidly, automatically, and predictably to the receipt of alarms at the security center.

Alarm printers. Alarm printers provide a hard copy of all alarm events and system activity, as well as limited backup in case the visual display fails.

Alarm priority. A hierarchy of alarms by order of importance. This is often used in larger systems to give priority to alarms with greater importance.

Annunciation. A visual, audible, or other indication by a security system of a condition.

Antiterrorism (AT). Defensive measures used to reduce the vulnerability of individuals, forces, and property to terrorist acts.

Area Commander. A military commander with authority in a specific geographical area or military installation.

Area lighting. Lighting that illuminates a large exterior area.

Areas of potential compromise. Categories where losses can occur that will impact either a department's or an agency's minimum essential infrastructure and its ability to conduct core functions and activities.

Assessment. The evaluation and interpretation of measurements and other information to provide a basis for decision making.

Assessment System elements. Detection measures used to assist guards in visual verification of Intrusion Detection System Alarms and Access-Control System functions and to assist in visual detection by guards. Assessment System elements include closed circuit television and protective lighting.

Asset.   A resource of value requiring protection. An asset can be tangible (e.g., people, buildings, facilities, equipment, activities, operations, and information) or intangible (e.g., processes or a company's information and reputation).

Asset protection.   Security program designed to protect personnel, facilities, and equipment, in all locations and situations, accomplished through planned and integrated application of combating terrorism, physical security, operations security, and personal protective services, and supported by intelligence, counterintelligence, and other security programs.

Asset value.   The degree of debilitating impact that would be caused by the incapacity or destruction of an asset.

Attack.   A hostile action resulting in the destruction, injury, or death to the civilian population, or damage or destruction to public and private property.

Audible alarm device.   An alarm device that produces an audible announcement (e.g., bell, horn, siren, etc.) of an alarm condition.

B

Balanced magnetic switch.   A door position switch utilizing a reed switch held in a balanced or center position by interacting magnetic fields when not in alarm condition.

Ballistics attack.   An attack in which small arms (e.g., pistols, submachine guns, shotguns, and rifles) are fired from a distance, and rely on the flight of the projectile to damage the target.

Barbed tape or concertina.   A coiled tape or coil of wires with wire barbs or blades deployed as an obstacle to human trespass or entry into an area.

Barbed wire.   A double strand of wire with four-point barbs equally spaced along the wire deployed as an obstacle to human trespass or entry into an area.

Barcode.   A black bar printed on white paper or tape that can be easily read with an optical scanner.

Biological agents.   Living organisms or the materials derived from them that cause disease in or harm to humans, animals, or plants or cause deterioration of material. Biological agents may be used as liquid droplets, aerosols, or dry powders.

Biometric reader.   A device that gathers and analyzes biometric features.

Biometrics.   The use of physical characteristics of the human body as a unique identification method.

Blast curtains.   Heavy curtains made of blast-resistant materials that could protect the occupants of a room from flying debris.

Blast-resistant glazing.   Window opening glazing that is resistant to blast effects because of the interrelated function of the frame and glazing material properties frequently dependent upon tempered glass, polycarbonate, or laminated glazing.

Blast vulnerability envelope.   The geographical area in which an explosive device will cause damage to assets.

Bollard.   A vehicle barrier consisting of a cylinder, usually made of steel and sometimes filled with concrete, placed on end in the ground and spaced about three feet apart to prevent vehicles from passing, but allowing entrance of pedestrians and bicycles.

Boundary penetration sensor.   An interior intrusion detection sensor that detects attempts by individuals to penetrate or enter a building.

Building hardening.   Enhanced construction that reduces vulnerability to external blast and ballistic attacks.

Building separation.   The distance between closest points on the exterior walls of adjacent buildings or structures.

Business Continuity Program (BCP).   An ongoing process supported by senior management and funded to ensure that the necessary steps are taken to identify the impact of potential losses, maintain viable recovery strategies and recovery plans, and ensure continuity services through personnel training, plan testing, and maintenance.

C

Cable barrier.   Cable or wire rope anchored to and suspended off the ground or attached to chain-link fence to act as a barrier to moving vehicles.

Capacitance sensor.   A device that detects an intruder approaching or touching a metal object by sensing a change in capacitance between the object and the ground.

Card reader.   A device that gathers or reads information when a card is presented as an identification method.

Chemical agent.   A chemical substance that is intended to kill, seriously injure, or incapacitate people through physiological effects. Generally separated by severity of effect (e.g., lethal, blister, and incapacitating).

Chimney effect.   Air movement in a building between floors caused by differential air temperature (differences in density), between the air inside and outside the building. It occurs in vertical shafts, such as elevators, stairwells, and conduit/wiring/piping chases. Hotter air inside the building will rise and be replaced by infiltration with colder outside air through the lower portions of the building. Conversely, reversing the temperature will reverse the flow (down the chimney). Also known as stack effect.

Clear zone.   An area that is clear of visual obstructions and landscape materials that could conceal a threat or perpetrator.

Closed circuit television (CCTV).   An electronic system of cameras, control equipment, recorders, and related apparatus used for surveillance or alarm assessment.

CCTV pan-tilt-zoom camera (PTZ).   A CCTV camera that can move side to side, up and down, and zoom in or out.

CCTV pan-tilt-zoom control.   The method of controlling the PTZ functions of a camera.

CCTV pan-tilt-zoom controller.   The operator interface for performing PTZ control.

CCTV switcher.   A piece of equipment capable of presenting multiple video images to various monitors, recorders, etc.

Collateral damage.   Injury or damage to assets that are not the primary target of an attack.

Combating terrorism.   The full range of federal programs and activities applied against terrorism, domestically and abroad, regardless of the source or motive.

Community.   A political entity that has the authority to adopt and enforce laws and ordinances for the area under its jurisdiction. In most cases, the community is an incorporated town, city, township, village, or unincorporated area of a county; however, each state defines its own political subdivisions and forms of government.

Components and cladding.   Elements of the building envelope that do not qualify as part of the main wind-force resisting system.

Confidentiality. The protection of sensitive information against unauthorized disclosure and sensitive facilities from physical, technical, or electronic penetration or exploitation.

Consequence Management. Measures to protect public health and safety, restore essential government services, and provide emergency relief to governments, businesses, and individuals affected by the consequences of terrorism. State and local governments exercise the primary authority to respond to the consequences of terrorism.

Contamination. The undesirable deposition of a chemical, biological, or radiological material on the surface of structures, areas, objects, or people.

Continuity of services and operations. Controls to ensure that, when unexpected events occur, departmental/agency minimum essential infrastructure services and operations, including computer operations, continue without interruption or are promptly resumed, and that critical and sensitive data are protected through adequate contingency and business recovery plans and exercises.

Control center. A centrally located room or facility staffed by personnel charged with the oversight of specific situations and/or equipment.

Controlled area. An area into which access is controlled or limited. It is that portion of a restricted area usually near or surrounding a limited or exclusion area. Correlates with exclusion zone.

Controlled lighting. Illumination of specific areas or sections.

Controlled perimeter. A physical boundary at which vehicle and personnel access is controlled at the perimeter of a site. Access control at a controlled perimeter should demonstrate the capability to search individuals and vehicles.

Conventional construction. Building construction that is not specifically designed to resist weapons, explosives, or chemical, biological, and radiological effects. Conventional construction is designed only to resist common loadings and environmental effects such as wind, seismic, and snow loads.

Coordinate. To advance systematically an exchange of information among principals who have or may have a need to know certain information in order to carry out their roles in a response.

Counterintelligence. Information gathered and activities conducted to protect against espionage, other intelligence activities, sabotage, or assassinations conducted for or on behalf of foreign powers, organizations, or persons; or international terrorist activities, excluding personnel, physical, document, and communications security programs.

Counterterrorism (CT). Offensive measures taken to prevent, deter, and respond to terrorism.

Covert entry. Attempts to enter a facility by using false credentials or stealth.

Crash bar. A mechanical egress device located on the interior side of a door that unlocks the door when pressure is applied in the direction of egress.

Crime Prevention Through Environmental Design (CPTED). A crime prevention strategy based on evidence that the design and form of the built environment can influence human behavior. CPTED usually involves the use of three principles: natural surveillance (by placing physical features, activities, and people to maximize visibility); natural access control (through the judicial placement of entrances, exits, fencing, landscaping, and lighting); and territorial reinforcement (using buildings, fences, pavement, signs, and landscaping to express ownership).

Crisis Management (CM).   The measures taken to identify, acquire and plan the use of resources needed to anticipate, prevent, and/or resolve a threat or act of terrorism.

Critical assets.   Those assets essential to the minimum operations of the organization, and to ensure the health and safety of the general public.

Critical infrastructure.   Primary infrastructure systems (e.g., utilities, telecommunications, transportation, etc.) whose incapacity would have a debilitating impact on the organization's ability to function.

D

Damage assessment.   The process used to appraise or determine the number of injuries and deaths, damage to public and private property, and the status of key facilities and services (e.g., hospitals and other health care facilities, fire and police stations, communications networks, water and sanitation systems, utilities, and transportation networks) resulting from a man-made or natural disaster.

Data gathering panel.   A local processing unit that retrieves, processes, stores, and/or acts on information in the field.

Data transmission equipment.   A path for transmitting data between two or more components (e.g., a sensor and alarm reporting system, a card reader and controller, a CCTV camera and monitor, or a transmitter and receiver).

Decontamination.   The reduction or removal of a chemical, biological, or radiological material from the surface of a structure, area, object, or person.

Defense layer.   Building design or exterior perimeter barriers intended to delay attempted forced entry.

Defensive measures.   Protective measures that delay or prevent attack on an asset or that shield the asset from weapons, explosives, and CBR effects. Defensive measures include site work and building design.

Delay rating.   A measure of the effectiveness of penetration protection of a defense layer.

Design Basis Threat (DBT).   The threat (e.g., tactics and associated weapons, tools, or explosives) against which assets within a building must be protected and upon which the security engineering design of the building is based.

Design constraint.   Anything that restricts the design options for a protective system or that creates additional problems for which the design must compensate.

Design opportunity.   Anything that enhances protection, reduces requirements for protective measures, or solves a design problem.

Design team.   A group of individuals from various engineering and architectural disciplines responsible for the protective system design.

Detection layer.   A ring of intrusion detection sensors located on or adjacent to a defensive layer or between two defensive layers.

Detection measures.   Protective measures that detect intruders, weapons, or explosives; assist in assessing the validity of detection; control access to protected areas; and communicate the appropriate information to the response force. Detection measures include Detection Systems, Assessment Systems, and Access Control System elements.

Detection System elements.   Detection measures that detect the presence of intruders, weapons, or explosives. Detection System elements include Intrusion Detection Systems, weapons and explosives detectors, and guards.

Disaster.   An occurrence of a natural catastrophe, technological accident, or human-caused event that has resulted in severe property damage, deaths, and/or multiple injuries.

Disaster Field Office (DFO).   The office established in or near the designated area of a presidential-declared major disaster to support federal and state response and recovery operations.

Disaster Recovery Center (DRC).   Places established in the area of a presidential-declared major disaster, as soon as practicable, to provide victims the opportunity to apply in person for assistance, and/or obtain information relating to that assistance.

Domestic terrorism.   The unlawful use, or threatened use, of force or violence by a group or individual based and operating entirely within the United States or Puerto Rico without foreign direction committed against persons or property to intimidate or coerce a government, the civilian population, or any segment thereof in further-ance of political or social objectives.

Door position switch.   A switch that changes state based on whether or not a door is closed. Typically, a switch mounted in a frame that is actuated by a magnet in a door.

Door strike, electronic.   An electromechanical lock that releases a door plunger to unlock the door. Typically, an electronic door strike is mounted in place of or near a normal door strike plate.

Dose rate (radiation).   A general term indicating the quantity (total or accumulated) of ionizing radiation or energy absorbed by a person or animal, per unit of time.

Dosimeter.   An instrument for measuring and registering total accumulated exposure to ionizing radiation.

Dual technology sensor.   A sensor that combines two different technologies in one unit.

Duress alarm devices.   Also known as panic buttons, these devices are designated specif-ically to initiate a panic alarm.

E

Effective standoff distance.   A standoff distance at which the required level of protec-tion can be shown to be achieved through analysis or can be achieved through build-ing hardening or other mitigating construction or retrofit.

Electromagnetic pulse (EMP).   A sharp pulse of energy radiated instantaneously by a nuclear detonation that may affect or damage electronic components and equip-ment. EMP can also be generated in lesser intensity by non-nuclear means in specific frequency ranges to perform the same disruptive function.

Electronic emanations.   Electromagnetic emissions from computers, communications, electronics, wiring, and related equipment.

Electronic-emanations eavesdropping.   Use of electronic-emanation surveillance equipment from outside a facility or its restricted area to monitor electronic emana-tions from computers, communications, and related equipment.

Electronic Entry Control Systems (EECS).   Electronic devices that automatically verify authorization for a person to enter or exit a controlled area.

Electronic Security System (ESS).   An integrated system that encompasses interior and exterior sensors, closed circuit television systems for assessment of alarm con-ditions, Electronic Entry Control Systems, data transmission media and alarm reporting systems for monitoring, control and display of various alarm and system information.

Emergency.   Any natural or human-caused situation that results in or may result in substantial injury or harm to the population or substantial damage to or loss of property.

Emergency Alert System (EAS).   A communications system of broadcast stations and interconnecting facilities authorized by the Federal Communications Commission (FCC). The system provides the president and other national, state, and local officials the means to broadcast emergency information to the public before, during, and after disasters.

Emergency Environmental Health Services.   Services required to correct or improve damaging environmental health effects on humans, including inspection for food contamination, inspection for water contamination, and vector control; providing for sewage and solid waste inspection and disposal; cleanup and disposal of hazardous materials; and sanitation inspection for emergency shelter facilities.

Emergency Medical Services (EMS).   Services including personnel, facilities, and equipment required to ensure proper medical care for the sick and injured from the time of injury to the time of final disposition, including medical disposition within a hospital, temporary medical facility, or special care facility; release from the site; or declared dead. Further, Emergency Medical Services specifically include those services immediately required to ensure proper medical care and specialized treatment for patients in a hospital and coordination of related hospital services.

Emergency Mortuary Services.   Services required to assure adequate death investigation, identification, and disposition of bodies; removal, temporary storage, and transportation of bodies to temporary morgue facilities; notification of next of kin; and coordination of mortuary services and burial of unclaimed bodies.

Emergency Operations Center (EOC).   The protected site from which state and local civil government officials coordinate, monitor, and direct emergency response activities during an emergency.

Emergency Operations Plan (EOP).   A document that describes how people and property will be protected in disaster and disaster threat situations; details who is responsible for carrying out specific actions; identifies the personnel, equipment, facilities, supplies, and other resources available for use in the disaster; and outlines how all actions will be coordinated.

Emergency Planning Zones (EPZ).   Areas around a facility for which planning is needed to ensure prompt and effective actions are taken to protect the health and safety of the public if an accident or disaster occurs. In the Radiological Emergency Preparedness Program, there are two EPZs. **Plume Exposure Pathway** (ten-mile EPZ): A circular geographic zone (with a ten-mile radius centered at the nuclear power plant) for which plans are developed to protect the public against exposure to radiation emanating from a radioactive plume caused as a result of an accident at the nuclear power plant. **Ingestion Pathway** (fifty-mile EPZ): A circular geographic zone (with a fifty-mile radius centered at the nuclear power plant) for which plans are developed to protect the public from the ingestion of water or food contaminated as a result of a nuclear power plant accident. In the Chemical Stockpile Emergency Preparedness Program (CSEPP), the EPZ is divided into three concentric circular zones: **Immediate Response Zone (IRZ):** A circular zone ranging from ten to fifteen kilometers (six to nine miles) from the potential chemical event source, depending on the stockpile location on-post. Emergency response plans developed for the IRZ must provide for the most rapid and effective protective actions possible, because the IRZ will have the highest concentration of agent and the least amount of warning time. **Protective Action Zone (PAZ):** An area that extends beyond the IRZ to approximately sixteen to fifty kilometers (ten to thirty miles) from the stockpile location. The PAZ is that area where public protective actions may still be necessary in case of an accidental release of chemical agent, but where the available warning and response time is such that most people could evacuate. However, other responses (e.g., sheltering) may be appropriate for institutions and special populations that could not evacuate within the available time. **Precautionary Zone** (PZ). The outermost portion of the EPZ for CSEPP, extending from the PAZ outer boundary to a distance where the risk of adverse impacts to humans is negligible. Because of the increased warning and response time available for implementation of response actions in the PZ, detailed local emergency planning is not required, although Consequence Management planning may be appropriate.

Emergency Public Information (EPI). Information that is disseminated primarily in anticipation of an emergency or at the actual time of an emergency and, in addition to providing information frequently directs actions, instructs, and transmits direct orders.

Emergency Response Team (ERT). An interagency team, consisting of the lead representative from each federal department or agency assigned primary responsibility for an ESF and key members of the FCO's staff, formed to assist the FCO in carrying out his or her coordination responsibilities.

Emergency Response Team Advance Element (ERT-A). For federal disaster response and recovery activities under the Stafford Act, the portion of the ERT that is first deployed to the field to respond to a disaster incident. The ERT-A is the nucleus of the full ERT.

Emergency Response Team National (ERT-N). An ERT that has been established and rostered for deployment to catastrophic disasters where the resources of the FEMA Region have been, or are expected to be, overwhelmed. Three ERT-Ns have been established.

Emergency Support Function (ESF). In the Federal Response Plan (FRP), a functional area of response activity established to facilitate the delivery of federal assistance required during the immediate response phase of a disaster to save lives, protect property and public health, and maintain public safety. ESFs represent those types of federal assistance that the state will most likely need because of the impact of a catastrophic or significant disaster on its own resources and response capabilities, or because of the specialized or unique nature of the assistance required. ESF missions are designed to supplement state and local response efforts.

Emergency Support Team (EST). An interagency group operating from FEMA Headquarters. The EST oversees the national-level response support effort under the FRP and coordinates activities with the ESF primary and support agencies in supporting federal requirements in the field.

Entity-wide security.   Planning and management that provides a framework and continuing cycle of activity for managing risk, developing security policies, assigning responsibilities, and monitoring the adequacy of the entity's physical and cyber security controls.

Entry control point.   A continuously or intermittently manned station at which entry to sensitive or restricted areas is controlled.

Entry control stations.   Entry control stations should be provided at main perimeter entrances where security personnel are present. Entry control stations should be located as close as practical to the perimeter entrance to permit personnel inside the station to maintain constant surveillance over the entrance and its approaches.

Equipment closet.   A room where field control equipment, such as data gathering panels and power supplies, are typically located.

Evacuation.   Organized, phased, and supervised dispersal of people from dangerous or potentially dangerous areas.

Evacuation, mandatory or directed.   This is a warning to persons within the designated area that an imminent threat to life and property exists and individuals MUST evacuate in accordance with the instructions of local officials.

Evacuation, spontaneous.   Residents or citizens in the threatened areas observe an emergency event or receive unofficial word of an actual or perceived threat and, without receiving instructions to do so, elect to evacuate the area. Their movement, means, and direction of travel are unorganized and unsupervised.

Evacuation, voluntary.   This is a warning to persons within a designated area that a threat to life and property exists or is likely to exist in the immediate future. Individuals, issued this type of warning or order, are NOT required to evacuate; however, it would be to their advantage to do so.

Evacuees.   All persons removed or moving from areas threatened or struck by a disaster.

Exclusion area.   A restricted area containing a security interest. Uncontrolled movement permits direct access to the item. *See* controlled area and limited area.

Exclusion zone.   An area around an asset that has controlled entry with highly restrictive access. See controlled area.

Explosives disposal container.   A small container into which small quantities of explosives may be placed to contain their blast pressures and fragments if the explosive detonates.

F

Facial recognition.   A biometric technology that is based on features of the human face.

Federal Coordinating Officer (FCO).   The person appointed by the FEMA Director to coordinate federal assistance in a presidential-declared emergency or major disaster.

Federal On-scene Commander.   The FBI official designated upon JOC activation to ensure appropriate coordination of the overall U.S. government response with federal, state, and local authorities, until such time as the attorney general transfers the LFA role to FEMA.

Federal Response Plan (FRP).   The FRP establishes a process and structure for the systematic, coordinated, and effective delivery of federal assistance to address the consequences of any major disaster or emergency.

Fence protection.   An intrusion detection technology that detects a person crossing a fence by various methods, such as climbing, crawling, cutting, etc.

Fence sensor.   An exterior intrusion detection sensor that detects aggressors as they attempt to climb over, cut through, or otherwise disturb a fence.

Fiber optics.   A method of data transfer by passing bursts of light through a strand of glass or clear plastic.

Field Assessment Team (FAsT).   A small team of pre-identified technical experts that conducts an assessment of response needs (not a PDA) immediately following a disaster.

Field of view.   The visible area in a video picture.

First responder.   Local police, fire, and emergency medical personnel who first arrive on the scene of an incident and take action to save lives, protect property, and meet basic human needs.

Flash flood.   Follows a situation in which rainfall is so intense and severe and runoff so rapid that it precludes recording and relating it to stream stages and other information in time to forecast a flood condition.

Flood.   A general and temporary condition of partial or complete inundation of normally dry land areas from overflow of inland or tidal waters, unusual or rapid accumulation or runoff of surface waters, or mudslides/mudflows caused by accumulation of water.

Forced entry.   Entry to a denied area achieved through force to create an opening in fence, walls, doors, etc., or to overpower guards.

Fragment retention film (FRF).   A thin, optically clear film applied to glass to minimize the spread of glass fragments when the glass is shattered.

Frame rate.   In digital video, a measurement of the rate of change in a series of pictures, often measured in frames per second (fps).

Frangible construction.   Building components that are designed to fail to vent blast pressures from an enclosure in a controlled manner and direction.

G

Glare security lighting.   Illumination projected from a secure perimeter into the surrounding area, making it possible to see potential intruders at a considerable distance while making it difficult to observe activities within the secure perimeter.

Glass-break detector.   An intrusion detection sensor that is designed to detect breaking glass either through vibration or acoustics.

Glazing.   A material installed in a sash, ventilator, or panes (e.g., glass, plastic, etc., including material, such as thin granite installed in a curtain wall).

Governor's Authorized Representative (GAR).   The person empowered by the governor to execute, on behalf of the state, all necessary documents for disaster assistance.

Grid wire sensor.   An intrusion detection sensor that uses a grid of wires to cover a wall or fence. An alarm is sounded if the wires are cut.

H

Hand geometry.   A biometric technology that is based on characteristics of the human hand.

Hazard.   A source of potential danger or adverse condition.

Hazard mitigation.   Any action taken to reduce or eliminate the long-term risk to human life and property from hazards. The term is sometimes used in a stricter sense to mean cost-effective measures to reduce the potential for damage to a facility or facilities from a disaster event.

Hazardous material (HazMat).   Any substance or material that, when involved in an accident and released in sufficient quantities, poses a risk to people's health, safety, and/or property. These substances and materials include explosives, radioactive materials, flammable liquids or solids, combustible liquids or solids, poisons, oxidizers, toxins, and corrosive materials.

High-hazard areas.   Geographic locations that, for planning purposes, have been determined through historical experience and vulnerability analysis to be likely to experience the effects of a specific hazard (e.g., hurricane, earthquake, hazardous materials accident, etc.), resulting in vast property damage and loss of life.

High-risk target.   Any material resource or facility that, because of mission sensitivity, ease of access, isolation, and symbolic value, may be an especially attractive or accessible terrorist target.

Human-caused hazard.   Human-caused hazards are technological hazards and terrorism. They are distinct from natural hazards primarily in that they originate from human activity. Within the military services, the term "threat" is typically used for human-caused hazard. *See* definitions of technological hazards and terrorism for further information.

Hurricane.   A tropical cyclone, formed in the atmosphere over warm ocean areas, in which wind speeds reach seventy-four miles per hour or more and blow in a large spiral around a relatively calm center or "eye." Circulation is counter-clockwise in the Northern Hemisphere and clockwise in the Southern Hemisphere.

I

Impact analysis.   A management-level analysis that identifies the impacts of losing the entity's resources. The analysis measures the effect of resource loss and escalating losses over time in order to provide the entity with reliable data upon which to base decisions on hazard mitigation and continuity planning.

Incident Command System (ICS).   A standardized organizational structure used to command, control, and coordinate the use of resources and personnel that have responded to the scene of an emergency. The concepts and principles for ICS include common terminology, modular organization, integrated communication, unified command structure, consolidated action plan, manageable span of control, designated incident facilities, and comprehensive resource management.

Insider compromise.   A person, authorized access to a facility (an insider), compromises assets by taking advantage of that accessibility.

Intercom door/gate station.   Part of an intercom system where communication is typically initiated, usually located at a door or gate.

Intercom master station.   Part of an intercom system that monitors one or more intercom door/gate stations; typically, where initial communication is received.

Intercom switcher.   Part of an intercom system that controls the flow of communications between various stations.

Intercom System.   An electronic system that allows simplex, half-duplex, or full-duplex audio communications.

International terrorism.   Violent acts or acts dangerous to human life that are a violation of the criminal laws of the United States or any state, or that would be a criminal violation if committed within the jurisdiction of the United States or any state. These acts appear to be intended to intimidate or coerce a civilian population, influence the policy of a government by intimidation or coercion, or affect the conduct of a government by assassination or kidnapping. International terrorist acts occur outside the United States, or transcend national boundaries in terms of the means by which they are accomplished, the persons they appear intended to coerce or intimidate, or the locale in which their perpetrators operate or seek asylum.

Intrusion Detection Sensor.   A device that initiates alarm signals by sensing the stimulus, change, or condition for which it was designed.

Intrusion Detection System (IDS).   The combination of components, including sensors, control units, transmission lines, and monitor units, integrated to operate in a specified manner.

Isolated fenced perimeters.   Fenced perimeters with a hundred feet or more of space outside the fence that is clear of obstruction, making approach obvious.

J

Jersey barrier.   A protective concrete barrier initially and still used as a highway divider that now also functions as an expedient method for traffic speed control at entrance gates and to keep vehicles away from buildings.

Joint Information Center (JIC).   A central point of contact for all news media near the scene of a large-scale disaster. News media representatives are kept informed of activities and events by Public Information Officers who represent all participating federal, state, and local agencies that are collocated at the JIC.

Joint Information System (JIS).   Under the FRP, connection of public affairs personnel, decision makers, and news centers by electronic mail, fax, and telephone when a single federal-state-local JIC is not a viable option.

Joint Interagency Intelligence Support Element (JIISE).   An interagency intelligence component designed to fuse intelligence information from the various agencies participating in a response to a WMD threat or incident within an FBI JOC. The JIISE is an expanded version of the investigative/intelligence component that is part of the standardized FBI command post structure. The JIISE manages five functions, including security, collections management, current intelligence, exploitation, and dissemination.

Joint Operations Center (JOC).   Established by the LFA under the operational control of the federal OSC, as the focal point for management and direction of on-site activities, coordination/establishment of state requirements/priorities, and coordination of the overall federal response.

Jurisdiction.   Typically counties and cities within a state, but states may elect to define differently in order to facilitate their assessment process.

L

Laminated glass.   A flat lite of uniform thickness consisting of two monolithic glass plies bonded together with an interlayer material as defined in Specification C1172. Many different interlayer materials are used in laminated glass.

Landscaping.   The use of plantings (shrubs and trees), with or without landforms and/or large boulders, to act as a perimeter barrier against defined threats.

Laser card.   A card technology that uses a laser reflected off of a card for uniquely identifying the card.

Layers of protection.   A traditional approach in security engineering using concentric circles extending out from an area to be protected as demarcation points for different security strategies.

Lead Agency.   The federal department or agency assigned lead responsibility under U.S. law to manage and coordinate the federal response in a specific functional area.

Lead Federal Agency (LFA).   The agency designated by the president to lead and coordinate the overall federal response is referred to as the LFA and is determined by the type of emergency. In general, an LFA establishes operational structures and procedures to assemble and work with agencies providing direct support to the LFA in order to provide an initial assessment of the situation, develop an action plan, monitor and update operational priorities, and ensure each agency exercises its concurrent and distinct authorities under U.S. law and supports the LFA in carrying out the president's relevant policy. Specific responsibilities of an LFA vary, according to the agency's unique statutory authorities.

Level of protection (LOP).   The degree to which an asset is protected against injury or damage from an attack.

Liaison.   An agency official sent to another agency to facilitate interagency communications and coordination.

Limited area.   A restricted area within close proximity of a security interest. Uncontrolled movement may permit access to the item. Escorts and other internal restrictions may prevent access to the item. *See* controlled area and exclusion area.

Line of sight (LOS).   Direct observation between two points with the naked eye or hand-held optics.

Line-of-sight sensor.   A pair of devices used as an intrusion detection sensor that monitor any movement through the field between the sensors.

Line supervision.   A data integrity strategy that monitors the communications link for connectivity and tampering. In Intrusion Detection System sensors, line supervision is often referred to as two-state, three-state, or four-state in respect to the number of conditions monitored. The frequency of sampling the link also plays a big part in the supervision of the line.

Local government.   Any county, city, village, town, district, or political subdivision of any state, and Indian tribe or authorized tribal organization, or Alaska Native village or organization, including any rural community or unincorporated town or village or any other public entity.

M

Magnetic lock.   An electromagnetic lock that unlocks a door when power is removed.

Magnetic stripe. A card technology that uses a magnetic stripe on the card to encode data used for unique identification of the card.

Mail-bomb delivery. Bombs or incendiary devices delivered to the target in letters or packages.

Man-trap. An access-control strategy that uses a pair of interlocking doors to prevent tailgating. Only one door can be unlocked at a time.

Mass care. The actions that are taken to protect evacuees and other disaster victims from the effects of the disaster. Activities include providing temporary shelter, food, medical care, clothing, and other essential life support needs to those people who have been displaced from their homes because of a disaster or threatened disaster.

Mass notification. Capability to provide real-time information to all building occupants or personnel in the immediate vicinity of a building during emergency situations.

Microwave motion sensor. An intrusion detection sensor that uses microwave energy to sense movement within the sensor's field of view. These sensors work similar to radar by using the Doppler effect to measure a shift in frequency.

Military installations. Army, Navy, Air Force and Marine Corps bases, posts, stations and annexes (both contractor- and government-operated), hospitals, terminals, and other special mission facilities, as well as those used primarily for military purposes.

Minimum essential infrastructure resource elements. The broad categories of resources, all or portions of which constitute the minimal essential infrastructure necessary for a department, agency or organization to conduct its core mission(s).

Minimum measures. Protective measures that can be applied to all buildings regardless of the identified threat. These measures offer defense or detection opportunities for minimal cost, facilitate future upgrades, and may deter acts of aggression.

Mitigation. Those actions taken to reduce the exposure to and impact of an attack or disaster.

Motion detector. An intrusion detection sensor that changes state based on movement in the sensor's field of view.

Moving vehicle bomb. An explosive-laden car or truck driven into or near a building and detonated.

Mutual Aid Agreement. A prearranged agreement developed between two or more entities to render assistance to the parties of the agreement.

N

Natural hazard. Naturally occurring events, such as floods, earthquakes, tornadoes, tsunami, coastal storms, landslides, and wildfires, that strike populated areas. A natural event is a hazard when it has the potential to harm people or property (*FEMA 386–2, Understanding Your Risks*). The risks of natural hazards may be increased or decreased as a result of human activity; however, they are not inherently human-induced.

Natural protective barriers. Natural protective barriers are mountains and deserts, cliffs and ditches, water obstacles, or other terrain features that are difficult to traverse.

Non-exclusive zone. An area around an asset that has controlled entry, but shared or less-restrictive access than an exclusive zone.

Non-persistent agent.   An agent that, upon release, loses its ability to cause casualties after ten to fifteen minutes. It has a high evaporation rate, is lighter than air, and will disperse rapidly. It is considered to be a short-term hazard; however, in small, unventilated areas, the agent will be more persistent.

Nuclear, biological, or chemical weapons.   Also called Weapons of Mass Destruction (WMD). Weapons that are characterized by their capability to produce mass casualties.

Nuclear detonation.   An explosion resulting from fission and/or fusion reactions in nuclear material, such as that from a nuclear weapon.

O

On-Scene Coordinator (OSC).   The federal official pre-designated by the EPA and U.S. Coast Guard to coordinate and direct response and removals under the National Oil and Hazardous Substances Pollution Contingency Plan.

Open systems architecture.   A term borrowed from the IT industry to claim that systems are capable of interfacing with other systems from any vendor, which also uses open system architecture. The opposite would be a proprietary system.

Operator interface.   The part of a security management system that provides that user interface to humans.

Organizational areas of control.   Controls consist of the policies, procedures, practices, and organization structures designed to provide reasonable assurance that business objectives will be achieved and that undesired events will be prevented or detected and corrected.

P

Passive infrared motion sensor.   A device that detects a change in the thermal energy pattern caused by a moving intruder and initiates an alarm when the change in energy satisfies the detector's alarm-criteria.

Passive vehicle barrier.   A vehicle barrier that is permanently deployed and does not require response to be effective.

Patch panel.   A concentrated termination point that separates backbone cabling from devices cabling for easy maintenance and troubleshooting.

Perimeter barrier.   A fence, wall, vehicle barrier, landform, or line of vegetation applied along an exterior perimeter used to obscure vision, hinder personnel access, or hinder or prevent vehicle access.

Persistent agent.   An agent that, upon release, retains its casualty-producing effects for an extended period of time, usually anywhere from thirty minutes to several days. A persistent agent usually has a low evaporation rate and its vapor is heavier than air; therefore, its vapor cloud tends to hug the ground. It is considered to be a long-term hazard. Although inhalation hazards are still a concern, extreme caution should be taken to avoid skin contact as well.

Physical security.   The part of security concerned with measures/concepts designed to safeguard personnel; to prevent unauthorized access to equipment, installations, materiel, and documents; and to safeguard them against espionage, sabotage, damage, and theft.

Planter barrier.   A passive vehicle barrier, usually constructed of concrete and filled with dirt (and flowers for aesthetics). Planters, along with bollards, are the usual street furniture used to keep vehicles away from existing buildings. Overall size and the depth of installation below grade determine the vehicle stopping capability of the individual planter.

Plume.   Airborne material spreading from a particular source; the dispersal of particles, gases, vapors, and aerosols into the atmosphere.

Polycarbonate glazing.   A plastic glazing material with enhanced resistance to ballistics or blast effects.

Predetonation screen.   A fence that causes an anti-tank round to detonate or prevents it from arming before it reaches its target.

Preliminary Damage Assessment (PDA).   A mechanism used to determine the impact and magnitude of damage and the resulting unmet needs of individuals, businesses, the public sector, and the community as a whole. Information collected is used by the state as a basis for the governor's request for a presidential declaration, and by FEMA to document the recommendation made to the president in response to the governor's request. PDAs are made by at least one state and one federal representative. A local government representative familiar with the extent and location of damage in the community often participates; other state and federal agencies and voluntary relief organizations also may be asked to participate, as needed.

Preparedness.   Establishing the plans, training, exercises, and resources necessary to enhance mitigation of and achieve readiness for response to, and recovery from, all hazards, disasters, and emergencies, including WMD incidents.

Pressure mat.   A mat that generates an alarm when pressure is applied to any part of the mat's surface, such as when someone steps on the mat. Pressure mats can be used to detect an intruder approaching a protected object, or they can be placed by doors and windows to detect entry.

Primary asset.   An asset that is the ultimate target for compromise by an aggressor.

Primary gathering building.   Inhabited buildings routinely occupied by fifty or more personnel. This designation applies to the entire portion of a building that meets the population density requirements for an inhabited building.

Probability of detection (POD).   A measure of an intrusion detection sensor's performance in detecting an intruder within its detection zone.

Probability of intercept.   The probability that an act of aggression will be detected and that a response force will intercept the aggressor before the asset can be compromised.

Progressive collapse.   A chain-reaction failure of building members to an extent disproportionate to the original localized damage; such damage may result in upper floors of a building collapsing onto lower floors.

Protective barriers.   Define the physical limits of a site, activity, or area by restricting, channeling, or impeding access and forming a continuous obstacle around the object.

Protective measures.   Elements of a protective system that protect an asset against a threat; protective measures are divided into defensive and detection measures.

Protective system.   An integration of all of the protective measures required to protect an asset against the range of threats applicable to the asset.

Proximity sensor.   An intrusion detection sensor that changes state based on the close distance or contact of a human to the sensor; these sensors often measure the change in capacitance as a human body enters the measured field.

Public Information Officer (PIO).   A federal, state, or local government official responsible for preparing and coordinating the dissemination of emergency public information.

R

Radiation.   High-energy particles or gamma rays that are emitted by an atom as the substance undergoes radioactive decay. Particles can be either charged alpha or beta particles or neutral neutron or gamma rays.

Radiation sickness.   The symptoms characterizing the sickness known as radiation injury, resulting from excessive exposure of the whole body to ionizing radiation.

Radiological monitoring.   The process of locating and measuring radiation by means of survey instruments that can detect and measure (as exposure rates) ionizing radiation.

Recovery.   The long-term activities beyond the initial crisis period and emergency response phase of disaster operations that focus on returning all systems in the community to a normal status or to reconstitute these systems to a new condition that is less vulnerable.

Regional Operations Center (ROC).   The temporary operations facility for the coordination of federal response and recovery activities located at the FEMA Regional Office (or Federal Regional Center) and led by the FEMA regional director or deputy director until the DFO becomes operational. After the ERT-A is deployed, the ROC performs a support role for federal staff at the disaster scene.

Report printers.   A separate, dedicated printer attached to the Electronic Security Systems used for generating reports utilizing information stored by the central computer.

Request-to-exit device.   Passive infrared motion sensors or push buttons that are used to signal an Electronic Entry Control System that egress is imminent or to unlock a door.

Resolution.   The level to which video details can be determined in a CCTV scene is referred to as resolving ability or resolution.

Resource Management.   Those actions taken by a government to identify sources and obtain resources needed to support disaster response activities; coordinate the supply, allocation, distribution, and delivery of resources so that they arrive where and when most needed; and maintain accountability for the resources used.

Response.   Executing the plan and resources identified to perform those duties and services to preserve and protect life and property, as well as provide services to the surviving population.

Response force.   The people who respond to an act of aggression; depending on the nature of the threat, the response force could consist of guards, special reaction teams, military or civilian police, an explosives ordnance disposal team, or a fire department.

Response time.   The length of time from the instant an attack is detected to the instant a security force arrives on site.

Restricted area.   Any area with access controls that is subject to these special restrictions or controls for security reasons. *See* controlled area, limited area, exclusion area, and exclusion zone.

Retinal pattern.   A biometric technology that is based on features of the human eye.

RF data transmission.   A communications link using radio frequency to send or receive data.

Risk.   The potential for loss of, or damage to, an asset; it is measured based upon the value of the asset in relation to the threats and vulnerabilities associated with it.

Rotating drum or rotating plate vehicle barrier.   An active vehicle barrier used at vehicle entrances to controlled areas based on a drum or plate rotating into the path of the vehicle when signaled.

Routinely occupied.   For the purposes of these standards, an established or predictable pattern of activity within a building that terrorists could recognize and exploit.

RS-232 data.   IEEE Recommended Standard 232; a point-to-point serial data protocol with a maximum effective distance of fifty feet.

RS-422 data.   IEEE Recommended Standard 422; a point-to-point serial data protocol with a maximum effective distance of four thousand feet.

RS-485 data.   IEEE Recommended Standard 485; a multi-drop serial data protocol with a maximum effective distance of four thousand feet.

S

Sacrificial roof or wall.   Roofs or walls that can be lost in a blast without damage to the primary asset.

Safe haven.   Secure areas within the interior of the facility. A safe haven should be designed such that it requires more time to penetrate by aggressors than it takes for the response force to reach the protected area to rescue the occupants. It may be a haven from a physical attack or air-isolated haven from CBR contamination.

Scramble keypad.   A keypad that uses keys on which the numbers change pattern with each use to enhance security by preventing eavesdropping observation of the entered numbers.

Secondary asset.   An asset that supports a primary asset and whose compromise would indirectly affect the operation of the primary asset.

Secondary hazard.   A threat whose potential would be realized as the result of a triggering event that of itself would constitute an emergency (e.g., dam failure might be a secondary hazard associated with earthquakes).

Secure/access mode.   The state of an area monitored by an intrusion detection system in regards to how alarm conditions are reported.

Security analysis.   The method of studying the nature of and the relationship between assets, threats, and vulnerabilities.

Security console.   Specialized furniture, racking, and related apparatus used to house the security equipment required in a control center.

Security engineering.   The process of identifying practical, risk-managed, short- and long-term solutions to reduce and/or mitigate dynamic manmade hazards by integrating multiple factors, including construction, equipment, manpower, and procedures.

Security engineering design process.   The process through which assets requiring protection are identified, the threat to and vulnerability of those assets is determined, and a protective system is designed to protect the assets.

Security Management System database.   In a Security Management System, a database that is transferred to various nodes or panels throughout the system for faster data processing and protection against communications link downtime.

Security Management System distributed processing.   In a Security Management System, a method of data processing at various nodes or panels throughout the system for faster data processing and protection against communications links downtime.

Segregation of duties.   Policies, procedures, and an organizational structure established so that one individual cannot control key aspects of physical and/or computer-related operations and thereby conduct unauthorized actions or gain unauthorized access to minimum essential infrastructure resource elements.

Semi-isolated fenced perimeters.   Fence lines where approach areas are clear of obstruction for sixty to a hundred feet outside of the fence and where the general public or other personnel seldom have reason to be in the area.

Senior FEMA Official (SFO).   The official appointed by the director of FEMA, or his representative, that is responsible for deploying to the JOC to serve as the senior interagency consequence management representative on the Command Group, and to manage and coordinate activities taken by the Consequence Management Group.

Serial interface.   An integration strategy for data transfer where components are connected in series.

Shielded wire.   Wire with a conductive wrap used to mitigate electromagnetic emanations.

Situational crime prevention.   A crime prevention strategy based on reducing the opportunities for crime by increasing the effort required to commit a crime, increasing the risks associated with committing the crime, and reducing the target appeal or vulnerability (whether property or person). This opportunity reduction is achieved by management and use policies, such as procedures and training, as well as physical approaches, such as alteration of the built environment.

Smart card.   A newer card technology that allows data to be written, stored, and read on a card typically used for identification and/or access.

Software level integration.   An integration strategy that uses software to interface systems. An example of this would be digital video displayed in the same computer application window and linked to events of a security management system.

Specific threat.   Known or postulated aggressor activity focused on targeting a particular asset.

Standoff distance.   A distance maintained between a building or portion thereof and the potential location for an explosive detonation or other threat.

Standoff weapons.   Weapons, such as anti-tank weapons and mortars, that are launched from a distance at a target.

State Coordinating Officer (SCO).   The person appointed by the governor to coordinate state, commonwealth, or territorial response and recovery activities with FRP-related activities of the federal government, in cooperation with the FCO.

State Liaison.   A FEMA official, assigned to a particular state, who handles initial coordination with the state in the early stages of an emergency.

Stationary vehicle bomb.   An explosive-laden car or truck stopped or parked near a building.

Storm surge.   A dome of seawater created by the strong winds and low barometric pressure in a hurricane that causes severe coastal flooding as the hurricane strikes land.

Strain sensitive cable.   Strain sensitive cables are transducers that are uniformly sensitive along their entire length and generate an analog voltage when subjected to mechanical distortions or stress resulting from fence motion. They are typically attached to a chain-link fence about halfway between the bottom and top of the fence fabric with plastic ties.

Structural protective barriers.   Man-made devices (e.g., fences, walls, floors, roofs, grills, bars, roadblocks, signs, or other construction) used to restrict, channel, or impede access.

Superstructure.   The supporting elements of a building above the foundation.

Supplies-bomb delivery.   Bombs or incendiary devices concealed and delivered to supply or material handling points, such as loading docks.

System events.   Events that occur normally in the operation of a security management system. Examples include access-control operations and changes of state in intrusion detection sensors.

System software.   Controls that limit and monitor access to the powerful programs and sensitive files that control the computer hardware and secure applications supported by the system.

T

Tactics.   The specific methods of achieving the aggressor's goals to injure personnel, destroy assets, or steal materiel or information.

Tamper switch.   Intrusion detection sensor that monitors an equipment enclosure for breach.

Tangle-foot wire.   Barbed wire or tape suspended on short metal or wooden pickets outside a perimeter fence to create an obstacle to approach.

Taut wire sensor.   An intrusion detection sensor utilizing a column of uniformly spaced horizontal wires, securely anchored at each end and stretched taut. Each wire is attached to a sensor to indicate movement of the wire.

Technical assistance.   The provisioning of direct assistance to states and local jurisdictions to improve capabilities for program development, planning, and operational performances related to responses to WMD terrorist incidents.

Technological hazards.   Incidents that can arise from human activities, such as manufacture, transportation, storage, and use of hazardous materials. For the sake of simplicity, it is assumed that technological emergencies are accidental and that their consequences are unintended.

TEMPEST.   An unclassified short name referring to investigations and studies of compromising emanations. It is sometimes used synonymously for the term "compromising emanations" (e.g., TEMPEST tests, TEMPEST inspections).

Terrorism.   The unlawful use of force and violence against persons or property to intimidate or coerce a government, the civilian population, or any segment thereof, in furtherance of political or social objectives.

Thermally tempered glass (TTG).   Glass that is heat-treated to have a higher-tensile strength and resistance to blast pressures, although with a greater susceptibility to airborne debris.

Threat.   Any indication, circumstance, or event with the potential to cause loss of or damage to an asset.

Threat analysis.   A continual process of compiling and examining all available information concerning potential threats and human-caused hazards. A common method to evaluate terrorist groups is to review the factors of existence, capability, intentions, history, and targeting.

Time/date stamp.   Data inserted into a CCTV video signal with the time and date of the video as it was created.

TNT equivalent weight.   The weight of TNT (trinitrotoluene) that has an equivalent energetic output to that of a different weight of another explosive compound.

Tornado.   A local atmospheric storm, generally of short duration, formed by winds rotating at very high speeds, usually in a counter-clockwise direction. The vortex, up to several hundred yards wide, is visible to the observer as a whirlpool-like column of winds rotating about a hollow cavity or funnel. Winds may reach three hundred miles per hour or higher.

Toxic-free area.   An area within a facility in which the air supply is free of toxic chemical or biological agents.

Toxicity.   A measure of the harmful effects produced by a given amount of a toxin on a living organism.

Triple-standard concertina (TSC) wire.   This type of fence uses three rolls of stacked concertina. One roll will be stacked on top of two other rolls that run parallel to each other while resting on the ground, forming a pyramid.

Tsunami.   Sea waves produced by an undersea earthquake; such sea waves can reach a height of eighty feet and can devastate coastal cities and low-lying coastal areas.

Twisted pair wire.   Wire that uses pairs of wires twisted together to mitigate electro-magnetic interference.

Two-person rule.   A security strategy that requires two people to be present in or gain access to a secured area to prevent unobserved access by any individual.

U

Unobstructed space.   Space around an inhabited building without obstruction large enough to conceal explosive devices 150 mm (6 inches) or greater in height.

Unshielded wire.   Wire that does not have a conductive wrap.

V

Vault.   A reinforced room for securing items.

Vertical rod.   Typical door hardware often used with a crash bar to lock a door by inserting rods vertically from the door into the doorframe.

Vibration sensor.   An intrusion detection sensor that changes state when vibration is present.

Video intercom system.   An intercom system that also incorporates a small CCTV system for verification.

Video motion detection.   Motion detection technology that looks for changes in the pixels of a video image.

Video multiplexer.   A device used to connect multiple video signals to a single location for viewing and/or recording.

Visual displays.   A display or monitor used to inform the operator visually of the status of the electronic security system.

Visual surveillance.   The aggressor uses ocular and photographic devices (such as binoculars and cameras with telephoto lenses) to monitor facility or installation operations or to see assets.

Voice recognition.   A biometric technology that is based on nuances of the human voice.

Volumetric motion sensor.   An interior intrusion detection sensor that is designed to sense aggressor motion within a protected space.

Vulnerability.   Any weakness that can be exploited by an aggressor or, in a non-terrorist threat environment, make an asset susceptible to hazard damage.

W

Warning.   The alerting of emergency response personnel and the public to the threat of extraordinary danger and the related effects that specific hazards may cause.

Watch.   Indication in a defined area that conditions are favorable for the specified type of severe weather (e.g., flash flood watch, severe thunderstorm watch, tornado watch, tropical storm watch).

Waterborne contamination.   Chemical, biological, or radiological agent introduced into and fouling a water supply.

Weapons-grade material.   Nuclear material considered most suitable for a nuclear weapon. It usually connotes uranium enriched to above 90 percent uranium-235 or plutonium with greater than about 90 percent plutonium-239.

Weapons of Mass Destruction (WMD).   Any device, material, or substance used in a manner, in a quantity or type, or under circumstances showing intent to cause death or serious injury to persons, or significant damage to property. An explosive, incendiary, or poison gas, bomb, grenade, rocket having a propellant charge of more than four ounces, or a missile having an explosive incendiary charge of more than 0.25 ounce, or mine or device similar to the above; poison gas; weapon involving a disease organism; or weapon that is designed to release radiation or radioactivity at a level dangerous to human life.

Weigand protocol.   A security industry standard data protocol for card readers.

Z

Zoom.   The ability of a CCTV camera to close and focus or open and widen the field of view.

Chemical, Biological, and Radiological Glossary

CHEMICAL TERMS

Acetylcholinesterase.   An enzyme that hydrolyzes the neurotransmitter acetylcholine; the action of this enzyme is inhibited by nerve agents.

Aerosol.   Fine liquid or solid particles suspended in a gas (e.g., fog or smoke).

Atropine.   A compound used as an antidote for nerve agents.

Blister agents.   Substances that cause blistering of the skin; exposure is through liquid or vapor contact with any exposed tissue (eyes, skin, lungs). Examples are distilled mustard (HD), nitrogen mustard (HN), lewisite (L), mustard/lewisite (HL), and phenodichloroarsine (PD).

Blood agents.   Substances that injure a person by interfering with cell respiration (the exchange of oxygen and carbon dioxide between blood and tissues). Examples are arsine (SA), cyanogens chloride (CK), hydrogen chloride (HCl), and hydrogen cyanide (AC).

Casualty (toxic) agents.   Produce incapacitation, serious injury, or death, and can be used to incapacitate or kill victims. They are the blister, blood, choking, and nerve agents.

Central nervous system depressants.   Compounds that have the predominant effect of depressing or blocking the activity of the central nervous system. The primary mental effects include the disruption of the ability to think, sedation, and lack of motivation.

Central nervous system stimulants.   Compounds that have the predominant effect of flooding the brain with too much information. The primary mental effect is loss of concentration, causing indecisiveness and the inability to act in a sustained, purposeful manner. Examples of the depressants and stimulants include agent 15 (suspected Iraqi BZ), BZ (3-quinulidinyle benzilate), canniboids, fentanyls, LSD (lysergic acid diethylamide), and phenothiazines.

Chemical agents.   Substances that are intended for use in military operations to kill, seriously injure, or incapacitate people through their physiological effects. Excluded from consideration are riot control agents, and smoke and flame materials. The agent may appear as a vapor, aerosol, or liquid; it can be either a casualty/toxic agent or an incapacitating agent.

Choking/lung/pulmonary agents.   Substances that cause physical injury to the lungs; exposure is through inhalation. In extreme cases, membranes swell and lungs become filled with liquid. Death results from lack of oxygen; hence, the victim is "choked." Examples are chlorine (CL), diphosgene (DP), cyanide (KCN), nitrogen oxide (NO), perfluororisobutylene (PHIB), phosgene (CG), red phosphorous (RP), sulfur trioxide-chlorosulfonic acid (FS), Teflon and PHIB, titanium tetrachloride (FM), and zinc oxide (HC).

Cutaneous.   Pertaining to the skin.

Decontamination.   The process of making any person, object, or area safe by absorbing, destroying, neutralizing, making harmless, or removing the hazardous material.

G-series nerve agents.   Chemical agents of moderate to high toxicity developed in the 1930s. Examples are tabun (GA), sarin (GB), soman (GD), phosphonofluoridic acid, ethyl-, 1-methylethyl ester (GE), and cyclohexyl sarin (GF).

Incapacitating agents.   Produce temporary physiological and/or mental effects via action on the central nervous system. Effects may persist for hours or days, but victims usually do not require medical treatment; however, such treatment speeds recovery.

Industrial agents.   Chemicals developed or manufactured for use in industrial operations or research by industry, government, or academia. These chemicals are not primarily manufactured for the specific purpose of producing human casualties or rendering equipment, facilities, or areas dangerous for use by man. Hydrogen cyanide, cyanogen chloride, phosgene, chloropicrin, and many herbicides and pesticides are industrial chemicals that also can be chemical agents.

Liquid agents.   Chemical agents that appear to be an oily film or droplets. The color ranges from clear to brownish amber.

Nerve agents.   Substances that interfere with the central nervous system; exposure is primarily through contact with the liquid (skin and eyes) and secondarily through inhalation of the vapor. Three distinct symptoms associated with nerve agents are pinpoint pupils, an extreme headache, and severe tightness in the chest. *See also* G-series and V-series nerve agents.

Nonpersistent agents.   Agents that, upon release, lose the ability to cause casualties after ten to fifteen minutes; they have a high evaporation rate and are lighter than air and will disperse rapidly. They are considered to be short-term hazards; however, in small, unventilated areas, these agents will be more persistent.

Organophosphorous compound.   A compound containing the elements phosphorus and carbon, whose physiological effects include inhibition of acetylcholinesterase. Many pesticides (malathione and parathion) and virtually all nerve agents are organophosphorous compounds.

Percutaneous agents.   Agents that are able to be absorbed by the body through the skin.

Persistent agents.   Agents that, upon release, retain their casualty-producing effects for an extended period of time, usually anywhere from thirty minutes to several days. A persistent agent usually has a low evaporation rate and its vapor is heavier than air. Therefore, its vapor cloud tends to hug the ground. They are considered to be long-term hazards. Although inhalation hazards are still a concern, extreme caution should be taken to avoid skin contact as well.

Protection.   Any means by which an individual protects his or her body. Measures include masks, self-contained breathing apparatuses, clothing, structures, such as buildings, and vehicles.

Tear (riot control) agents.   Produce irritating or disabling effects that rapidly disappear within minutes after exposure ceases. Examples are bromobenzylcyanide (CA), chloroacetophenone (CN or commercially known as Mace), chloropicrin (PS), CNB (CN in benzene and carbon tetrachloride), CNC (CN in chloroform), CNS (CN and chloropicrin in chloroform, CR (dibenz-(b,f)-1,4-oxazepine, a tear gas), CS (tear gas), and Capsaicin (pepper spray).

V-series nerve agents.   Chemical agents of moderate to high toxicity developed in the 1950s. They are generally persistent. Examples are VE (phosphonothioic acid, ethyl-, S-(diethylamino)ethyl] O-ethylester), VG (phosphorothioic acid, S-[2-(diethylamino)ethyl] O, O-diethyl ester), VM (phosphonothioic acid, methyl-, S-[2-(diethylamino) ethyl] O-ethyl ester), VS (phosphonothioic acid, ethyl, S-[2-[bis(1-methylethyl)amino] ethyl] O-ethyl ester), and VX (phosphonothioic acid, methyl-, S-[2-[bis(1-methylethyl)amino]ethyl] O-ethyl ester).

Vapor agents.   A gaseous form of a chemical agent. If heavier than air, the cloud will be close to the ground. If lighter than air, the cloud will rise and disperse more quickly.

Volatility.   A measure of how readily a substance will vaporize.

Vomiting agents.   Produce nausea and vomiting effects; can also cause coughing, sneezing, pain in the nose and throat, nasal discharge, and tears. Examples are adamsite (DM), diphenylchloroarsine (DA), and diphenylcyanoarsine (DC).

BIOLOGICAL TERMS

Aerosol.   Fine liquid or solid particles suspended in a gas (e.g., fog or smoke).

Antibiotic.   A substance that inhibits the growth of or kills microorganisms.

Antisera.   The liquid part of blood containing antibodies that react against disease-causing agents, such as those used in biological warfare.

Bacteria.   Single-celled organisms that multiply by cell division and that can cause disease in humans, plants, or animals.

Biochemicals.   The chemicals that make up or are produced by living things.

Biological warfare.   The intentional use of biological agents as weapons to kill or injure humans, animals, or plants, or to damage equipment.

Biological warfare agents.   Living organisms or the materials derived from them that cause disease in or harm to humans, animals, or plants, or cause deterioration of material. Biological agents may be used as liquid droplets, aerosols, or dry powders.

Bioregulators.   Biochemicals that regulate bodily functions. Bioregulators that are produced by the body are termed "endogenous." Some of these same bioregulators can be chemically synthesized.

Causative agents.   The organism or toxin that is responsible for causing a specific disease or harmful effect.

Contagious.   Capable of being transmitted from one person to another.

Culture.   A population of microorganisms grown in a medium.

Decontamination.   The process of making people, objects, or areas safe by absorbing, destroying, neutralizing, making harmless, or removing the hazardous material.

Fungi.   Any of a group of plants mainly characterized by the absence of chlorophyll, the green-colored compound found in other plants. Fungi range from microscopic single-celled plants (such as molds and mildews) to large plants (such as mushrooms).

Host.   An animal or plant that harbors or nourishes another organism.

Incapacitating agents.   Agents that produce physical or psychological effects, or both, that may persist for hours or days after exposure, rendering victims incapable of performing normal physical and mental tasks.

Infectious agents.   Biological agents capable of causing disease in a susceptible host.

Infectivity.   (1) The ability of an organism to spread. (2) The number of organisms required to cause an infection to secondary hosts. (3) The capability of an organism to spread out from the site of infection and cause disease in the host organism. Infectivity also can be viewed as the number of organisms required to cause an infection.

Line-source delivery system.   A delivery system in which the biological agent is dispersed from a moving ground or air vehicle in a line perpendicular to the direction of the prevailing wind. *See also* point-source delivery system.

Microorganism.   Any organism, such as bacteria, viruses, and some fungi, that can be seen only with a microscope.

Mycotoxin.   A toxin produced by fungi.

Nebulizer.   A device for producing a fine spray or aerosol.

Organism.   Any individual living thing, whether animal or plant.

Parasite.   Any organism that lives in or on another organism without providing benefit in return.

Pathogen.   Any organism (usually living), such as bacteria, fungi, and viruses, capable of producing serious disease or death.

Pathogenic agents.   Biological agents capable of causing serious disease.

Point-source delivery system.   A delivery system in which the biological agent is dispersed from a stationary position. This delivery method results in coverage over a smaller area than with the line-source system. *See also* line-source delivery system.

Route of exposure (entry). The path by which a person comes into contact with an agent or organism (e.g., through breathing, digestion, or skin contact).

Single-cell protein.   Protein-rich material obtained from cultured algae, fungi, protein, and bacteria, and often used as food or animal feed.

Spore.   A reproductive form some microorganisms can take to become resistant to environmental conditions, such as extreme heat or cold, while in a "resting stage."

Toxicity.   A measure of the harmful effect produced by a given amount of a toxin on a living organism. The relative toxicity of an agent can be expressed in milligrams of toxin needed per kilogram of body weight to kill experimental animals.

Toxins.   Poisonous substances produced by living organisms.

Vaccine.   A preparation of killed or weakened microorganism products used to artificially induce immunity against a disease.

Vector.   An agent, such as an insect or rat, capable of transferring a pathogen from one organism to another.

Venom.   A poison produced in the glands of some animals (e.g., snakes, scorpions, or bees).

Virus.   An infectious microorganism that exists as a particle rather than as a complete cell. Particle sizes range from 20 to 400 nanometers (one-billionth of a meter). Viruses are not capable of reproducing outside of a host cell.

RADIOLOGICAL TERMS

Acute radiation syndrome.   Consists of three levels of effects: hernatopoletic (blood cells, most sensitive); gastrointestinal (GI cells, very sensitive); and central nervous system (brain/muscle cells, insensitive). The initial signs and symptoms are nausea, vomiting, fatigue, and loss of appetite. Below about 200 rems, these symptoms may be the only indication of radiation exposure.

Alpha particles.   Alpha particles have a very short range in air and a very low ability to penetrate other materials, but also have a strong ability to ionize materials. Alpha particles are unable to penetrate even the thin layer of dead cells of human skin and consequently are not an external radiation hazard. Alpha-emitting nuclides inside the body as a result of inhalation or ingestion are a considerable internal radiation hazard.

Beta particles.   High-energy electrons emitted from the nucleus of an atom during radioactive decay. They normally can be stopped by the skin or a very thin sheet of metal.

Cesium-137 (Cs-137).   A strong gamma ray source and can contaminate property, entailing extensive cleanup. It is commonly used in industrial measurement gauges and for irradiation of material. Its half-life is 30.2 years.

Cobalt-60 (Co-60).   A strong gamma ray source, and is extensively used as a radio-therapeutic for treating cancer, food and material irradiation, gamma radiography, and industrial measurement gauges. Its half-life is 5.27 years.

Curie (Ci).   A unit of radioactive decay rate defined as 3.7 x 1010 disintegrations per second.

Decay.   The process by which an unstable element is changed to another isotope or another element by the spontaneous emission of radiation from its nucleus. This process can be measured by using radiation detectors, such as Geiger counters.

Decontamination.   The process of making people, objects, or areas safe by absorbing, destroying, neutralizing, making harmless, or removing the hazardous material.

Dose.   A general term for the amount of radiation absorbed over a period of time.

Dosimeter.   A portable instrument for measuring and registering the total accumulated dose to ionizing radiation.

Gamma ray.   A high-energy photon emitted from the nucleus of atoms; similar to an X-ray. It can penetrate deeply into body tissue and many materials. Cobalt-60 and Cesium-137 are both strong gamma-emitters. Shielding against gamma radiation requires thick layers of dense materials, such as lead. Gamma rays are potentially lethal to humans.

Half-life.   The amount of time needed for half of the atoms of a radioactive material to decay.

Highly enriched uranium (HEU).   Uranium that is enriched to above 20 percent. Uranium-235 (U-235). Weapons-grade HEU is enriched to above 90 percent in U-235.

Ionize.   To split off one or more electrons from an atom, thus leaving it with a positive electric charge. The electrons usually attach to one of the atoms or molecules, giving them a negative charge.

Iridium-192.   A gamma ray emitting radioisotope used for gamma radiography. Its half-life is 73.83 days.

Isotope.   A specific element always has the same number of protons in the nucleus. That same element may, however, appear in forms that have different numbers of neutrons in the nucleus. These different forms are referred to as "isotopes" of the element; for example, deuterium (2H) and tritium (3H) are isotopes of ordinary hydrogen (H).

Lethal dose   (50/30).   The dose of radiation expected to cause death within 30 days to 50 percent of those exposed without medical treatment. The generally accepted range is from 400–500 rem received over a short period of time.

Nuclear reactor.   A device in which a controlled, self-sustaining nuclear chain reaction can be maintained with the use of cooling to remove generated heat.

Plutonium-239 (Pu-239).   A metallic element used for nuclear weapons. Its half-life is 24,110 years.

Rad.   A unit of absorbed dose of radiation defined as deposition of 100 ergs of energy per gram of tissue. A rad amounts to approximately one ionization per cubic micron.

Radiation.   High-energy alpha or beta particles or gamma rays that are emitted by an atom as the substance undergoes radioactive decay.

Radiation sickness.   Symptoms resulting from excessive exposure to radiation of the body.

Radioactive waste.   Disposable, radioactive materials resulting from nuclear operations. Wastes are generally classified into two categories, high-level and low-level.

Radiological Dispersal Device (RDD).   A device (weapon or equipment), other than a nuclear explosive device, designed to disseminate radioactive material in order to cause destruction, damage, or injury by means of the radiation produced by the decay of such material.

Radioluminescence.   The luminescence produced by particles emitted during radioactive decay.

Roentgen Equivalent Man (REM or rem).   A unit of absorbed dose that takes into account the relative effectiveness of radiation that harms human health.

Shielding.   Materials (lead, concrete, etc.) used to block or attenuate radiation for protection of equipment, materials, or people.

Special Nuclear Material (SNM).   Plutonium and uranium enriched in the isotopes Uranium-233 or Uranium-235.

Uranium 235 (U-235).   Naturally occurring U-235 is found at 0.72 percent enrichment. U-235 is used as a reactor fuel or for weapons; however, weapons typically use U-235 enriched to 90 percent. Its half-life is 7.04×108 years.

X-ray.   An invisible, highly penetrating electromagnetic radiation of much shorter wavelength (higher frequency) than visible light. Very similar to gamma rays.

Bibliography

American Society of Heating, Refrigerating, and Air-Conditioning Engineers, Defensive Filtration, ASHRAE Journal, December 2002, James D. Miller
   http://resourcecenter.ashrae.org/store/ashrae/newstore.cgi?itemid=9346&view=item& categoryid=409&page=1&loginid=29483

Building Security Through Design: A Primer for Architects, Design Professionals, and Their Clients, November 2001, The American Institute of Architects (book)
   www.aia.org/security

Blast Effects on Buildings: Design of Buildings to Optimize Resistance to Blast Loading, 1995, G.C. Mays and P.D. Smith, London: Thomas Telford, Ltd., American Society of Civil Engineers, ISBN: 0–7277–2030–9
   www.pubs.asce.org/BOOKdisplay.cgi?9990338

Centers for Disease Control and Prevention/ National Institute for Occupational Safety and Health Publication No. 2002–139, Guidance for Protecting Building Environments from Airborne Chemical, Biological, or Radiological Attacks, May 2002, Cincinnati, OH
      www.cdc.gov/niosh/bldvent/2002–139.html

   Publication No. 2003–136, Guidance for Filtration and Air Cleaning Systems to Protect Building Environments from Airborne Chemical, Biological, or Radiological Attacks, April 2003, Cincinnati, OH
   www.cdc.gov/niosh/docs/2003–136/2003–136.html

Central Intelligence Agency. Chemical, Biological, Radiological Incident Handbook, October 1998
  www.cia.gov/cia/publications/cbr_handbook/cbrbook.htm
Cost Impact of ISC Security Criteria, GSA & Applied Research Associates, Inc., L. Bryant and J. Smith, Vicksburg, MS [Restricted Access]
  www.oca.gsa.gov/specialphp/References.php
Council on Tall Buildings and Urban Habitat Building Safety Enhancement Guidebook, 2002
  www.ctbuh.org
Crime Prevention Through Environmental Design and Community Policing, August 1996, Dan Fleissner and Fred Heinzelmann, Washington, DC
  www.ncjrs.org/pdffiles/crimepre.pdf
Crime Prevention Through Environmental Design in Parking Facilities, April 1996, Mary S. Smith, Washington, DC
  www.ncjrs.org/pdffiles/cptedpkg.pdf
Dwyer, K., Osher, D & C. Warger, A Guide to Safe Schools, 1998.
Facility Standards for the Public Building Service (PBS-P100); Chapter 8, Security Design, Revised November 2000
  http://hydra.gsa.gov/pbs/pc/facilitiesstandards/
Federal Emergency Management Agency FEMA 152, Seismic Considerations: Apartment Buildings, Earthquake
  Hazards Reduction Series 37, November 1988, Washington, DC (not available on Internet) Contact FEMA Distribution Center, P.O. Box 2012, 8231 Stayton Drive, Jessup, MD 20794–2012, Telephone: 1–800–480–2520, Fax: 301–362–5335
FEMA 153, Seismic Considerations: Office Buildings, Earthquake Hazards Reduction Series 38, November 1988, Washington, DC (not available on Internet) Contact FEMA Distribution Center, P.O. Box 2012, 8231 Stayton Drive, Jessup, MD 20794–2012, Telephone: 1–800–480- 2520, Fax: 301–362–5335
FEMA 154, Rapid Visual Screening of Buildings for Seismic Hazards: A Handbook (2nd Edition), 2002, 1988, Washington, DC (not available on Internet) Contact FEMA Distribution Center, P.O. Box 2012, 8231 Stayton Drive, Jessup, MD 20794–2012, Telephone: 1–800–480- 2520, Fax: 301–362–5335
FEMA 277, The Oklahoma City Bombing: Improving Building Performance through Multi-Hazard Mitigation, August 1, 1996, Washington, DC
  www.fema.gov/mit/bpat/bpat009.htm
FEMA 372, Mitigation Resources for Success (CD-ROM), October 2001, Washington, DC
  www.fema.gov/pdf/library/poster_fnl2.pdf
FEMA 386–2, Understanding Your Risks, Identifying Hazards and Estimating Losses, August 2001
  www.fema.gov/ima/planning_toc3.shtm
FEMA 386–7, Integrating Human-Caused Hazards Into Mitigation Planning, September 2002
  www.fema.gov/ima/antiterrorism/resources.shtm
FEMA 403, World Trade Center Building Performance Study: Data Collection, Preliminary Observations, and Recommendations, May 2002, Washington, DC
  www.fema.gov/library/wtcstudy.shtm
FEMA 424, Design Guide for Improving Schools in Earthquakes, Floods and High Winds, January 2004
  www.fema.gov/plan/prevent/rms/rmsp424.shtm
FEMA 428, Primer to Design Safe School Projects in case of Terrorist Attacks, December 2003
  www.fema.gov/plan/prevent/rms/rmsp428

Florida Department of Education: Florida Safe School Design Guidelines, 2
www.firn.edu/doe/edfacil/safe_schools.htm 003

General Services Administration Balancing Security and Openness: A Thematic Summary of a Symposium on Security and the Design of Public Buildings, November 30, 1999
http://hydra.gsa.gov/pbs/pc/gd_iles/SecurityOpenness.pdf

Healthy Building International, Inc. Vulnerability Assessments and Counter Terrorist Protocols
www.healthybuildings.com/s2/vacbt.pdf

Institute of Medicine. Reducing Underage Drinking: A Collective Responsibility, 2004.

Interagency Security Committee (executive agent—GSA) ISC Security Design Criteria for New Federal Office Buildings and Major Modernization Projects, May 28, 2001, [For Official Use Only] [Restricted Access]
www.oca.gsa.gov/specialphp/References.php

Institute of Transportation Engineers The Influence of Traffic Calming Devices upon Fire Vehicle Travel Times, Michael A. Coleman, 1997, ITE Annual Meeting Compendium, 1997 pp. 838–845
http://webservices.camsys.com/fhwa/cmn/cmn33.htm

Lawrence Berkeley National Lab Protecting Buildings From a Biological or Chemical Attack: actions to take before or during a release. LBNL/PUB-51959, January 10, 2003
http://securebuildings.lbl.gov/images/bldgadvice.pdf

Mail Center Manager's Security Guide—Second Edition, October 22, 2002
www.gsa.gov//attachments/GSA_PUBLICATIONS/extpub/MailCenterManagersSecurity GuideV2.pdf

Minimum Design Loads for Buildings and Other Structures, ASCE 7–02,2002, American Society of Civil Engineers, ISBN: 0–7844–0624–3 [Note: revision of 7–98 does not include building security or antiterrorism, but covers all natural hazards]
www.pubs.asce.org/ASCE7.html?9991330

National Academy of Sciences Combating Terrorism: Prioritizing Vulnerabilities and Developing Mitigation Strategies, Project Identification Number: NAEP-R-02–01- A, National Academy of Engineering on-going project—results to be published.
www.nationalacademies.org/webcr.nsf/ProjectScopeDisplay/

National Association on Alcohol Abuse and Alcoholism. Understanding Underage Drinking, 2002.

National Association on Alcohol Abuse and Alcoholism. National Survey on Drug Use and Health 2004.

National Capital Planning Commission Designing for Security in the Nation's Capital, October 2001
www.ncpc.gov/planning_init/security/DesigningSec.pdf

National Capital Planning Urban Design and Security Plan, October 2002
www.ncpc.gov/publications/udsp/Final%20UDSP.pdf

National Highway Traffic Safety Administration. Annual Report 2003.

National Institute of Building Sciences Whole Building Design Guide: Provide Security for Building Occupants and Assets
www.wbdg.org/design/index.php?cn=2.7.4&cx=0

National Institute of Justice (NIJ) The Appropriate and Effective Use of Security Technologies in U.S. Schools: A Guide for Schools and Law Enforcement Agencies, September 1999, with U.S. Department of Education, Safe and Drug-Free Schools Program; and U.S. Department of Energy, Sandia National Laboratories
www.ncjrs.org/school/home.html

National Research Council Protecting Buildings and People from Terrorism: Technology

Transfer for Blast-effects Mitigation, 2001, National Academy Press, Washington, DC, ISBN 0–309–08286–2

  http://books.nap.edu/books/0309082862/html/index.html

NIJ Guide 100–00, Guide for the Selection of Chemical Agent and Toxic Industrial Material Detection Equipment for Emergency First Responders, June 2000

  www.ncjrs.org/pdfiles1/nij/184449.pdf

NIJ Guide 101–00, An Introduction to Biological Agent Detection Equipment for Emergency First Responders, December 2001

  www.ncjrs.org/pdfiles1/nij/190747.pdf

NIJ Guide 102–00, Guide for the Selection of Personal Protective Equipment for Emergency First Responders, Volumes I-IV, November 2002

  www.ncjrs.org/pdfiles1/nij/191518.pdf

NIJ Guide 602–00, Guide to the Technologies of Concealed Weapon and Contraband Imaging and Detection, February 2001

  www.ncjrs.org/pdfiles1/nij/184432.pdf

NIJ Standard 0108.01, Blast Resistant Protective Materials, September 1985 [Subscription Required]

  www.ccb.org

Protecting Buildings From Bomb Blast, Transfer of Blast-Effects Mitigation Technologies from Military to Civilian Applications, 1995, National Academy Press, Washington, DC, ISBN 0–309–05375–7

  http://books.nap.edu/books/0309053757/html/index.html

Progressive Collapse Analysis and Design Guidelines for New Federal Office Buildings and Major Modernization Projects, November 2000 [Restricted Access]

  www.oca.gsa.gov/specialphp/References.php

Protection of Federal Office Buildings Against Terrorism, 1988, Committee on the Protection of Federal Facilities Against Terrorism, Building Research Board, National Academy Press, Washington, DC, ISBN 0–309–07691–9

  http://books.nap.edu/books/0309076463/html/index.html

Security Reference Manual, Part 3: Blast Design and Assessment Guidelines, July 31, 2001 [For Official Use Only] [Restricted Access]

  www.oca.gsa.gov/specialphp/References.php

Split Speed Bump, 1998, Kathy Mulder, Washington, DC, TE International Conference, 1998

  www.ite.org/trafic/documents/CCA98A33.pdf

Society of American Military Engineers National Symposium of Comprehensive Force Protection, October 200l, Charleston, SC, Lindbergh & Associates. For a list of participants, access

  www.same.org/forceprot/force.htm

State and Local Guide 101, Guide for All-Hazard Emergency Operations Planning, Chapter 6, Attachment G, Terrorism, April 2001

  www.fema.gov/rrr/allhzpln.shtm

Task Force on Tall Buildings: "The Future," October 15, 2001

  www.lehigh.edu/ctbuh/htmliles/hot_links/report.pdf or www.ctbuh.org/htmliles/hot_links/report.pdf

Technical Support Working Group (TSWG) Terrorist Bomb Threat Standoff Card with Explanation of Use

  www.tswg.gov/tswg/prods_pubs/newBTSCPress.htm

The House National Security Committee Statement of Chairman Floyd D. Spence on the Report of the Bombing of Khobar Towers, August 1996, Washington, DC

  www.house.gov/hasc/Publications/104thCongress/ Reports/saudi.pdf

University of Michigan. Johnston, L. D., O'Malley, P. M., & Bachman, J. G. (2002). Monitoring the Future national survey results on drug use, 1975–2001. Volume I: Secondary school students (NIH Publication No. 02–5106). Bethesda, MD: National Institute on Drug Abuse, 503 pp.

U.S. Department of Education Practical Information on Crisis Planning: A Guide for Schools and Communities, May 2003
  www.ed.gov/emergencyplan

U.S. Department of Justice, National Institute of Justice, The Appropriate and Effective Use of Security Technologies in U.S. Schools, September 1999
  www.ncjrs.gov/school/home.html

U.S. Secret Service, Threat Assessment in Schools: A Guide to Managing Threatening Situations and to Creating Safe School Climates, May 2002
  www.ed.gov/admins/lead/safety/threatassessmentguide.pdf

Organizations and Associations

Air-Conditioning and Refrigeration Institute, Inc.
  www.ari.org
Alliance for Fire & Smoke Containment & Control
  www.afscconline.org
American Council of Engineering Companies (ACEC)
  www.acec.org
American Institute of Architects (AIA), Security Resource Center
  www.aia.org/security
American Planning Association
  www.planning.org
American Society of Civil Engineers (ASCE)
  www.asce.org
American Society of Heating, Refrigerating, and Air-Conditioning Engineers (ASHRAE)
  www.ashrae.org
American Society of Mechanical Engineers (ASME)
  http://www.asme.org
Architectural Engineering Institute (AEI) of ASCE
  www.asce.org/instfound/aei.cfm
Associated General Contractors of America
  www.agc.org
Building Futures Council
  www.thebfc.com
Building Performance Assessment Team
  www.fema.gov/mit/bpat
Civil Engineering Research Foundation (CERF) of ASCE
  www.cerf.org
Construction Industry Institute
  http://construction-institute.org
Federal Emergency Management Agency (FEMA)
  www.fema.gov
National Crime Prevention Institute
  www.louisville.edu/a-s/ja/ncpi/courses.htm

National Fire Protection Association
   www.nfpa.org
National Institute of Standards and Technology (NIST), Building and Fire Research Laboratory
   www.bfrl.nist.gov
Office of Domestic Preparedness (ODP)
   www.ojp.usdoj.gov/odp
Protective Glazing Council
   www.protectiveglazing.org
Sandia National Laboratories (SNL)
   www.sandia.gov
Structural Engineering Institute (SEI) of ASCE
   www.seinstitute.org
Sustainable Buildings Industry Council
   www.sbicouncil.org
The Infrastructure Security Partnership (TISP)
   www.tisp.org
U.S. Department of Energy
   www.energy.gov
U.S. Department of Homeland Security
   www.whitehouse.gov/deptofhomeland
U.S. Green Building Council
   www.usgbc.org
U.S. Marshals Service (USMS)
   www.usdoj.gov/marshals
Vulnerability and Protection of Infrastructure Systems: The State of the Art, An ASCE Journals
   Special Publication compiling articles from 2002 and earlier, available online
   https://ascestore.aip.org/OA_HTML/aipCCtpItmDspRte.jsp?a=b

Index